# Telecom Management in Emerging Economies

AF793423

Murali Krishna Medudula
Mahim Sagar · Ravi Parkash Gandhi

# Telecom Management in Emerging Economies

## Evolutionary and Contemporary Perspectives

Springer

Murali Krishna Medudula
Indian Institute of Technology Delhi
New Delhi
India

Ravi Parkash Gandhi
Indian Institute of Technology Delhi
New Delhi
India

Mahim Sagar
Indian Institute of Technology Delhi
New Delhi
India

ISBN 978-81-322-3828-7 ISBN 978-81-322-2749-6 (eBook)
DOI 10.1007/978-81-322-2749-6

© Springer India 2016
Softcover reprint of the hardcover 1st edition 2016
This work is subject to copyright. All rights are reserved by the Publisher, whether the whole or part of the material is concerned, specifically the rights of translation, reprinting, reuse of illustrations, recitation, broadcasting, reproduction on microfilms or in any other physical way, and transmission or information storage and retrieval, electronic adaptation, computer software, or by similar or dissimilar methodology now known or hereafter developed.
The use of general descriptive names, registered names, trademarks, service marks, etc. in this publication does not imply, even in the absence of a specific statement, that such names are exempt from the relevant protective laws and regulations and therefore free for general use.
The publisher, the authors and the editors are safe to assume that the advice and information in this book are believed to be true and accurate at the date of publication. Neither the publisher nor the authors or the editors give a warranty, express or implied, with respect to the material contained herein or for any errors or omissions that may have been made.

Printed on acid-free paper

This Springer imprint is published by Springer Nature
The registered company is Springer (India) Pvt. Ltd.

# Contents

# Authors Biography

**Murali Krishna Medudula** is presently pursuing his doctoral study at IIT Delhi in the area of Mobile Data Security. In the past he has been associated with various organizations such as Aditya Birla Group (Transworks) and Wipro Technologies. He worked at a Sr. Executive level as the Bid Manager for Asia-Pacific region in Wipro Technologies. He was the Head Faculty and Knowledge Partner in the Ace Academy, Avikar Educational and Cultural Society (New Delhi, India) before joining as a research scholar at IIT Delhi. He holds B.Tech degree in Information Technology from CBIT, Hyderabad and MBA degree from IIT Delhi. His research areas include telecommunication policy and regulation, consumer behaviour, and technology absorption and adoption issues. He actively takes part in organizing and attending several workshops and conferences in the area of marketing, telecommunication technology and management. He can be reached at murali.iitphd@gmail.com

**Dr. Mahim Sagar** is a faculty at IIT Delhi. He works in the area of Marketing and Telecommunication Policy. His research has appeared in leading international journals as well as in public media. He has developed a unique concept on Ethical Positioning Index and has worked in the area of aware consumer and informed choice. In telecom area, his work focuses on policy issues, MVNO, OTT as well as telecom market models. He is the recipient of Teaching Excellence Award at IIT Delhi. He can be reached at mahim@dms.iitd.ac.in; mahimsagar@gmail.com

**Ravi Parkash Gandhi** is presently pursuing his doctoral study and is a part-time research scholar at IIT Delhi. He has been associated with various institutes of reputation like National Institute of Technology, Kurukshetra and Indian Institute of Management, Kozhikode. He has several journal and international conference publications to his credit and has rich experience in regulatory, licensing, policy and strategy of telecom sector, and management of large size mobile and fixed line telecom networks. He currently works as the Chief Regulatory Officer (CRO) at Bharti Airtel Limited and also serves as Chairman of the Strategy and Policy Committee of Cellular Operators Association of India (COAI). He is also member of GSMA's Chief Policy and Regulatory Officer Group (CPROG) and Spectrum Strategy and Management Group (SSMG). He had been part of Government of India as a member of civil services (Indian Telecommunication Service) during a major part of his career (1993–2007) where he had served in various capacities such as public policy, telecom licensing, license enforcement, business head, project management, installation and commissioning of telecom networks, both fixed line and mobile network. One of his major contributions includes setting up Telecom Enforcement, Resources and Monitoring Cells while at Department of Telecommunication. He can be reached at ravi.p.gandhi@gmail.com

# Abbreviations

| Term | Expanded Title |
|---|---|
| 0G | Zero Generation Mobile Standards |
| 1G | First Generation Mobile Standards |
| 2G | Second Generation Mobile Standards |
| 3G | Third Generation Mobile Standards |
| 3GPP | 3rd Generation Partnership Project |
| 3GPP2 | 3rd Generation Partnership Project2 |
| 4G | Fourth Generation Mobile Standards |
| AAG | Asia-America Gateway |
| AAS | Adaptive Antenna System |
| ABC | Activity-Based Costing |
| AFIS | Automated Fingerprint Identification System |
| AGR | Adjusted Gross Revenue |
| AIP | Administrative Incentive Pricing |
| AMPS | Advance Mobile Telephone System |
| APAC | Asia-Pacific |
| APCN2 | Asia Pacific Cable Network 2 |
| API | Application Program Interface |
| AQM | Application Quality Management |
| ARIB | Association of Radio Industries and Businesses |
| ARPU | Average Revenue Per User |
| ASON | Automatically Switched Optical Network |
| ATM | Asynchronous Transfer Mode |
| AUSPI | Association of Unified Telecom Service Providers of India |
| BIS | Bureau of Indian Standards |
| BRAN | Broadband Radio Access Network |
| BRTI | Badan Regulasi Telekomunikasi Indonesia |
| BSC | Base Station Controller |
| BSNL | Bharat Sanchar Nigam Limited |
| BSO | Basic Service Operator |
| BTS | Base Transceiver Station |
| BWA | Broadband Wireless Access |

| | |
|---|---|
| BYOD | Bring Your Own Device |
| C2C | City-to-City Cable |
| CAGR | Compound Annual Growth Rate |
| CAPEX | Capital Expenditure |
| CAPM | Capital Asset Pricing Model |
| CCA | Current Cost Accounting |
| CCSA | China Communications Standards Association |
| CDMA | Code Division Multiple Access |
| CEN | Carrier Ethernet Technology |
| CIS | Commonwealth of Independent States |
| CMSP | Cellular Mobile Service Providers |
| CMTS | Cellular Mobile Telephone Service |
| COAI | Cellular Operator Association of India |
| CP | Content Providers |
| CPE | Customer-Premises Equipment |
| CPI | Cost Performance Index |
| CPP | Calling Party Pays |
| CSP | Cellular Service Provider |
| CWTS | China Wireless Telecommunication Standard Group |
| D-AMPS | Digital Advanced Mobile Phone Service |
| DARPA | Defense Advanced Research Project Agency |
| DB | Decibel |
| DC | Domain Controller |
| DC-HSPA+ | Dual-carrier HSPA+ |
| DECT | Digital Enhanced Cordless Telecommunications |
| DL | Downlink |
| DLC | Domestic Leased Circuit |
| DoS | Denial-of-Service |
| DoT | Department of Telecommunications |
| DP | Distribution Point |
| DS-CDMA | Direct-Sequence Code Division Multiple Access |
| DSL | Digital Subscriber Line |
| DSLAM | Digital Subscriber Line Access Multiplexer |
| DTH | Direct-to-Home |
| DWDM | Dense Wavelength Division Multiplexing |
| E1 | E-carrier |
| EASSy | Eastern Africa Submarine Cable System |
| EC | European Commission |
| EDGE | Enhanced Data rates for GSM Evolution |
| E-GSM | Extended GSM |
| EIG | Europe India Gateway |
| EIR | Equipment Identity Register |
| EMC | Electromagnetic Compatibility |
| EMEA | Europe, Middle East and Africa |
| EMF | Electromagnetic Field |

| | |
|---|---|
| ENOC | Enhanced Network Operations Center |
| EoSDH | Ethernet Over SDH |
| EPS | External Power Supply |
| ETSI | European Telecommunications Standards Institute |
| EU | European Union |
| FAC | Fully Allocated Cost |
| FCC | Federal Communication Commission |
| FDD | Frequency Division Duplex |
| FDI | Foreign Direct Investment |
| FDMA | Frequency Division Multiple Access |
| FFT | Fast Fourier Transform |
| FIDIS | Future of Identity in the Information Society |
| FLLRIC | Forward-Looking Long Run Incremental Cost |
| FTA | Free-to-air |
| GAN | Generic Access Network |
| Gbps | Giga bits per second |
| GDP | Gross Domestic Product |
| GGSN | Gateway GPRS Support Node |
| GPRS | General Packet Radio System |
| GPS | Global Positioning System |
| GSM | Global System for Mobile Communication |
| GSMA | GSM Association |
| HARQ | Hybrid Automatic Repeat Request |
| HCA | Historical Cost Accounting |
| HHI | Herfindahl–Hirschman Index |
| HLR | Home Location Register |
| HSCSD | High-Speed Circuit-Switched Data |
| HSDPA | High-Speed Downlink Packet Access |
| HSPA | High Speed Packet Access |
| HSPA+ | Evolved High Speed Packet Access |
| HSS | Home Subscriber Server |
| IAMAI | Internet and Mobile Association of India |
| IAP | Internet Access Provider |
| IBSG | Internet Business Solutions Group |
| ICNIRP | International Commission for Non-Ionising Radiation Protection |
| ICRIER | Indian Council for Research on International Economic Relations |
| ICT | Information and Communications Technologies |
| IDC | International Data Corporation |
| IEEE | Institute of Electrical and Electronics Engineers |
| IETF | Internet Engineering Task Force |
| ILD | International Long Distance |
| ILP | Internet Leased Port |
| IMEI | International Mobile Equipment Identity |
| iMPLS | International Multiprotocol Label Switching |
| IMS | Integrated Management Services |

| | |
|---|---|
| IMSI | International Mobile Subscriber Identity |
| IMT-2000 | International Mobile Telecommunications-2000 |
| IMT-DS | International Mobile Telecommunications Direct Spread |
| IMT-FC | International Mobile Telecommunications Frequency Time |
| IMT-MC | International Mobile Telecommunications Multi-Carrier |
| IMTS | Improved Mobile Telephone Service |
| IMT-SC | International Mobile Telecommunications Single Carrier |
| IMT-TC | International Mobile Telecommunications Time Code |
| IMW | India-Middle East-Western Europe |
| iOS | Apple Operating System |
| IP | Internet Protocol |
| IP-I | Infrastructure Provider Category-I |
| IPLC | International Private Leased Circuits |
| IPv6 | Internet Protocol version 6 |
| IRU | Indefeasible Right of Use |
| ISDN | Integrated Service Digital Network |
| ISO | International Organization for Standardization |
| ISP | Internet Service Provider |
| ITFS | International Toll Free Service |
| ITS | Intelligent Transport System |
| ITU | International Telecommunication Union (ITU) |
| ITU-D | ITU Telecommunication Development Sector |
| ITU-R | ITU Radiocommunication Sector |
| ITU-T | ITU Telecommunication Standardization Sector |
| IUC | Interconnection Usage Charges |
| JNNURM | Jawaharlal Nehru National Urban Renewal Mission |
| JUS | Japan-US Submarine Cable System |
| KBPS | Kilobits per second |
| LCD | Liquid Crystal Display |
| LED | Light Emitting Diode |
| LRIC | Long Run Incremental Cost |
| LTE | Long-Term Evolution |
| M2M | Machine-to-Machine |
| MAC | Media Access Control |
| MAN | Metropolitan Area Networks |
| MIMO | Multiple-Input Multiple-Output |
| MITM | Man-in-the-Middle Attacks |
| MM | Multimedia |
| MME | Mobile Management Entity |
| MNP | Mobile Number Portability |
| MPBN | Maine Public Broadcasting Network |
| MPLS | Multiprotocol Label Switching |
| MSC | Mobile Switching Centre |
| MSS | Mobile-Satellite Service |
| MSU | Main Switching Unit |

| | |
|---|---|
| MTD | Swedish Mobile Telephony System D |
| MTNL | Mahanagar Telephone Nigam Limited |
| MTS | Mobile Telephone Service |
| MVNO | Mobile Virtual Network Operators |
| NDNC | National Do Not Call |
| NFAP | National Frequency Allocation Plan |
| NLD | National Long Distance |
| NMT | Nordic Mobile Telephone |
| NN | Net Neutrality |
| NOC | Network Operations Center |
| NOFN | National Optic Fibre Network |
| NRA | National Regulatory Authorities |
| NRA[1] | Network Remote Access |
| NTP94 | National Telecom Policy 1994 |
| NTP99 | New Telecom Policy 1999 |
| NTT | Nippon Telegraph and Telephone |
| O2 | Telefonica UK Limited |
| Ofcom | Office of Communications |
| OFDMA | Orthogonal Frequency Division Multiple Access |
| OFTA | Office of the Telecommunications Authority, Hong Kong |
| Oftel | Office of Telecommunications |
| OLT | Norwegian for Offentlig Landmobil Telefoni |
| OLTE | Optical Line Termination Equipment |
| Opex | Operational Expenditure |
| OPs | Organizational Partners |
| ORI | Open Radio Equipment Interface |
| OTN | Optical Transport Network |
| OTT | Over The Top |
| OVCC | Open Visual Communications Consortium |
| P&T | Post & Telecommunications |
| PABX | Private Branch Automatic Exchange |
| PCRF | Policy and Charging Rule Function |
| PCS | Personal Communications Services |
| PCs | Personal Computers |
| PDN | Packet Data Network |
| PDS | Packet Data Service |
| POI | Point of Interconnection |
| PRIME | Privacy and Identity Management for Europe |
| PSTN | Public Switched Telephone Network |
| PTT | Push-to-Talk |
| QAM | Quadrature Amplitude Modulation |

[1]The abbreviation is part of Chap. 1.

| | |
|---|---|
| QoS | Quality of Service |
| QPSK | Quadrature Phase-Shift Keying |
| RBOC | Regional Bell Operating Companies |
| RF | Radio Frequency |
| RFC | Request for Comments |
| RFID | Radio Frequency Identification |
| ROR | Rate of return |
| RoW | Right of Way |
| RRS | Reconfigurable Radio System |
| RSU | Remote Switching Unit |
| RTMI | Radio Telefono Mobile Integrato |
| SACFA | Standing Advisory Committee on Radio Frequency Allocation |
| SAE | System Architecture Evolution |
| SCM | Supply Chain Management |
| SCPC | Single Carrier Per Channel |
| SD | Secure Digital |
| SDH | Synchronous Digital Hierarchy |
| SDO | Standard Development Organization |
| SE | Secure Element |
| SEAS | Seychelles East Africa Submarine Cable |
| SES | Satellite Earth Stations and Systems |
| SGSN | Serving GPRS Support Node |
| SGW | Serving Gateway |
| SIMO | Single Input Multiple Output |
| SLA | Service-Level Agreement |
| SMP | Significant Market Power |
| SMS | Short Message Service |
| SMW | SEA-ME-WE |
| SOFDMA | Scalable Orthogonal Frequency Division Multiplexing Access |
| STC | Saudi Telecom Company |
| STM1 | Synchronous Transport Module Level 1 |
| SVoD | Subscription Video on Demand |
| T1 | T-carrier |
| TACS | Total Access Communication System |
| TAT-14 | Trans-Atlantic Cable System |
| TC | Technical Committee |
| TCP | Transmission Control Protocol |
| TDD | Time-Division Duplexing |
| TDM | Time-Division Multiplexing |
| TDMA | Time Division Multiple Access |
| TDSAT | Telecom Disputes Settlement and Apellate Tribunal |
| TD-SCDMA | Time Division Synchronous Code Division Multiple Access |
| TEAMS | The East African Marine System |
| TETRA | Terrestrial Trunked Radio |
| TIA | Telecommunications Industry Association |

| | |
|---|---|
| TMF | TeleManagement Forum |
| TMSI | Temporary Mobile Subscriber Identity |
| TRAI | Telecom Regulatory Authority of India |
| TSP | Telecommunications Service Provider |
| TTA | Telecommunications Technology Association |
| TTC | Telecommunications Technology Committee |
| TTO | Telecommunication Tariff Order |
| TTSL | Tata Teleservices Limited |
| UAS | Unified Access Service |
| UE | User Equipment |
| UICC | Universal Integrated Circuit Card |
| UL | Uplink |
| UMTS | Universal Mobile Telecommunications System |
| USO | Universal Service Obligation |
| UTRAN | Universal Terrestrial Radio Access Network |
| UWB | Ultra-Wide Band |
| UWC | Universal Wireless Communications |
| VAS | Value-Added Service |
| VC | Video Conference |
| VCM | Value Chain Management |
| VDSL | VeryHigh-Bit-Rate Digital Subscriber Line |
| VHF | Very High Frequency |
| VLR | Visitor Location Register |
| VNI | Visual Networking Index |
| VoIP | Voice over Internet Protocol |
| VoLTE | Voice over LTE |
| VPN | Virtual Private Network |
| VSAT | Very Small Aperture Terminal |
| VSNL | Videsh Sanchar Nigam Limited |
| WACC | Weighted Average of Cost of Capital |
| WACS | West Africa Cable System |
| WCDMA | Wideband CDMA |
| Wi-Fi | Wireless Fidelity |
| WiMAX | Worldwide Interoperability for Microwave Access |
| WiMAX 2 | Worldwide Interoperability for Microwave Access Release 2 |
| WLAN | Wireless Local Area Network |
| WLL | Wireless in Local Loop |
| WPC | Wireless Planning & Coordination |
| WTO | World Trade Organization |

# Chapter 1
# Telecommunication Standards and Growth: Evolutionary Process

Telecommunication networks are fundamental for the overall economic development of any nation. According to a study by ICRIER (2009), Indian States which achieve an increment of 10 % in mobile penetration can expect to have 1.2 % increase in their average growth rate. A similar report on the penetration of Internet services by the World Bank indicates that a 10 % increase in broadband or Internet penetration improves the economic growth by 1.38 % in low- and middle-income countries (Qiang et al. 2009). This trend can be observed in the growth of many emerging economies. It is an undisputed fact that the most developed economies have a strong underlying telecommunication network that allows for higher orders of business efficiency and inclusive development.

Telecommunication technologies play a pivotal role in shaping the modern world. The collective efforts of the scientific communities, the academicians and the industrial sector have ushered in a new age of communications that support ubiquitous access with a high quality of service and blazing fast speeds. Such has been the success of this industry that the global telecom subscriber base has crossed the 7-billion mark.

As is the case with every endeavour of humankind, the growth of telecommunications is a story of evolution. Ever-increasing demands for better quality of services and higher data rates, the industry kept pace and often exceeded expectations. Each new generation of mobile communication technology provided increased reliability, higher speeds, and a plethora of applications and services for subscribers. The pace of evolution and the adoption of various generations of mobile standards have become a differentiating factor among subscribers, operators and countries.

Several international bodies such as the ITU-T and ETSI help design and develop globally applicable standards for fixed-line, mobile, broadcast, Internet, aeronautical and other sectors. The International Telecommunication Union consists of three sectors (ITU-R, ITU-T and ITU-D), and several study groups in each sector of the

© Springer India 2016

M.K. Medudula et al., *Telecom Management in Emerging Economies*,
DOI 10.1007/978-81-322-2749-6_1

ITU help define the new technologies and standards for the global telecommunication industry. More information on ITU will be explained in Chap. 2.

## 1.1 Mobile Wireless Generations

Based on the level of performance, data speeds and other technical details, telecommunication standards/technologies have been classified into several mobile wireless generations. Technologies before 3G were not completely standardized, and the lack of global standards led the ITU to undertake extensive standardization efforts. Standardization allowed only specific technologies to qualify and be included in the standards. With continuous improvement in technology, the use of mobile networks was not limited to just connect mobile phones but has been extended for any technical instrument that requires connectivity.

New-generation telecommunication standards have four main features as depicted in Fig. 1.1.

There are several other features as well which distinguish the standards. Let us look at these main features which clearly help us in better understanding of these standards. The four points mentioned in the Fig. 1.1 help to realize the potential of technology in terms of growth, adoption and reliability.

Time-division duplex (TDD) and frequency-division duplex (FDD) are two popular duplexing techniques used for creating full-duplex telecommunication services which have the capability of two-way communication. TDD makes use of

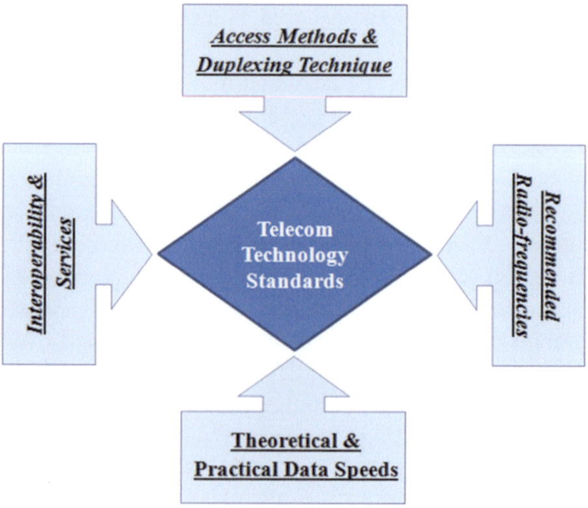


**Fig. 1.1** Key features of telecommunication technology standards

same frequency channel for two-way communication by maintaining different time slots for uplink and downlink. On the contrary, in FDD, we make use of two different frequency channels taking measures to avoid interference. Within a given telecom circle/network, operators can make use of TDD or FDD or both in order to improve the network efficiency. Those technologies which make use of both the duplexing techniques in the same band would require measures to minimize the interference level.

Access methods provide network access to multiple users by defining the rules for sharing the resources. Several access methods in use today include time-division multiple access (TDMA), frequency division multiple access (FDMA), code division multiple access (CDMA), wideband code division multiple access (WCDMA), frequency–time division multiple access (FTDMA), multi-frequency time-division multiple access (MFTDMA), orthogonal frequency-division multiple access (OFDMA), scalable orthogonal frequency-division multiple access (SOFDMA), high-speed packet access (HSPA), and evolved high-speed packet access (HSPA+).

Recommended radio frequency becomes an important part for the deployment as it becomes the base for worldwide interoperability of standards and international regulations. ITU through its radio regulations plays an important role in identifying the frequency bands that are ideal for various telecommunication standards. The recommended bands help in efficient and effective use of the spectrum in providing the services to the subscribers. Nations who are the members of ITU make use of these recommendations in planning their spectrum allocations. Nations may make use of other frequencies if the recommended bands are not available to use for telecom services.

Practical and theoretical data speeds are the measures for network efficiency, and new generation of telecommunication standards provide better speeds when compared to the older generations. Practical data speeds would be lesser than the theoretical data speed because of the network inefficiencies. The data speed may also be used in associating the standard to a particular technology generation. ITU expects that 3G standards (IMT-2000) provide a minimum of 2 Mb/s for stationary or waking users, whereas 348 kb/s for a moving vehicle.

Interoperability is an essential factor for the technology to be integrated to the existing networks and provide seamless connectivity to the users. Interoperability is defined by ETSI as "the ability of equipment from different manufacturers (or different systems) to communicate together on the same infrastructure (same system), or on another while roaming" (Van der Veer and Wiles 2008). Interoperability is key for convergence and for the networks to be scalable and efficient. Standards that are interoperable and efficient could provide plethora of value-added services to the subscribers. As per the testing body (such as ITU and ETSI), a minimum level of interoperability at various levels such as device to device, network to device and between networks is required for the standards to be approved for large-scale deployment.

Let us look at several generations of telecommunication standards and the improved capabilities of these standards during their evolution.

### *1.1.1 Zero Generation (0G): PTT, MTS, IMTS, AMTS, OLT and MTD*

0G refers to the first wireless analog mobile communication service that made use of radio waves for communication. The service characteristics and technologies that were used differentiated 0G from other generations. Some main features of zero-generation mobile standards included push to talk, selective calling and half duplex.

Lack of standardization efforts led to limited roaming capability for devices. Some technologies used in 0G systems included push to talk (PTT), mobile telephone service (MTS), improved mobile telephone service (IMTS), advanced mobile telephone system (AMTS), Norwegian for Offentlig Landmobil Telefoni, Public land mobile telephony (OLT) and Swedish mobile telephony system D (MTD) (Bhalla and Bhalla 2010). The numerous limitations and drawbacks of these technologies led to the creation of next-generation technology standards and technologies. Some of the limitations of 0G include:

1. Limited roaming facility,
2. One person at a time since the systems were half duplex and
3. Availability of limited number of channels.

Certainly 0G systems had their limitations, but it has provided the momentum and growth to leap forward for better network technologies and handsets. Brief overview of 0G features is presented in Fig. 1.2.

### *1.1.2 First Generation (1G): AMPS, NMT, RTMI, TACS and NTT*

Limitations associated with half-duplex systems and technologies were rectified with the birth of the 1G mobile standards. Full-duplex networks allowed subscribers to listen and talk to others on the same connection, a feature that we take for granted today and consider a bare necessity. 1G made use of FDMA protocols and was far better than zero generation (0G). However, the biggest drawback of first generation mobile technology and the standards ecosystem was the inherent variability in the implementation of these standards in different parts of the world—advanced mobile telephone system (AMPS) was followed in America, Nordic

**Fig. 1.2** Summary of 0G telecom system

**Fig. 1.3** Summary of 1G telecom system

mobile telephone (NMT) was followed in Nordic countries such as Norway, Radio Telefono Mobile Integrato (RTMI) was followed in Italy, total access communication system (TACS) was followed in Europe and NTT (system developed and used by NTT) was followed in Japan. This was the single largest roadblock that prevented roaming services from reaching the realm of reality (Kano 2000). These standards operated on different frequencies, e.g. AMPS used frequencies 824–849 MHz for uplink and 869–894 MHz for downlink, whereas NMT was using frequency bands in 450 MHz. These systems were purely voice based and presented no need for next-generation mobile standard and new technologies for subscribers. It was however at this stage that the industry and various associations worked towards the development of a new standard that provided additional data capabilities to subscribers (Fig. 1.3).

### *1.1.3 Second Generation (2G): CdmaOne, TDMA and GSM*

2G mobile systems were first implemented in the 1990s. These systems proved to be a major success as they made use of digital technologies that were capable of providing both voice and data services to subscribers. Even though these systems offered data services, voice services still dominated as a major utility among subscribers. Digital modulation such as time-division multiple access (TDMA) and code-division multiple access (CDMA) offered the advantages of improved system efficiency and radically improved the capacity of networks to handle a higher number of subscribers in a given time frame. These networks also make use of FMDA access method in dividing the frequency allocated into several carrier frequencies.

Based on the methods mentioned above, three primary 2G mobile communication systems were developed. The first CDMA-based digital cellular standard Interim Standard 95 (IS-95) was developed by Qualcomm with the brand name cdmaOne (Park and Adachi 2007). This system consisted of a physical layer implemented by CDMA and the commonly used modulation scheme of quadrature-phase shift keying (QPSK). The data transfer rates achieved ranged from 9.6 to 11.5 kb/s. Interim Standard-136 (IS-136) was the first TDMA cellular and is also referred as digital advanced mobile phone service. IS-136 made us of dual mode operation which was cost effective for migration from AMPS (Faccin et al. 1999). Global system for mobile communication (GSM) is another 2G technology which was developed by European Telecommunications Standards Institute (ETSI) as a digital standard with certain benefits which the analog networks could not provide, i.e. the ability to have roaming facility. When compared to 1G technology, 2G offered significant improvements in terms of handling a higher number of subscribers, greater quality parameters and enhanced security.

### *1.1.4 General Packet Radio System—GPRS (2.5G)*

GSM was a successful standard for mobile phones, but was used primarily for voice-based services and limited data services. There was a need for another standard that could facilitate transfer of large volumes of text and pictures. This need led to the creation of the next standard, which brought with it even higher data rates with dial-up speed of 30–90 kb/s. General Packet Radio System (GPRS) was developed to fill the gap and was essentially based on GSM. GPRS helped achieve higher transmission speeds and was capable of sending two to three times the information compared to earlier 2G standards.

### *1.1.5 Enhanced Data Rates for GSM Evolution—EDGE (2.75G)*

With the utility for data services on the rise, customer demands for faster data speeds were increased. There was a need for further standardization of any future technologies so services could be accessed seamlessly from most networks. The standardization for 2.75G was finalized by 3GPP in the year 2000 which resulted in growth of EDGE networks in telecom sector.

EDGE network delivered faster data rates and was proved to be the easier upgradation upon existed GSM networks. For most of the GSM/GPRS networks, upgrading to an EDGE network merely required software modifications. EDGE today can enable user bit rates of up to 250 kb/s with a latency of 150 ms. Essentially, this next step in the evolution of mobile communications standard allowed networks to handle four times the traffic supported by the standard GPRS, increase the usability of mobile data services, enhance customer satisfaction and boost data revenues (Ericsson 2009).

Theoretically, EDGE has the capability to provide data rates of up to 384 kb/s. EDGE networks were proved to be cost effective and are able to support most multimedia applications, and for the first time ever, these networks allowed subscribers to stream videos.

Initially thought of as 2.75G, EDGE actually enabled 3G applications such as mobile broadband over current GSM networks and provided seamless services by improved spectral efficiency. Its role as a key enabler for the next standard led the

**Fig. 1.4** Summary of 2G, 2.75G and 2.75G systems

International Telecommunication Union (ITU) to approve EDGE as a 3G standard in July 2000 (Fig. 1.4).

### *1.1.6 CDMA2000, WCDMA, TD-SCDMA, HSPA and WiMAX (3G)*

ITU defined the minimum data rates for the 3G standards in its IMT-2000 initiative. These standards have the capabilities of providing seamless triple play services (data, voice and video streaming). Wide use of CDMA started from this generation of mobile technology because it offered higher capacity, improved performance in multipath by diversity and a longer battery life, which led to standards such as CDMA2000 and wideband CDMA (WCDMA). Today, there exist three widely adopted 3G cellular network standards—CDMA2000 from America, WCDMA from Europe and TD-SCDMA from China. CDMA2000 is the trademark for the technical nomenclature that specifies the standards of the organizational partners (OPs) of 3GPP2. The WCDMA offered better efficiency over CDMA2000 networks due to higher carrier spacing (5 MHz in WCDMA and 3.75 MHz in CDMA2000) (Ziemer and Peterson 2001).

While WCDMA is a more mature standard and has been deployed in many countries, it should not be compared with TD-SCDMA. TD-SCDMA is more appropriate for areas with demand for Internet services and high bandwidth, and WCDMA would be ideal for sparsely populated areas (Hallne 2006). Looking at 3G from ITU's point of view, IMT-2000 offers a family of radio interfaces for 3G services as shown in Fig. 1.5. IMT-2000 took standardization to a level that a single network standard was implemented in the Americas, Europe and Japan. The International Telecommunication Union (ITU) has sanctioned the five following terrestrial IMT-2000 standards in its 3G standardization process.

Worldwide Interoperability for Microwave Access (WiMAX) is a standard proposed by IEEE 802.16 specifications. This standard was accepted as a 3G standard by ITU. WiMAX functions on both unlicensed and licensed frequencies. Generally for commercial use, the licensed frequencies are used. WiMAX forum certifies the broadband wireless products based on IEEE 802.16 specifications. Because of the high speeds and benefits, some suggested that WiMAX technology may turn out to be the 4G of wireless communications (Dekleva et al. 2007). But

**Fig. 1.5** IMT-2000 standards. *Source* ITU (2011)

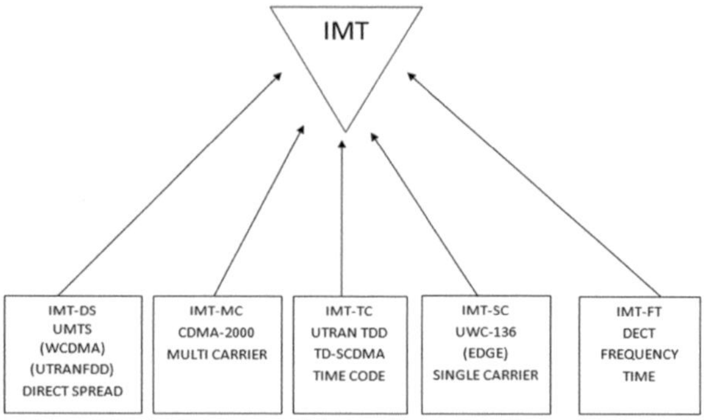


due to its limitations of low bit rates over large distances and speed of connectivity, the standard was not upgraded for a very long time. Some of the systems recommend WiMAX as 4G systems, whereas others regard them as 3G systems because of the non-achievement of true 4G speeds.

High-speed packet access (HSPA) is another 3G standard which has come to be known as an upgrade to WCDMA networks for higher data speeds. Several other standards such as HSPA+ and HSDPA preceded HSPA and aimed to reduce the latency and improve the downlink and uplink speeds. According to ITU statistics, more than 160 countries have launched 3G services and 50 % of the world population has access to a 3G mobile network.

### *1.1.7 LTE (IMT Advanced) and WiMAX 2: 4G Networks*

The 4G mobile system is an all IP-based network system, and all features of 4G may be summarized with one word—integration (Ruscelli and Cecchetti 2007). 4G technology should integrate with the current existing and future wireless network technologies to ensure freedom of movement and seamless roaming from one technology to another (Li et al. 2009). ITU's Radio communication sector (ITU-R) has officially designated LTE-advanced and Wireless MAN-advanced (802.16m) as the global 4G mobile wireless broadband technology, otherwise known as IMT-advanced (Li et al. 2008). Initiated in 2004, the long-term evolution (LTE) project focused on enhancing Universal Terrestrial Radio Access (UTRA) and optimizing 3GPP's radio access architecture (3GPP n.d.).

LTE-advanced is a natural evolution of LTE that can support spectrum aggregation up to 100 MHz and peak data rates up to 1 GB/s (Murai et al. 2008). The second IMT-advanced standard, Wireless MAN-advanced is an IEEE Standard 802.16-2001, completed in October 2001 and published on 8 April 2002 defines the Wireless MAN air interface specification for wireless metropolitan area networks (MANs) (Eklund et al. 2002). WiMAX release 2 (WiMAX 2) is capable of achieving true 4G speeds which were difficult for earlier versions. More information on 4G technologies will be covered in subsequent chapters.

With 3G networks implemented in most of the developed and developing countries, network and mobile operators started to look forward to the implementation of 4G services that could offer integration of all services onto a mobile platform and provide seamless roaming from one technology to another, leading to improved global mobile wireless broadband for subscribers.

## 1.2 Telecommunication Standards Development Through Partnerships

Technological transformations from analog to circuit-based switching and finally to IP-based packet delivery enabled establishment of new optimized core and radio access networks with open standards allowing for true convergence of both networks and services. Several international organizations have worked together in developing the standards for new technologies through mutual agreements and partnership projects. Two notable partnership projects in the field of telecommunications include 3GPP and 3GPP2.

### *1.2.1 3GPP (3rd Generation Partnership Project)*

This partnership project which initially released specifications on UMTS technologies (WCDMA) now works in several other areas including specifications for 4G technologies. 3GPP is involved in the standardization activities of various technologies and released specifications for wideband code-division multiple access (WCDMA), high-speed downlink (DL) packet data access (HSDPA), high-speed

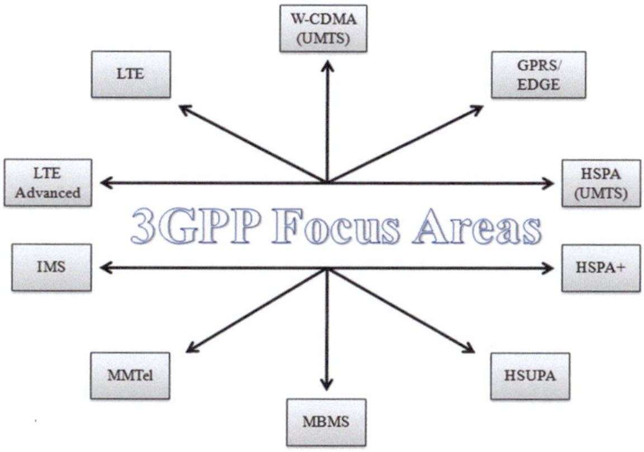


**Fig. 1.6** 3GPP specifications focus areas. *Data source* http://www.3gpp.org/

UL packet data access (HSUPA), evolved high-speed packet access (HSPA+), long-term evolution (LTE) and LTE advanced (Nakamura 2009). Universal Mobile Telecommunications System (UMTS) is used to collectively refer to all 3G standards specified under 3GPP. Figure 1.6 shows the focus of all 3GPP focus areas in the field of telecommunications. More details on 4G technologies will be discussed in Chap. 5. Currently, 3GPP is working on describing the 5G features and technologies through the initial phase of Release 14 and is planning to deliver initial features by the year 2020.

## 1.2.2 3GPP2 (3rd Generation Partnership Project 2)

3GPP2 is another important partnership for the development of 3G standard specifications in telecommunications sector. This was an ITU initiative which aims at developing IP-based standards to support seamless multimedia services and enable global roaming. The partnership firms in standard development organization (SDO) include organizational partners from various committees and associations based in five different nations. Association of Radio Industries and Businesses, Japan (ARIB), China Communications Standards Association (CCSA), Telecommunications Industry Association, North America (TIA), Telecommunications Technology Association, Korea (TTA), and Telecommunications Technology Committee, Japan (TTC), are the SDOs in 3GPP2 imitative. This partnership firm has two technical specification groups (TSG) working in the areas of "access networks and air interfaces" and "system aspects and core network" as depicted in Fig. 1.7. For more details please refer the website mentioned in the source.

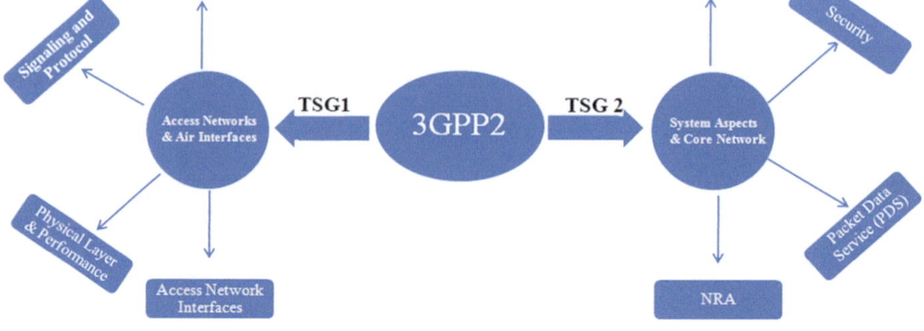


**Fig. 1.7** 3GPP specifications focus areas. *Data source* http://www.3gpp2.org/

## 1.3 Key Indicators of Telecom Growth World Wide

Monitoring the growth rate of various regions in the world gives us an idea of overall growth in telecommunications and the industry dynamics that drive this growth. These statistics present important information regarding the performance and growth of telecom industry worldwide.

### 1.3.1 ITU's Grouping of Regions in the World

According to ITU Statistics, the key statistics of telecommunication subscriptions and growth rates of various services can be analysed under the following six groups, namely

(i) Africa (44 regions)
Angola, Benin, Botswana, Burkina Faso, Burundi, Cameroon, Cape Verde, Central African Rep., Chad, Congo (Rep. of the), Congo (Dem. Rep.), Côte d'Ivoire, Equatorial Guinea, Eritrea, Ethiopia, Gabon, Gambia, Ghana, Guinea, Guinea-Bissau, Kenya, Lesotho, Liberia, Madagascar, Malawi, Mali, Mauritius, Mozambique, Namibia, Niger, Nigeria, Rwanda, Sao Tomé and Principe, Senegal, Seychelles, Sierra Leone, South Africa, South Sudan, Swaziland, Tanzania, Togo, Uganda, Zambia and Zimbabwe.

(ii) The Americas (35 regions)
Antigua and Barbuda, Argentina, Bahamas, Barbados, Belize, Bolivia, Brazil, Canada, Chile, Colombia, Costa Rica, Cuba, Dominica, Dominican Rep., Ecuador, El Salvador, Grenada, Guatemala, Guyana, Haiti, Honduras, Jamaica, Mexico, Nicaragua, Panama, Paraguay, Peru, Saint Kitts and Nevis, Saint Lucia, Saint Vincent, Grenadines, Suriname, Trinidad and Tobago, USA, Uruguay and Venezuela.

(iii) Arab States (21 regions)
Algeria, Bahrain, Comoros, Djibouti, Egypt, Iraq, Jordan, Kuwait, Lebanon, Libyan Arab Jamahiriya, Mauritania, Morocco, Oman, Qatar, Saudi Arabia, Somalia, Sudan, Syrian Arab Republic, Tunisia, United Arab Emirates and Yemen.

(iv) Asia and Pacific (39 regions)
Afghanistan, Australia, Bangladesh, Bhutan, Brunei Darussalam, Cambodia, China, Democratic People's Rep. of Korea, Fiji, India, Indonesia, Iran, Japan, Kiribati, Korea (Rep. of), Lao P.D.R., Malaysia, Maldives, Marshall Islands, Micronesia, Mongolia, Myanmar, Nauru, Nepal, New Zealand, Pakistan, Papua New Guinea, Philippines, Samoa, Singapore, Solomon Islands, Sri Lanka, Thailand, Timor-Leste, Tonga, Tuvalu, Vanuatu and Vietnam.

(v) CIS (12 regions)
Armenia, Azerbaijan, Belarus, Georgia, Kazakhstan, Kyrgyzstan, Moldova, Russian Federation, Tajikistan, Turkmenistan, Ukraine and Uzbekistan.

(vi) Europe (44 regions)
Albania, Andorra, Austria, Belgium, Bosnia and Herzegovina, Bulgaria, Croatia, Cyprus, Czech Republic, Denmark, Estonia, Finland, France, Germany, Greece, Hungary, Iceland, Ireland, Israel, Italy, Latvia, Liechtenstein, Lithuania, Luxembourg, Malta, Monaco, Montenegro, the Netherlands, Norway, Poland, Portugal, Romania, San Marino, Serbia, Slovakia, Slovenia, Spain, Sweden, Switzerland, The Former Yugoslav Rep. of Macedonia, Turkey, UK and Vatican.

### *1.3.2 Global Telecom Statistics*

Among the 6 major groups, APAC telecom sector comprises over 50 % of both fixed-line telephone subscriptions and mobile cellular subscriptions. Fixed-line telephone subscriptions in a vast majority of regions have witnessed a sharp decline in terms of annual growth rate. Mobile subscriptions have steadily increased, and the penetration of mobile subscriptions has exceeded 100 % in Arab States, The Americas, Arab States, CIS and Europe.

Generally IT organizations follow these classifications in creating several teams and allocate heads for each of the above groups to maintain their clients. For example, if the client is a telecom firm from Japan which requires a billing system from an IT organization, then the project will be allocated internally within the organization to the Asia–Pacific team. APAC team members assume the responsibility to deal with client requirements. It is in the interest of organizations to maintain their teams according to the six groups above and monitor their performance separately. Some key statistics derived from ITU data during 2000–2011 include the following
(ITU 2013):

1. Top 10 regions in fixed-line telephone subscriptions include: China, USA, Japan, Germany, Russia, Brazil, France, Indonesia, UK and India.
2. Top 10 regions in mobile cellular telephone subscriptions include: China, India, USA, Russia, Indonesia, Brazil, Japan, Vietnam, Germany, Pakistan and Italy.
3. Top 10 regions in terms of fixed-line telephone penetration (subscriptions per 100 inhabitants) include: Monaco, Gibraltar, Taiwan, Falkland (Malvinas) Is., Cayman Islands, France, Germany, Hong Kong, Korea (Rep.) and Switzerland.
4. Top 10 regions in terms of mobile telephone penetration(subscriptions per 100 inhabitants) include: Macao, Hong Kong, Antigua and Barbuda, Saudi Arabia, Panama, Russia, Suriname, Kuwait, Oman and Cayman Islands.

5. Over 50 % of regions have seen negative growth in fixed-line subscriptions during 2010–2011.
6. Over 90 % of the countries have seen positive growth in mobile subscriptions during 2010–2011.
7. Top 10 regions that have witnessed maximum percentage increase of Internet subscriptions include: Qatar, Antigua and Barbuda, Bahrain, Andorra, Cayman Islands, Luxembourg, Barbados, Kuwait, Latvia and France.

A detailed description of the subscriptions data can be accessed from the ITU's website. ITU also presents a chronological time series statistical analysis which is one of the most authoritative sources of data on telecom evolution, and the availability and usage of ICTs by subscribers.

## 1.4 Telecom Opportunities—Mapping the World Countries

Understanding telecom technology implementations and other key indicators such as teledensity, CAGR and ARPU figures worldwide would certainly give us an idea to map the countries. An attempt has been made using the telecom statistics (2008–2009) to create such a map where the countries were mapped under six categories. Several key terms were used in finalizing the category for the country, and different colour codings were used for each category to make the visual representation better. The indicator used to decide the category was valid during the year 2009, and the same indicator may give us different results presently. It is worth noting the methodology in creating the map, and hence, it is included for readers in this chapter.

Five indicators primarily were used in deciding the category/metaphor for a country. These include penetration, technology, growth, ARPU and markets. **Penetration** include four subcategories, namely low penetration (teledensity < 30 %), moderate penetration (30 % < teledensity < 60 %), high penetration (teledensity > 60 %) and very high penetration (teledensity > 150 %). **Technology** includes low technology (everything below 3G) and high technology (high penetration + 3G (at least 20 % adoption)/very high penetration + 3G). **Growth** is categorized as low growth (teledensity < 60 % and CAGR < 35 %/teledensity < 40 % and CAGR < 60 %), moderate growth (40 % < teledensity < 60 % and 35 % < CAGR < 60 %) and high growth (teledensity > 60 % and CAGR > 35 %/teledensity > 40 % and CAGR > 60 %). **ARPU** includes low ARPU (ARPU < USD 5), moderate ARPU (USD 5 < ARPU < USD 10) and high ARPU (ARPU > USD 10). **Markets** are subcategorized as nascent market (moderate penetration, low growth, low technology and low ARPU), highly developed markets (high penetration + high technology (at least 20 % 3G adoption)/very high penetration + high technology/high penetration + high ARPU) and high potential markets (moderate penetration, moderate growth and moderate growth). Mapping the world countries was done to give an outlook of the opportunities in telecommunication domain.

Each country as per the indicators has been categorized under one of the six metaphors. These metaphors include: **Snail** (low penetration, low technology), **Koala** (nascent market, low growth, low technology, low ARPU), **Primate** (highly developed market, high ARPU, high technology), **Leopard** (high growth, moderate/high penetration), **Cow** (high ARPU, 3G, high penetration) and **Elephant** (high potential market—moderate penetration, moderate growth). Countries that have deployed mobile number portability (MNP) are marked as "##". ARPU figures have been obtained from variety of sources and are hence belong to a time period of 2007–2009. But this does not significantly affect the "Mapping Rule" as ARPU ranges are broadly defined. **MAPPING RULE** countries across the globe have been mapped based on the criteria (RULE) specified in the Table 1.1. The

**Table 1.1** Mapping Rule

| No | Metaphor | Explanation | Criterion | Indicators | | | |
|---|---|---|---|---|---|---|---|
| | | | | Teledensity[3] 2008 | CAGR[5] 2003–08 | ARPU[4] 2007–09 | Technology[7] 2008 |
| | | | | % | % | USD | 2G/3G |
| 1 | Snail | ***Low penetration,*** *Low technology* | | <30 | NC[1] | NC | 2G |
| 2 | Koala | ***Nascent market, low growth,*** *low technology, low ARPU* | *A* | <60 | <35 | NC | NC |
| | | | *B* | 30–40 | <60 | NC | NC |
| | | | *C* | 30–40 | NC | <$5 | NC |
| 3 | Primate | ***Highly developed*** *market, high ARPU, high Technology* | *A* | >100 | NC | >$30 | NC |
| | | | *B* | >100 | NC | NC | 3G (at least 20 % adoption)[7] |
| | | | *C* | >150 | NC | NC | 3G |
| 4 | Leopard | ***High growth,*** *moderate/high penetration* | *A* | 40–65 | 60–40 | NC | NC |
| | | | *B* | >85 | 30–40 | NC | NC |
| 5 | Cow | ***High ARPU, 3G,*** *high penetration* | | 75–100 | NC | $10–30 | NC |
| 6 | Elephant | ***High potential market***—*moderate penetration, moderate growth* | | >40 | >35 | >$5 | NC |

Countries that have deployed MNP[2] are marked as "##"
*Source* Sagar et al. (2009)

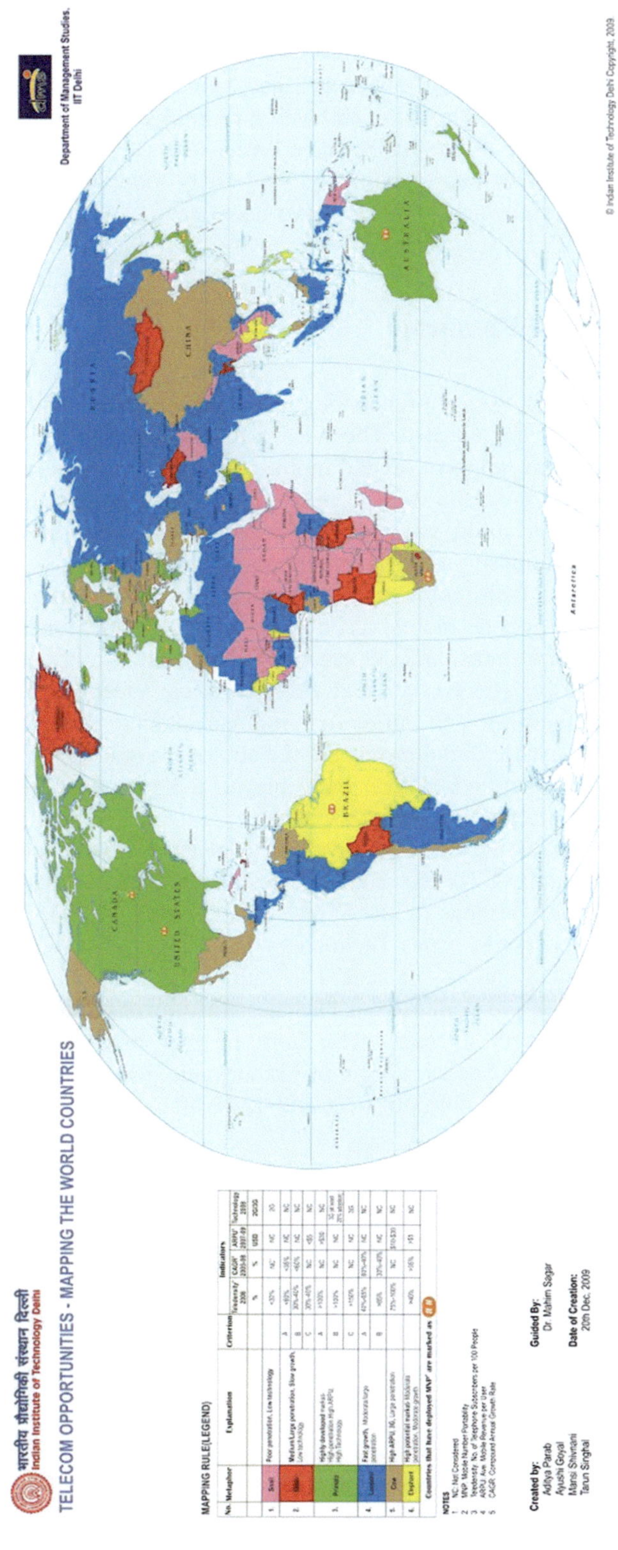


**Fig. 1.8** Telecom technology map. *Source* Sagar et al. (2009)

**Order** of assigning a specific metaphor to a country is same as described in the table. For some (15–20) countries, whose values of indicators are in the vicinity (3 %) of defined range, a judgemental call has been taken to associate them with one of the metaphor. We have classified level of technology as either 2G or 3G. The Level 2G also includes all the intermediate levels such as EDGE (2.5G). In some cases, we have also taken into account the Level of 3G adoption (in %). Using these rules and statistics, the world countries have been mapped as depicted in Fig. 1.8.

## 1.5 Concluding Remarks

Consumer adoption and usage of technological advancements promote the research and development of an industry. The need for better mobile services and technologies led to the invention of several mobile generations, and a sector once only voice-centric started providing basic data services which eventually propelled the industry and academic circles to come up with better standards with the potential to make mobile communications truly ubiquitous.

0G systems used radio communication which were half duplex and are considered to be precell phone mobile technologies. 1G networks facilitated two-way full-duplex communications, and 2G systems fostered the use of data services. 3G systems supported high-speed data and video services. Video on demand became possible with 3G networks. Seamless roaming and making the mobile a one stop portal for all conceivable digital needs are the aim of the 4G networks. Partnership projects such as 3GPP and 3GPP2 have played a key role in establishing the new-generation telecommunication standards.

ITU is an international body that monitors telecom growth and helps in the development of standards for the sector. In this chapter, we looked at key telecom statistics among the 6 regions as classified by ITU, which helps in monitoring the growth of the sector every year. Technology map helps us in understanding the level of technology adoption and market growth in this sector across the globe.

In the next chapter, we shall use this ITU classification of regions and understand more about the growth in telecom sector from the year 2000–2011. We shall also look at top 30 telecom firms in terms of brand value and present you the information about the market, telecom acts and governing bodies in telecom sector worldwide.

## References

3GPP (nd) LTE historical information. Available at: http://www.3gpp.org/technologies/keywords-acronyms/98-lte. Accessed 2 May 2014

Bhalla M, Bhalla A (2010) Generations of mobile wireless technology: a survey. Int J Comput Appl 5(4):26–32

Dekleva S, Shim J, Varshney U, Knoerzer G (2007) Evolution and emerging issues in mobile wireless networks. Commun ACM 50(6):38–43

Eklund C, Marks R, Stanwood K, Wang S (2002) IEEE standard 802.16: A technical overview of the WirelessMAN/sup TM/ air interface for broadband wireless access. IEEE Commun Mag 40 (6):98–107

Ericsson (2009) The evolution of EDGE. Available at: http://www.iwpc.org/Workshop_Folders/08_03_GSM_EDGE_Extensions/3107_The_evolution_of_EDGE_A.pdf. Accessed 30 Mar 2014

Faccin S, Hsu Liangchi, Koodli R, Le Khiem, Purnadi R (1999) GPRS and IS-136 integration for flexible network and services evolution. IEEE Pers Commun 6(3):48–54

Hallne M (2006) WCDMA and TD-SCDMA: European 3G vs. Chinese 3G. Available at: http://www.nada.kth.se/~mikeh/WCDMA_vs_TD-SCDMA-v2.0.pdf. Accessed 11 Apr 2015

ICRIER (2009) India: the impact of mobile phones. Available at: http://www.icrier.org/pdf/public_policy19jan09.pdf. Accessed 13 May 2014

ITU (2011) All about the technology. Available at: https://www.itu.int/osg/spu/ni/3G/technology/index.html. Accessed 21 Mar 2014

ITU (2013) Statistics. Available at: http://www.itu.int/ITU-D/ict/statistics/. Accessed 28 May 2014

Kano S (2000) Technical innovations, standardization and regional comparison—A case study in mobile communications. Telecommun Policy 24(4):305–321

Li X, Gani A, Yang L, Zakaria O, Jumaat B (2008) Mix-bandwidth data path design for 5G real wireless world. In: The proceeding of WSEAS 13th international conferences on multimedia and communication, pp 216–221

Li X, Gani A, Salleh R, Zakaria O (2009) The future of mobile wireless communication networks. In: International conference on communication software and networks

Murai H, Edvardsson M, Dahlman E (2008) LTE advanced—The solution for IMT-advanced. Available at: http://www.3g4g.co.uk/LteA/LteA_Pres_0806_Ericsson.pdf. Accessed 12 June 2014

Nakamura T (2009) Proposal for candidate radio interface technologies for IMT-advanced based on LTE Release 10 and Beyond (LTE-advanced). Available at: http://www.3gpp.org/IMG/pdf/2009_10_3gpp_IMT.pdf. Accessed 9 Apr 2015

Park Y, Adachi F (2007) Enhanced radio access technologies for next generation mobile communication. Springer, Dordrecht, pp 1–37

Qiang C, Rossotto C, Kimura K (2009) Economic impacts of broadband. Available at: http://siteresources.worldbank.org/EXTIC4D/Resources/IC4D_Broadband_35_50.pdf. Accessed 21 Feb 2014

Ruscelli A, Cecchetti G (2007) Toward the QoS support in 4G wireless systems. In: Proceeding of 18th Tyrrhenian workshop on digital communications, pp 245–252

Sagar M, Parab A, Goyal A, Shivani M, Singhal T (2009) Telecom technology map. In Working Paper, IIT Delhi

Van der Veer H, Wiles A (2008) Achieving technical interoperability. European Telecommunications Standards Institute. Available at: http://www.etsi.org/images/files/ETSIWhitePapers/IOP%20whitepaper%20Edition%203%20final.pdf. Accessed 12 May 2014

Ziemer R, Peterson R (2001) Introduction to digital communication. Prentice Hall, Upper Saddle River

# Chapter 2
# Telecom Players, Regulatory Bodies, International Organizations and Regional Telecom Statistics: Global Overview

Technology and regulation are key drivers for telecom growth in emerging economies. Technology facilitates improved services and creates market conducive for growth. The evolution of technology decreases costs and facilitates rapid growth phase that appeals to many industry players. With an increasing number of players, each striving for larger market shares, regulation is critical and necessary to promote growth and harmony in the sector. Regulations ensure that fair practices are adopted by telecom operators in their efforts to increase and maintain market shares.

Globalization ensured faster roll-out of new technologies, decreased costs, reduced significant market power (SMP) by any single player and promoted competitiveness in the market place. Many economies have seen foreign direct investment as an accelerator for the growth of the telecom business. Due to an increasing number of players in the market and the increased role of regulators, it is critical for one to have basic familiarity with the major telecom players and regulators of the world. This chapter presents the information about the regulator, ministry & operators of top 5 countries chosen on the basis of mobile subscriptions. The chapter presents the list of top telecom firms in terms of brand value (2013 Statistics).

As per the ITU's mobile subscription statistics 2011, the top 15 regions in terms of mobile subscriptions include:

1. China,
2. India,
3. USA,
4. Russia,
5. Indonesia,
6. Brazil,
7. Japan,
8. Vietnam,
9. Germany,

© Springer India 2016

M.K. Medudula et al., *Telecom Management in Emerging Economies*,
DOI 10.1007/978-81-322-2749-6_2

10. Pakistan,
11. Italy,
12. Mexico,
13. Nigeria,
14. Philippines and
15. United Kingdom.

The top 15 regions represent over 50 % of the total mobile subscriptions in the world. During 2011, India and China accounted for over 50 % of the total APAC mobile subscriptions. In this chapter, we carry out a comparative analysis of some of the top regions in terms of average year on year growth rate, mobile penetration and subscription figures.

## 2.1 China

China, officially "The People's Republic of China" is the first nation to reach the 1 billion mark in terms of telecom subscriber growth. China's overall economic growth was achieved by its three-step development strategy, set in place in 1987. China was economically weak prior to 1949 and is today among one of the fastest developing nations in the telecom sector. China in its 12th Five Year plan talked about high bandwidth applications, spectrum usage and reframing, 4G services and improved information access for both public and private services.

### *2.1.1 Regulatory and Government Bodies: MII, MIIT and TAB*

The Ministry of Industry and Information Technology (MIIT) in China is the body responsible for regulating telecom services and the equipment manufacturing industry. MIIT was established in 2008, prior to which The Ministry of Information Industry (MII) had established full regulation and operations in the telecom sector. The Telecommunications Administration Bureau (TAB) was set up in 2000 and was given the responsibilities to formulate plans, policies and measures for telecommunications development in China.

### *2.1.2 Mobile Operators: China Mobile, China Unicom and China Telecom*

China Mobile, China Unicom and China Telecom hold most of the market share in China. As per company reports circa December 2012, China Mobile is the leading mobile operator in the country with over 710.3 Million subscribers followed by China Unicom with a subscriber base of 239.31 million subscribers and China Telecom with 160.62 million subscribers.

## 2.2 India

India, officially the Republic of India, is known for its diversity in region, religion, culture and consumer behaviour. Looking at the growth trajectory as per ITU statistics, the following graph shows a clear picture of year on year growth rate of wireless subscription of India which stood at over 64 % during 2000–2011 (Fig. 2.1).

As per the figures from a TRAI press release date 31 July 2015, the total subscriber base stood at 1009.31 million over 983.21 million wireless subscribers (TRAI 2015). India has the 2nd largest mobile subscriber base and is often recognized as one of the most competitive markets for operators.

### *2.2.1 Regulatory and Government Bodies: DOT, TRAI and TDSAT*

At the ministry level, the "Department of Telecommunications (DOT)" performs the role of a licensor and policy maker, while TRAI, established in 1997 by an act of parliament, acts as an independent legal authority to regulate telecommunications and associated services. An amendment to the TRAI Act in the year 2000 led to the setting up of Telecom Disputes Settlement and Appellate Tribunal (TDSAT) which looks after settlements and disputes in the telecom industry. More information about the various roles and responsibility of TRAI and TDSAT will be described in the next unit.

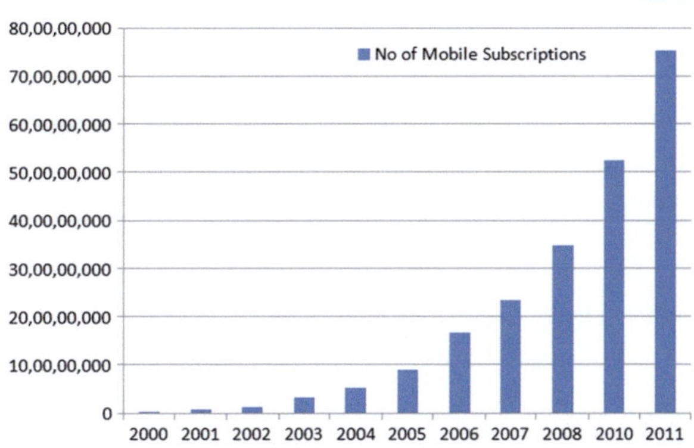


**Fig. 2.1** Yearwise Indian mobile subscription growth rate. *Data source* ITU statistics (2013) (*Year 2009 statistic is not available in the ITU statistics)

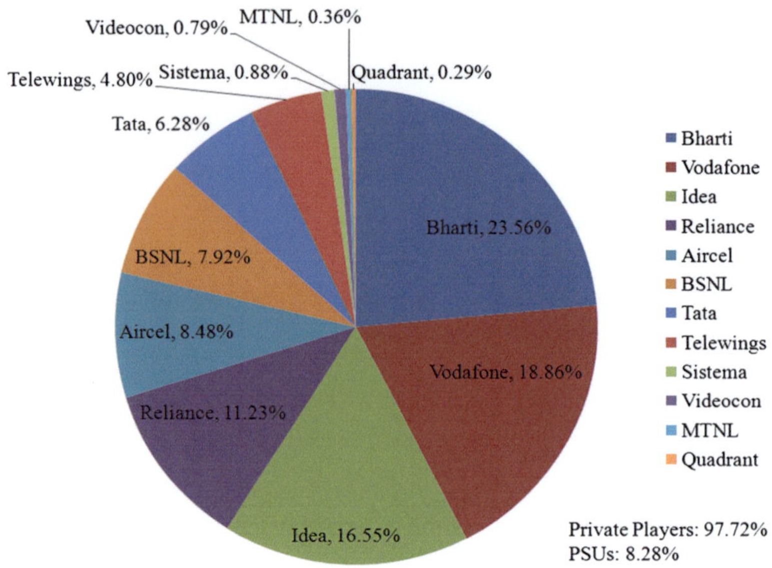


**Fig. 2.2** Access service provider-wise market shares in the wireless subscribers as on 31st July 2015. *Source* TRAI (2015)

### 2.2.2 *Mobile Operators: Incumbents and Private Players*

India is a highly competitive market for existing and new entrants in telecommunications. As of July 2015, there were 12 service providers where Bharti Airtel, Vodafone and Idea holding approximately 59 % of the wireless market whereas BSNL and MTNL had a combined market share of 74.31 % in the fixed-line (wireline) segment.

Bharti Airtel is India's first private operator to launch landline services for subscribers. With 18 years of experience in providing telecom services, Bharti Airtel went on to become the world's third largest operator in terms of subscribers with operations in 20 countries. It is the 1st player to reach 100 and 200 million subscribers in the Indian telecom market. As on 31st July, 2015 (Fig. 2.2), Bharti Airtel had 23.56 % of total wireless subscriber share and occupies the top position. Vodafone which acquired controlling stake in Hutchison Essar in 2007 is currently the 2nd largest mobile operator in India in terms of subscribers. Idea Cellular headquartered in Mumbai is the third largest operator.

## 2.3 USA

The USA has always assumed the role of a technology leader and is a front runner in the testing and adoption of various mobile standards. With over 100 % mobile penetration and extremely mature market, growth rate in terms of subscriber base has seen a downturn. When MCI Communications filed the antitrust lawsuit against Bell Systems, it resulted in the breakup of Bell Systems into seven Regional Bell Operating Companies (RBOCs). Over time, these divisions in the Bell Systems facilitated the formation of the current top two mobile operators—AT&T and Verizon.

### 2.3.1 *Regulatory Body: FCC*

Established in the year 1934 by the Communication Act, the Federal Communications Commission (FCC) regulates the Telecommunication sector for the entire US territory. FCC is further charted out into seven offices and six Bureaus which are further broken down into various divisions. It is the task of the "Wireless Telecommunication Bureau" to regulate mobile, broadband and spectrum usage in the US telecom industry. Enforcement Bureau of FCC is responsible to settle market disputes and handle customer complaints. Communication Act (1934) and Telecommunication Act (1996) are two important telecom acts in this sector.

### 2.3.2 *Mobile Operators: AT&T, Verizon, Sprint and T-Mobile*

Top mobile operators in terms of subscriber base include AT&T, Verizon, Sprint and T-Mobile, respectively. Verizon leads the mobile market with 31.2 % market share followed by AT&T (27.3 %), Sprint (10.3 %) and T-mobile (8.4 %) (Fig. 2.3).

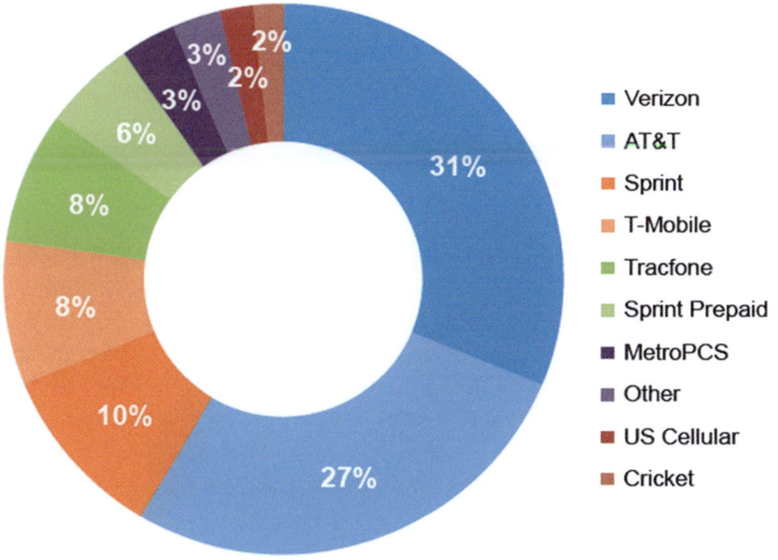


**Fig. 2.3** USA mobile service providers market share as on Q4, 2012. *Source* comScore Inc (2013)

These four operators hold more than 75 % of the mobile market share leaving behind Altel, US Cellular, Tracfone, Cricket MetroPCS, Sprint and other operators to share the rest 10–15 % of the mobile market. With decreasing voice ARPU in this region, data ARPU is chalked up as the most appropriate driver of future growth.

## 2.4 Russia

Russia, officially The Russian Federation is the largest country in terms of area and 9th largest in terms of population. As per ITU statistics, Russia had 237 million wireless subscribers in 2011 with an annual mobile growth rate of 3.32 % and a mobile penetration of over 179 %. Telecom markets are at a high maturity level and most operators develop strategies for customer retention. The Russian telecommunications industry is known to be mainly driven by data services.

### *2.4.1 Regulatory Body: Minkomsvyaz*

The Ministry of Telecom and Mass Communications of the Russian Federation (Minkomsvyaz) is the federal body that oversees and regulates the telecommunications sector in Russia. The ministry has the duties of both the policy maker and the regulator and takes care of allocation and conversion of the radio frequency spectrum. In its recent objective statements for the period 2012–2018, the ministry aims at providing the Internet to all the towns and villages by achieving 90 % penetration for broadband services.

### *2.4.2 Mobile Operators: MTS, Megafon, Vimplecom and Tele2*

Established in the year 1993, MTS was acquired by Sistema. MTS has been the leader in terms of implementing new technologies and acquiring market share.

Founded in 1993, Megafon is headquartered in Moscow and operates both as a fixed-line and a mobile service provider. Another operator Vimplecom has completed 20 years of operations in 2012 with a presence in over 18 countries worldwide. With over 10 different brands, Vimplecom provides mobile services in Russia under the brand "Beeline". Tele2, a Pan European telecom operator, entered the Russian market in 2001 and launched its first commercial GSM network in the year 2003. Tele2 has a presence in over 11 countries, out of which the Russian Market is one of the biggest. The telecom market is dominated by these service providers with MTS (31 %) being the leader followed by MegaFon (27 %) and VimpleCom (25 %), respectively, and the telecom market has entered the maturity stage (GSMA Intelligence 2012).

## 2.5 Indonesia

Indonesia, officially The Republic of Indonesia, is the third largest mobile market in APAC with over 211 million subscribers and more than 100 % mobile penetration. Indonesia has registered an average annual growth rate of mobile subscriptions of over 45 % during the period 2000–2011. By the end of 2017, mobile penetration is expected to reach 173.5 %, with nearly 444 million mobile subscribers (Business Monitor International 2013).

### *2.5.1 Regulatory and Government Body: BRTI and MCIT*

Established in the year 2003, BRTI (Badan Regulasi Telekomunikasi Indonesia) is the Indonesian Telecommunication Regulatory Authority which reports to the Ministry of Communication and Information Technology. BRTI is divided into the Telecom Regulatory Committee and the Director General of Posts and Telecom.

### *2.5.2 Mobile Operators: Telkomsel, XL Axiata and Indosat*

With growth in voice revenues approaching stagnation, Indonesian operators have increased focus on revenue from data streams. Usage of mobile commerce and social media on the mobile platform has increased in the past few years, and operators are focusing on non-voice streams for revenue growth by introducing data centric services in the market.

Established in the year 1995, Telkomsel is the leading mobile operator in Indonesia with over 120 million subscribers and one of the largest rural networks in the country. Telkomsel is the first mobile operator to reach 100 million subscribers and is one of the first operators to launch 3G services in Indonesia. XL Axiata started operations in 1996 and is currently the second largest mobile operator with over 42 million subscribers. Indosat is the third largest operator and offers mobile broadband services under the service names IM3, Mentari and Matrix.

The detailed list of countries with the name of the ministry, regulator, important laws, incumbent and private operators list can be found in table presented under Appendix A. This table gives the reader a brief overview of most of the telecom regions worldwide. It can be observed that most of the regions have created the laws for establishment-independent regulators and transformed the regulatory roles from the ministry. The table also presents the Websites of the ministry/regulator where the reader can look at for detailed information of the telecommunication sector in those particular regions. The incumbent operators in many regions of the world have been partially privatized and the liberalization process has resulted in establishing competitive environment for the service providers.

## 2.6 International Organizations in Telecom Sector

Most of the regions in the world have initiated regulations in form of telecom policies, laws and acts to invite participation from foreign and domestic players to put an end to monopoly. Establishment of independent regulator has created a level playing field for the new players among the established incumbents and protecting their interest by promoting healthy competition and reducing the SMP of incumbents. Privatization has benefitted the subscribers with improved services and faster deployments of next-generation networks in the sector. To achieve full globalization in terms of connectivity, several international bodies had played a significant role in establishing standards that enabled international roaming. This section gives you a brief of several organizations and associations who have contributed significantly to the welfare and growth of telecom industry. ITU plays a key role in maintaining the numbering system, recommending ideal radio frequencies for different technologies, assessing future requirements for telecom growth and collaborating for the development of new-generation technological standards.

### *2.6.1 International Telecommunication Union (ITU)*

ITU is the United Nations specialized agency for Information and Communication Technologies—ICTs. In Chap. 1, we have discussed three main areas of ITU where the agency works towards international cooperation between the Governments and private sector. ITU organizes its activities among various study groups which are part of the three main focus areas (radiocommunications, standardization and development) as depicted in Fig. 2.4.

ITU provides a platform for exchange of knowledge among the stakeholders which help in development of ICT sector. As a member of United Nations Development Group, ITU is committed to the development of ICT sector by establishing a platform for exchange of knowledge and international cooperation among various stakeholders in this sector. One of the significant works ITU performed was in the area of international radio frequency administration. The regulations regarding the international radio frequency are being approved by all the ITU member states. ITU-T is committed in development of standards for newer

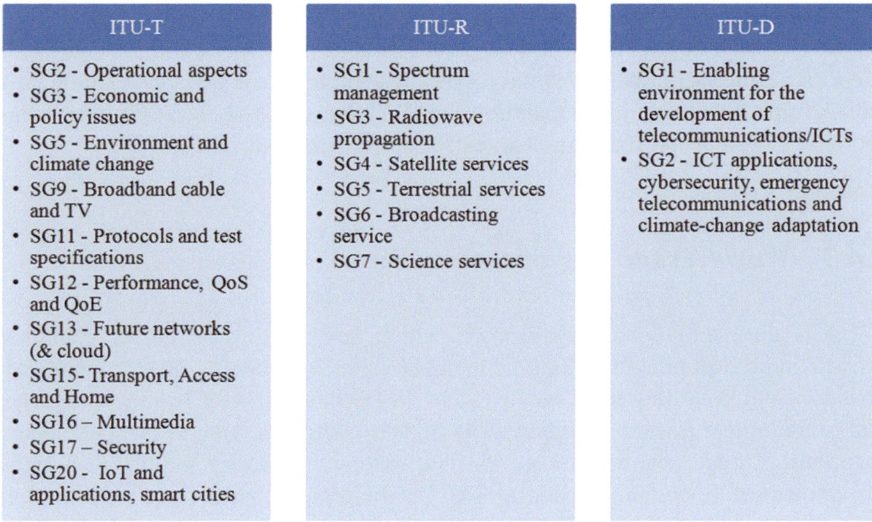


**Fig. 2.4** ITU study groups. *Data source* www.itu.int/

technologies in this sector and one of the focus groups (IMT-2020) is currently working on network standardization requirements for 5G. ITU-D aims at sustainable development and to spread equitable and affordable access for social and economic development. Another landmark activity undertaken by ITU was in drafting the "International Telecommunication Regulations (ITRs)" with document on final acts being presented at World Administrative Telegraph and Telephone Conference (WATTC). ITRs discuss the telecommunications service rules operating at international borders with the aim of promoting global connectivity.

### 2.6.2 *European Union (EU)*

The regulations and directives of European Union are being adopted by all the 28 member states of the Union. European Commission is EU's executive body responsible for protecting the interest of the Union by proposing legislations, enforcing laws and managing EU policies. EU legislation (Directive 2002/21/EC) has brought in a new chapter in the history of telecommunications in the member states. This directive on "common regulatory framework for electronic communications networks and services" has transformed the telecommunication sector by stimulating investment, liberalizing the sector and benefitting the consumers with more choices and improved service quality. This directive also mandated the member states to establish National Regulatory Authorities (NRAs) who take care of the regulatory functions of the sector. This separation of operation and regulatory functions has been coupled with granting independence to NRAs to perform their duties without any partialities. These steps have resulted in a more liberalized economy which helped the sector to attract foreign investment and provide better services for the subscribers. Several recent legislations of the European Union have led to further increase in cooperation among NRAs (No. 1211/2009) and better services with reduced roaming charges for consumers (No. 531/2012).

### 2.6.3 World Trade Organization (WTO)

WTO is an international organization which strives towards global economic growth and developments among its member states by reducing international trade obstacles and providing level playing field. WTO has currently 161 member states and is committed towards building trade capacity, implementing WTO agreements, involving in trade negotiations and dispute settlements among the member states. Department of Telecommunications (DoT) is the representative from India through Department of Commerce. Indian Government under the agreement with WTO has liberalized the telecommunication sector by allowing foreign equity in private firm that is registered in India. The discussions and negotiations among member states in during and post-Uruguay Round led to the development of regulatory framework for the basic telecommunications services. Member states who have submitted their commitments and signed the agreement have liberalized their telecom sector by lowering the entry barriers. Figure 2.5 highlights the various functions of WTO.

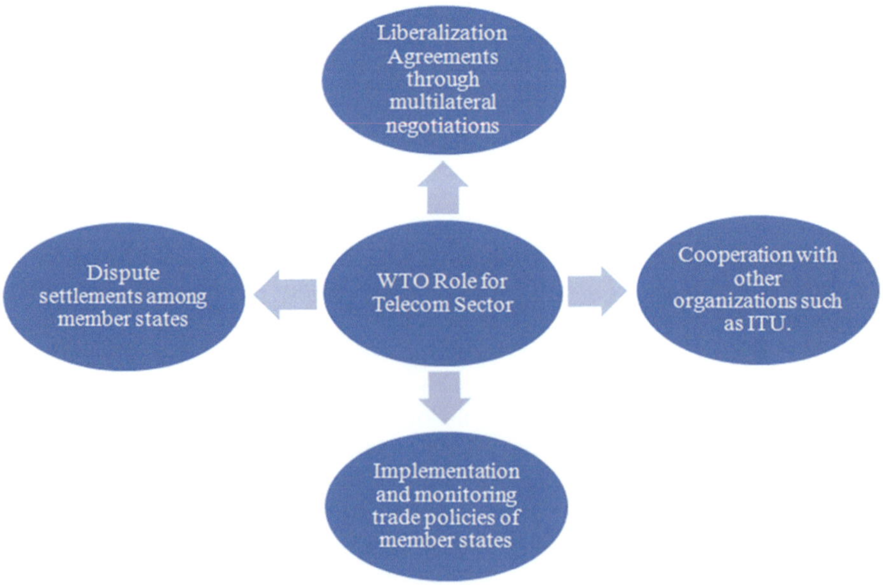


**Fig. 2.5** Activities and functions of WTO. *Data source* https://www.wto.org/english/thewto_e/whatis_e/what_we_do_e.htm

### 2.6.4 European Telecommunications Standards Institute (ETSI)

ETSI is an international standardization organization committed towards producing standards in the area of ICT that are recognized and accepted globally. This not-for-profit organization has several types of committees who work towards fulfilling the sector, and technological area needs through standardization activities and cooperation with other international organizations. In the area of 3G and 4G mobile communications, ETSI is a partner in 3rd Generation Partnership Project (3GPP) where it collaborated with several other organizations such as Association of Radio Industries and Businesses (ARIB); Alliance for Telecommunications Industry Solutions (ATIS); China Communications Standards Association (CCSA); Telecommunications Standards Development Society, India (TSDSI); Telecommunications Technology Association (TTA); and Telecommunication Technology Committee (TTC). ETSI has also partnered with TIA, ATIS and CCSA in global oneM2M partnership which is committed towards developing technical specifications and standards for machine-to-machine (M2M) and Internet of Things. Figure 2.6 shows the various committees that handle the functions of ETSI.

TC Broadband Radio Access Network (BRAN) works in the area of BWA spectrum and is committed towards producing standards and specifications. This committee produced standards such as HiperLan1, HiperLan2 and HiperACCESS. TC Digital Enhanced Cordless Telecommunications (DECT) is working towards DECT technology developments in ultra-low energy and new generation. As discussed earlier, ETSI has partnered in 3GPP which has developed several technologies such as EDGE (44 and 45 Series), HSPA, LTE, LTE advanced, UMTS and WCDMA. TC ERM [Electromagnetic Compatibility (EMC) and Radio Spectrum Matters] looks after the ETSI harmonized standards and coordinates with several committees in issue related to radio equipments and radio spectrum usage.

TC Satellite Earth Stations and Systems (SES) works in the area of satellite navigation systems and equipments and looks at the implemented protocols in this area. TC TETRA and Critical Communications Evolution (TCCE) works towards the development of standards in critical broadband communications and maintenance of existing TETRA standards. Reconfigurable Radio System (TC RRS) has four working groups with tasks in system aspects, security of RRS systems, radio equipment architecture and synergies establishment for public safety. ISG Open Radio equipment Interface (ORI) works towards the interoperability issues and strives towards making the elements between the base stations fully interoperable. More information about these committees and groups can be accessed from the official ETSI website.

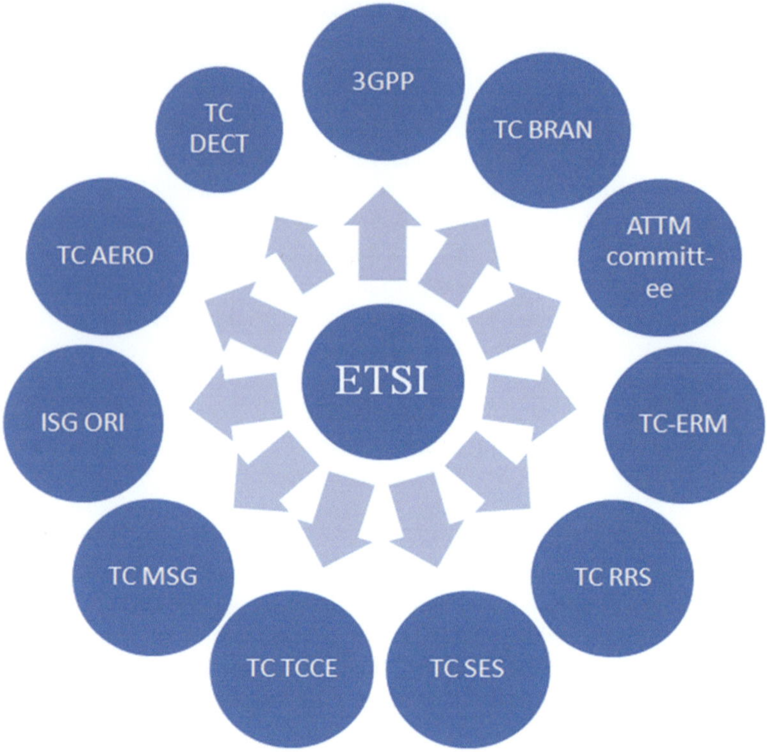


**Fig. 2.6** ETSI committees and groups in wireless systems. *Data source* http://www.etsi.org/technologies-clusters/clusters/wireless-systems

## 2.6.5 International Organization for Standardization (ISO)

National standard bodies of countries become the members of ISO. Bureau of Indian Standards (BIS) is the Indian member of ISO working towards development of standards and certifications. ISO standards help the MNCs, small and medium enterprises to build trust and gain consumer confidence which results in more business opportunities in the market place. ISO develops the standards for telecommunications sector in six stages as illustrated in Fig. 2.7.

ISO is working towards development of standards in several fields of telecommunications such as telecommunication infrastructure, telecommunication services and applications, telecommunication systems, telecommunication terminal equipment, radiocommunications, mobile services, Integrated Services for Digital Network (ISDN), fibre-optic communications, telecontrol telemetering, electromagnetic compatibility and in many other areas in this sectors.

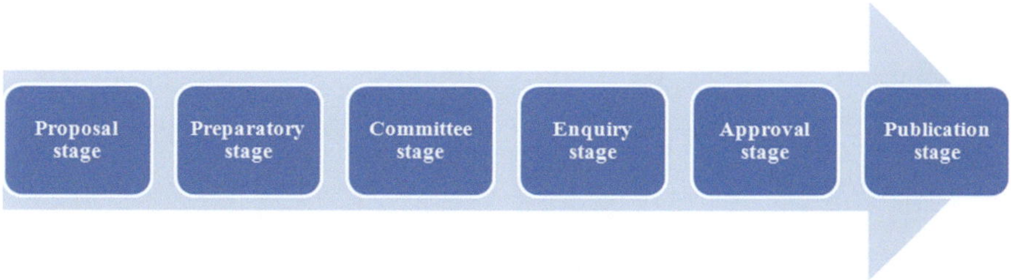


**Fig. 2.7** Stages in telecommunication standard development process of ISO. *Data source* http://www.iso.org/iso/home/standards_development/resources-for-technical-work/support-for-developing-standards.htm

### *2.6.6 GSM Association (GSMA)*

Mobile operator becomes an important entity in telecom value chain. GSMA represents the interests of mobile operators across the globe in various events and international forms. GSMA works towards building consensus among stakeholders involved in setting the frameworks and standards in respect of operational and technical matters (http://www.gsma.com/aboutus/leadership/committees-and-groups/working-groups). GSMA has several working groups and committees who work in several areas and programmes such as public policy, personal data, mobile for development, female digital economy, mobile economy, digital commerce, Network 2020, OneAPI, managed services and connected living programmes. Figure 2.8 highlights various areas where GSMA records the industry perspectives towards introducing pro-investment telecommunication policies.

GSMA is focussed on these areas with the aim to achieve their programme goals. As the representative of GMS operators in many international forums, GSMA aims at achieving the following goals:

- Defining best practices in disaster management process.
- Creation of scalable, replicable and commercially sustainable agricultural information and advisory services.
- To reduce global mobile gender gap and improve socio-economic benefits to women.

The list of various other international organizations is mentioned in Appendix B.

## 2.7 Top Telecom Firms in Terms of Brand Value

Brand equity is defined by David Aaker as the value a brand generates for the product (Aaker 1991). Brand equity is the output of any branding effort which reflects the dominance of the organization in the market place. Brand equity plays a

**Fig. 2.8** GSMA mobile policy areas. *Data source* http://mph.gsma.com/publicpolicy/handbook

critical role in helping companies gain a competitive edge over others in the business. Brand equity also represents the intangible part (good will) of an enterprise and defines the enterprise core value. As capital intensive as the telecom is, brand equity pays an important role and is one of the top parameters considered during mergers and acquisitions and joint ventures. Brand equity and brand value are two terminologies that measure the firms value. Brand value gets reported in the balance sheet of an organization.

Brand equity and brand value are being measured by several consulting firms that use proprietary methods to value a firm, product and consumer level. Interbrand, a leading brand consulting firm releases the list of top global brands. "Brand Finance" is the world's leading brand valuation consulting firm which periodically releases a list of the top 500 brands in terms of brand value. Top 36 telecom firms in terms of brand value released by Brand Finance are being depicted in the following diagrams.

As per the 2013 statistics, eleven firms in the telecom sector made it to the top 100 most valuable brands with only one firm among the top 10 list. Among the top 500 firms, 49 firms from the telecom sector made the list and include firms headquartered in USA, India, South Africa, Taiwan, Sweden, Saudi Arabia, Russian Federation, Norway, the Netherlands, Mexico, Republic of Korea, Japan, Italy, Hong Kong, United Kingdom, France, Finland, Spain, Germany, China, Switzerland, Canada, Brazil, Australia and UAE.

USA registered the most number of firms in top 500 brands followed by the Russian Federation, China, Japan and Canada, each with 3 firms in the list. Bharti Airtel is the only firm from India that made the list but with a drop of 126 ranks compared to its previous year rank (Fig. 2.9).

**Fig. 2.9** **a–c** Top telecom companies (operators+infrastructure service providers) in terms of brand value. *Data source* Brand Directory (2013)

(c)

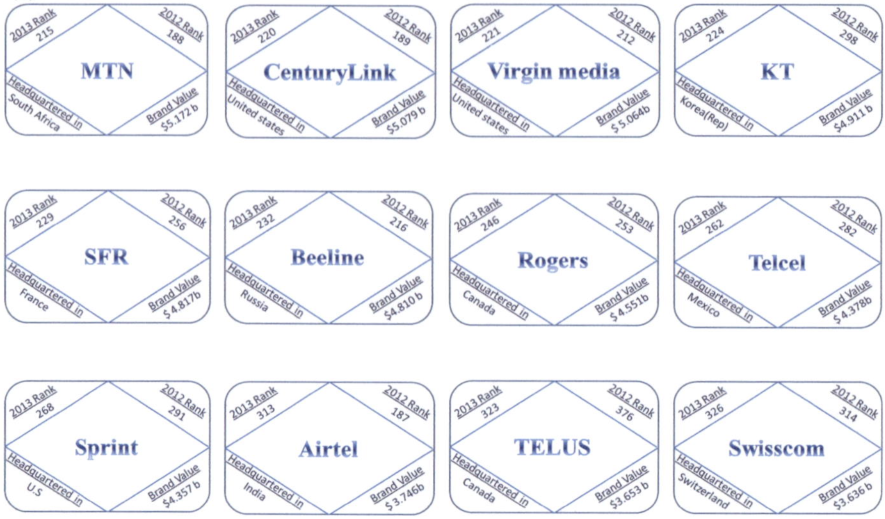


**Fig. 2.9** (continued)

## 2.8 Telecom Growth Rate Statistics

Growth rate analyses give an idea of market attractiveness and dynamics of the industry which helps us in identifying markets that are in growth, maturity and decline stages for particular services and products. The telecom industry has seen positive growth in most regions for the past decade with APAC and African geographies clearly emerging as the next major areas for growth. These two geographies are driving growth for most organizations and presenting enormous opportunities for new operators.

### *2.8.1 Growth Rate Statistics of Top Regions in Mobile Subscriptions*

Many regions have maintained a healthy growth rate during the past 10–15 years. This growth rate has led to over 100 % mobile penetration and improved rural access to telecom services. As per the ICT statistics, we have calculated near approximate figures for a 11-year period (2000–2011) and 5-year period (2006–2011). During the 11-year period, Nigeria has seen the highest average year on year growth rate of an impressive 169.24 % followed by Pakistan at 80.04 % followed by India at 66.94 % (Fig. 2.10).

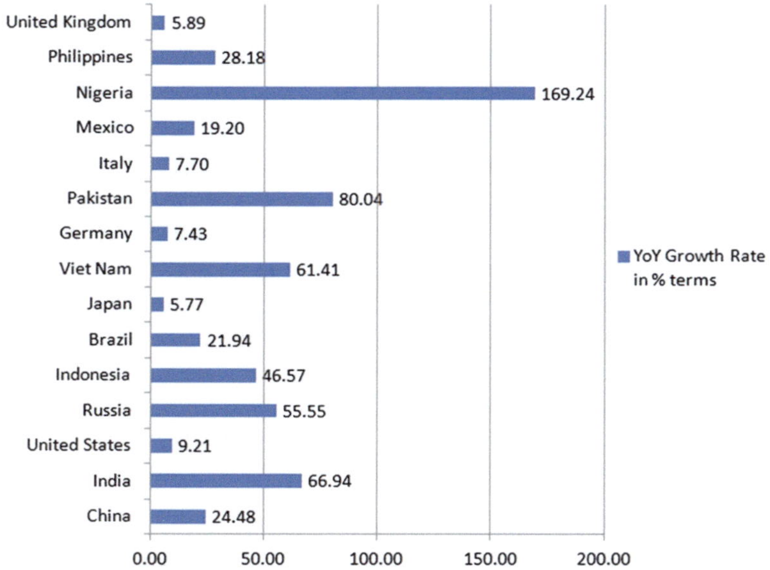


**Fig. 2.10** Average year on year growth rate of mobile subscriptions during 2000–2011. *Data source* ITU (2013)

UK registered the least average year on year growth rate of 5.89 % whereas average year on year growth rates for Philippines, Mexico, Italy, Germany, Vietnam, Japan, Brazil, Indonesia, Russia, USA and China has registered in at 28.18, 19.20, 7.70, 7.43, 61.41, 5.77, 21.94, 46.57, 55.55, 9.21 and 24.48 %, respectively.

Closer examination of 5-year growth rates during 2006–2011 reveals Vietnam to have witnessed the highest mobile subscription growth rate of 49.88 %. India has registered the next highest growth rate of 36.76 % followed by Pakistan at 26.90 %. Germany, Japan and USA have registered lowest average year on year growth rates among top 15 regions in terms of subscriber base (Fig. 2.11).

Of all the top regions with at least 1 million subscriptions during 2011, Uzbekistan, Uganda, Vietnam, Afghanistan and India have registered the top 5 average year on year growth rates in the world. Only those regions with maximum available information were chosen for this statistic. The chart below presents an overview of top regions that have registered over 20 % of average year on year growth rate during the period 2006–2011. Out of these 26 regions, Africa has seen 20 % average year on year growth rate in over 9 regions: Uganda, Côte d'Ivoire, Sudan, Egypt, Tanzania, Kenya, Ghana, Congo (Dem. Rep.) and Nigeria.

APAC registered more than 20 % average year on year growth rate in over 8 regions: Vietnam, Afghanistan, India, Iran (I.R.), Bangladesh, Indonesia, Sri Lanka and Pakistan, whereas 5 regions from Arab States, 2 regions from CIS and 2 regions from the Americas have registered more than 20 % average year on year growth rate during 2006–2011 and none of the regions from Europe registered growth rates of over 20 % (Fig. 2.12).

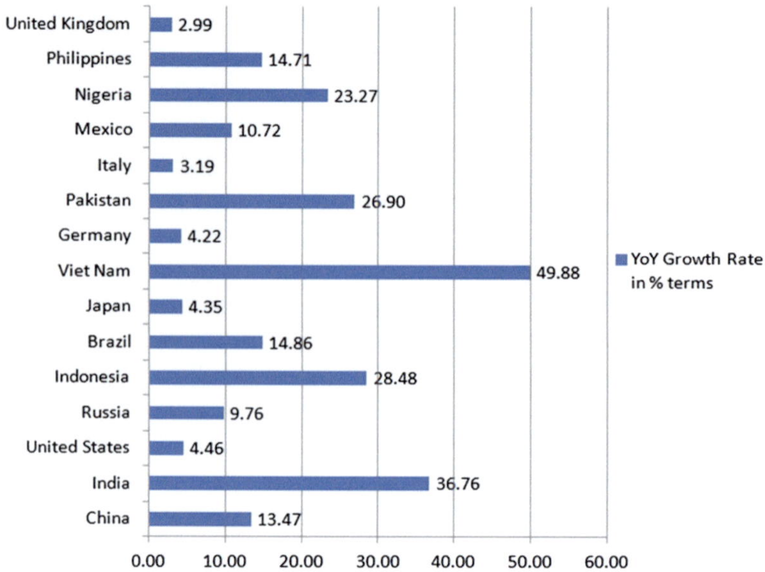


**Fig. 2.11** Average year on year growth rate of mobile subscriptions of Top 15 regions during the year 2006–2011. *Data source* ITU (2013)

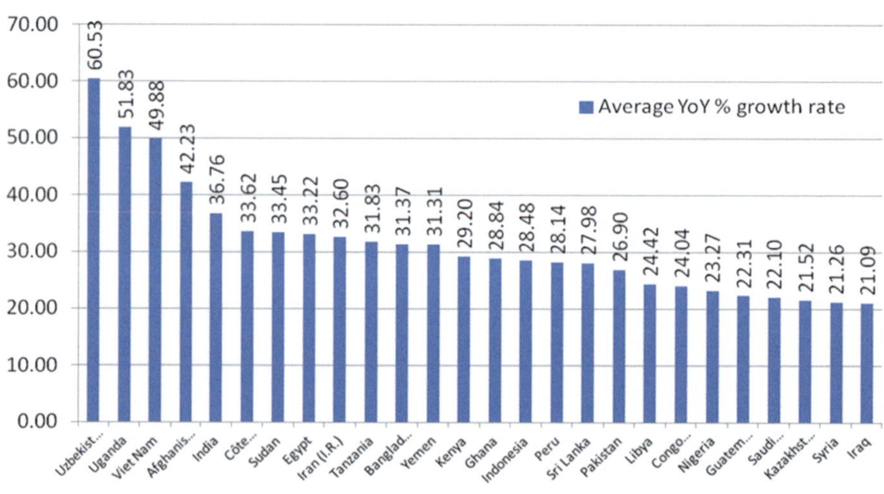


**Fig. 2.12** Average year on year growth rate for all the regions during the year 2006–2011 (mobile subscriptions > 1 million). *Data source* ITU (2013)

### 2.8.2 *Growth Rate Statistics of Top Regions in Fixed-Line Telephony Subscriptions*

With mobile penetration in many regions of the world moving towards or exceeding 100 %, the number of fixed-line telephone subscriptions has seen a major setback in terms of growth rates. In many regions, mobile operators have devoted resources towards the development of marketing strategies, and brand communication efforts directed towards the mobile platform. Very few advertisements and promotions schemes talk about the operators' fixed-line telephone service with most of the publicity efforts of the telecom companies being directed towards mobile services.

Due to more focus from the industry on wireless services, customers were ignorant on the schemes and latest gadgets available on fixed-line telephone subscriptions. In many regions, fixed-line telephone subscriptions and handsets have come with on-demand video services, but a simple pilot survey suggests that subscribers have no idea of such devices and services in the market place.

For our study on fixed-line telephone subscriptions, we relied on ITU's statistics during the period 2006–2011. In many regions of the world during the period 2006–2011, mobile penetration rates have improved tremendously which led to the decreased use of fixed-line telephone services.

During the year 2011, India stood 11th across all regions in the world and 4th in APAC in terms of fixed-line telephone subscriptions. China stands No.1 with over 28 million fixed-line telephone subscriptions followed by USA and Japan at 14.58 and 6.46 million, respectively.

These top 10 regions account for more than 50 % of all the fixed-line telephone subscriptions in the world. During the period 2006–2011, out of the top 10 regions, 5 regions have recorded negative growth rate and only 1 region registered a double-digit growth rate.

Figure 2.13 gives a clear outlook of growth rates of all the regions with more than 1 million fixed-line subscriptions in the world. It can be plausibly inferred that a majority of regions have faced negative or single-digit growth rates, suggesting that the overall market for the fixed-line telephone is on a decline. This would result in reduced price for services and less number of players who rely purely on fixed-line telephone subscribers.

Among all the regions in the chart below, only Indonesia registered a double-digit growth rate and 12 regions have registered less than 1 or negative growth rates. China, India, Turkey, Italy and USA had the least growth rate among these 22 regions. The negative and slow growth rate can be attributed to high mobile subscriptions and improved mobile access and penetration levels.

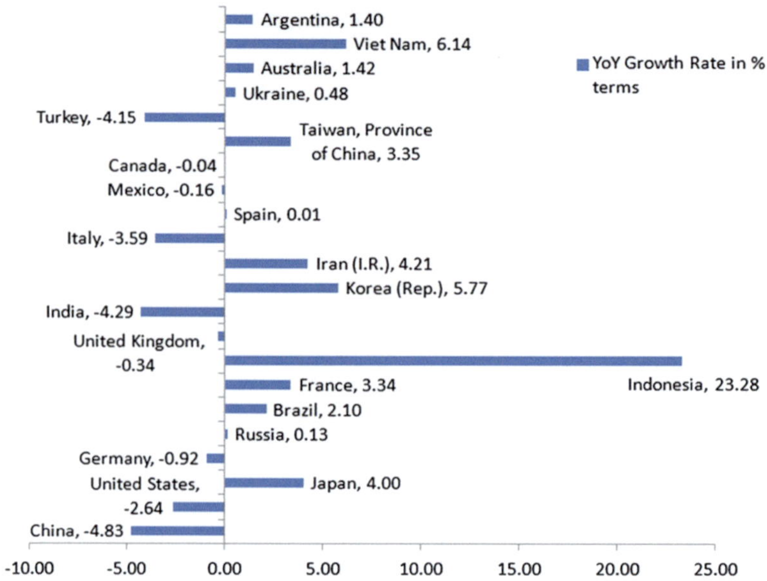


**Fig. 2.13** Average year on year growth rate during the year 2006–2011 for fixed-line subscriptions. *Data source* ITU (2013)

## 2.9 Concluding Remarks

Mobile subscriptions have helped the nations to improve the connectivity, and several regions in the world have achieved teledensity of over 100 %. This achievement would not have been possible by private sector participation and liberalization polices put into effect by their respective Governments. The transformational changes in both the technology front and the industry and regulatory practices could not be achieved without the involvement of various international organizations which helped in liberalizing the sector and have a healthy growth stage. The international organizations discussed in this chapter have played a key role in promoting growth in this sector and harmonizing all the effort towards providing better services for next generations. Telecom statistics presented in the chapter provides basic understanding to readers about the growth rate of mobile and fixed-line telephony subscriptions in top regions of the world. Many regions that were once dominated by fixed-line telephone services have seen a gradual fall in the number of subscriptions and the market growth is primarily in mobile services. India is not an exception to this global trend and liberalization policies have encouraged private players to enter and dominate the telecom sector in terms of subscriptions and growth rates.

In the next chapter, we present the duties of the regulator and its important role in improving teledensity, broadband services and rural coverage particularly in Indian Telecommunication sector.

# References

Aaker D (1991) Managing brand equity. Free Press, New York

Adiwiyoto B (2004) The role of a sectoral regulator: case of Indonesia in telecommunication sector. Available at: http://www.apeccp.org.tw/doc/Workshop/w2004/04010.pdf. Accessed 16 Oct 2014

Brand Directory (2013) Best global brands | brand profiles & valuations of the world's top brands. Available at: http://brandirectory.com/league_tables/table/global-500-2013. Accessed 3 Apr 2014

Business Monitor International (2013) Indonesia telecommunications report Q1 2013. Available at: http://www.researchandmarkets.com/reports/2355075/. Accessed 6 Sept 2014

comScore, Inc (2013) 2013 Mobile future in focus. Available at: http://www.comscore.com/Insights/Presentations_and_Whitepapers/2013/2013_Mobile_Future_in_Focus. Accessed 21 Jan 2015

GSMA Intelligence (2012) Russia hits mobile saturation point. Available at: https://gsmaintelligence.com/research/2012/06/russia-hits-mobile-saturation-point/339/. Accessed 11 Mar 2015

ITU (2013) Statistics. Available at: http://www.itu.int/ITU-D/ict/statistics/. Accessed 28 May 2014

TRAI (2015) Press release. Available at: http://www.trai.gov.in/WriteReadData/PressRealease/Document/PR-TSD-30092015.pdf. Accessed 15 Sept 2015

# Chapter 3
# Telecom Evolution and Role of Regulatory Bodies: The Indian Perspective

The invention of the electric telegraph in 1837 and the telephone by Alexander Graham Bell in 1876 led to the birth of a new industry that had the vision and the very real potential to broadcast voice and music and eventually become a platform for data services. The introduction of PSTN by Bell Systems afforded commercial viability and investment incentives to businesses. PSTN relied on circuit switching which became the core concept to provide voice services to the public.

As discussed in Chap. 1, the telecom industry plays a key role in the development of any nation and contributes significantly to GDP growth. As per TRAI press releases, the Indian telecom sector has come a long way from a mere 0.6 teledensity in 1990 to an impressive 81.83 as on 31st Dec, 2015 (TRAI 2016). An Urban teledensity of 152.45 and rural teledensity of 49.94 suggest that the Indian market has a lot to offer to telecom operators in terms of growth prospects. The evolution of the Indian telecom sector is a story of phenomenal growth rates and ambitious milestones. This chapter examines key transitions in this sector from the point of liberalization till the publication of the National Telecom Policy of 2012.

Two time frames accurately classify the overall telecommunication growth story in India. In the years prior to 1994, only three Government run operators [Department of Telecom (DoT), Mahanagar Telephone Nigam Limited (MTNL) and Videsh Sanchar Nigam Limited (VSNL)] were authorized to provide telecommunication services, and DoT maintained a monopoly across the subcontinent. MTNL, under the purview of DoT, was set up in 1986 to provide telephony services in Mumbai and Delhi circles, while VSNL was set up to provide international calling services.

Efforts to liberalize this sector in 1994 were a response to inadequate public funds, a need for faster roll-out of services and the objective to promote competition in the marketplace. This liberalization allowed new players to enter the marketplace. At the time, India was in the midst of a deep fiscal crisis, and liberalization of this sector presented an opportunity to reduce the fiscal deficit by opening up the telecommunication industry to private operators. Pager services were introduced by radio paging operators in 1992 and the industry was, for the very first time, opened

© Springer India 2016

M.K. Medudula et al., *Telecom Management in Emerging Economies*,
DOI 10.1007/978-81-322-2749-6_3

up to the private sector. Elaborate and ambitious plans were laid down in the 1994 Telecom Policy (NTP-94) with the aim of connecting the rural areas of India.

## 3.1 National Telecom Policy 1994 (NTP-94)

The key objectives of NTP-94 were to provide telecom services to everyone at affordable rates, maximum coverage of telephony services to the rural areas, establishing India as a manufacturing base and major exporter for telecom equipments and protecting the defence and security interests of the country. Due to the changes in technology taking place at that point in time, making India a technologically capable country was essential for reducing telecom infrastructure costs and facilitating faster network roll-outs.

NTP-94 was a big step for the ministry to enable and sustain growth in the telecom sector. NTP-94 facilitated the entry of private players to bridge the resource gap and opened up opportunities for players to provide telecom services on demand to everyone in the nation. India has been divided into 23 service areas which consist of 19 telecom circles and four metros. Licences were awarded to 8 CMTS operators in the four metros, 14 CMTS operators in 18 state circles, 6 BTS operators in 6 state circles and to paging operators in 27 cities and 18 state circles (DOT) (TRAI 1994).

Out of the 14 CMTS operators, only 9 were operational and the roll-out of services was never completed. Basic telecom services by private operators had only just commenced in a limited way in two of the six circles where licences were awarded. This slow rate of growth and the achievement of only 50 % rural coverage led the Government of India to recognize the need for a new telecom policy. NTP-94 certainly had shortcomings that were to an extent addressed in the next policy. During NTP-94, the privatization of the industry and service roll-out lagged because telecom providers spent excessive amounts on spectrum and lower financial resources prevented them from providing faster services (Sivasankari et al. 2008). Additionally, non-winning bidders had complained lack of transparency in the auction process. Plans were hence laid out for the new telecom policy to overcome these shortcomings, to meet the technical challenges and to aid the industry players in achieving faster and better growth rates.

## 3.2 Role of Regulatory Body (TRAI)

The entry of private operators and demands for independent regulation by these players led to the establishment of TRAI by an act of parliament as an independent legal authority to regulate telecommunication services.

### 3.2.1 Mandatory Functions

Mandatory/direct functions of TRAI include the following:

(a) Interconnectivity terms and conditions between operators.
(b) Compliance of terms and conditions of licence by the operators.
(c) Tariff and revenue sharing among operators.
(d) Quality of service.
(e) Ensure compliance of licence conditions.

TRAI issued regulations on number portability, quality of service, tariff orders, regulatory enforcements, commercial communication, mobile number portability (MNP), accounting and separation as well as many other areas. These regulations form part of the mandatory roles of TRAI. It can be observed from Fig. 3.1 that consumer protection is a top priority for the regulator.

Quality of service is important for service sectors, and minimum standards are to be maintained by the operators in telecom sector. Recent developments in Indian telecom sector suggest that TRAI has near zero tolerance when it comes to quality of service and the operators have been directed to compensate the customer/subscriber for call drops. This suggests that protecting the consumer right is of paramount importance and the time has come to work towards maintaining the quality standards.

Another key function of regulator is tariff restructuring where the subscriber would be able to use the services at affordable rates. TRAI through its tariff orders and amendments has regulated the prices from time to time for both fixed-line and cellular mobile telecom services. These tariff orders over a period of time had reduced the call rates, abolished charges for incoming calls and established the tariff ceilings for various other services. The sector has come a long way in improving the tariff structures which reduced the price difference between the local and domestic long distance calls. More details regarding the costing and pricing mechanisms of tariff will be detailed in Chap. 7.

Interconnection is the key for seamless connectivity. TRAI had protected both the consumer and operator interested towards providing best connectivity network through interconnection rules. The interconnection regulations (IUC) specify the charges and revenue sharing mechanism between the operators for local, domestic long distance and international calls. The call charges in roaming have been treated

**Fig. 3.1** Functions of TRAI. *Source* TRAI (2007)

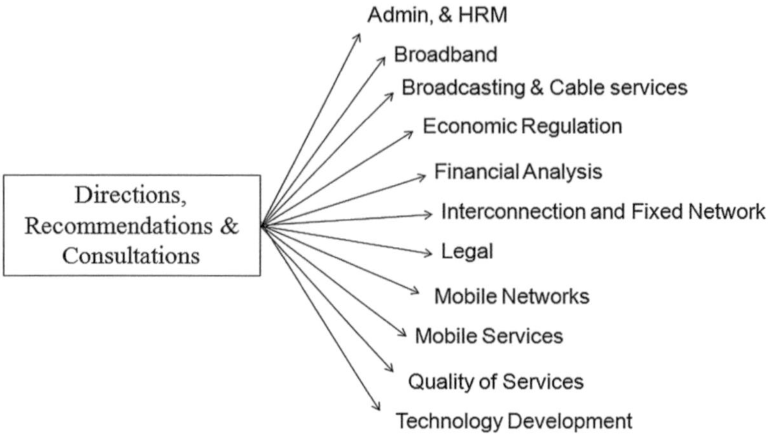


**Fig. 3.2** TRAI key focus areas in the telecom sector. *Data source* http://www.trai.gov.in/

at twice the cost of regular call by the initial regulations, but later on, the charges have been reduced considerably. Now, the operators provide free roaming for incoming calls on a nominal daily rental. The telecommunication interconnection usage charges are currently in twelfth amendment effective from 1 March 2015.

The regulator issues directions, recommendations and consultations in 11 key areas of the telecom sector as shown in Fig. 3.2.

With the establishment of the TDSAT (discussed in Sect. 3.4), TRAI was free from handling disputes which was earlier one of its key responsibilities. Detailed study of each of these directions, recommendations and consultations is out the scope of this chapter. More information can be found in the official Website of TRAI.

### *3.2.2 Recommendatory Functions*

Some of the key recommendatory functions of TRAI include the following:

(a) Licensing related issues such as terms and conditions of licence to service providers.
(b) Measures to facilitate competition and growth.
(c) Issues related to use of technology.
(d) Issues related to spectrum efficiency.
(e) Any other matter related to telecom industry in general, e.g. USO fund.

More information about the TRAI's contribution to the telecom sector can be found in its official Website "www.trai.gov.in".

## 3.3 New Telecom Policy 1999 (NTP-99)

Due to sluggish growth rates and the need for better policy architecture for promoting growth and to maintain the interests of the Nation, NTP-99 came as a major and key policy reform for this sector.

### *3.3.1 NTP 1999 Recommendations*

Key points in NTP-99 can be summarized as below (DoT 1999):

(a) Strengthen the objectives of NTP-94 by providing affordable services and telephony services on demand for everyone and by achieving entire rural coverage and teledensity of 7 by the year 2005 and teledensity of 15 by the year 2010.
(b) Operators were given the choice of connecting and sharing their infrastructure with any other operator within their service area and in consultation with TRAI for different service areas.
(c) Operators could provide last mile access by themselves without the intervention of DOT.
(d) Operators were allowed to move out from the licence fee payment regime to a revenue sharing regime. This provision is given for all telecom service providers including basic, cellular, paging and other value-added services.
(e) The licence period for cellular mobile service providers (CMSPs) was increased to 20 years which could be extended for another 10 years.
(f) To provide Internet access to all district headquarters by the year 2000.

NTP-99 reduced financial burdens by eliminating the annual licence fee and helped the operator to effectively utilize their networks by allowing network sharing. These measures improved teledensity to a greater extent, and TRAI played a major role in recommending the appropriate entry fee/revenue sharing structure between operators and the Government.

### *3.3.2 Impact of NTP 1999*

The failure of NTP-94, especially with respect to achieving the targets set by the policy, led authorities to revisit the framework. NTP-99 improved telecom growth, promoted privatization and deregulated the telecom sector to realize the benefits. Some of the objectives that were laid out in NTP-99 have been achieved with huge success, whereas others only attained limited success. Key outcomes of this policy were as follows:

(a) Teledensity increased by over 60 % by the year 2010.
(b) Implementation of calling party pay (CPP) regime and decreasing tariff costs resulted in telecom services becoming more affordable for subscribers.
(c) Rural teledensity crossed 30 % in 2011 with around 5.9 lakh villages connected.
(d) Internet access to all district headquarters by 2000 was not achieved.

## 3.4 Establishment of Telecom Disputes Settlement and Appellate Tribunal (TDSAT)

Due to the entry of private operators and the implementation of NTP-99, the telecom industry witnessed one of the fastest growth rates in the world. In the year 2000, an amendment of the TRAI Act 1997 resulted in functional clarity by clearly specifying the recommendatory and regulatory roles of TRAI. This amendment also led to the setting up of the TDSAT on 29 May 2000, empowering the tribunal to adjudicate any disputes between (a) the licensor and licensees, (b) service providers and (c) service providers and group of consumers (TRAI 2003a). TDSAT was empowered to appeal against directions, decisions and orders of TRAI. Establishment of the TDSAT led to the better functioning of the telecom sector and protected the interests of the consumers.

## 3.5 Wireless Local Loop (WLL)

Last mile access has been the single largest limiting factor for the provision of ubiquitous telephony services to rural areas. The costs involved in laying and maintaining copper lines were a costly process for providing services in low-demand regions. WLL offered cost-effective alternatives to copper and ensured faster roll-out of services.

WLL initially made use of licence-free spectrum bands worldwide, but due to an increasing number of interference problems and costly maintenance operations, service providers started using licensed bands by getting the licence from respective ministries. In the Indian landscape, last mile access was a serious issue and WLL provided an appropriate and affordable solution to this problem. In consultation with TRAI and as per TRAI recommendations, DOT permitted limited mobility services for WLL. Since technological advancements like WLL potentially benefitted people by providing cost-effectiveness and low maintenance solutions to last mile access issues, DOT allowed WLL only with limited mobility so as to maintain a boundary between the basic and wireless services and protect the interests of the mobile operators (Fig. 3.3).

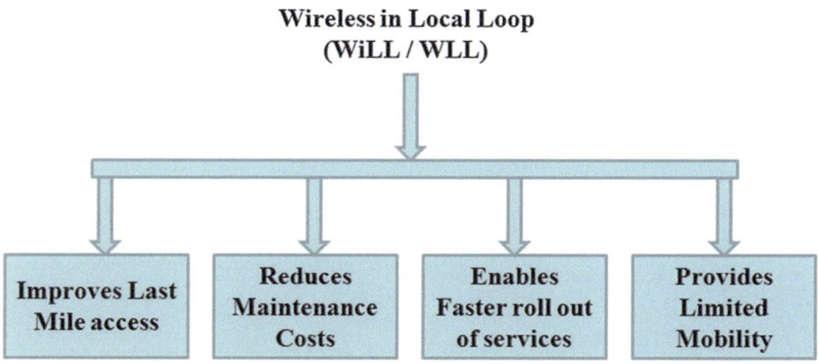


**Fig. 3.3** Advantages of wireless local loop network

The launch of CDMA technology resulted big firms like Reliance to enter the basic telephony market and provide services using WLL technology. This was objected to by incumbent operators who presented many criticisms and this resulted in arguments between CDMA and GSM operators. The Government realized that technological advancements worldwide should not be restricted by licensing conditions and opined that the way in which landline and fixed telephony services were provided was vague and the time had come to free licensing issues from these categorizations. DOT, as per the recommendations of TRAI, mandated the issue of Unified Licenses in the year 2003. This emphasized the Government view point that benefits of technological advancements should reach the end-user and regulation must take necessary steps to protect consumers' interest.

## 3.6 Unified Licensing Regime

Advancements in telecommunications technology and the need for technology neutral licenses formed the impetus for the removal of fundamental distinctions between fixed-line and wireless services. WLL possesses the capability to provide both local and long distance calls at almost the same cost. The end result of the implementation of the unified Licensing regime was that the geographic boundaries in terms of circles created under NTP-94 started falling apart as fixed telephony and mobile telephony were provided at similar tariff structures. In 2006, Reliance Infocomm launched the IndiaOne tariff plan. The following benefits led to the launch of unified licensing regime by DOT (Fig. 3.4).

Since the telecom sector is highly capital-intensive and operators must invest huge amounts of capital to roll-out networks, it is important for the industry to not be limited in its use of technology. TRAI recommended that the industry gets the full advantages of new technology and be on par with global technical standards. The industry was in the midst of a rapid growth stage and in urgent need of market

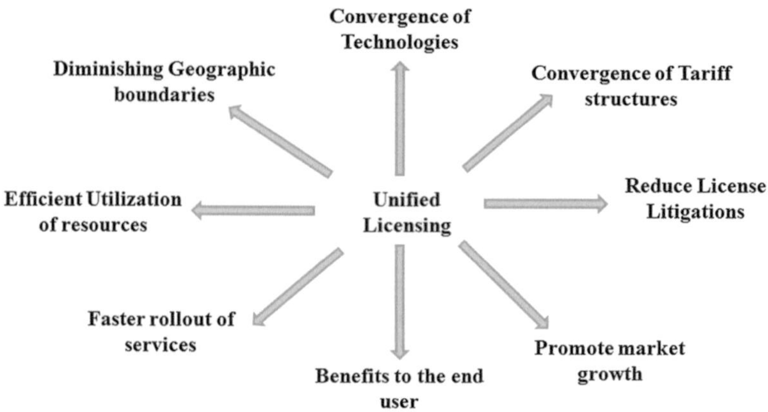


**Fig. 3.4** Factors that led to a unified Licensing Regime in Indian telecommunication sector

growth and faster roll-out of services. There was also a clear and present need to improve quality of services and provide better last mile access.

By means of an addendum to NTP-99, the Ministry of Communications and Information Technology established two categories of licences (TRAI 2003b):

(a) Unified Licence for telecommunication services permitted licensees to provide all telecommunication/telegraph services covering various geographical areas using any technology;
(b) Licence for Unified Access (Basic and Cellular) Services permitted licensees to provide basic and/or cellular services using any technology in defined service area/(s).

The Unified Licence has given the operator the right to launch services throughout the nation, subject to the availability of adequate amounts of spectrum. Unified Licensing has eradicated the segmentation for operators by region and the type of service provided. This licensing framework has removed the limitation of NTP-94 that restricted a single operator from providing telephony services in more than three circles in category "A" and "B".

This unified Licensing Regime was followed by a new set of recommendations from TRAI in the year 2010. In its recommendations on "Spectrum Management and Licensing Framework" dated 11 May 2010, the regulator recommended that all future licences be unified and highlighted the need to delink spectrum from the licence.

Due to the technology and policy advancements in the sector, teledensity had improved to 7 and the subscriber base had crossed 70 million by the year 2003. "A", "B" and "C" circles witnessed over 100 % growth rates during 2003–2004. The figures on broadband Internet remained low with the penetration of broadband and Internet at 0.02 and 0.4 %, respectively, by December 2003. Lower penetration and a lack of standards led to the design and development of the Broadband Policy in the year 2004.

## 3.7 Broadband Policy, Plan and Growth Rate Statistics

### *3.7.1 Broadband Policy 2004*

To promote Internet growth, the Government opened up the sector to ISPs in November 1998. The Broadband Policy helped identify service characteristics and established targets of 3, 9 and 20 million broadband connections to be achieved by the years 2005, 2007 and 2010, respectively. The policy framework laid out various technological options and pointed out the limitations of broadband services offered through copper loops. DOT (BSNL) and MTNL had an extensive copper network, but due to the technical reasons, only 7 million lines could be leveraged for broadband services. Some access technologies identified by this policy are represented in Fig. 3.5.

BSNL and MTNL targeted 1.5 million connections by the end of 2005. DSL technology was used to fulfil the targets set by the policy. A growth in broadband would in turn fuel the growth of other sectors in the country, i.e. education, governance, medicine and entertainment. A provision for quarterly review of the performance of the private players and PSUs was also put into place.

During the first year of the policy implementation, only 0.61 million broadband connections were achieved, which was far below the 3 million target (TRAI 2005). TRAI once again recommended to the ministry to unbundle the local loop so as to fully utilize the network. In an effort to promote competition and bring down tariffs/charges for international connectivity and broadband services, TRAI, by virtue of its powers, imposed binding price controls for International Private Leased Circuits (IPLCs) and Domestic Leased Line. To improve broadband services for mobility, TRAI recommended the allocation of permanent IP addresses for broadband and migration to IPv6 from IPv4 protocols.

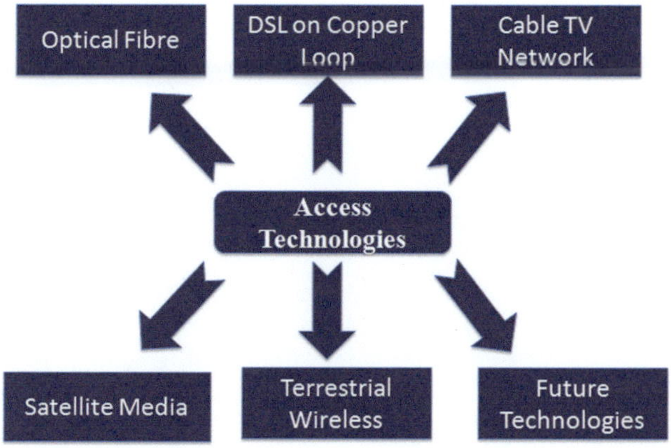


**Fig. 3.5** Access technologies for broadband provide (TRAI 2005)

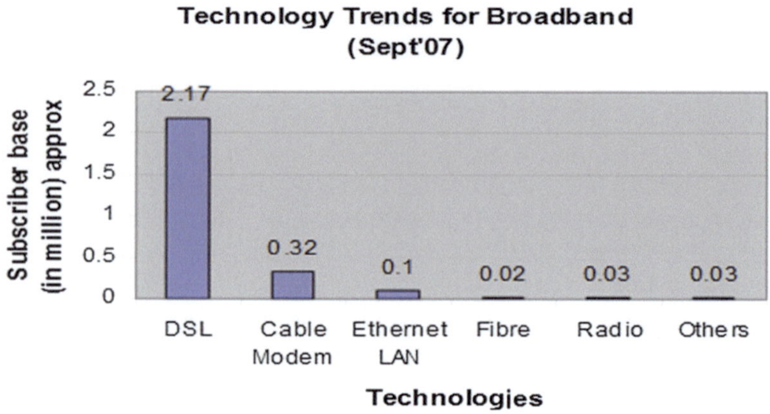


**Fig. 3.6** Broadband technological trends. *Source* TRAI (2008)

A look at broadband growth rate statistics for the year 2007 suggests that broadband uptake was not very encouraging with a mere 2.67 million connections as of September 2007 (TRAI 2008). Technological trends suggested that DSL was the most sought after by operators to provide broadband connections (Fig. 3.6).

The Ministry of Telecom and IT could foresee that for the second time targets set by the Broadband policy were not going to be achieved. China added more than 40 times the number of broadband connections in India in the quarter during 2007. At the same time, the Government was also drafting out the National e-governance plan and envisioning the establishment of statewide area networks for greater information access to the public. The urgency to improve broadband penetration and usage led to the declaration of the year 2007 as "Year of Broadband". To make efficient use of the local loop, TRAI recommended the franchisee model as an alternative to unbundling the local loop. Such a model held a possible solution to the shortage of customer-premises equipments (CPEs). Release of spectrum for 3G and WiMAX was critical to the growth of broadband in the nation, and TRAI recommended this move in the same policy.

### 3.7.2 *Broadband Plan 2010*

A review of the National Broadband Plan in the year 2010 revealed that the target of 20 million broadband connections was far from reality. As of September 2010, there were 10.30 million broadband connections with Chennai, Bangalore, Delhi and Mumbai leading the pack as the top 4 cities in terms of subscriber base. BSNL alone accounted for over 50 % of subscribers. The National Broadband Plan recommended the establishment of an open access broadband networks on optical fibre, connecting all habitation with population of 500 and above. The setting up of this network was to be established in two phases. The first phase covering all cities, urban areas and Gram Panchayats was scheduled for completion by the year 2012. Phase II would see the extension of this network to all habitations with a population over 500 by 2013. The objectives of this plan were to provide 75 million broadband connections (17 million DSL, 30 million cable and 28 million wireless broadband) by the year 2012 and 160 million broadband connections (22 million DSL, 78 million cable and 60 million wireless broadband) by the year 2014. This plan also aimed at providing fibre to homes in 63 cities covered under JNNURM and fibre to the kerb in all other cities (TRAI 2011).

### 3.7.3 *Wireless Broadband Statistics*

In line with the recommendations of TRAI, 3G spectrum and BWA spectrum were released and auctioned in 2010, providing operators with a plethora of opportunities to improve broadband penetration and provide value-added services. The launch of 3G and 4G services resulted in better penetration of broadband Internet and affordability of services. Service providers have implemented several pricing strategies according to the needs of various customer groups. The statistics released by TRAI shows us a clear picture of significant improvement in wireless broadband subscribers when compared to wireline broadband subscribers. Figure 3.7 highlights the growth of broadband subscribers during the year 2014–2015.

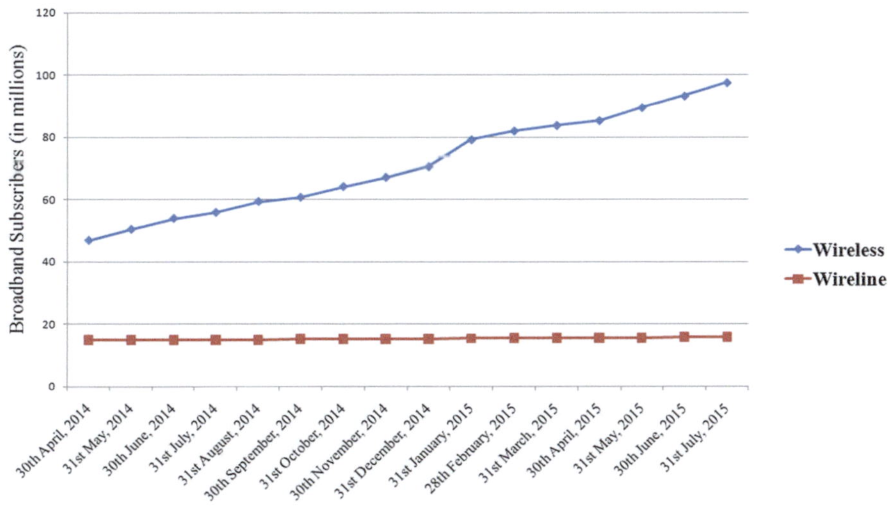


**Fig. 3.7** Telecom broadband growth rate statistics. *Data source* http://www.trai.gov.in/

## 3.8 Mobile Number Portability

In an effort to further develop the telecom sector for both customers and the industry, TRAI and DoT implemented several regulations and policies to initiate some key changes in the sector.

MNP is one such initiative for mobile telephony subscribers who desire to switch from one operator to another while retaining their mobile number. MNP has been implemented in most regions worldwide. First implemented in Singapore in 1997, the policy was replicated across the world in countries such as the UK, Hong Kong and Netherlands by 1999. The introduction of MNP resulted in a more competitive environment where the service providers strive towards offering better quality services and innovative products to attract subscribers.

MNP is considered a winning proposition for all key stakeholders such as regulators, operators and subscribers, in the long run (Iconectiv 2013). The Government announced guidelines for MNP service licence in the country on 1 August 2008 and brought in a separate licence for MNP service w.e.f. 20.03.2009.

### *3.8.1 Key Aspects for MNP Construction*

As per TRAI (2009), MNP regulations issued in September 2009, the key aspects of the MNP framework are as follows:

(a) Clear unambiguous eligibility conditions for the porting of mobile numbers.
(b) Definition of rights and obligations of all stakeholders—the donor operator, the recipient operator and the MNP service provider.
(c) Procedure to be followed by each player in the chain in processing porting request.
(d) Specification of time limits for the completion of steps by each player in the chain.
(e) Envisaging least disruption of services to the consumer.

### *3.8.2 Imperatives for MNP Adoption*

For MNP to be successful, the following have to be considered.

(a) Simplicity: The cost structure for both operators and end subscribers.
(b) Subscriber friendliness: Subscription fees have been kept extremely low (maximum of INR 19) to ensure negligible barrier to porting.
(c) Equitable: Fees have to be equitable.
(d) Stability: The MNP system must be driven by the goal of maximizing the success of implementation.

DoT guidelines have geographically divided the country into two Number Portability Zones (zone 1 and zone 2), each comprising 11 licensed service areas. MNP can be implemented in 2 different ways—donor-led porting and recipient-led porting. India, like the international and European standards, has adopted the "recipient-led" porting standard. Internationally, MNP is free of charge for the subscriber and costs are borne by operators.

## 3.9 National Telecom Policy 2012

The increasing presence of India as a leading developing economy provided for vast growth potentials for telecom players. To tap into this potential and emerge as a global leader, India needs to work hard at creating basic infrastructure for growth. The telecommunication sector has the potential to be a key driver of growth, and the Telecom Policy of 2012 stresses on the need to provide affordable and quality telecommunication services in rural and remote areas. According to DoT (2012), the major objectives are as follows:

- To provide secure, affordable and high-quality telecommunication service to all citizens.
- To aim at empowering citizens through the use and implementation of telecom services by enabling their participation in e-governance in key sectors such as health, banking, education, governance and employment. and by repositioning the mobile phone as an empowerment device that combines communication with proof of identity, financial transactions and other related facilities.
- To achieve One Nation—Free Roaming and strive to create One Nation—One Licence across services and service areas.
- To provide high-quality and affordable broadband services to all villages and habitations taking access to every nook and corner of the country. NTP-2012 also talks of issues such as protection of consumer interests and the adoption of a green policy in telecom.

Encouraged by the success of New Telecom Policy 1999 which resulted in an increased teledensity and very low tariff rates. National Telecom Policy 2012 went a step ahead by taking forward the ideology of inclusive growth and increased focus on making the Internet and mobile tools for not only communication but also towards empowering the common man.

The policy addresses to decrease the gap between rural teledensity and urban teledensity and other telecom services with special focus on addressing the needs of rural India. While the Telecom Policy of 1999 focused on creating basic infrastructure, the Telecom Policy of 2012 addressed current issues of prime importance such as consumer awareness, sustainability and health concerns. It also talked about creating an investor friendly environment and promoting indigenous R&D.

## 3.10 Growth of Indian Telecom Sector: Trends

Subscriber statistics present an interesting picture of the growth and maturity stages of Indian telecom sector. The statistics reveal that during period of December 2008 till December 2011, there was a positive growth in number of wireless subscribers and improvement in teledensity. During the year 2012, for the first time, a slight decrease is visible in these numbers. The growth stage of Indian telecom sector is very impressive with many of the operators more than doubled their subscriber base. Today, the market is very competitive and more number of players in each circle presenting challenges to maintain the subscriber base and sustain growth. Figure 3.8 shows the growth story of wireless subscriptions of top four private telecom mobile network operators in India.

During these years, there has been a gradual decrease in number of subscription in wireline segment as more number of subscribers preferred wireless services. The overall teledensity has increased twofold with significant improvement in rural teledensity. During this period, overall teledensity improved with average YoY growth rate of 16.17 %. The digital divide improved during these years and yet there is a lot of scope for further growth in this sector. Figure 3.9 shows the growth rate in telecom subscribers which shows the fixed-line market is in maturity stage with gradual decline in subscriptions. Wireless segment has increased nearly threefold clearly dominating the sector and paving the way towards improved teledensity and mobile broadband for subscribers.

PSUs dominate the wireline market with more than 70 % of the market share, whereas they have collectively less than 9 % of the wireless subscriber market share (TRAI 2015). Another key indicator to telecom growth is teledensity. Teledensity is often looked at an important parameter in analysing the digital divide of the nation.

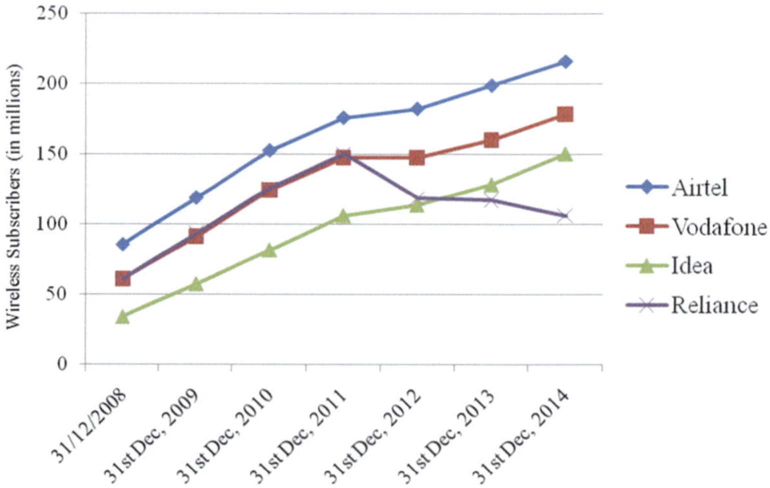


**Fig. 3.8** MNO wireless subscriber growth rate. *Data source* http://www.trai.gov.in

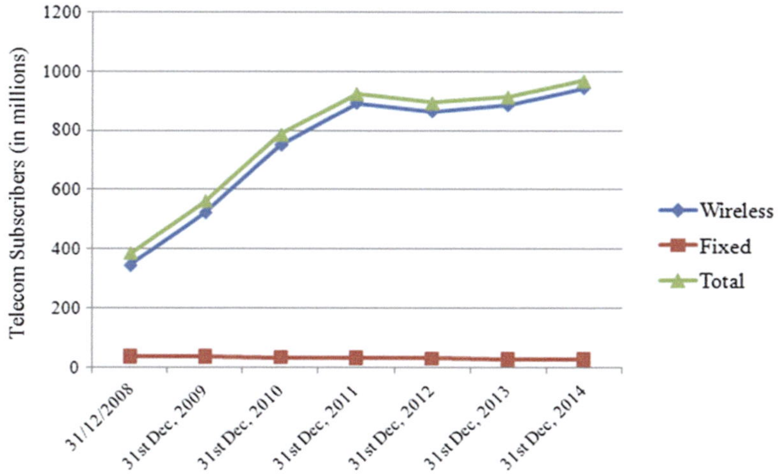


**Fig. 3.9** Telecom subscribers (fixed-line and wireless) growth rate. *Data source* http://www.trai.gov.in

Overall, teledensity helps us in understanding the penetration of telecom services, and rural and urban teledensities give us the disparity figure in terms of connectivity. Figure 3.10 presents the increase in rural and overall teledensities in Indian telecom sector.

The urban teledensity is over 100 suggesting more than 1 subscription per person. With launch of 3G and 4G services, mobile services are seen as an important tool to increase ICT adoption, bridge the digital divide and improve citizen participation in governance-related activities. To make use of this phenomenal growth in Indian telecommunication sector, Department of Electronics and Information Technology

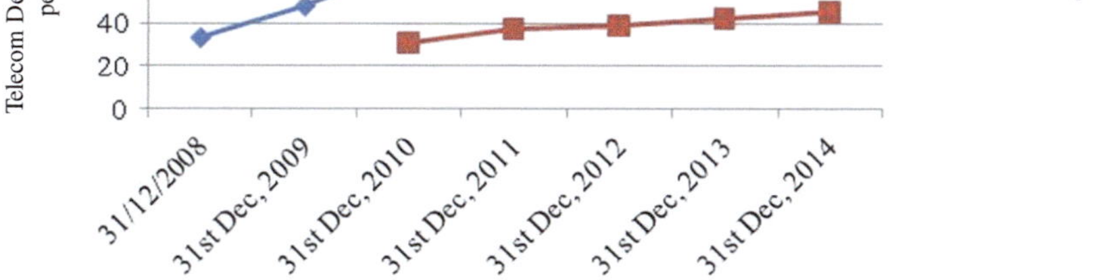


**Fig. 3.10** Teledensity statistics. *Data source* http://www.trai.gov.in

(DeitY), Government of India has formulated a revolutionary framework "Mobile Seva" in providing citizen services such as rail ticket, Kisaan SMS, Aadhar, PAN, EPF and passport on mobile platform (http://india.gov.in).

The phenomenal growth of any sector includes active industry participation and consumer involvement through adoption. Liberalization policies and FDI play a key role in the growth cycle of an industry. During the introductory phase of mobile services, each sector had not more than two service providers in wireless market. India adopted the duopoly during the initial phase slowly progressing towards more liberalized initiatives to attract more investment and players. Resultantly, there was a healthy growth cycle coupled with new technological deployments for better services for subscribers. Presently, the sector is highly competitive with 12 wireless access service providers and not less than 5 operators/service providers per telecom circle. It is interesting to examine the trend in competition growth rate in this sector over a period of time in last two decades. Herfindahl–Hirschman Index (HHI) gives us an idea of the market concentration and is equal to the squares of the individual firm's percentage market share (HHI 2015). In a monopolistic market, single firm has 100 % market share and the HHI would come to be 10,000. Whereas theoretically in a pure competitive market, each firm has near 0 % market share; hence, HHI value would approach zero. Looking at this index over a period of time gives us some information about the market concentration of the sector and presents some insights on market/sector competitiveness. Figure 3.11 shows the trend in HHI for wireless market, and Fig. 3.12 presents the trend for wireline market for the past 5 years.

It can be observed that HH index in wireless sector is below 1500 for over a period of six years suggesting a competitive market environment in this segment. On the contrary, the HH index values in the range of 4000–6000 suggest that the wireline market is less competitive in nature in comparison with wireless market.

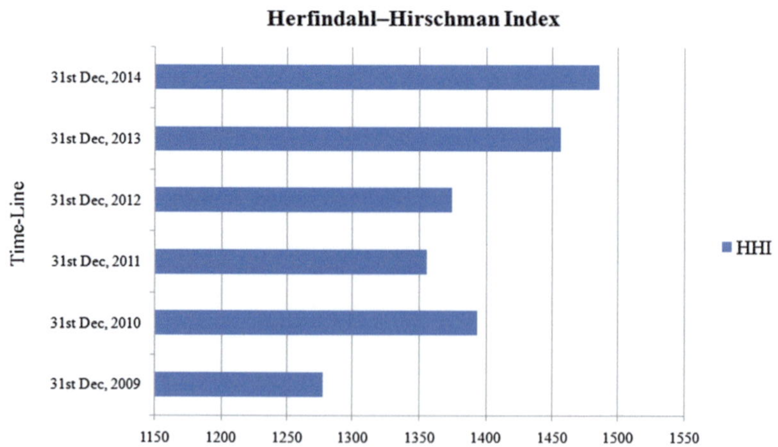


**Fig. 3.11** HHI for Indian wireless access market. *Data source* http://www.trai.gov.in

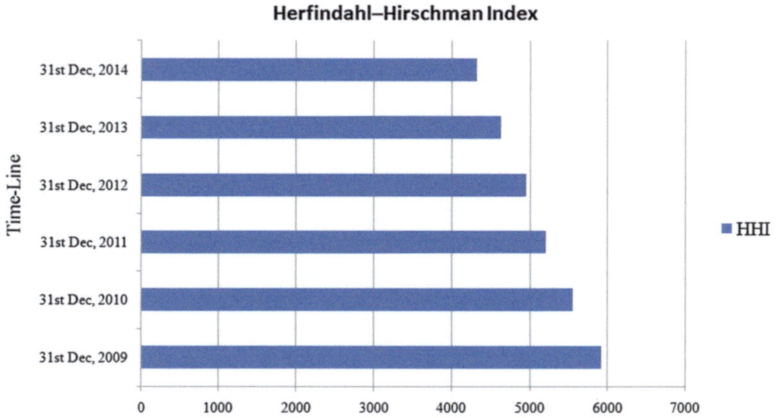


**Fig. 3.12** HHI for Indian wireline access market. *Data source* http://www.trai.gov.in

Over a period of time, the wireline market has entered the maturity stage and the numbers of subscriptions have started declining. HH index suggests that there is lesser competition in wireline segment which may be the result of reduced attractiveness and consumer adoption. The HHI statistics suggest that competiveness may give us some insights about the market growth. Wireless subscribers prefer the best network quality provider with better customer service and plethora of value-added services (Sharma et al. 2015). Hence, the growth of wireless telecom market can be attributed to value-added services being offered which acts as a motivator for consumer adoption.

## 3.11 Timeline of Major Events in Indian Telecom Sector

The Indian telecom sector is the third largest in terms of network and second largest in terms of subscriptions. During the period 18–19 years after liberalization, the Indian telecom sector transitioned through many changes in terms of technology, policy architectures, number of players in the market and the type of services offered to subscribers. We can look at the entire evolutionary process in telecom industry in four major time intervals as shown in Fig. 3.13.

**Fig. 3.13** Telecom evolution time frames

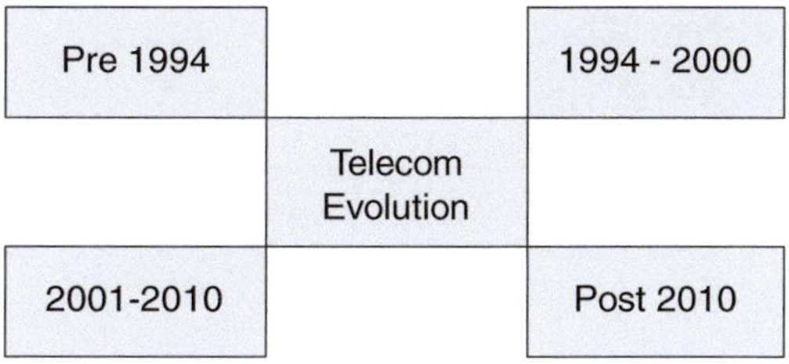

During each of these time frames, several technical and policy level changes took place in the sector with the aim of improving teledensity, rural coverage, quality of services and broadband in the country. Telecom commission was set up in 1989 to work collaboratively with DoT in policy formulation and spectrum management. Indian Wireless Act (1993) was put into effect to regulate the possession of wireless telegraphy apparatus. The Broadband Policy (2004), initiation of National Optic Fibre Network (NOFN) in 2011 and launch of 3G and 4G services aims at providing high-speed information access to the citizens and improve their quality of life. NOFN aims at proving broadband services to all the states covering cities, district headquarters and till the Gram Panchayat level. The broadband subscribers as on 31 July 2015 stood at 113.32 million, out of which approximately 86 % of the subscribers are on wireless broadband (TRAI 2015). In the year 2012, for the first time in the history of liberalized Indian telecommunication sector, the Supreme Court of India had cancelled all the 122 2G licences and stated that the eligibility criteria were not followed during the allocations properly. Figure 3.14 presents the key events according to the time frames which established the present telecom industry.

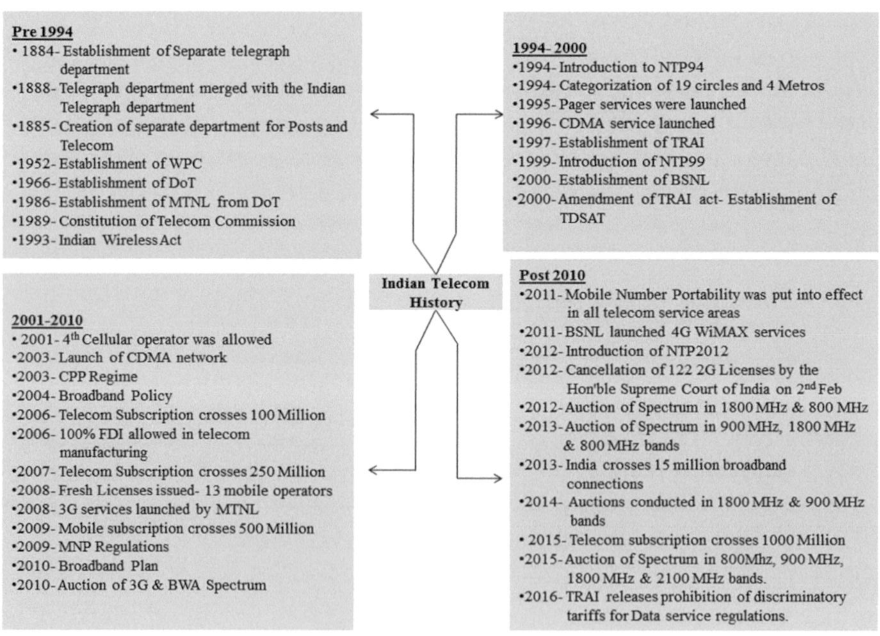


**Fig. 3.14** Major events in Indian telecom history

## 3.12 Concluding Remarks

The Indian telecom industry is capable of providing world-class services to subscribers with the latest technological standards at affordable rates. Remarkable improvements have led to an increase in the subscriber base and quality standard, due to favourable policies that promoted competition and fair practices in the sector. The new paradigms for the industry are greater access to information, growth of broadband and empowerment of the individual. Privatization and liberalization have enabled faster roll-out and improved quality of services. NTP-1994 has liberalized the sector enabling the growth and with NTP-1999 put into effect the sector registered a healthy growth rate in terms of mobile subscriber growth which eventually drove the industry to become the second largest region in terms of mobile subscriptions in the world. The establishment of independent bodies such as TRAI and TDSAT enabled the adoption of fair practices by all industry players and also helped build investor confidence in this sector.

With industry forecasts of future growth driven by data services, many operators started providing mobile Internet services. The Government introduced the Broadband Policy in 2004 and Broadband Plan in 2010 with the aim of connecting the entire nation through broadband. NTP-2012 focuses on empowering the citizen and making mobile the one-stop resource for all information and communication needs. With the mobile assuming an important role in the life of the ordinary citizen and the launch of 4G services in India, it is now extremely important to ensure full utilization of spectrum for mobile services. The growth trends in subscriber base, teledensity and HH index present the overall picture of Indian telecom sector. The next chapter focuses on the need for spectrum management and existing policies and recommendations on spectrum allocation and its efficient utilization.

## References

DoT (1999) New telecom policy, 1999. Available at: http://www.dot.gov.in/telecom-polices/new-telecom-policy-1999. Accessed 21 Feb 2015

DoT (2012) National telecom policy 2012. Available at: http://www.dot.gov.in/sites/default/files/NTP-06.06.2012-final.pdf. Accessed 3 Jan 2015

HHI (2015) Herfindahl-Hirschman Index. Available at: http://www.justice.gov/atr/herfindahl-hirschman-index. Accessed 2 Sept 2015

Iconectiv (2013) Best practices for number portability success. Available at: http://www.iconectiv.com/collateral/whitepapers/number_port_best_practices_wp.pdf. Accessed 2 Jan 2015

Sharma A, Medudula M, Patro S (2015) Marketing flexibility interaction matrix and consumer clusters preference criteria in telecommunication sector. Glob J Flexib Syst Manage 16(3):295–307

Sivasankari S, Sagar M, Agrawal D (2008) Spectrum auctioning and licensing in telecom industry. Econ Political Weekly 44(3):17–20

TRAI (1994) National telecom policy 1994. Available at: http://www.trai.gov.in/Content/telecom_policy_1994.aspx. Accessed 12 Sept 2014

TRAI (2003a) Addendum to NTP 99. Available at: http://www.dot.gov.in/sites/default/files/Addendum%20to%20NTP-99_11-11-03.pdf. Accessed 8 Feb 2015
TRAI (2003b) Recommendations on unified licensing. Available at: http://www.trai.gov.in/WriteReadData/Recommendation/Documents/Recomodifiedfinal.pdf. Accessed 14 Feb 2015
TRAI (2005) Broadband Policy 2004—targets and achievement. Available at: http://www.trai.gov.in/WriteReadData/Recommendation/Documents/letter3nov05.pdf. Accessed 14 Jan 2015
TRAI (2007) A journey towards excellence in telecommunications. Available at: http://www.trai.gov.in/WriteReadData/UserFiles/Aboutus/History/achievment.pdf. Accessed 7 Feb 2015
TRAI (2008) Recommendations on growth of broadband. Available at: http://www.trai.gov.in/WriteReadData/Recommendation/Documents/recom2jan08.pdf. Accessed 10 Feb 2015
TRAI (2009) Telecommunication mobile number portability per port transaction charge and dipping charge regulations, 2009. Available at: http://www.trai.gov.in/content/Regulation/0_9_REGULATIONS.aspx. Accessed 23 Jan 2015
TRAI (2011) Broadband Plan 2011. Available at: http://www.trai.gov.in/WriteReadData/Recommendation/Documents/Rcommendation81210.pdf. Accessed 11 Feb 2015
TRAI (2015) Press release. Available at: http://www.trai.gov.in/WriteReadData/PressRealease/Document/PR-TSD-30092015.pdf. Accessed 15 Sep 2015
TRAI (2016) Press release. Available at: http://trai.gov.in/WriteReadData/WhatsNew/Documents/Press_Release_No_15.pdf. Accessed 24 Feb 2106

# Chapter 4
# Introduction to Spectrum Management

Radio spectrum is the invisible lifeline for mobile communications. The invention of the base station architecture by Bell Labs and the development of technological standards enabled handsets to become truly mobile. Spectrum (radio frequency spectrum/radio waves) is a scare resource which lies between the "very low frequency" and "microwaves" in the electromagnetic spectrum. Hence, even though the spectrum is renewable in nature, it is available in limited quantities for the usage by telecommunication sector. Technological changes in the industry present many challenges for effective spectrum management, which requires a flexible management approach. With the mobile becoming increasingly ubiquitous, and with the pace of integration of ICT, the need for spectrum management has become critical. Increasing mobile subscriber base and the introduction of newer technologies such as 3G and 4G have made it essential to carefully allocate and regulate the usage of spectrum. Spectrum allocation is a long-term commitment to operators, and one has to look at future changes, challenges and opportunities in the sector before allocation. In this chapter, we take a look at the National Frequency Allocation Plan (NFAP) and TRAI guidelines on spectrum management. A comparative analysis of spectrum allocation and usage with some other countries has also been included.

## 4.1 Spectrum Management in India

The operations and functions of the Indian telecom industry were monopolized until 1994. The DoT which was set up in 1984 acted as the policy maker, regulator and operator for all those services that existed in the industry then. The allocation of spectrum for different purposes was managed by the Wireless Planning and Coordination Wing (WPC) of Ministry of Communications. Eventually, in 1994, National Telecom Policy was released, after almost 10 years since the establishment of the DoT, which envisaged that telecom services on demand at affordable and reasonable prices combined with a world-class standard for their quality of services

© Springer India 2016

M.K. Medudula et al., *Telecom Management in Emerging Economies*,
DOI 10.1007/978-81-322-2749-6_4

must be provided. NTP-94 recognized that the required resources for achieving these targets must also come through private investments and the involvement of the private sector is mandatory to bridge the resource gap.

A clearly defined spectrum management policy is essential for stakeholders to comprehend licensing procedures, frequency allocations, pricing, service standards, spectrum use, necessary certifications, etc. Spectrum management is an important duty of the regulator who drafts out plans for allocating frequencies and monitoring their usage.

### 4.1.1 Role of Wireless Planning and Coordination Wing

The WPC is a wing of the Ministry of Communications created in 1952 and is the National Radio Regulatory Authority with the following roles (www.wpc.co.in) (WPC 2014):

(a) WPC is responsible for spectrum management including licensing and caters to the needs of all wireless users (Government and Private) in the country.
(b) WPC exercises the statutory functions of the central government and issues licences to establish, maintain and operate wireless stations.

WPC is divided into major sections such Licensing and Regulation (LR), New Technology Group (NTG) and Standing Advisory Committee on Radio Frequency Allocation (SACFA). SACFA makes recommendations on major frequency allocation issues, formulation of frequency allocation plans and other issues related to the International Telecom Union (ITU).

### 4.1.2 National Frequency Allocation Plan (NFAP) and Its Importance

Based on the recommendations of the regulator, the government allocates licences in recommended spectrum bands. At the international level, ITU-R is the entity within ITU responsible for allocating spectrum for different services around the world.

As per ITU recommendations, every region/country has to have a clear idea of the spectrum being used for civilian as well as non-civilian purposes. In order to be in line with international regulations, the Wireless Planning Commission of India implemented the NFAP on January 2000. This plan has since been revised at regular intervals and the latest revision was published in October 2011. The objectives of the NFAP are indicated below (WPC 2011):

**Table 4.1** Recommended frequency bands

| Technology | Recommended frequency |
|---|---|
| GSM 900 | 890–915 MHz paired with 935–960 MHz |
| GSM 1800 | 1710–1785 MHz paired with 1805–1880 MHz |
| CDMA 800 | 824–844 MHz paired with 869–889 MHz |
| Cor-DECT | 1880–1900 MHz (TDD—unpaired) |
| IMT 2000 (3G) | 1920–1980 MHz paired with 2110–2170 MHz and 2010–2025 MHz (TDD—unpaired) |
| BWA (4G) | 2300–2400 MHz (TDD—unpaired) |

*Data source* WPC (2011)

(a) To be in line with the radio regulations of ITU-R.
(b) To cater to the needs of newly emerging technologies such as ultra-wide band (UWB), intelligent transport system (ITS) and Short Range Devices.
(c) To enable provisions in few frequency bands for indigenous development and manufacturing.
(d) To ensure protection of existing services.
(e) To keep in view the requirement projected by all stakeholders.

It is extremely important for nations to be in line with International Frequency Allocation guidelines to avoid interference. Table 4.1 and Fig. 4.1 detail the recommended frequency bands classified by WPC for different technologies.

NFAP 2011 has identified that the 700 MHz band can be used for mobile broadband services with greater efficiency. TRAI in its recommendations has also noted that India was lagging behind in the introduction, implementation and uptake of 3G access and needs to catch up with rest of the world in 4G/LTE, for which the 700 MHz band offers immense potential. Given the benefits of 700 MHz band,

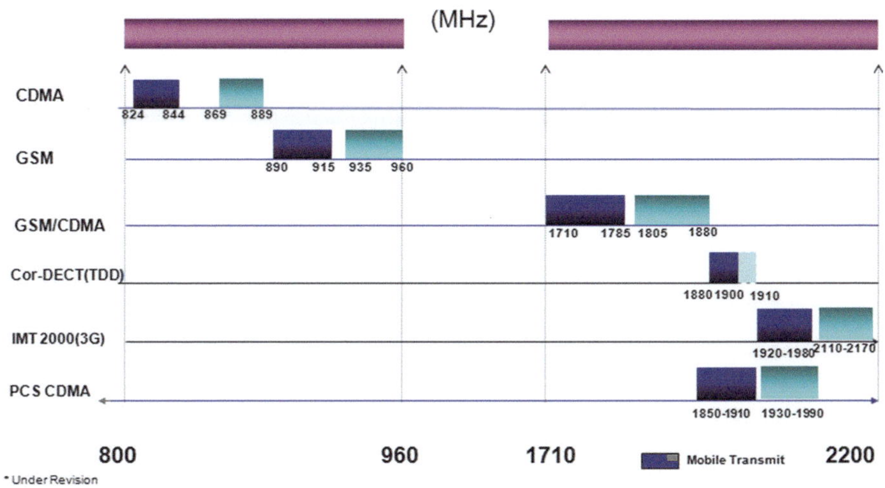


**Fig. 4.1** Recommended frequency band chart. *Data source* WPC (2011)

TRAI suggested the reserve price of Rs 11,485 cr/Mhz in its recent recommendations. TRAI also recommended the usage of 800/900 MHz bands for IMT services. Liberalization of spectrum has reached the stage that spectrum auctioned in 1800 MHz/900 MHz can now be used for deployment of any technology.

### *4.1.3 Policies of the Indian Government*

The Indian government has followed a traditional "command and control" approach to manage radio spectrum. The first two 2G licences in India were auctioned in 1995 after the defence sector agreed to give up a certain band of spectrum to the telecommunication industry. The third licence was auctioned in 2001, and spectrum access was granted after payment of a fixed licence fee. The fourth licence was granted in 2001 to state-owned operators, and they were required to pay the amount decided in an auction. The operators were also required to pay a fixed percentage of their annual revenues to the government. Additional spectrum was granted to existing operators if their subscriber base exceeded a critical threshold. In August 2007, Telecom Regulatory Authority of India (TRAI) in its reforms on licensing policy for access service provisions mentioned that no cap would be placed on the number of access service provided in any telecom service area nationwide (TRAI 2007).

In the 2G spectrum auctions in 2008, small slices of spectrum were granted to several new firms which led to excessive fragmentation in the radio frequency spectrum. In 2010, 3G spectrum was auctioned by the Indian government using "Simultaneous, Controlled and Ascending e-auctions". In November 2012, after a Supreme Court verdict ruled in favour of cancelling 122 licences awarded in 2008, auctions for spectrum in 1800 and 800 MHz bands were conducted. There were no takers for spectrum in the 800 MHz band, and spectrum in the 1800 MHz band was bought primarily by licensees whose licences had been cancelled. The lack of proper response from the market was primarily on account of a high reserve price. Another round of auctions was conducted in Mar 2013 after some reductions in the reserve price of 1800 and 800 MHz bands. In this auction, only one operator bid for 800 MHz in 8 circles and there were no takers for spectrum in the 1800 and 900 MHz bands.

After the failure of two consecutive auctions in Nov 12 and Mar 13, the licensor sought support from TRAI to determine a reserve price that reflected market realities and viability. Recommendations from TRAI caused a considerable decline in reserve prices of spectrum in the 1800 MHz band. Another round of auctions in Feb 2014 witnessed aggressive bidding by operators, and an overwhelming majority of the spectrum put up for auction was acquired.

While auctions maximize revenues for the government, they may in certain cases lead to overbidding by firms, which can deter the growth of the industry as a whole, and may not necessarily promote faster deployment of networks and services. The average spectrum holding per operator in India is well below the international average, and due to the large number of operators, telecom markets are highly competitive. Tremendous competition and low efficiency are major impediments to sustained growth of this sector in India. The immense competition, the policies of Indian government and a rapidly growing telecom market have had three important effects on scarce radio frequency spectrum.

(i) **Excessive Fragmentation**

The telecommunications sector witnesses increasing returns to scale. This implies that between two operators with the same infrastructure, the one that holds a greater amount of spectrum would be able to provide the same services to the same set of subscribers at a greatly reduced cost. In the absence of sufficient spectrum, operators need to deploy, maintain and operate a greater number of BTS's and this increases the unit cost.

Due to a large number of operators and the policies of the Indian government, radio frequency spectrum has become excessively fragmented. Excessive fragmentation coupled with inefficient use of BTS's has led to a low level of allocative efficiency in the Indian telecom sector which has limited the rate of growth of mobile services in India (Sridhar and Prasad 2011).

(ii) **High spectrum prices**

The Indian government has tried to maximize its revenue by allocating spectrum through auctioning. 3G/BWA/1800 MHz/900 MHz spectrum in India was allocated through the process of simultaneous, controlled and increasing e-auctions from 2010 to 2014. It is, however, true that maximizing auction pricing neither guarantees maximum social welfare nor indicates the efficiency of public policy. In scenarios of high uncertainty, auctioning may cause firms to overbid which is detrimental to the growth of the industry as a whole.

(iii) **Underutilization of spectrum**

A highly competitive telecom sector with a large number of operators can sometimes accompany the unfortunate side effect of underutilization of spectrum by many operators. This is especially true for new entrants as they typically do not have a large subscriber base to utilize allocated spectrum efficiently.

### *4.1.4 Nomenclature for Spectrum Allocation*

TRAI plays a critical role as a recommending authority and, after genuinely sophisticated analyses, recommends how and how much spectrum should be issued to existing and new operators. As per TRAI recommendations, the prescribed limit of spectrum for GSM should be 2 × 8 MHz for all service areas other than in Delhi and Mumbai where 2 × 10 MHz would be appropriate. In the case of CDMA, the authority recommends 2 × 5 MHz for all service areas and 2 × 6.25 MHz in the metro areas of Delhi and Mumbai (Table 4.2).

**Table 4.2** Nomenclature for spectrum assignment

| Nomenclature used | Amount of spectrum for GSM | Amount of spectrum for CDMA |
|---|---|---|
| Initial/start-up spectrum | 2 × 4.4 MHz | 2 × 2.5 MHz |
| Contracted/committed spectrum | 2 × 6.2 MHz | 2 × 5 MHz |
| Prescribed limit of spectrum | 2 × 8 MHz (other than Delhi and Mumbai) | 2 × 5 MHz (other than Delhi and Mumbai) |
| Excess spectrum | Beyond contracted spectrum | Beyond contracted spectrum |
| Additional spectrum | Beyond initial spectrum and includes excess spectrum | Beyond initial spectrum and includes excess spectrum |

*Source* TRAI (2011)

When operators bid for spectrum, it is awarded in accordance with the relevant provisions of the Service License Agreement. The current policy allows any operator to hold up to 50 % of available spectrum in a given band and no more than 25 % of the total spectrum in all bands together.

## 4.2 Improving Spectrum Efficiency and Management

Newer standards and improved mobile technologies are the result of innovation and research work in telecommunications. Radio spectrum has to accommodate new technologies and pass on associated benefits to subscribers. The need for improved spectrum efficiency and management is compounded by the rising demands from an ever-increasing subscriber base. Innovative means to improve efficiency and effectively manage this national resource should be embraced and aid in ushering in new and improved iterations of prevailing regimes.

### *4.2.1 Spectrum Refarming*

Technological progress often necessitates replanning and reassigning government-regulated spectrum. With the passage of time, new technologies become available which use spectrum more efficiently. Also new technologies permit introduction of new services that were simply not available with earlier technologies. Demand for better services mandates that spectrum be freed up and put to use for new and improved technologies. This mechanism is referred to as refarming, and many countries have adopted it to manage spectrum efficiently (TRAI 2012).

Refarming is more often than not a complex exercise and can present some very real and daunting challenges for regulators as well as the industry. A considerable amount of trial and error globally suggests that practices like amending existing licensing conditions to allow new technology implementations is often required when refarming. Abolishing dated technology, reassigning spectrum and/or redistributing spectrum are some other methods to refarm.

Harmonization is one such process, wherein Department of Telecommunications has realigned spectrum assigned through auctions in 1800 MHz bands to various TSPs in to their contiguous holdings. The process is distributed in 5 phases, encompassing 17 telecom service areas. The contiguous spectrum so allocated, will improve the spectral efficiency as well as will also reduce the interference of the communication band with the defence band.

### *4.2.2 Secondary Spectrum Markets*

It is important to note that refarming is just one mechanism to effectively manage radio spectrum. Secondary markets and spectrum trading can be equally effective at managing spectrum, but should in no way be considered in isolation. A well-designed spectrum management policy would have elements from the principle of refarming to ensure optimum allocation, as well as secondary markets that would help operators reduce costs and service their customers better. Two approaches have traditionally been used by authorities to manage public assets—"Market-based Mechanism" and the "command and control" approach. It has been argued by many that a market-based mechanism would make for a better approach to manage radio frequency spectrum due to several reasons (Valletti 2001). Spectrum trading involves renting out or selling the licence for using the spectrum in part to other operators who cannot or have not achieved full roll-out or do not hold a licence for spectrum usage. Spectrum trading is not permitted in India, but intra-circle spectrum sharing is allowed. Operators can share spectrum within the circle and allow roaming facilities to subscribers. Development of efficient secondary spectrum markets and spectrum trading is of critical importance for the following reasons.

(a) **Correcting Misallocations**

The traditional "command and control" approach does not guarantee efficient allocation of spectrum. When using this approach, spectrum is allotted for a particular use and then assigned to various operators. Since this gives the operator exclusive access to spectrum, it solves the problem of network congestion. Even though this form of spectrum management does not reduce technical efficiency, it does not ensure allocative efficiency. For instance, the portion of spectrum allocated to television broadcasting may be used more efficiently in telecommunication industry. Since regulatory authorities neither possess the required information nor have visibility on what classifies as optimal use of a particular spectrum band, such mechanisms may lead to situations wherein spectrum is not utilized optimally. Development of spectrum markets presents a unique opportunity to fill this gap and ensure efficient allocation of radio frequency spectrum.

(b) **Consolidation of Telecom Market**

The Indian telecom market is highly competitive with about 9–11 operators per licence area. Tremendous competition has led to excessive fragmentation of spectrum and has reduced the average spectrum holding per operator, leading to lower efficiency and pricing that goes against consumer interest. The allocative efficiency of the Indian telecom industry is low and impedes the growth of the sector. Secondary markets would ensure that spectrum is allocated to firms that value it most. A firm operating suboptimally would be able to acquire more spectrum, would increase its efficiency and would be able to provide the same set of services at a lower unit cost, leading to maximum social welfare.

#### 4.2.2.1 Possible Concerns

There are however some major concerns that need to addressed or evaluated by regulators before the formation of secondary markets.

(a) **Spectrum Hoarding**

The traditional "command and control" mechanism ensures that no firm has excessive market power by limiting the amount of spectrum that can be assigned to a single operator. In the Indian scenario, additional spectrum was awarded to telecom operators when and only when their subscriber base crossed a certain threshold. The development of secondary markets may give rise to anti-competitive behaviour in spectrum markets and lead to spectrum hoarding by major players. This would be as if not more detrimental to the objective of social welfare than the absence of secondary markets, as market power would be concentrated in the hands of a few. However, this issue can be addressed by state intervention in spectrum markets (Cave 2010). The regulators can put ceilings on the maximum amount of spectrum an operator can hold. This would ensure that no single firm has excessive market power or pursues monopolistic practices. Other measures such as a "use it or lose it" clause could also prevent spectrum hoarding by telecom operators. Regulatory measures such as spectrum auditing would help curb any spectrum hoarding by telecom operators.

(b) **Lack of Information**

The most important feature of an efficient market is that both buyers and sellers possess information which is far from the truth in the case of spectrum markets. Buyers and sellers may not have sufficient information about the market price of spectrum and would abstain from trading. This knowledge gap can be addressed by the intervention of appropriate authorities. Publishing information related to spectrum pricing and conducting more auctions can act as important sources of information for secondary markets (Crocioni 2009). It is also difficult to measure the actual cost of radio frequency spectrum, and a framework which quantifies the actual value of a spectrum block is absolutely essential.

(c) **Capital-Intensive Nature**

The telecom industry is capital-intensive and requires huge investments to set up radio infrastructure required for providing mobile services. Such costs can effectively deter new firms from entering the market. Regulatory and administrative changes are warranted and absolutely essential to the growth of secondary markets. In order to arrive at an appropriate spectrum fee, several factors must be taken into consideration, and regulators need to lead the charge by carrying out consultations, research and discussions with the industry.

## 4.3 Spectrum Auctioning in India (Sivasankari et al. 2008)

In 1995, spectral auctioning began for global system for mobile (GSM) cellular operations only. According to the NFAP, the frequency ranges between 890–915 and 935–960 MHz were identified and earmarked for GSM operations. Similarly, bands from 824–844 to 869–889 MHz were allocated for code division multiple access (CDMA) operations by the WPC. However, it was absolutely essential, especially in the case of a nation as large as India, to classify the zones in which services could be provided. Only once such a classification existed did the government assign this spectrum to operators. India was divided into 21 circles—six states as six "A" circles, eight states as eight "B" circles and 12 states split up into seven "C" circles. The four metros—Delhi, Mumbai, Chennai and Kolkata—were considered as separate areas of operations. This auction of 2G spectrum was based on "direct auctioning" and was conducted in two stages.

Two qualified bidders who quoted the highest prices for the circle emerged as the winners in the second stage. This approach had its shortcomings: first, even though there was considerable privatization in the telecom industry, service roll-out still remained slow, owing partly to the fact that winners had shelled out huge sums to win a circle and were financially strained to provide faster services. Second, various non-winners of the bidding process complained of a lack of transparency in the auctioning process, while the winners complained of high inter-circle interconnection costs fixed by the DoT. These and other factors were believed to be the reasons for the slow service roll-outs.

In order to resolve the above issues and to create a regulatory structure, the TRAI was set up and the New Telecom Policy '99 (NTP-99) was announced. NTP-99 offered a new scheme to the bidders called the "migration package", under which existing operators could make a one-time payment called "entry fee" and subsequently pay a part of their Adjusted Gross Revenue (AGR) as a quarterly licence fee.

At the end of the bidding process, winners were allocated a spectrum bandwidth of 4.4 MHz for GSM operations (2×, i e, inclusive of uplink and downlink) and 2.5 MHz (2×) for CDMA operations. GSM operators today hold a maximum spectral width of 11.2 MHz in metros, 9.2 MHz in circle A, 8.2 MHz in circle B and 6.2 MHz in circle C. The maximum in any circle for a GSM operator is 15 MHz. Some GSM operators, however, are demanding spectral widths as large as 22.5 MHz for 2G network expansion and have raised separate spectral claims for 3G services.

In such scenarios, there arise questions regarding the efficiency with which these operators utilize allocated frequency bands. GSM operators need to use the spectrum they already have much more efficiently, noting that they serve 3.9 million subscribers per MHz, as opposed to Chinese operators who serve up to 8.5 million subscribers per MHz. GSM operators are also criticized for cartelizing and hoarding spectrum. Lessons learned from 2G spectrum auctions led authorities to carefully consider the following before conducting 3G auctions:

(i) deciding the frequency band for spectrum allocation;
(ii) the minimum reserve price; and
(iii) auction design.

## 4.4 Spectrum Assigning Methodologies

Globally, several methods are used to assign spectrum to operators. Available spectrum is typically divided into blocks, based on recommendations from the regulator. These blocks are then allocated to operators using one of the following methodologies:

(a) First-come, first-served;
(b) Auction/bidding methodology (competitive, sealed/open bid and simultaneous ascending auction and Anglo-Dutch auction);
(c) Beauty contest methodology.

### 4.4.1 First-Come, First-Served Basis

The first-come, first-served methodology allocates spectrum blocks to operators in a chronological way. The number of operators is limited by the number of blocks available, the process ends when all blocks are assigned, and no more requests are entertained once the blocks are completely assigned. The biggest drawback of this process is that the allocating methodology may not account for market forces and the price of the spectrum may not reflect market realities. Repercussions of adopting this method can be severe in nature and can upon critical scrutiny lead to the cancellation of licences as in the case of the Indian telecom sector in 2012 when 122 2G spectrum licences were cancelled because of the use of this approach.

### 4.4.2 Auction/Bidding Methodology

The auction/bidding approach to assign spectrum is followed by most countries and takes the marketplace and market price of spectrum into consideration. The success of this method depends on its ability to prevent collusion among bidders, an appropriate minimum reserve price and the total number of players participating in the auction. Bidding may involve sealed/open bidding amounts where the highest bid is awarded the licence followed by the next highest bidders.

Competitive bidding is a variant of auction methodology where in the initial round, the spectrum block would be available only to those operators who match the highest bidder. If no other players are willing to pay for the block, the left over blocks are typically reauctioned. India followed this process in 1995 for the award of 2G licences for 14 CMTS, 6 BTS and paging licences. The simultaneous ascending auction approach will be discussed in the subsequent units.

Proposed by Binmore and Klemperer (2002), the Anglo-Dutch auction starts with a base price and price increments at regular intervals ensure that most players drop out until two remain. These two players participate in a sealed bid where the one with the highest quoted price gets the licence to use the allocated spectrum. If there are n blocks of spectrum available, the auction process will continue till there are $n + 1$ bidders left. These $n + 1$ bidders then participate in a sealed bid, where the top n participants get licences for spectrum usage.

### 4.4.3 Beauty Contest Methodology

The beauty contest is an auctioning procedure, which is not wholly dependent on the pricing. With much similarities to an actual "beauty contest", here too, every contestant will have to convince the auctioneers of their ability to provide services. Based on answers to questions such as—how wide the service area will be, how fast and efficiently services will be rolled out and what will be the customer usage charges—a contestant will be selected as the winner of this "beauty contest" and will be provided the licence (Sivasankari et al. 2008).

The biggest drawback of the auction/bidding approach is that the liquidity in the market gets used up in the acquisition of licences and spectrum. As a result, roll-out of service may not live up to the vision of the government/ministry. Faster roll-outs may be an essential condition for some nations, and the auction/bidding approach while maximizing revenues for the exchequer may hinder industrial progress at the infrastructure level.

To achieve these objectives, spectrum would be awarded to operators based not only on the price but also on the competencies of the bidding operators. Participants are compared to benchmarks set by the ministry. This method of assigning spectrum is generally known as a beauty contest and is embraced by several countries. Finland, Japan and France have used this method for assigning 3G licences. The licensing methodology for all spectrum blocks can be based on beauty contest or can be a mix of both the beauty contest and auction methodologies as in the case of 3G licensing in France.

## 4.5 3G Spectrum Auctioning and Allocation Process

Spectral auction is one of the major sources of revenue available to a government. With a booming telecom sector and its net worth of approximately $30 billion, the contribution of communication sector to Indian GDP has increased from about 1.59 % in 2000 to 3.97 % in 2006. It becomes imperative for India to choose a proper auction design to maximize government revenue comparable to other countries such as the USA, UK, Germany and Switzerland. At the same time, emphasis must be given to safeguard the interests of telecom operators and ensure the future growth of the telecom sector and not just keep in mind the profits from auctions. Worldwide, the third-generation licences were awarded through either a beauty contest or other auctioning methods such as sealed bidding, open bidding, simultaneous multiple round auctions and Vickrey auction (Sivasankari et al. 2008).

Comparative International Scenario for 3G Auction: some of the methods followed by various countries and their profitability rating are shown in Table 4.3. The advantage of a beauty contest, when compared to open auctions, is that the operators will be able to work on 3G side by side, even as they keep on focusing on the provision of mobile services to those who are still unconnected and remain a priority. Also, financial problems due to direct auctions (where bidders quote extremely high prices) and major delays in roll-out after 3G auctions, a scenario that occurred in Europe after 3G auctions, can be deterred. To develop a spectrum auctioning plan for 3G, we should refer to the countries who have already auctioned 3G spectrum. Finland was the first country to award the 3G licences using the beauty contest methodology. The auctioning process was not based purely on pricing, and four operators were awarded the spectrum. Japan in the year 2000

**Table 4.3** Comparative international scenario for 3G auction

| Country | Method of licence distribution | Key aspects | Year | S and P[a] profitability rating |
|---|---|---|---|---|
| Finland | Beauty contest | First country to award 3G licences. It was not price based. Four operators | 1999 | Average |
| Japan | Beauty contest | Three operators | 2000 | Excellent |
| France | Beauty contest + auction | $4.5 billion per licence for the first two licences and later auctioning for remaining two licences | 2001 | Very good |
| UK | Auction | Five licences—four for established operators and only one for a new operator | 2000 | Very good |
| USA | Simultaneous multiple round auction | Reserve price set to $10 billion | 2004 | Good |

*Source* Sivasankari et al. (2008)
[a]Standard and Poor's (S&P) is a division of McGraw-Hill that publishes financial research and analysis

awarded 3G licences to three operators based on the beauty contest method. France in the year 2001 used the method of both beauty contest and auction as depicted in Table 4.3.

Having examined the international spectrum allocation methods used in various countries, the key learning would be in identifying the variables which play an important role in a successful spectrum allocation process. The spectrum allocation process should be able to balance the interest of government, industry and subscribers. The process should be objective in nature with transparency as the key parameter during the allocation process. The process should be able to avoid collusion and excessive speculation as well. The entire process of allocation of 3G spectrum should result in an environment which help to foster competition and spectrum being allocated to those players who value it the most.

Indian spectrum allocation process for 3G has aimed to be fair and transparent. There existed several key challenges at the time of auctions. The industry was highly fragmented, and the completion levels in the wireless segment were at its peak with decreasing ARPU levels which impacted the EBITA margins for the service providers. Apart from this, the spectrum was scarce and hence the government planned for the best efficient way of allocating the spectrum. The consultation provided by NM Rothschild & Sons (India) Private Limited and DotEcon Limited resulted in choosing the auctioning method for allocation of 3G spectrum by the government where three-staged process of "Controlled, Simultaneous, Ascending e-auction" was conducted. The auction which started during April 2010 had 3 to 4 blocks of paired spectrum to be auctioned in each of the 22 service areas. The entire process followed was aimed at efficient utilization of the resources and to foster competition towards better allocation practices. The auction process was conducted for 34 days from the start with around 183 rounds of bidding which resulted in revenue generation of Rs. 67,719 crore from the private player to the exchequer. The success of the auction can be attributed to several key decisions made by the government before and during the auction process.

As discussed earlier, the auction process has to consider three important things which are as follows: deciding the frequency band for spectrum allocation, the minimum reserve price and auction design. During 3G spectrum auctioning for the 22 circles, the radio frequencies allocated were 1920–1980 MHz paired with frequencies in the range 2110–2170 MHz in 2.1 GHz band. These frequencies are allocated as per the NFAP recommendations. Spectrum awarded will be valid for 20-year period until it is being surrendered or revoked. The minimum reserve price plays a key role in determining the successful of the auction process and arriving at the optimum reserve price has been the key for 3G auctioning process. The reserve price for 3G was set at Rs. 320 cr for metros (Delhi and Mumbai), Rs. 320 cr for "A" category circles (Maharashtra, Gujarat, Andhra Pradesh, Karnataka and Tamil Nadu), Rs. 120 cr for "B" category circles and Rs. 30 cr for "C" category circles (DoT 2010). The third important element is the auction design where a three-staged process was followed.

### *4.5.1 3G Spectrum Auction Design*

The auction was conducted online where the eligible bidders were given access to the electronic auction system using standard Web browsing software. As stated in the Notice Inviting Applications document (DoT 2010), the 3G auction design had three stages as depicted below:

(a) Pre-Qualification Stage:
During this stage, the eligibility of the bidder is being examined and the qualification process is being implemented. This stage is very crucial as it determines the number of players who will enter the auctioning process. There are chances for bias to be introduced in this stage, and hence, the eligibility criteria should be objective and transparent. Readers can find the eligibility criteria details in the Notice Inviting Applications document (DoT 2010). The prospective bidders were not compared to each other at this stage, and each prospective bidder had been checked independently. The roll-out obligations have been specified and the spectrum had been delinked from the licence. The award of spectrum does not necessarily provide the right to provide 3G services. The winning bidders would be required to apply for the UAS licence separately, and this licence would be provided to the Indian telecom player only. Foreign player can get the licence only when they form or acquire an Indian player with at least 26 % stake. This clause prevented the participation of foreign player in 3G auctions which resulted in no participation from players outside India.

(b) Clock Stage (Auction Rules):
The prospective bidders who met the eligibility criteria were allowed to take part in the auctioning process which is governed by the auction rules. To conduct the auction over EAS, qualified bidders are given cryptographic authentication tokens and passwords. Earnest money deposit in the form of bank guarantee (12.5–25 % of the minimum reserve price depending upon the service area) is an eligibility condition for participating in the clock round for each of the service area. Each service area is independently being monitored, and the bidders can bid for all the areas depending upon the earnest money deposited (Rs 505 cr for all 22 circles). The price for the 1st clock round is equal to the minimum reserve price for the circle. Clock stage consists of several rounds depending on the activity generated during the bidding process. Activity rules were defined for regulating the bidding activity for each clock round. For the 1st clock round, earnest money will become the eligibility criteria, and for subsequent clock round, the activity level and requirement specified by the auctioneer become the eligibility for the bidder to take part in next clock round. Every round will see an increment in the price of the generic spectrum block unless the demand equals the number of blocks available, and no opportunity exists for increasing the price. The maximum price increment according to the auction rule is 10 % of the bidding price in the previous round. The final clock round would have the activity requirement of 100 % and the excess demand is either zero or negative. All provisional winning bidders after the final clock round would pay the same fee for the generic block in the particular circle. The ranking criteria are used in determining the winning bidders where the highest bids are ranked in descending order of value. More details on activity rules can be found in the Notice Inviting Applications document (DoT 2010).

(c) Frequency Identification Stage:
This is the final stage in the auctioning process where the provisional winning bidders would be awarded the spectrum block through random allocation method. Each winning bidder will be allocated the paired spectrum block (2 * 5 MHz) and not more than one paired spectrum will be awarded to each winning bidder.

There were necessary checks put in the process to avoid collusion and to control speculation through timely updates to all the bidders. All the provisional bidder identities were revealed before the auction process after pre-qualification stage. The prices for bidding in the clock round, the number of block available for the round, number of bids received and the demand figures were informed to the bidders during and after each clock round. The identities of the bidders were not revealed in between the clock rounds and are revealed only after the final clock round. The price increment was determined by the auctioneer rather than the bidders to prevent speculation. Stringent time bound roll-out obligations and payment terms were specified so that only serious player can take part in the auction. These rules in the auction process helped the auctioneer to achieve the market price for the spectrum which was more than twice the price which the government expected. The auction process prevented spectrum hoarding since the roll-out obligations have to be fulfilled and the break even time would be high due to high spectrum fees paid by the service providers. Overall, the process proved to be a major success from the regulator point of view where the entire spectrum put for auctioning has been taken.

## 4.6 Spectrum Allocation and Pricing—UK

In the UK, spectrum allocation and management are handled by the Department of Trade and Industry's "Radio Communication Agency". To meet evolving spectrum needs for changing technology and identify innovate ways of allocation, two acts—Wireless Telegraph Act in 1998 and Communication Act in 2003—were implemented. At present, Office of Communications (Ofcom) formed by the Communication Act is the independent agency responsible for spectrum management and allocation in the country (Cave 2010).

An independent study in the year 2001 favoured spectrum trading to manage spectrum through the market. The UK, however, chose to use administrative incentive pricing (AIP) where a certain amount of the value of spectrum is linked to the economy or the society. Such a practice has the potential to discourage spectrum hoarding and generally enables efficient use of spectrum. Spectrum valuations in such cases are typically based on opportunity costs (alternative efficient use of the spectrum). The study revealed that in competitive markets, both AIP and spectrum trading generate the same amount of revenue for the government.

Due to the unwillingness to pay the price determined by AIP, the auctioning method was used for 3G auctions in 2000. For the first time, unidentical licences were awarded to promote the entry of new operators. The simultaneous ascending auction was used to award licences. Due to huge investments in the acquisition of licences, the next fixed wireless broadband licence auctions attracted few entrants and lasted for a relatively shorter period. This duality of results essentially led to the use of "spectrum trading" in the marketplace. The advantages and the need for this method have been covered in previous sections.

## 4.7 Spectrum Management in Australia

The establishment of the Radio Communications Act 1992 and the Australian Communications Authority Act 1997 was the trigger events for regulated spectrum management in Australia (ITU Report). Australia's spectrum has been divided into the following seven frequency band plans (Table 4.4; Fig. 4.2).

The pie chart above states that mobile occupies the 2nd largest share with 20 % spectrum.

**Table 4.4** Frequency band plans of Australia

| Frequency band plan | Utility |
|---|---|
| VHF mid-band frequency band plan (70–87.5 MHz) 1991 | Land mobile services and technologies and support for narrowband area services |
| VHF high band frequency band plan (148–174 MHz) 1991 | Encouraged the use of land mobile services and a more efficient use of spectrum by accommodating two frequency systems |
| 900 MHz band plan (820–960 MHz) 1992 | Allocations for cordless telephone services and for the transition from analogue to digital cellular mobile telephone services (using GSM technology) |
| 1.5 GHz band plan (1427–1535 MHz) 1996 | Point-to-multipoint, mobile satellite and aeronautical mobile telemetry services |
| 1.9 GHz band plan (1880–1900 MHz) 1996 | Cordless telecommunication systems, wireless local area network, wireless local loop and wireless PABX |
| 2.1 GHz band frequency band plan 2002 | Fixed point-to-point services and introduction of 3G mobile |
| Mobile satellite service band plan (2 GHz) | New MSS and set out the conditions of the incumbent licensees who operate in the 2 GHz bands |

*Source* ITU (n.d.)

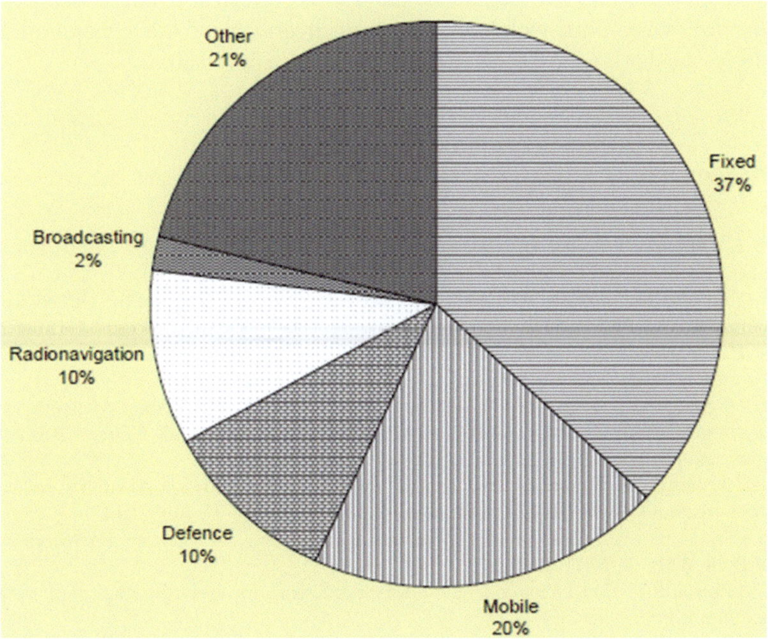


**Fig. 4.2** Spectrum allocations to major spectrum uses in Australia. *Source* ITU (n.d.)

## 4.8 Concluding Remarks

Spectrum management and planning is an important activity for the ministry and regulator. Protecting the interest of industry players and subscribers is of critical importance, and technologies that can potentially benefit subscribers must not be prohibited on account of scarcity of spectrum. Several methods such as spectrum refarming and trading have been suggested as efficient ways of managing spectrum.

Spectrum auctioning and licensing have been discussed in this unit leaving the readers with three key factors the authorities must consider—frequency bands, minimum reserve price and auction design. From the regulatory and policy perspective, spectrum auctions ensure efficient usage by allocating it to those entities that value it the most, while also generating revenues for governments. However, auctions may lead to unexpected outcomes as, for example, when regulatory agencies have inadequate market information, there may be a mismatch between expected and actual bidder behaviour or auctions may be poorly designed. The key challenge before regulatory agencies is to design auctions in such a way as to meet the objective of fostering competition, while at the same time, ensuring that bidders can effectively use the spectrum for their business. 3G spectrum auctioning process in India was a successful process where the activity rules and eligibility conditions resulted in true market price for the spectrum. The 3G auction process also put a check on collusion and avoided speculation to the greatest extent possible.

In the following unit, we shall present an overview of 4th generation mobile technology standards and the technology ecosystem in detail.

## References

Binmore K, Klemperer P (2002) The biggest auction ever: the sale of the British 3G telecom licences. Econ J 112(478):C74–C96

Cave M (2010) Spectrum management for a converged world: case study of the United Kingdom. Available at: http://www.itu.int/osg/spu/ni/spectrum/UK-RSM.pdf. Accessed 21 Mar 2014

Crocioni P (2009) Is allowing trading enough? Making secondary markets in spectrum work. Telecommun Policy 33(8):451–468

DoT (2010) Auction of 3G and BWA spectrum: notice inviting applications. Available at: http://www.dot.gov.in/sites/default/files/3G%20%26%20BWA%20Auctions_Notice%20Inviting%20Applications_0.pdf. Accessed 13 Dec 2014

ITU (n.d.) Spectrum management for a converged world: case study on Australia. Available at: http://www.itu.int/osg/spu/ni/spectrum/aust-rsm.pdf. Accessed 21 July 2014

Sivasankari S, Sagar M, Agrawal D (2008) Spectrum auctioning and licensing in telecom industry. Econ Polit Wkly 44(3):17–20

Sridhar V, Prasad R (2011) Towards a new policy framework for spectrum management in India. Telecommun Policy 35(2):172–184

TRAI (2007) A journey towards excellence in telecommunications: commitment to provide world class quality service. Available at: http://www.trai.gov.in/WriteReadData/UserFiles/Aboutus/History/achievment.pdf. Accessed 6 Sept 2014

TRAI (2011) Recommendations—telecom regulatory authority of India. Available at: http://www.trai.gov.in/WriteReadData/Recommendation/Documents/Final2011.pdf. Accessed 16 June 2014

TRAI (2012) Clarifications on the prescribed limit for spectrum, retention of spectrum on renewal of licences and refarming of spectrum. Available at: http://www.trai.gov.in/WriteReadData/Miscelleneus/Document/201211010456564904825ResponsetoDoT-30OCT-12.pdf. Accessed 21 May 2014

Valletti T (2001) Spectrum trading. Telecommun Policy 25(10–11):655–670

WPC (2011). National frequency allocation plan 2011. Available at: http://www.wpc.dot.gov.in/Docfiles/National%20Frequency%20Allocation%20Plan-2011.pdf. Accessed 21 June 2014

WPC (2014) WPC home. Available at: http://www.wpc.dot.gov.in/. Accessed 20 Jan 2014

# Chapter 5
# Overview of Fourth-Generation Mobile Technology

The growth of mobile communications can most appropriately be paralleled with the scope and pace advocated by the very general yet strangely accurate Moore's Law. Such has been the nature of technological development over the last decade that even consumers have come to expect growth at such momentum. With every passing generation of mobile technology, what can be consistently observed is the proportionally larger set of features and benefits each generation delivers over its predecessor. Devices are now more efficient and capable of supporting higher data rates for data-intensive applications. This growth in mobile communication technology would not have been possible in the absence of technical evolution and standards. With the widespread adoption of mobile broadband, 4G, the fourth generation of mobile communication technology, is poised to further enrich user experiences and support more applications such as mobile video, advanced gaming, interactive TV and many others. 4G is sometimes referred to as IMT-Advanced, is based on **IP packet-switched network** and does not support circuit-switched systems.

Designed to facilitate improved service capabilities, higher network speeds and improved user experiences, 4G ensures seamless services over wireless networks with enhanced data rates and smoother handoffs. It also offers a wide array of compelling data services on a real-time basis, and long-term, efficient and friendlier interactive experiences on high-speed platforms.

As per ITU recommendations of 2008, 4G has a peak data rate of up to approximately 100 Mb/s for high mobility and up to approximately 1 Gb/s for low mobility. In December, 2010, the International Telecommunication Union (ITU) relaxed the definition of 4G to include technologies that do not fulfil the IMT-Advanced requirements and support much less speed than 100 Mb/s for full mobility and 1 Gb/s for limited mobility. Prevailing contenders, LTE and WiMAX, fell short by some margin and failed to achieve the transfer rates envisioned by ITU. The biggest roadblock was the "resource accessing" techniques used at the physical layer of existing systems, which rely on FDMA, TDMA, DS-CDMA or a combination, to provide access to multiple users (Shah et al. 2011). In 2010, ITU

© Springer India 2016

M.K. Medudula et al., *Telecom Management in Emerging Economies*,
DOI 10.1007/978-81-322-2749-6_5

recognized LTE, WiMAX and HSPA+ as technologies that do not fulfil the IMT-Advanced requirements, but classified them as "4G" since they were for all intents and purposes the forerunners to IMT-Advanced compliant versions and provided substantial improvements in performance/capabilities over 3G systems.

Mobile WiMAX Release 2 (Wireless MAN-Advanced or IEEE 802.16m) and LTE-Advanced (LTE-A) are IMT-Advanced compliant versions of WiMAX and LTE, respectively, promising speed of 1 Gbps and likely to be deployed in 2013.

## 5.1 Technologies and Standards for 4G

ITU-R, the Radio Communication Division of ITU, has issued various requirements with respect to International Mobile Telecommunications-Advanced (IMT-Advanced). IMT-Advanced is the ITU description for systems beyond IMT-2000, is essentially synonymous with fourth-generation mobile communication technologies, and with the following sets the eligibility of systems to be classified as truly fourth generation (ITU 2003).

> The new radio access interface(s) are envisaged to handle a wide range of supported data rates according to economic and service demands in multi-user environments with target peak data rates of up to approximately 100 Mbit/s for high mobility such as mobile access and up to approximately 1 Gbit/s for low mobility such as nomadic/local wireless access

IMT-Advanced standards include minimum performance requirements for peak and average channel spectral efficiency, cell edge user spectral efficiency, VOIP capacity, control and user plane latency, handover, mobility and channel bandwidth. It also includes QoS, roaming and other inter-operator parameters.

IEEE 802.16m was developed to meet or exceed the requirements of IMT Advanced and came as an amendment to the IEEE 802.16 Wireless MAN-OFDMA specification. LTE parameters and objectives such as channel BW, peak DL and UL spectral efficiency, latency, mobility support, frame structure, antenna systems supported are defined in IEEE 802.16m.

LTE (Rel-8), LTE Advanced (Rel-10), WiMAX (IEEE 802.16e2005), WiMAX 2(IEEE 802.16m) and HSPA+ (Rel-7, Rel-8 and Rel-9) are few dominant technologies categorized as 4G.

### *5.1.1 High-Speed Packet Access Evolved (HSPA+)*

HSPA+ is an evolved version of HSPA (WCDMA/UMTS)-based 3G networks and works in FDD mode with a channel bandwidth requirement of 2 × 5 MHz. HSPA Rel-6 supports peak data rates of 14 Mb/s for downlink and 5.8 Mb/s for uplink.

HSPA+ with enhanced modulation efficiency supports much higher speeds. Release 7 of this standard supports 64 QAM in the downlink and 16 QAM in the uplink and hence supports peak data rates of 28 Mb/s for downloads and 11 Mb/s for uploads. Release 8 with 64 QAM in uplink and (2 × 2) MIMO in downlink supports 42 Mb/s download and 11 Mb/s upload speeds.

Features such as multiple input–multiple output, multicarrier operation and high-order modulation are supported by this standard, and HSPA+ with 64 QAM and dual carrier operations is spectrally very efficient.

The essential difference between HSPA and HSPA+ is that while HSPA supports up to 16 QAM for downlinks, up to QPSK for uplink and (1 × 2) SIMO for BS antenna and MS antenna, whereas HSPA+ supports up to 64 QAM with an option of (2 × 2) MIMO.

HSPA+ offers advantages of speedy deployment and the availability of a large number of multimode user handsets and devices. Recently developed networks can be upgraded to HSPA+ networks with software and hardware changes, just like upgradation of GSM networks to EDGE networks.

### *5.1.2 Worldwide Interoperability for Microwave Access (WiMAX)*

WiMAX has been designed to operate in both FDD and TDD schemes. For proper functioning, a minimum channel bandwidth of 2 × 5 MHz and 10 MHz is required for FDD and TDD, respectively. Current deployments of WiMAX have primarily been in TDD mode.

Some major WiMAX technologies are as follows:

(1) **Scalable orthogonal frequency division multiplexing access (SOFDMA)** is an advanced version of OFDMA and offers the added advantage of scaling the size of the FFT to the channel bandwidth to keep subcarrier spacing constant across different channel bandwidths.
(2) **Adaptive antenna system (AAS)** is a group of antennas and associated signal processing equipment that together are able to change antenna radiation patterns dynamically to adjust to the noise environment, interference and multipath. It has the ability to carry out spatial multiplexing and can steer antenna beams towards mobile nodes and the nulls towards interferers.
(3) **Hybrid automatic repeat request (HARQ)** is a system in which information blocks are encoded for partial error correction at receiving ends and additionally uncorrected errors are retransmitted.
(4) **Multiple input–multiple output (MIMO)** is a smart antenna technology for wireless communications in which multiple antennas are used at both the source (transmitter) and the destination (receiver). The antennas at each end of the communications circuit are combined to minimize errors and optimize data speeds.

While standards for voice over WiMAX also exist, the same have not been standardized. The availability of multimode handsets/user devices is also a big constraint in the promotion of this technology.

### *5.1.3 Long-Term Evolution (LTE)*

LTE can also be deployed in either time division duplexing (TDD) or frequency division duplexing (FDD) schemes. FDD requires paired spectrum with sufficient frequency separation, whereas TDD does not require such restrictions.

The most significant feature of LTE is its scalability which allows it to be used in different channel sizes/configurations, viz. 1.4, 3, 5, 10, 15 and 20 MHz in both TDD/FDD. This feature sets LTE apart from other standards which require a fixed bandwidth for deployment. The spectral efficiency of LTE is substantially higher than other mobile technologies.

LTEs arrival on the scene a year later than WiMAX, allowed it to incorporate or adopt most, if not all the key features such as OFDM, MIMO and HARQ. Key technologies used in LTE are as follows:

(1) **Orthogonal frequency division multiplexing (OFDM)** is a multicarrier system in which available bandwidth is divided into many narrowbands and data is transmitted in these bands parallely.
(2) **System architecture evolution (SAE)** is a system architectural framework for the evolution of the core network to LTE. It provides a packet-optimized system that supports multiple radio access technologies and lower latency.
(3) **Beam forming** or **spatial filtering** is a signal processing technique used in sensor arrays for directional signal transmission or reception. This is achieved by combining elements in a phased array in a way that signals at particular angles experience constructive interference while others experience destructive interference. Beam forming can be used at both transmitting and receiving ends in order to achieve spatial selectivity.
(4) **Multiple input–multiple output (MIMO)** is a smart antenna technology for wireless communications in which multiple antennas are used at both the source (transmitter) and the destination (receiver). The antennas at each end of the communications circuit are combined to minimize errors and optimize data speeds.

**Voice over LTE (VoLTE)**

Voice can be delivered over LTE in several ways. Some of these are listed below.

(1) Simultaneous voice LTE—circuit-switched voice services are run in parallel with packet-switched data services. This approach can have a negative impact on battery life as it requires two radios to run simultaneously. Additionally, the popular CSFB-based voice service affects IP-based data sessions in these networks by causing throughput drops, lost 4G connectivity and application aborts for data sessions. The interference between voice and data services is

mutual in these cases as users may miss voice calls when turning on data access (Tu et al. 2013).

(2) Circuit-switched fallback—enables the service to fall back on the 2G or 3G network before a circuit-switched voice call is initiated.

(3) Voice over LTE using GAN—provides voice services using a generic access network.

Voice over LTE (VoLTE) has been launched in South Korea and is being deployed in many countries such as Canada, USA, UAE, Sweden, India and Slovenia. The standards for voice are near finalization, and there are many multi-mode devices that facilitate roaming and ensure seamless connectivity by falling back to older generations.

## 5.2 Technology Ecosystem

### *5.2.1 Worldwide Interoperability for Microwave Access (WiMAX)*

There is no uniform global licensed spectrum for WiMAX; however, the WiMAX forum has published three licensed spectrum profiles, 2.3, 2.5 and 3.5 GHz, in an effort to drive standardization and decrease costs. The fixed profiles have channel sizes of 3.5, 5, 7 and 10 MHz, whereas mobile profiles require channel bandwidths of 5, 8.75 and 10 MHz. (Note: the 802.16 standard allows a far wider variety of channels, but only the above subsets are supported as WiMAX profiles.) WiMAX covers over 800 million subscribers and has been commercially deployed in more than 150 countries such as by SKT in Korea, UQ in Japan, VMAX and VEE in Taiwan, Yota-Scartel in Russia, Wateen in Pakistan, Packet One in Malaysia and Imagine in Europe (Senza Fili Consulting 2010).

WiMAX has been majorly deployed in 2.3, 2.5 and 3.5 GHz bands. It may be deployed in the 700 MHz band as this band has among the lowest propagation losses. Benefits such as better building penetration, lower Doppler effect and low path loss may be realized in the 700 MHz band (Sprint n.d.).

Widespread adoption of the technology and economies of scale are driving the prices of WiMAX equipment to levels lower than ever. Devices and equipment are now readily available and have attracted the attention of many large equipment manufacturers. It is however important to note that WiMAX is not perfect and has a few drawbacks. It is not a natural successor to any technology/previous generations, and the non-availability of multimodal handsets/user devices restricts roaming of users who opt for this network.

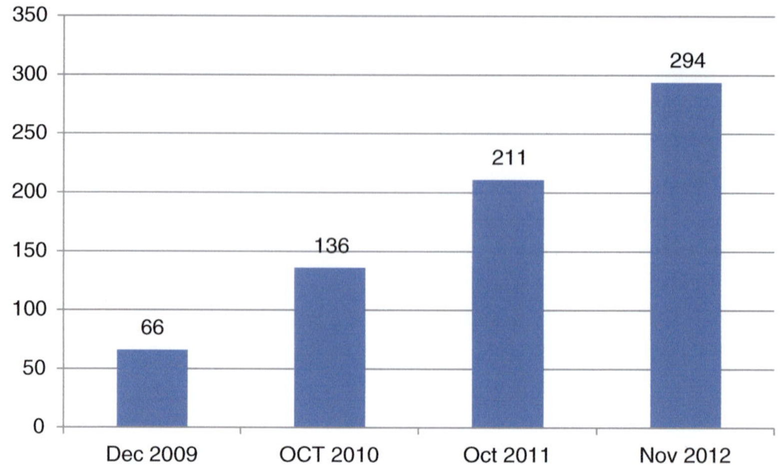


**Fig. 5.1** HSPA+ network commitments and deployments. *Data Source* GSA (2013a)

## 5.2.2 *High-Speed Packet Access Evolved (HSPA+)*

HSPA+ is an evolved version of HSPA, and presently deployed HSPA networks can be upgraded to HSPA+ with a few software and hardware changes. The graphs below show that 100 % of WCDMA networks have been upgraded to HSPA and over 50 % have been upgraded to HSPA+. This is incontrovertible evidence that HSPA is a developed and accepted technology worldwide (Figs. 5.1 and 5.2).

The world's first HSPA network was deployed and tested in June 2008 by Telstra Next G. Since then many operators around the world have deployed HSPA+

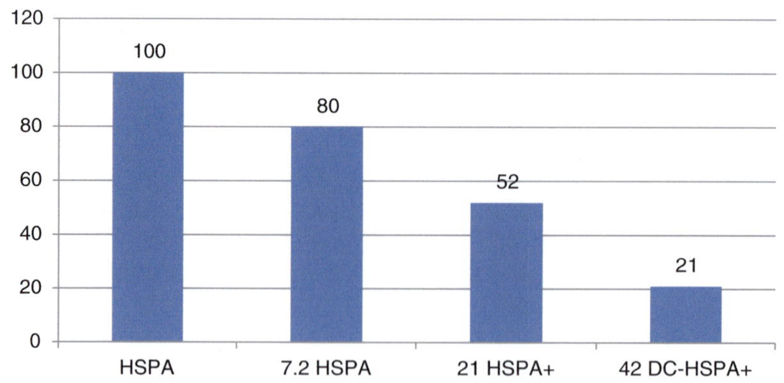


**Fig. 5.2** Percentage of WCDMA networks upgraded to HSPA family till 2012. *Data Source* GSA (2013a)

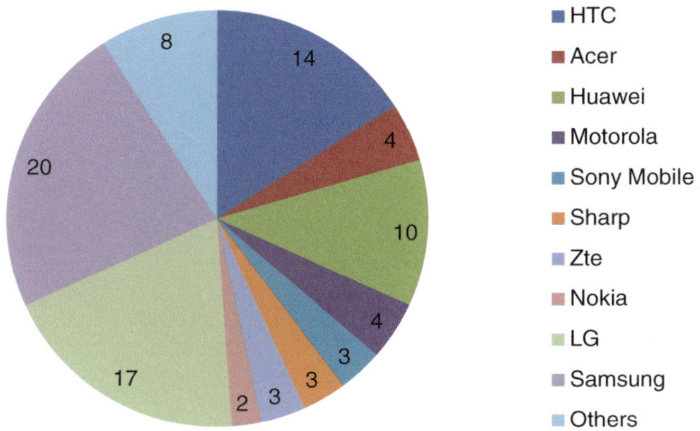


**Fig. 5.3** HSPA device vendor share. *Source* HSPA+ smartphone devices (GSA 2012)

networks, and as of October, 2015, 415 commercial HSPA+ systems in 173 countries have been launched (GSA 2015).

The HSPA+ ecosystem is quite mature, and many suppliers offer various devices such as data cards, notebook, handsets, USB modems and routers. This is due in part to features such as reduced power consumption of user equipment. A survey conducted in 2012 confirmed the launch of a total of 3847 HSPA (HSPA+ and DC-HSPA+) devices up to that point in time, with a whopping 620 devices added in the previous year alone (GSA 2012) (Figs. 5.3 and 5.4).

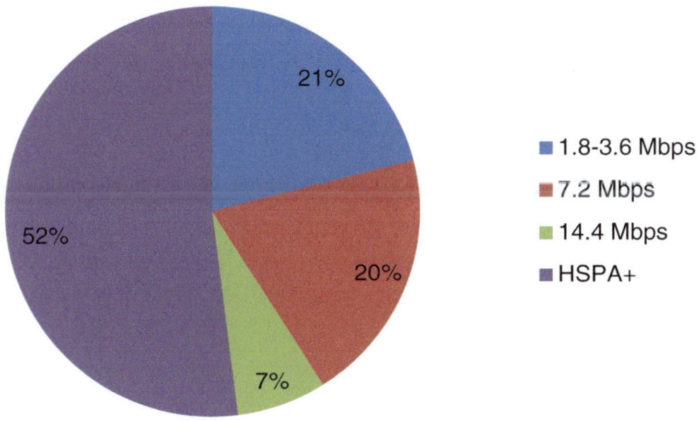


**Fig. 5.4** HSPA+ network peak DL data speed. *Source* GSA (2013b)

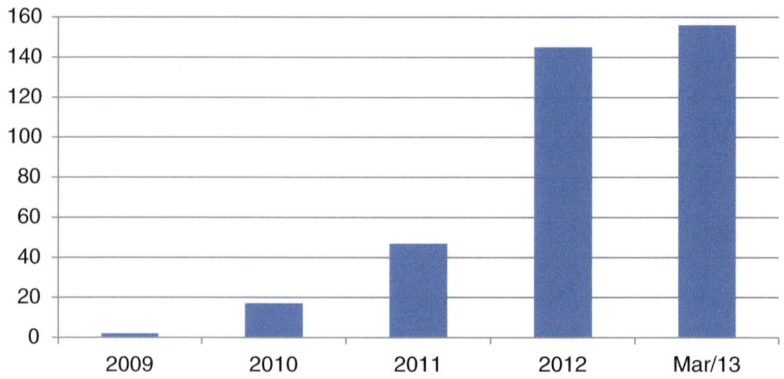


**Fig. 5.5** Growth in number of LTE networks during the year 2009–2013. *Data Source* GSA (2013c)

### *5.2.3 Long-Term Evolution (LTE)*

In 2009, TeliaSonera acquired the title of the first operator in the world to launch commercial 4G LTE services for customers in Stockholm, Sweden, Oslo and Norway (LteWorld n.d.). Many operators in many countries have since deployed LTE networks: Antel, AT&T, Bharti Airtel, China Mobile, Chunghwa Telecom, Etisalat, Interdnestrcom, KDDI, LightSquared, MetroPCS, NTT DoCoMo, SK TELECOM, Sky Telecom, Sprint, STC, T-Mobile, Telecom Italia, Telefonica, Telenor, Teliasonera, Telstra, UNE EPM Telecomunicaciones, Verizon Wireless, Vodafone and Zain are just a few.

LTE is without a doubt the fastest growing wireless technology ever with the number of commercially deployed networks increasing at a tremendous rate and more number of operators committing to the technology. As of 2013, LTE has been commercially deployed in 67 countries in 156 networks (GSA 2013c). Figure 5.5 shows the growth in number of LTE networks in the last few years.

LTE can be deployed in FDD mode in various bands, viz. 700, 800, 850, 900, 1800, 1900, 2100 and 2600 MHz. The number of LTE networks deployed and under deployment in different bands is indicated in Fig. 5.6.

Deployment of LTE network may also be done in TDD mode in several bands, viz. 2.3, 2.6 and 3.5 GHz. As of March, 2013, 14 LTE-TDD networks have been commercially launched.

### *5.2.4 Device Ecosystem for LTE*

The popularity and acceptability of mobile networks is largely driven by the presence and availability of a large number of user devices. Architecture and

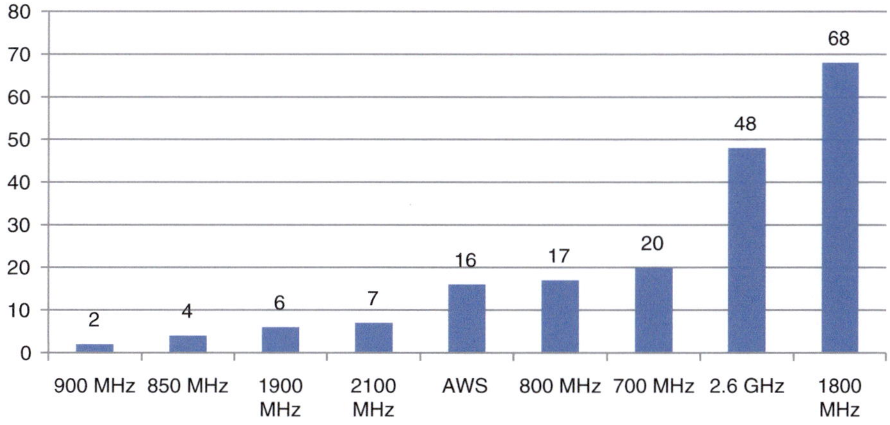


**Fig. 5.6** LTE (FDD) deployments in the different bands. *Data Source* GSA (2013d)

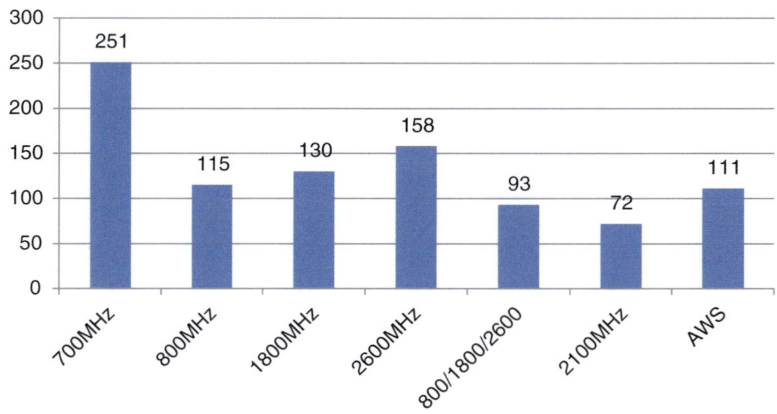


**Fig. 5.7** LTE FDD devices in different bands. *Data Source* GSA (2013e)

specifications of user equipment (UE) have been defined by international bodies such as ITU, 3GPP and IEEE. It is ideal that UE meets certain basic performance characteristics such as interoperability and protocol conformance and should be compatible with existing networks, so there is seamless transition from one network to another for users. Figures 5.7 and 5.8 show the number of LTE-FDD and LTE-TDD devices available in different bands.

The adoption of LTE has been fast, and the number of subscribers opting for LTE is increasing at a very fast rate.

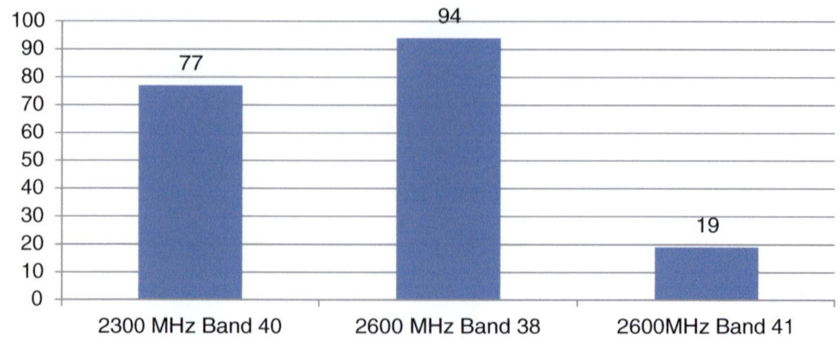


**Fig. 5.8** LTE-TDD devices in different bands. *Data Source* GSA (2013e)

## 5.3 Security Concerns

A key difference between 3G and 4G networks is that the latter will be based entirely on TCP/IP architecture and a suite of protocols designed to drive down costs as IP is already the ubiquitous choice for data networking across heterogeneous technologies. However, one important consequence of moving to a relatively open set of protocols (TCP/IP) is the expected increase in security issues compared to earlier generations. LTE and WiMAX have been developed with security protocols in place, and both are at an advanced specification level. In 2010, at the Eighth International Conference on Privacy, Security and Trust, members of the Canadian telecommunications industry along with representatives from the defence sector demonstrated that both WiMAX and LTE suffered from some physical layer vulnerabilities that made these networks susceptible to various kinds of attacks. At the MAC layer, WiMAX is susceptible to DoS attacks, eavesdropping, replay attack, service degradation and other vulnerabilities due in part to faulty key management (Seddigh et al. 2010). LTE was found to be similarly susceptible at the MAC layer and was vulnerable to illegal use of user and mobile equipment, location tracking, DoS attacks and data integrity attacks.

It is also important to note that many of these vulnerabilities have been addressed in future revisions of these standards (802.16e and 802.16m), but later research, at the time of writing this book, i.e., 2014, still points to vulnerabilities that need to addressed. Leong et al. (2014) in their paper on "Unveiling the Hidden Dangers of Public IP Addresses in 4G/LTE Cellular Data Networks" demonstrated with tests conducted on three 4G/LTE networks in Singapore that it is still easy for attackers to initiate three different types of attacks, viz. data quota drain, DoS flooding and battery drain.

It is important to consider these and other security issues when undertaking efforts to operationalize 4G networks. This new generation brings with it real measurable benefits but accompanies some risks and security concerns. The transition from previous generations should therefore be calm and carefully planned.

# 5.4 4G in India

## *5.4.1 Auction of BWA Spectrum in 2010*

The auction of spectrum in the 2.3 GHz band for BWA services was conducted by DoT in 2010. Two slots of 20 MHz spectrum (unpaired) in 2.3 GHz were assigned through this auction. BSNL and MTNL were allocated spectrum in 20 MHz (unpaired) in 2.5 GHz band at the auction determined price.

The summary of the auction results along with the amount paid by different operators is given in Table 5.1.

**Table 5.1** Auction results of BWA spectrum allocation

| Auction of BWA spectrum in 2010 | | | | | | | | |
|---|---|---|---|---|---|---|---|---|
| Service areas | Price in Rs. Crs. for 20 years | Airtel | Infotel | Qualcomm | Tikona | Augere | Aircel | BSNL/MTNL |
| Delhi | 2241.02 | | 20 | 20 | | | | 20 |
| Mumbai | 2292.95 | | 20 | 20 | | | | 20 |
| Maharashtra | 915.64 | 20 | 20 | | | | | 20 |
| Gujarat | 613.85 | | 20 | | 20 | | | 20 |
| Andhra Pradesh | 1059.12 | | 20 | | | | 20 | 20 |
| Karnataka | 1543.25 | 20 | 20 | | | | | 20 |
| Tamil Nadu | 2069.45 | | 20 | | | | 20 | 20 |
| Kolkata | 523.20 | 20 | 20 | | | | | 20 |
| Kerala | 258.67 | | 20 | 20 | | | | 20 |
| Punjab | 332.27 | 20 | 20 | | | | | 20 |
| Haryana | 119.90 | | 20 | 20 | | | | 20 |
| UP (E) | 142.50 | | 20 | | 20 | | | 20 |
| UP (W) | 183.87 | | 20 | | 20 | | | 20 |
| Rajasthan | 97.32 | | 20 | | 20 | | | 20 |
| Madhya Pradesh | 124.66 | | 20 | | | 20 | | 20 |
| West Bengal | 70.97 | | 20 | | | | 20 | 20 |
| Himachal Pradesh | 20.66 | | 20 | | 20 | | | 20 |
| Bihar | 99.28 | | 20 | | | | 20 | 20 |
| Orissa | 63.63 | | 20 | | | | 20 | 20 |
| Assam | 33.02 | | 20 | | | | 20 | 20 |
| North East | 21.27 | | 20 | | | | 20 | 20 |
| Jammu and Kashmir | 21.27 | | 20 | | | | 20 | 20 |
| **No of circles** | **22** | **4** | **22** | **4** | **5** | **1** | **8** | **22** |
| **Total in Rs. Crs.** | **12,847.77** | **3314.36** | **12,847.77** | **4912.54** | **1058.20** | **124.66** | **3438.01** | **12,847.77** |

BWA spectrum allocated to operators is unpaired

*Data Source* www.dot.gov.in

Reliance Infotel was the only private operator who was assigned 20 MHz (unpaired) spectrum in the 2.3 GHz band on a Pan India basis. Other players who were assigned 20 MHz of spectrum in the 2.3 GHz included Airtel, Qualcomm, Augere, Aircel and Tikona.

### 5.4.2 *Auction of Spectrum in November 2012 in 1800 MHz Band*

In November 2012, the DoT for the first time conducted the auction of spectrum in 1800 MHz. Total 127.50 MHz of paired spectrum in 1800 MHz band was acquired by the operators which fetched the Government exchequer Rs. 9407.64 Crs (Table 5.2).

**Table 5.2** Auction results in 1800 MHz band (November 2012)

| Auction of spectrum in November 2012 in 1800 MHz band | | | | | | |
|---|---|---|---|---|---|---|
| Service area | Price per MHz for 20 years in Rs. Crs. | Airtel | Idea | Telenor | Vodafone | Videocon |
| Andhra Pradesh | 229.53 | – | – | 5.00 | – | – |
| Assam | 6.94 | 1.25 | 5.00 | – | 2.50 | – |
| Bihar | 37.14 | – | 1.25 | 5.00 | 2.50 | 5.00 |
| Delhi | – | – | – | – | – | – |
| Gujarat | 179.87 | – | – | 5.00 | – | 5.00 |
| Haryana | 37.22 | – | – | – | 2.50 | 5.00 |
| Himachal Pradesh | 6.22 | – | – | – | 1.25 | – |
| Jammu and Kashmir | 5.06 | – | 5.00 | – | 2.50 | – |
| Karnataka | – | – | – | – | – | – |
| Kerala | 52.24 | – | – | – | 1.25 | – |
| Kolkata | 90.98 | – | 5.00 | – | – | – |
| Madhya Pradesh | 43.19 | – | – | – | 2.50 | 5.00 |
| Maharashtra | 210.25 | – | – | 5.00 | 1.25 | – |
| Mumbai | – | – | – | – | – | – |
| North East | 7.07 | – | 5.00 | – | 2.50 | – |
| Orissa | 16.22 | – | 5.00 | – | 2.50 | – |
| Punjab | 53.82 | – | – | – | 1.25 | – |
| Rajasthan | – | – | – | – | – | – |
| Tamil Nadu | 244.87 | – | 5.00 | – | – | – |
| Uttar Pradesh (East) | 60.94 | – | – | 5.00 | 1.25 | 5.00 |
| Uttar Pradesh (West) | 85.93 | – | – | 5.00 | 2.50 | 5.00 |
| West Bengal | 20.67 | – | 6.25 | – | 2.50 | – |
| **Total in Rs. Crs.** | | **8.67** | **2031.31** | **4018.28** | **1127.94** | **2221.44** |

Spectrum in 1800 MHz band is paired
*Data Source* www.dot.gov.in

Out of 127.50 MHz paired spectrum sold during the auction, 95 MHz paired spectrum is in contiguous block size of 5 MHz paired which is LTE-FDD ready and can be used for deployment of LTE-FDD networks. Videocon acquired 5 MHz of paired spectrum in 1800 MHz band in 6 circles and has expressed its intent to start LTE-FDD services in the near future.

### 5.4.3 *Auction of Spectrum in February 2014 in 1800 MHz Band*

In February 2014, the DoT conducted the auction of spectrum in 1800 and 900 MHz bands. Total 307.20 MHz of paired spectrum was acquired by the operators in 1800 MHz Band which fetched the Government exchequer Rs. 37,572.60 Crs.

Contiguous spectrum in blocks of 5 MHz was acquired by the operators, and out of the total spectrum acquired by the operators, i.e. 307.20, 200 MHz was available in contiguous blocks of 5 MHz of paired spectrum (Table 5.3).

### 5.4.4 *Auction of Spectrum in March 2015 in 1800 MHz Band*

In March 2015, the DoT conducted the auction of spectrum in 1800, 900, 800 and 2100 MHz bands. Total 93.80 MHz of paired spectrum in 1800 MHz band was acquired by the operators which fetched the Government exchequer Rs. 9636.17 Crs (Table 5.4).

Out of total 93.80 MHz of paired spectrum, 40 MHz is in contiguous blocks of 5 MHz paired and can be used for deployment of LTE-FDD networks.

## 5.5 Future Ahead

It is not in question that data requirements are on an increase and will continue to do so in the near future. All 3 flavours of 4G described above are potential candidates, but the following may hold the key to their adoption and sustenance:

**Table 5.3** Auction results in 1800 MHz band (February 2014)

| Auction of spectrum in February 2014 in 1800 MHz band | | | | | | | | |
|---|---|---|---|---|---|---|---|---|
| Service area | Price per MHz for 20 years in Rs. Crs. | Airtel | Vodafone | Reliance Jio | Idea | Aircel | Uninor | R. Com. |
| Andhra Pradesh | 163.00 | 8.80 | 0.60 | 5.80 | 6.00 | – | 1.40 | – |
| Assam | 36.10 | – | – | 5.40 | – | – | 6.00 | – |
| Bihar | 43.10 | – | – | – | – | – | 2.20 | – |
| Delhi | 364.00 | 7.00 | 8.00 | 5.40 | 0.60 | – | – | – |
| Gujarat | 237.80 | – | 4.40 | 6.00 | 1.60 | – | – | – |
| Haryana | 27.00 | – | 2.40 | – | 6.00 | – | – | – |
| Himachal Pradesh | 6.00 | 10.20 | – | – | – | – | – | – |
| Jammu and Kashmir | 6.10 | 2.60 | – | – | – | 1.80 | – | – |
| Karnataka | 155.00 | 8.80 | 5.00 | 5.00 | 5.00 | – | – | – |
| Kerala | 52.00 | 5.00 | 7.00 | 5.00 | 10.00 | – | – | – |
| Kolkata | 73.00 | 5.00 | 8.00 | 5.00 | – | – | – | – |
| Madhya Pradesh | 50.40 | 5.80 | – | 6.40 | 7.00 | – | – | – |
| Maharashtra | 290.35 | – | – | 5.00 | 9.00 | – | – | – |
| Mumbai | 272.00 | 6.00 | 8.20 | 6.60 | 2.00 | – | – | 0.60 |
| North East | 7.00 | 7.00 | – | 6.40 | 5.00 | 1.80 | – | – |
| Orissa | 16.00 | 5.00 | – | 5.00 | – | – | – | – |
| Punjab | 54.00 | 8.20 | 0.60 | – | 8.00 | – | – | – |
| Rajasthan | 26.00 | 8.20 | 0.80 | – | – | 1.60 | – | – |
| Tamil Nadu | 208.00 | 5.00 | – | 6.20 | – | – | – | – |
| Uttar Pradesh (East) | 64.00 | – | 4.00 | – | – | 1.80 | 1.80 | – |
| Uttar Pradesh (West) | 94.95 | – | – | – | – | – | 2.00 | – |
| West Bengal | 24.60 | 4.40 | – | 5.60 | – | 1.20 | – | – |
| **Total in Rs. Crs.** | | **9906.02** | **8383.52** | **11,054.41** | **7010.83** | **209.90** | **844.72** | **163.20** |

Spectrum in 1800 MHz band is paired
*Data Source* www.dot.gov.in

**Table 5.4** Auction results in 1800 MHz band (March 2015)

| Auction of spectrum in Mar 2015 in 1800 MHz band | | | | | | | | | |
|---|---|---|---|---|---|---|---|---|---|
| Service area | Price per MHz for 20 years in Rs. Crs. | Airtel | Vodafone | Idea | RJIO | RCOM | Tata | Uninor | Aircel |
| Andhra Pradesh | 242.80 | 1.20 | – | – | – | – | 2.60 | – | – |
| Bihar | 62.00 | – | | – | – | – | – | – | – |
| Gujarat | 238.00 | – | 3.40 | – | – | – | – | – | – |
| Haryana | 46.60 | 3.40 | – | – | 4.00 | 0.60 | – | – | – |
| Himachal Pradesh | 15.90 | – | – | 4.80 | 5.40 | – | – | – | – |
| Karnataka | 185.00 | – | – | 1.00 | – | 0.60 | – | – | – |
| Kerala | 83.45 | – | 1.00 | – | – | – | – | – | – |
| Kolkata | 149.10 | 2.00 | – | – | 5.00 | – | – | – | – |
| North East | 11.00 | 1.60 | – | 1.00 | | 5.00 | – | – | – |
| Odisha | 33.10 | 6.20 | – | 5.00 | – | 5.00 | – | – | – |
| Punjab | 71.00 | 1.00 | – | – | – | 0.60 | – | – | – |
| Rajasthan | 72.75 | – | – | – | 10.00 | – | – | – | – |
| Tamil Nadu | 225.00 | – | – | 6.40 | 0.60 | – | – | – | 10.00 |
| Uttar Pradesh (East) | 106.95 | – | 1.20 | – | 3.00 | – | – | – | – |
| Uttar Pradesh (West) | 95.95 | – | – | 2.20 | – | – | – | – | – |
| **Total in Rs. Crs.** | | **1041.82** | **1020.99** | **2088.91** | **2201.11** | **402.06** | **631.28** | **–** | **2250.00** |

Spectrum in 1800 MHz band is paired
*Data Source* www.dot.gov.in

(1) **WiMAX**:

- The popularity and acceptability of mobile networks are largely driven by the presence and availability of a large number of user devices. The absence of multimodal handsets/user devices in WIMAX restricts the roaming capability of users.
- WIMAX is not a natural successor of any technology/previous generations; hence, its adoption by the service providers may be restrained.

(2) **HSPA+**:

- HSPA+ is an evolution over HSPA networks already deployed by a large number of service providers. The existing HSPA networks can be made HSPA+ with software and hardware upgrades. This makes it a natural choice for the service providers to migrate to a better technology at minimal cost.
- The affordable user devices/handsets are readily available which helps in early adoption by end-users.

(3) **LTE**:

- All technologies and all bands evolve to LTE.
- The most significant feature of LTE is its scalability which allows it to be used in different channel sizes/configurations, viz. 1.4, 3, 5, 10, 15 and 20 MHz in both TDD/FDD. This feature alone places it way above the other technologies.
- Although the present cost of deployment is very high, it is likely to reduce due to increased commitments by operators.
- The device ecosystem is also developing rapidly.
- LTE is also highly spectral efficient. Due to the high costs of spectrum and its scarcity, LTE emerges as the natural choice.

## 5.6 Concluding Remarks

Supported spectrum bands and device ecosystem play a very important role in the adoption of any technology. It may be conclusive to say that both HSPA+ and LTE will grow and adopted by the masses in the near future. However, the inherent advantage of LTE, i.e. higher spectral efficiency, scalability and compliance to IMT-Advanced, will make it the technology of future and we will see a large number of operators around the world directly migrating their networks from 2G to 4G.

In the next chapter, we introduce mobile virtual network operators (MVNOs) as a new business model for the Indian telecom sector.

# References

GSA (2012) GSA HSPA devices survey key findings, August, 2012. Available at: http://www.gsacom.com/gsm_3g/info_papers.php4 [Accessed 17 Feb 2015]
GSA (2013a) Mobile broadband wallchart: 3GPP systems deployments, devices (WCDMA-HSPA/HSPA+, LTE). Available at: http://www.gsacom.com/gsm_3g/info_papers.php4#htmlElement_2233 [Accessed 19 Oct 2014]
GSA (2013b) GSA market update—LTE developments worldwide. Available at: http://www.gsacom.com/gsm_3g/info_papers.php4#htmlElement_2242 [Accessed 28 Nov 2014]
GSA (2013c) GSA Evolution to LTE report: 156 commercial networks launched; 412 operators investing in LTE. Available at: http://www.gsacom.com/gsm_3g/info_papers.php4#htmlElement_2253 [Accessed 9 Nov 2014]
GSA (2013d) Spectrum used in commercially launched LTE FDD networks. Available at: http://www.gsacom.com/gsm_3g/info_papers.php4#htmlElement_2254 [Accessed 16 Nov 2014]
GSA (2013e) Status of the LTE ecosystem. Available at: http://www.gsacom.com/gsm_3g/info_papers.php4#htmlElement_2237 [Accessed 3 Dec 2014]
GSA (2015) Fast facts. Available at: http://www.gsacom.com/news/gsa_fastfacts.php4 [Accessed 15 Oct 2015]
ITU (2003) M.1645 : Framework and overall objectives of the future development of IMT-2000 and systems beyond IMT-2000. Available at: https://www.itu.int/rec/R-REC-M.1645/en [Accessed 29 Apr 2015]
IXIA (2011) Deconstructing LTE/4G testing. Available at: http://www.ixiacom.com/node/2925 [Accessed 20 Feb 2015]
Leong W, Kulkarni A, Xu Y, Leong B (2014) Unveiling the hidden dangers of public IP addresses in 4G/LTE cellular data networks. ACM, New York, p 16
LteWorld (n.d.) Teliasonera|LteWorld. Available at: http://lteworld.org/operator/teliasonera [Accessed 30 Feb 2015]
Seddigh N, Nandy B, Makkar R, Beaumont J (2010) Security advances and challenges in 4G wireless networks. In: 2010 eighth annual international conference on privacy, security and trust. IEEE, New York, pp 62–71
Senza Fili Consulting (2010) Reaching sustained growth in the WiMAX market A survey of WiMAX operators, with a subscriber forecast for 2009–2014. Available at: http://www.goingwimax.com/wp-content/uploads/SenzaFili_WXforecast.pdf [Accessed 29 Apr 2015]
Shah S, Umrani A, Memon A (2011) Performance comparison of OFDM. MCCDMA and OFCDM for 4G wireless broadband access and beyond. In: PIERS Proceedings.
Sprint (n.d.) Mobile WiMAX: The 4G revolution has begun, Version 1
Tu G, Peng C, Wang H, Li C, Lu S (2013) How voice calls affect data in operational LTE networks. In: 19th annual international conference on mobile computing and networking. ACM, New York, pp 87–98

# Chapter 6
# Mobile Virtual Network Operators (MVNOs): An Emerging Business Model

Currently, India stands second in the world in terms of the number of mobile subscribers. This success can be attributed to the regulatory strategy of encouraging private players and maintaining a competitive environment. There has been an exponential growth in the number of wireless subscribers over the years and the telecommunications sector has reinforced the economic growth wave of the country. There are challenges to optimal usage of resources and bringing services within the reach of all at affordable prices. The Department of Telecommunication (DoT) is considering the potential of mobile virtual network operators (MVNOs) in meeting these demands. The Telecom Regulatory Authority of India (TRAI) released its recommendation paper in August 2008 about MVNOs following consultation with various stakeholders.

Considering all these aspects, this study is very significant in analysing the entry of the MVNO in India. TRAI defines an MVNO as "a licensee in any service area that does not have spectrum of its own for access service, but can provide wireless (mobile) access services to its own customers through an agreement with the licensed access provider, UAS/CMTS Licensee" (TRAI 2008a). Other countries have adopted different views when defining the MVNO. ITU considers an MVNO as an operator that offers mobile services but does not own its own radio frequency (ITU 2011). Usually, this operator has its own network code and, in many cases, issues its own SIM card. The mobile VNO can be a mobile service provider or a value-added service (VAS) provider. Ovum defines an MVNO as 'an organization that offers mobile services to customers, has its own mobile network code, issues its own SIM card, operates its own mobile switching centre (MSC) and does not have its own radio frequency allocation (Lewin 2001). The US Federal Communications Commission (FCC) defines MVNOs as resellers that purchase airtime from facilities-based providers and resell services to the public for profit (FCC 2001).

---

Reproduction: Kumar, P. M., and Sagar, M. (2010). Entry of Mobile Virtual Network Operators (MVNOs) in India: A strategic analysis. Journal of Telecommunications Management, 3(2), pp. 148–163.

© Springer India 2016 
M.K. Medudula et al., *Telecom Management in Emerging Economies*,
DOI 10.1007/978-81-322-2749-6_6

Oftel defined MVNO as 'an organization that offers mobile subscription and call services to customers but does not have an allocation of spectrum' (Ofcom 2009). From all these definitions, there is unanimous agreement about MVNOs not having their own spectrum while they are varying in infrastructure requirements and operational processes. Thus, the MVNO model is suited for both telecommunications and non-telecommunications organizations which have facilities and opportunities to provide mobile services without the need for spectrum licenses, which are restricted in number.

The main objective of this chapter is to assess the need for, timing of, regulatory approach to and impact on the cellular market of MVNO entry from a policy perspective in India. The analysis is based on the history and the current market conditions.

This chapter highlights the following:

- The classification of MVNOs across the world is presented based on business models to understand their operations and service offerings to assess the possible MVNO business models in India.
- The history of various countries has been studied with reference to MVNOs—how MVNO entry happened, the evolution of these business models, the regulatory role, the effect on the mobile market, etc.—MNOs and customers, the successes and failures, mergers and acquisitions of MVNOs and challenges faced by MVNOs, with the final goal being to derive implications relevant to the Indian mobile market scenario.
- In the light of the above analysis, an inspection of the views of various stakeholders—incumbent MNOs like Airtel, Vodafone, Reliance, TRAI, DOT, service providers from various countries and others—was conducted.
- The possible implications and suggestions were inferred with regard to the existing planned guidelines given by TRAI.

## 6.1 MVNO Business Models

The MVNO is a globally emerging trend in cellular markets with diverse core concepts of business which include the purpose, strategies, infrastructure, services and operational aspects, resulting in various business models. Of all these aspects, MVNOs are distinguished by the infrastructure and the strategies they choose.

### *6.1.1 Infrastructure-Based Classification*

This classification is made on the basis of the infrastructure facilities owned and managed by the MVNO (Pousttchi and Hufenbach 2009). It can be explained with respect to the mobile value chain (see Fig. 6.2). The main components of a value chain for mobile operators are sales, marketing, customer services, billing, operation of the core network and operation of the access network. Since MVNOs do not have any allotted spectrum, the operation of the access network (composed of base stations) is left to MNO(s). Depending on the extent to which the MVNO integrates into this value chain, it can be categorized into branded resellers, service providers, enhanced service providers and full MVNO (Fig. 6.1).

Branded resellers are the simplest version of an MVNO. They buy network capacity from the MNO and sell it to the customers by following their own marketing strategies and using their distribution channels. They may or may not take up customer care and services. They are generally companies with a high brand reputation. Service providers are the next level of MVNOs which take care of billing and pricing along with sales and marketing. They also provide customer support but do not own any network elements. The enhanced service provider differs from

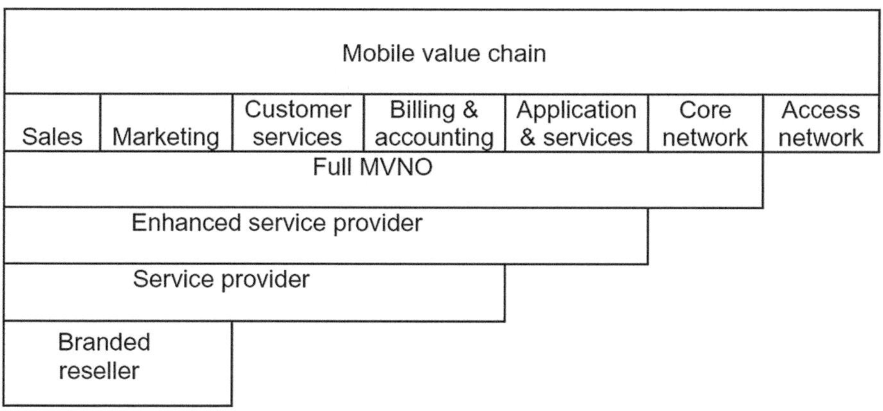


**Fig. 6.1** MVNO categorization with respect to the mobile value chain

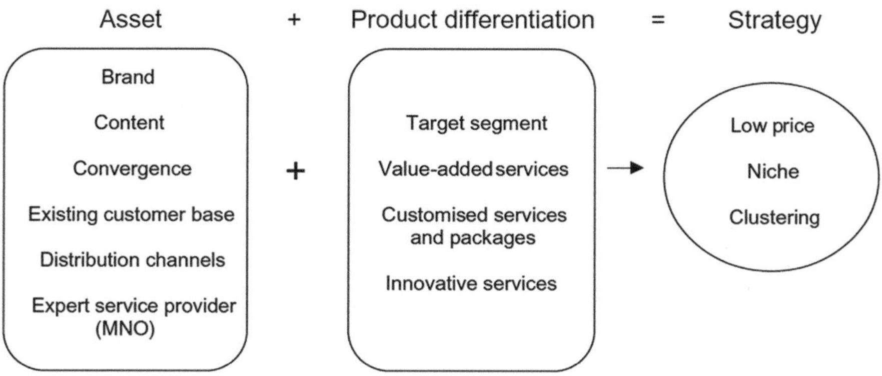


**Fig. 6.2** Evolution of MVNO strategies

service providers in that they additionally offer VASs. They do this by operating their own intelligent network and application platforms. They have a higher level of control over their services and less dependence on MNOs compared to the previous two types. The full MVNO is the deepest level value chain for an MVNO.

Full MVNOs own and maintain all aspects of the mobile value chain barring radio access networks. They have maximum independence over the services offered, pricing and billing. They also enter into interconnection and call termination agreements with other operators, generally telecommunications companies. Considerable start-up capital and operational expenditure (Opex) are required at this level and it is more risky. TRAI considers branded resellers and service providers to be thin MVNOs and enhanced service providers to be intermediate MVNOs.

### *6.1.2 Strategy-Based Classification*

Strategy refers to the plan of action to operate in the market which is reflected in the services and offerings to customers. MVNOs have the assets of brand appeal, content, convergence, customer base and distribution channels. MVNOs opt for the strategies which are in line with leveraging the existing assets to produce product differentiation (Friend 2009). Various strategies (Ofcom 2006) chosen by MVNOs include: discount, niche, brand extension, portfolio expansion and clustering approaches (Kiiski and Hammainen 2004). The discount strategy is also referred to as the low-cost, price leader or no frills strategy.

MVNOs compete based on price and offer low prices to consumers by minimizing their Opex. In order to survive with this strategy, a large customer base is required because of the small profit margins, as a significant amount of revenue goes towards the wholesale purchase of minutes, e.g. Tesco Mobile (UK) and Tracfone (USA). Niche MVNOs purely focus on a particular segment and offer services to attract customers, e.g. Lyca Mobile (UK), Virgin (USA, youth), Firefly (USA, children), Boost (USA, teenagers), YES (UK, business customers), Fujitsu Services (Finland, IT companies), Trident (Hong Kong, business travellers), ESPN mobile (USA, sports lovers) and Disney mobile (USA, schoolchildren).

Typically, the companies having a non-telecommunications background with strong brand values and customer bases, such as supermarkets, banks, high-street retailers or entertainment networks, choose the brand extension strategy. They target a larger customer base and have lesser marketing and promotion costs, e.g. Virgin (UK, USA and Canada), French market chain Carrefour (in Spain) and tourism group Globalia (Spain). Portfolio expansion is selected for leveraging the assets of convergence and content. Fixed-line operators, existing distributors and retailers, cable operators and internet service providers (ISPs) can provide bundled services on a single account, e.g. British Telecom (UK), internet provider Euskaltel (Spain), cable TV provider Telecable (Spain) and Japanese cable operator Japan

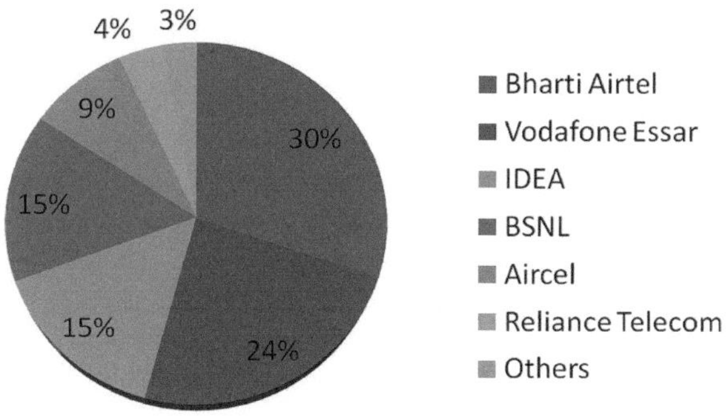


**Fig. 6.3** Indian mobile market share as of March 2010. *Sources* see http://www.coai.com/statistics.php and http://www.auspi.in/ (telecom statistics)

Communications, Inc. (JCI). Content providers are also called service leaders because they have the ability to develop differentiated VASs for the dynamic needs of the customer due to the company's core competence. They have multiple target segments that use the same services with different customized content, e.g. Blyk (UK) and MTV3 (Finland).

The clustering approach is taken by the established MNOs of other countries which choose to enter as an MVNO without any investment in spectrum and network infrastructure. Based on their existing expertise, they can have quick roll-out of services. As a drawback, they have to start from a zero subscriber base, e.g. UK mobile carrier Lebara Mobile entered into a wholesale agreement as an MVNO in Spain or Tele2 in Denmark. This whole discussion can be summarized as shown in Fig. 6.3.

## 6.2 Global Overview

The MVNO ecosystem, evolution of different business models, the regulatory standpoint and how MVNOs have influenced the markets in various countries are briefly described in this section.

### *6.2.1 USA*

The USA is one of the first countries where MVNOs have emerged (Dippon and Banerjee 2006). As the USA MNOs offered increased coverage area, competition increased between them. FCC, on the other hand, introduced MNP in June 2003. With increased competition, MNOs turned to the MVNO concept to differentiate themselves from competitors by targeting market-specific segments—youth, music lovers, sports fans, children, the rich, etc. Specifically, MVNO entry has redefined the prepaid market segment by focusing on budget-conscious people and offering services without any long-term contract, early termination fees, etc. Tracfone was the first MVNO in the USA, started in 1996. It offered a simple prepaid service that involved buying blocks of minutes and was found attractive by budget-conscious people and those who used mobiles for emergency calls only. Virgin, launched in 2002, is an example of a full MVNO. It attracted the youth segment by providing non-voice applications such as music, ringtones and song clips. Some MVNOs that targeted other niche segments include Firefly mobile targeting children aged between 8 and 13 years by offering special services such as emergency contacts and optional blocking of phone calls from numbers not stored in the mobile. ESPN mobile is an example of an MVNO leveraging the brand. Amp'd Mobile tried to leverage its content.

Voce mobile launched its services to serve those who do not hesitate to spend. Prepaid plans launched by MVNOs in the USA forced the other MNOs to introduce their respective prepaid packages. The MVNO subscriber base reached ten million by the first quarter of 2005 with Tracfone, Virgin and Boost Mobile having five million, three million and 1.7 million subscribers, respectively. FCC has not regulated the market as it was found to be effectively competitive.

### *6.2.2 United Kingdom*

In Europe, both prepaid and post-paid markets are popular, and hence, business models are mostly related to niche markets. The European regulatory authority has given guidelines to the National Regulatory Authority (NRA) to conduct a periodic survey to assess monopoly in the market by a single or a group of operators, termed significant market power (SMP) determination (Banerjee and Dippon 2009). If the market is found to have SMP, necessary steps have to be taken to induce competition and MVNOs have been one of the strategies chosen by the NRA. In the UK, the major MNOs—Vodafone, TMobile, Orange and O2—have nearly equal market share (Attenborough et al. 2007) which has led to the formation of voluntary relationships between MNOs and MVNOs. Virgin, the first MVNO in the UK, entered in 1999 targeting the youth market and, by the beginning of 2006, it had a market share of around 6 % (Ofcom 2006). Easy mobile has entered the market with a low-cost strategy. Tesco Mobile has offered prepaid plans at low prices. BT Mobile has targeted the high usage residential and business segment.

### *6.2.3 Finland*

Incumbent operators in Finland are TeliaSonera, Elisa and DNA capturing 49, 28 and 15 % of the market (as at March 2004), respectively. Finnish Communications Regulatory Authority has imposed on the SMP to enter into wholesale agreements with MVNOs. Tele2 is an ISP in Finland which has leveraged the convergence asset. It has entered the market with a price leader strategy. MTV3 is a television channel and offers services by exploiting its content capability. Saunalahti offers low-price content differentiated services and also has agreements with branded resellers; in 2005, it was acquired by Elisa MNO (Kiiski and Hammainen 2004).

### *6.2.4 Denmark*

In Denmark, the MNO TDC had a market share of 50 % and the MNO Sonofone had a market share of 30 % (Attenborough et al. 2007). Both were found to have SMP and the regulator mandated open access to MVNOs in 2000. Danish MVNOs selected the low-price strategy and triggered a price war which resulted in a decline in the average revenue per user (ARPU) and the subscriber base of the MNOs (Ofcom 2006). By 2003, 14 different MVNOs were competing with MNOs on voice and data with a low-price strategy. This has caused up to 50 % fall in prices. The ARPU and subscriber base of the incumbent MNO TDC reduced by 50 and 20 %, respectively, in 2003. Thus, TDC acquired Telmore MVNO and MNO Sonofone acquired CBB Mobil MVNO. This resulted in an increase in the ARPU and stabilized the retail pricing volatility. By 2006, MVNOs Tele2, Telmore, debitel (Denmark), CBB Mobil and DLG Tele had a combined subscriber base of 26.8 %; however, three of these MVNOs were acquired by MNOs reducing the MVNO market share to 8.4 % (Attenborough et al. 2007).

### *6.2.5 Hong Kong*

In Hong Kong, the market is competitive for 2G services; however in 2001, the regulator mandated open access to full MVNOs with 3G licensing to induce competition among the few licensees and also to enable quick roll-out of services and a wider reach of customers by separating service provision from network operation. OFTA has taken the risk of providing less of a commercial incentive for network operators to invest and build up their own networks and infrastructure. Here, again the prepaid market was an untapped segment as in the USA. MVNOs targeted the niche segments like business travellers with tailor-made prepaid plans. Trident was the first MVNO in Hong Kong which provided prepaid international plans for business travellers from non-GSM nations such as Japan, South Korea and the USA (Yan 2004). However, in Sweden MNOs allowed MVNOs to meet the coverage requirements set by the regulator.

### 6.2.6 *Spain*

In Spain, MNOs Telephonica and Vodafone were found to have dominance in the market and the regulator reduced the entry barriers for MVNOs in 2002. Since no successful agreements were formed between the MNOs and MVNOs until 2005, the regulator has mandated the network access. Carrefour, British phone retailer The Phone House and UK mobile carrier Lebara mobile (clustering MVNO) are the early MVNOs in Spain (Attenborough et al. 2007).

### 6.2.7 *Japan*

In Japan, the regulator gave the guidelines for MVNO entry in 2002; however, MNOs have no incentive to partner with them which resulted in no successful MNO–MVNO agreements. In 2007, the regulator reviewed the market competition and stated that MNOs should negotiate when approached by the potential MVNOs. If they could not reach an agreement, an MVNO can appeal to the Dispute Settlement Authority which will review the situation. JCI has secured a deal with NTT DoCoMo (MNO) through this approach. Jupiter Communication and JCI (cable TV operator) are the two MVNOs in Japan (Shoji 2009).

### 6.2.8 *Norway*

In Norway, as Telenor and Netcom had SMP in the market, wholesale agreements with MVNOs were mandated in 2003 (Attenborough et al. 2007). Chess and Tele2 had a significant market share but were later acquired by MNOs, thereby reducing the MVNO share in the market (Ofcom 2006). Note that Denmark, Finland and Norway had this similar trend: existence of SMP in the market followed by regulatory intervention, discount strategy resulting in a relatively large share for MVNOs; however, due to dwindling ARPUs, MVNOs with significant share were acquired by MNOs.

## 6.3 Inferences

Following the above discussion, the authors scrutinized the inferences from various perspectives which can be correlated with the Indian scenario. The following analysis of the stakeholders' debate in India has been based on this outlook.

### 6.3.1 Key Prime Movers for MVNO Entry

- Regulator: To induce competition in the market and to enhance consumer welfare by various innovative services.
- MNO: In a saturated market, to sustain competition or customer acquisition by product differentiation; also to increase the coverage area of services.
- MVNO: To leverage existing assets of brands, content, convergence, existing customer base and distribution channels.

### 6.3.2 Regulatory Stance on MVNO Entry

Regulators in the USA and UK did not impose any regulations on MNOs as the market was driven by the competition and MNOs were looking for MVNOs. They decided to intervene only when there was an SMP or anti-competitive behaviour. In Denmark, Norway, Finland and Spain, due to the dominant share of an MNO or a group of MNOs, regulators mandated MVNO agreements. In Hong Kong, this mandating was done only for 3G services. In Japan, the regulators decided to intervene only when the agreements failed between the MNO and MVNO. In all the countries, introduction of number portability reduced entry barriers because of the reduction in switching costs.

The study indicates that a regulatory mandate for MVNOs is required only after a competitive assessment of the market which shows symptoms of market failure, i.e. market forces cannot direct prices, services and offerings due to lack of competition, dominance of a single or group of service provider(s) and collusion among the operators. Otherwise, voluntary MNO–MVNO agreements should be encouraged. If they are not successful, the reasons can be the lack of a proper ecosystem (i.e. competition at the wholesale level has not evolved despite strong retail competition) or that other entry barriers have to be sorted out.

### 6.3.3 Infrastructure Requirements for MVNO

Hong Kong allowed only full MVNOs, while the USA and UK considered simple resellers also as MVNOs. Typically, MVNO infrastructure was determined by the degree to which its partner MNO could provide access to its functions and also the investment and risk factors of the MVNOs. In general, there were no restrictions on the infrastructure requirements of the MVNOs from the regulators.

### 6.3.4 Strategy, Acquisitions and Consumer Welfare

Although various strategies have been adopted globally depending on the earlier core competence of the MVNO, selection of the strategy suiting the market conditions is very crucial and should act as an adjunct for MNO services. Identifying the niche demographics ignored by the MNOs and offering unique customized services for that target segment is the most appreciated strategy. In Spain, MVNOs provided innovative services in the form of add-ons, upgrades and expensive items and got more ARPU from customers. Various niche segments were identified in all the countries and customized offerings were provided for them. Some of the niche segments are youth, children, university students, IT professionals, tourists, etc. MVNOs with content capabilities (television channels, music channels, etc.), convergence capabilities (ISPs, cable operators, etc.) and brand appeal have entered the market. With convergence, customers are offered broadband, television and mobile services with a single connection.

Acquisitions of MVNOs occur when MVNOs compete with the host MNOs and thereby hampering their growth. The low-cost strategy targeting the niche segments is the dominant strategy in Europe and the USA. Since there is a lot of scope in the reduction of tariffs, MVNOs embraced this opportunity. In some saturated markets such as Finland, Norway and Denmark, the low-price strategy has even threatened the growth of MNOs because MVNOs have caused a decline in the ARPUs of the MNOs. But MNOs have taken over those MVNOs with decent market share, regained their ARPUs and their sustainability in the market. So, MVNOs with a discount strategy have questionable future prospects for growth in a saturated market while the MVNOs with a niche strategy are expected to have long-term viability in the market. From the customer's view, they enjoy innovative customized services with a wide variety of choice at affordable prices.

### 6.3.5 Advantages for MVNOs

Because of low Opex and investments, MVNOs generally take less time to start generating profits. They can focus more on service innovation than technological aspects. Because of existing assets and economies of scale, customer acquisition is possible at a cost which is lower than the industry average. They need not own the spectrum to provide services.

### 6.3.6 Challenges for MVNOs

Selection of a suitable MNO, a viable contract and strategy are the key success factors. Some of the challenges for MVNO survival in the market include constant adaptation to the needs of the target segment and niche markets, i.e. ability to differentiate their services from those of others (particularly imitators), competition due to the convergence of technology, capitalizing on brand reputation, choice of billing system and quality of customer care services. For example, in the USA, ESPN mobile was unable to capitalize on its brand. Amp'd Mobile was unable to provide the promised services to its customers, and customers suffered disruption in streaming video services and poor bill collection as the provider could not realize payment for the post-paid services given to the youth market (Kharif 2007). Disney mobile was unable to provide sufficient differentiation and consequently exited the market. The contract between MVNO Trident (Hong Kong) and its MNO was scrapped leading to the closure of its services. Firefly ended its services after MNOs started coming after its target segment (children aged 8–13 years).

### 6.3.7 MVNO–MNO Relationship and Agreements

The common dilemma of how MVNOs slicing the retail market share of MNOs can benefit.

MNOs is clarified here. The two key factors are as follows:

- MVNOs' existing assets and
- Level of wholesale discount between the MNO and the MVNO.

MVNOs add value to products through their existing assets and try to serve the market segments which are ignored by MNOs, thereby widening and deepening the market in a way which a traditional MNO cannot. Under certain demand and sales conditions, MNOs generate more net economic benefits by wholesale access to MVNOs than retail operation alone (Banerjee and Dippon 2009). This level of wholesale discount is also crucial for the sustenance of a virtual operator. Thus, MVNOs bring new subscribers and traffic to the MNO's network at zero acquisition cost and share the network cost. But MNOs lose the direct relationship with the customer. It is also to be noted that the MNO is non-existent from the customer point of view, e.g. many Virgin Mobile (MVNO) customers are unaware of the Tmobile (MNO) role in their services. MVNOs with good market share can be threatened by MNOs because they can be acquired or price barriers can be increased against them.

### 6.3.8 Final Remarks

Some typical market conditions and observations in the majority of the countries where MVNO entry has happened were identified:

- The number of network operators is limited (typically 3–5).
- Availability of spectrum capacity with MNO leasing out to MVNO.

- The market is mature (market share of the operator tends to become stable) and highly penetrated. MNOs are finding it difficult to increase their subscriber base.
- Potential for reduction in ARPU levels.
- Many untapped customer segments.
- There are symptoms of market failure due to lack of competition and collusion among service providers.
- MVNOs which were the first movers had a good advantage and were able to get a decent market share compared to later entrants and imitators.
- Typically, the major subscriber base among MVNOs is shared among two or three MVNOs.
- MVNO strategy should supplement the host MNO's services rather than competing with the host MNOs: it should not give unwelcome competition to the host MNO. Otherwise, MVNOs have questionable prospects for their long-term viability in the market.

## 6.4 Indian Context

The authors consider four parameters: need for, timing of, infrastructure required for and regulatory approach to MVNO entry as suggested by TRAI, DoT, Association of Unified Telecom Service Providers in India (AUSPI), Airtel, etc., and analyse the pros and cons in the light of the inferences they have derived and propose some suggestions and changes to the planned guidelines. In this study, the authors focus specifically on the metros and rural areas, which are the two extremes in the current Indian cellular market scenario due to the contrasting market conditions and the digital divide.

### *6.4.1 Stakeholder Perspective*

Current challenges to the regulator in the Indian cellular market are as follows:

- To maintain the current exponential growth of subscribers which reflect an increase in teledensity;
- To bridge the digital divide and to provide services within the reach of all at affordable prices;
- To maintain or increase competition levels (Fig. 6.4 indicates the competition levels among the Indian Service Providers as of March 2010);
- To achieve all these goals with optimal utilization of resources—spectrum, infrastructure, etc. TRAI envisaged MVNO potential in attaining these goals (TRAI 2008b). The regulator and stakeholders such as AUSPI, Reliance, Tata Teleservices Limited (TTSL), BT Mobile support the need for and timing of

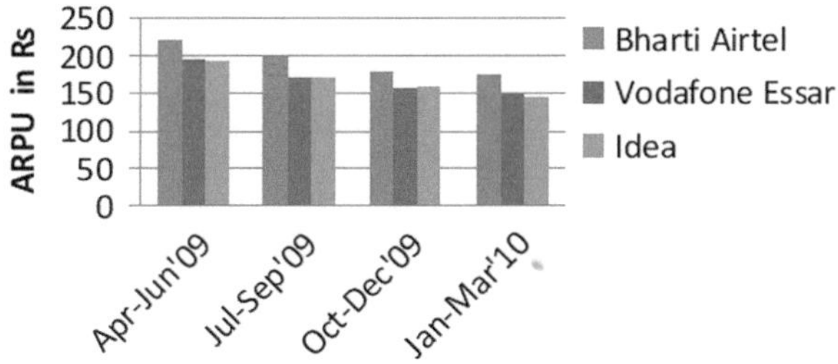


**Fig. 6.4** Dwindling ARPUs of Indian service providers from April 2009–March 2010. *Source* http://www.coai.com/revenue.php [Year 2009 and 2010 (accessed on 5 April 2010)]

MVNO entry in India currently, while Bharti Airtel, Cellular Operator Association of India (COAI), BSNL, etc., hold the opposite view. The reasons behind these conflicting views are as follows (TRAI 2008c).

### 6.4.2 *Metros*

**Supporting factors**

- Customer acquisition is becoming difficult, particularly in some metro cities where basic mobile services will become a common commodity and the need for product differentiation has arisen. In these areas, an MVNO with a strong retail chain effectively can address the needs of the unserved niche segments, thereby widening and deepening the market, in addition to promoting competition by effective product bundling and cross selling.
- Many service areas have vast geographical spread nearly equal to that of a European country. An MNO limited in its schemes, consumer understanding and resources cannot serve the niche and faraway customers in a satisfying manner.
- Falling ARPUs can be arrested by innovative VASs (Fig. 6.5).

**Constraints**

- Constraints are mostly in terms of the sustenance of MVNOs in the market. Low ARPU levels, high taxation levels of 17–26 % and an FDI limit of 74 % make it difficult for MVNOs with thin margins to operate.
- There are around ten access providers in each service area; 5–6 new operators will roll out their services and adopt aggressive strategies to capture the market meaning that MVNOs will face tough competition to acquire customers.
- In India, allocation of spectrum to MNOs is based on subscriber base and at least incumbent MNOs are facing challenges to meet the burgeoning demands of the market and may not have any surplus capacity to share with MVNOs.
- Other factors include that the Indian market has not reached sufficient penetration and maturity levels; MNOs are already focusing on innovations and

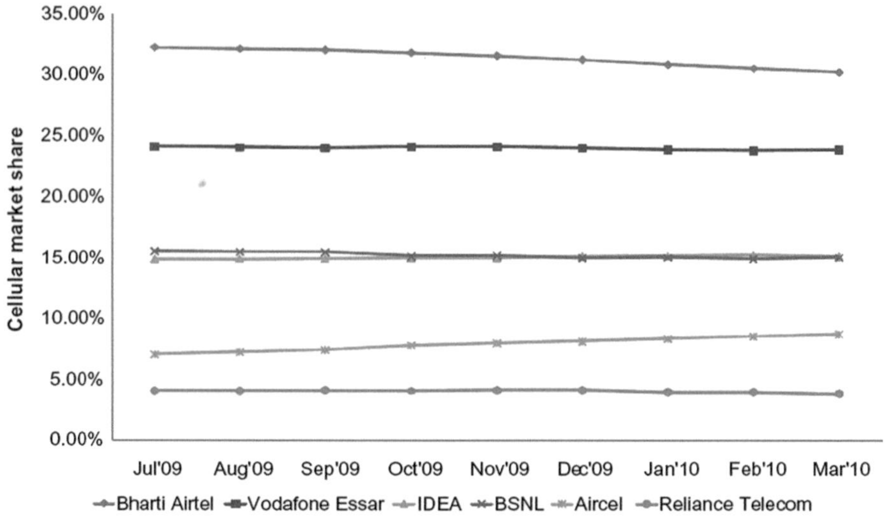


**Fig. 6.5** Mobile market share (tend to stable values) among the service providers in India. *Sources* see http://www.coai.com/statistics.php and http://www.auspi.in/ (telecom statistics)

VASs, leaving less scope for MVNOs; there is a common threat of dilution of incentives for network investments; and there are limited numbering resources (Attenborough et al. 2007).

### *6.4.3 Rural Areas*

**Supporting factors**

- MNOs are currently focusing on circles B and C, which are the least penetrated, to increase their subscriber base, and deploying infrastructure. MVNOs can focus on their services and acquire customers for MNOs which can focus on building network infrastructure without bothering about distribution and marketing.
- MVNOs can specifically address the niche markets like rural areas, thereby enhancing the teledensity of the country and can bridge the digital divide (TRAI 2008a).

**Constraints**

- Constraints for rural areas include that telecommunications networks in rural areas are much more capital intensive than in urban areas so that MVNOs have to pay more to MNOs and may not fetch sufficient revenues for them.

The MVNO is an urban concept which is famous for providing VASs where the basic services are already present, in general, MVNOs are not employed for providing basic services (TRAI 2009).

### 6.4.4 *Analysis of the Need for and Timing of Entry Factors in Metros and Rural Areas*

**Metros**

The Indian market can be considered competitive based on an operator's market share varying over certain values, e.g. Airtel, 30 %; Vodafone, 23–24 %; and Idea and BSNL around 15 % [July 2009–March 2010 statistics (Fig. 6.6) and falling ARPUs in Metros (Fig. 6.7)].[1,2] The prerequisites of maturity (market shares of the operators tend to become stable) and high penetration levels are indicative of a strong retail competitive market which is reflected in some metros in India. If MVNOs are restricted now due to the constraints previously discussed—number of operators, dwindling ARPUs (Fig. 6.7), etc., then they can never enter the Indian market. The authors' proposition is that there is still a viable business case and agreements available for MVNOs dependent mainly on their strategy and the level of wholesale discount that MNOs offer. An MVNO should not adopt the low-price strategy, which cannot lead to long-term viability in the market, rather it should identify niche segments and provide customized VASs which are expected by MNOs to increase ARPU levels. In this way, MVNOs will not be a threat to the growth of the MNOs, for they are acquiring niche customers using VASs and do not compete with the MNOs who are acquiring customers with basic services with few or no VASs. As even more MVNOs come into the market, they all will be competing on VASs only, which is a new type of competition in the cellular market. New MNOs might be more eager to have MVNO agreements than incumbent operators in order to increase their subscriber base against the competition and to promote their network and spectrum utilization. They have the initially allotted 4.4 MHz spectrum which can be shared. MVNO customers are also MNO customers but in an indirect way. Unless an MVNO's value proposition is so appealing to incumbent MNOs, they may be unwilling to share their spectrum with the MVNO, but doing so should add significant product differentiation to an MNO's services. In summary, the MVNO strategy will play a key role in making agreements and thereby achieving long-term sustainability in the market.

[1]See: http://www.coai.com/statistics.php (Year 2009 and Year 2010), (accessed 5 April 2010).

[2]See: http://www.auspi.in/show-subscribber.asp (Year 2009 and Year 2010), (accessed 5 April 2010).

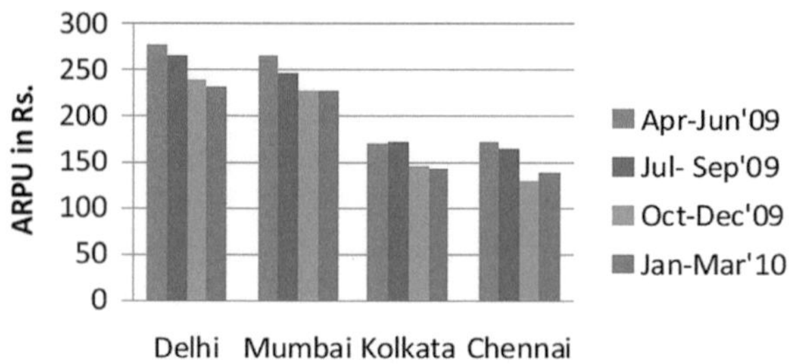


**Fig. 6.6** Falling ARPUs in metros during the period April 2009–March 2010. *Source* http://www.coai.com/revenue.php [Year 2009 and 2010 (accessed 5 April 2010)]

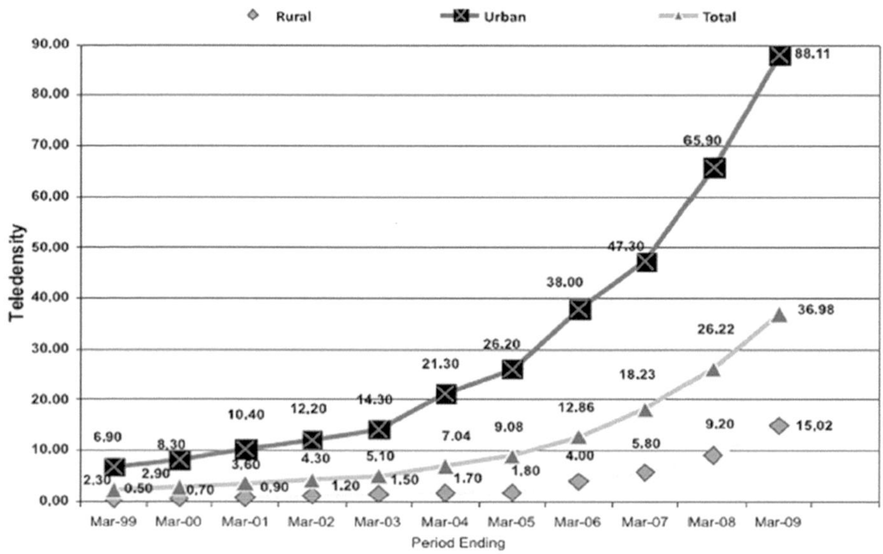


**Fig. 6.7** Comparison of teledensity in rural and urban areas. *Source* TRAI annual report 2008–09, available at: http://www.trai.gov.in/annualreport/TRAIAR2008-09E.pdf

### Rural areas

Rural areas are under-penetrated with low-income users, and deploying networks in these areas requires more capital than in urban areas. So MNOs did not address rural segments sufficiently. Even if MNOs provide their services, these excess costs may be transferred to the end customers. There is a considerable technology gap between the urban and rural areas (Fig. 6.7) and the needs of the people in these areas are totally different. A very customer-centric approach is required to work in these areas which can be best addressed only by MVNOs. So the traditional paradigm has been changed by proposing MVNOs for rural areas, which are under-penetrated. TRAI has proposed providing incentives to MVNOs so that local entrepreneurs who are well aware of the needs and habits of the local people can provide customized products and applications and thereby extending mobile services to these ignored segments (TRAI 2009).

In principle, the concept of using MVNOs for increasing the coverage area has already been implemented in Sweden and for 3G services in Hong Kong. Dilution of facility-based competition and disincentives to invest in networks by MNOs are the possible consequences. The current issue of rural areas resembles the 3G implementation in Hong Kong, where MNOs have to provide open access to MVNOs. OFTA stated that separating service provision from network operation would enhance competition and provide customers with a wide variety of services.

The potential drawbacks also were foreseen of less commercial incentive for the operators to build up their networks and infrastructures. But with limited spectrum availability, introduction of MVNOs was seen to promote competition and, by sharing the network costs of MNOs, customers did not get burdened with excess charges (Yan 2004). Even MNOs are exclusively given incentives to build their networks and provide basic services to rural areas, but they need more incentives, because of the high margins, compared to those of MVNOs, and the scope for providing VASs will be less in the future. Note that price is the important consideration for rural customers.

A possible trade-off could be to provide incentives for both MNOs and MVNOs and let them work together for rural penetration. This could be a win–win scenario. Even regulators could consider mandating open access in this scenario or intervene in case of failure in commercial agreements. MVNOs with foreign brands have much less scope in this scenario, while the rural brands which are well known to the rural people are the best MVNOs. Based on the economies of scale, MVNOs will be able to manage with the support of the regulator. To start with, MVNOs can operate with low-price strategy providing basic mobile services and can gradually add VASs to their services and offerings.

In conclusion, the regulator should support both MNOs and MVNOs to build networks and to offer services, thereby separating services from network deployment. In this case, it could consider taking an active role of mandating the agreements. This is the different approach that the authors are proposing as stated by TRAI, which wanted to encourage voluntary agreements between MNOs and MVNOs.

**Infrastructure**
With regard to the infrastructure, since MVNOs cannot have spectrum on their own, they should not install radio access networks, but can own other network elements until a core network exists in the supply value chain. Few stakeholders are of the view that MVNOs should be introduced in a phased manner, i.e. initially only service providers and enhanced service providers (thin MVNOs), who are resellers augmenting the product with their brand, etc., should be allowed (TRAI 2008c). But the majority suggest to give freedom to MVNOs to choose their business model, as posing restrictions would affect their agreements, innovation and prospects for future growth, etc., and MVNOs will not be attracted to the Indian market. By restricting entry to thin MVNOs, the desired goal of competition and VASs will not be served and incumbent MNOs will still have control of the market.

**Regulatory role**
With regard to regulation, all stakeholders are unanimous that there are no symptoms of market failure and hence voluntary MNO–MVNO agreements should be encouraged and no regulator intervention is required even if they fail. The presence of market failure is determined by a competitive assessment of the market, as done by any regulator in terms of the operator's shares, revenues and offerings over a period of time. In general, collusion is possible where the number of operators is limited and incumbent operators have similar competitive parameters. This is not the case in India's current scenario, as already mentioned. In the above discussion, the authors have suggested a slightly different approach for regulatory intervention. Even in metros, regulators should maintain a "watchdog" position to monitor the market dynamics.

**Entry barriers**
The following are the key barriers to market entry which the regulator should work on to enable MVNO entry:

- Number portability (under consideration in India);
- Limited number resources (under consideration in India);
- Despite retail competition, if wholesale-level completion has not emerged or matured, it can impede MVNO entry. To give trust to the potential MVNOs, an effort to create a wholesale environment should be in place where MNOs and MVNOs both invest in wholesale business development.

## 6.5 Concluding Remarks

A detailed analysis of the global emergence of MVNOs—time of entry, evolution of the business models, impact on the mobile market and regulatory standpoint—has been presented. This has been mapped to the current Indian cellular market. The authors analysed the pros and cons (impact) of the guidelines proposed by TRAI after reviewing the comments from all stakeholders in terms of need, timing, infrastructure requirements and regulatory role and offered some suggestions.

A different approach is needed in metros and rural areas due to contrasting market conditions in terms of competition and penetration. In metros, due to the strong retail competition, MVNOs should adopt a niche strategy and produce product discrimination instead of employing a discount strategy, which tends to compete with the host MNO. Only then can they have a long-term sustainable business model and voluntary relationships can be made, although the regulator needs to maintain a watchdog position.

In rural areas, MVNOs can start with low-price strategy but regulatory support is required for both MNOs and MVNOs because of capital intensive networks and low revenues. The principle of separating the service segment from network development has to be employed. This avoids disincentives for facility-based operators, and regulators could consider mandating open access to MVNOs. Some prerequisites such as number portability, numbering scheme and development of a wholesale market have to be in place to support MVNOs. With regard to the infrastructure, all types of MVNOs should be encouraged in the market which will support the innovation, consumer welfare and MVNO growth. Different MVNO value propositions and regulatory approaches in urban and rural areas and tackling entry barriers are the authors' suggestions for successful MVNO entry in India.

## References

Attenborough N, Dippon C, Sorensen S (2007) Mobile virtual network operators (MVNOs) in Israel: economic assesment and policy recommendation. Available at: http://www.moc.gov.il/sip_storage/FILES/8/1328.pdf. Accessed 30 Jun 2010

Banerjee A, Dippon CM (2009) Voluntary relationship among mobile network operators and mobile virtual network operators: an economic explanation. Inf Econ Policy 21(1):72–84

Dippon C, Banerjee A (2006) Mobile virtual network operators: blessing or curse? An economic evaluation of the MVNO relationship with mobile network operators, NERA Economic Consulting. Available at: http://www.nera.com/publications/archive/2006/mobile-virtual-network-operators-blessing-or-curse-an-economic.html.

FCC (2001) Biennial regulatory review spectrum aggregation limits. Available at: https://www.fcc.gov/document/2000-biennial-regulatory-review-spectrum-aggregation-limits

Friend G (2009) Critical success factors, mobile virtual network operators. Coleago consulting, April. Available at: http://www.coleago.co.uk/index.php?page=critical-successfactors-in-launching-an-mvno. Accessed 10 Sept 2009

ITU (2011) Regulatory resources on 3G mobile: MVNOs. Available at: http://www.itu.int/osg/spu/ni/3G/resources/MVNO/index.html. Accessed 17 Mar 2015

Kharif O (2007) Amp'd files for bankruptcy. Businessweek.com. Available at: http://www.businessweek.com/the_thread/the_thread/techbeat/archives/2007/06/ampd_

Kiiski A, Hammainen H (2004) Mobile virtual network operators: case Finland. ITS 15th biennial conference

Lewin D (2001) ITU MVNOs-competition policy and market development: ITU workshop on 3G mobile. Available at: https://www.itu.int/osg/spu/ni/3G/workshop/presentations/lewin_1.pdf. Accessed 4 Mar 2015

Ofcom (2006) The communications market. Interim report. Available at: http://www.ofcom.org.uk/research/cm/interim/feb06_report/comms_mkt.pdf. Accessed 30 Jun 2010

Ofcom (2009) Available at: http:// www.ofcom.org.uk/consult/condocs/mobile_call_termination/wmvct/annexf. Accessed 20 Nov 2009

Pousttchi K, Hufenbach Y (2009) Analyzing and categorization of the business model of virtual operators. In: Eighth international conference on mobile business. IEEE, pp 87–92

Shoji Y (2009) Evaluation of the competition policy to encourage MVNO system in Japan. In: SAINT'09: 2009 ninth annual international symposium on applications and the internet. IEEE, pp 220–222

TRAI (2008a) Recommendations on mobile virtual network operator (MVNO). Available at: http://www.trai.gov.in/writereaddata/recommendation/documents/recom6aug08952012.pdf. Accessed 22 Jan 2015

TRAI (2008b) Consultation paper on mobile virtual network operator (MVNO). Available at: http://trai.gov.in/WriteReaddata/ConsultationPaper/Document/cpaper5may08.pdf.

TRAI (2008c) Stakeholders comments on consultation paper on mobile virtual network operator (MVNO). Available at: http://trai.gov.in/Content/Consultation_ViewCommentDescription/515_1_ViewCommentDescription.aspx.

TRAI (2009) Recommendations on an approach to rural telephony â€ suggested measures for an accelerated growth. Available at: http://trai.gov.in/WriteReadData/Recommendation/Documents/recom19mar09[1].pdf

Yan X (2004) 3G licensing in Hong Kong: the debate. Telecommun Policy 28(2):213–226

# Chapter 7
# Costing and Pricing Mechanism of Telecom Services

The telecommunication (or telecom) sector is of critical importance to the economy of any country. Telecommunication services are vital for overall economic development. The Indian telecom sector has witnessed phenomenal growth over the past decades and is now the second largest telecom market in the world. Today, the telecom network coverage has been extended to most parts of the country. The competition in telecom sector has resulted in affordable access to communication and information. This has helped to improve the life of the people and led to socially inclusive growth. The sector has significance both as a direct independent economic activity in itself and also as a major means of facilitating and enhancing the activities in almost all other economic and social sectors. The cost of telecommunication services is an input for other economic activities. It therefore holds significance for all consumers, individual or collective (TRAI 2012).

The liberalization of telecom sector through the formation of the Telecom Regulatory Authority of India (TRAI or the Authority) in 1997 indeed revolutionised the industry. Prior to 1997, the Department of Telecommunications (DoT) was the sole operator and playing the dual and conflicting role of the regulator and an operator. The liberalization has led to a transition from a monopolistic to a competitive market and led to tremendous growth and development of the telecom sector. The consumers can now choose and subscribe to tariff plans according to their preference and needs. The deregulation in the sector has ushered

---

Contribution:
Dr. K.V. Damodharan
M.Com, M.A.[ECO], MBA, FICWA, Ph.d
[Former Joint Economic Advisor, TRAI]

© Springer India 2016

M.K. Medudula et al., *Telecom Management in Emerging Economies*,
DOI 10.1007/978-81-322-2749-6_7

in an improvement in performance and efficiency among the service providers. Owing to mobile number portability, a consumer can now retain his mobile number but change the service provider if the services are unsatisfactory. There is notable evidence that the efficiency gains are being passed on to the consumers. The economies of scale accompanied with rapid technological advances have resulted in lower costs, and the price charged to consumers does not exceed the marginal costs of providing the services. Thus, the Indian telecom service providers have been successful in providing services at one of the lowest tariffs in the world. Indian telecom has become an international paradigm in all respects and has set an example for the rest of the world.

The regulation formulated and implemented by TRAI has been the cornerstone in transforming a Government controlled, monopolistic and bureaucratic Indian telecom sector into a forward-looking, competitive, performance-oriented and efficient industry. Economic regulation is generally used to provide prices that reflect efficient costs and promote universal access to basic service (TRAI 2012).

In a regulated market, competition is the best regulator. Where there is effective competition in a mature market, the tariffs would be determined by the market forces and not by the regulator. For a well-organized tariff rule, a suitable pricing and costing mechanism is very important. Pricing refers to the value paid by the end consumer for the services consumed, whereas costing means determination of the worth of the resources consumed in provision of the services.

Although low prices are often the prime factor for a consumer in making his purchase decision, it is important to note that lowering the tariffs alone would not make the sector successful. The regulators need to understand the pricing economics and take into account the cost involved in producing a service. If cost involved in providing a service exceeds the tariff charged to consumers, it will adversely impact the business viability of the service provider and also impact the quality of service. If on the other hand the prices are high, then the demand will get blocked and will not attract the required investment. For policy maker, the telecom pricing is extremely important since the prices effect the economic decision of the investors, service providers and the users, and there is a close link between the underlying cost of providing a service and the tariff of the such service or product; hence, TRAI emphasized a cost-based prices for all telecom services at the same time ensuring a reasonable return to the investors.

Telecommunication is a complex capital-intensive industry. An efficient regulatory framework assists in the development of a telecommunication infrastructure that allows the consumers of telecommunication services, ubiquitous and affordable access to an increasing range of competitively provided basic and advanced products and services. Owing to the long useful lives of the assets, the service providers generally expect a stream of reasonable revenues consistently for a longer period. No business venture is free of risk, and the investors need to be rewarded for the risks assumed by appropriately considering a reasonable return on their investment, while determining the tariffs.

Telecom services being technologically intricate and multifaceted, it is not always easy to establish a clear relationship between the cost of inputs and the value of relevant outputs. Hence, the conventional methodologies may not always be appropriate for determining the price of a telecom service. Therefore, cost studies are essential to make pricing decisions. Once an appropriate costing methodology is determined, it is important to apply it on a consistent basis. This will avoid uncertainty for the service providers, protect the interest of the consumers and promote competition.

There are several widely accepted methodologies for the costing of telecom services in various regulatory regimes. Choosing the appropriate costing methodology is absolutely essential and a challenge too. Various costing and pricing methodologies and principles generally followed by the regulators are explained in the following paragraphs (Kathuria 2004; Sinha 2000; TRAI (n.d.); Kearney 2013; Melody 1997).

## 7.1 Various Costing Principles and Its Applications

Any costing model should be based on sound costing principles. These include principles such as cost causation [like in activity-based costing (ABC)], objectivity, consistency, transparency, auditability, practicality and efficiency. Sufficiently detailed cost data is necessary to arrive at the cost of services. In a liberalized market, service cost models can be a vital source of information both to operators (particularly new entrants/interconnection seekers) and regulators for the following purposes:

- Interconnection and access pricing;
- Understanding the net cost of universal service obligations;
- Assessments of potential anti-competitive behaviour;
- Retail tariff control and rebalancing;
- Can provide "build or buy" signals to new entrants;
- Help in taking decision whether to lease or construct an asset.

Tariff per unit in network or transportation infrastructure business is generally calculated based on a predetermined return on regulatory asset basis (RAB) explained in the following diagram. This method is called regulatory building block approach. Cost of capital is one of the important elements of regulatory building block approach. There are two methods to assess the cost of capital. One is return on capital employed (RoCE) and the other is called return on equity (RoE) method, which are further explained below with the help of flow charts (Fig. 7.1).

The regulated building block shows the flow for determining the tariff per unit. The unit can be a minute, a subscriber or an mb/s of data. The most decisive factor is the regulatory asset base (RAB). Under the regulatory asset base approach, an asset base is defined and valued for applying the return. As time progresses, capital expenditure (capex) is added to the RAB. The RAB drives two of the fundamental building blocks that make up the operator's revenue requirement: one is the cost of

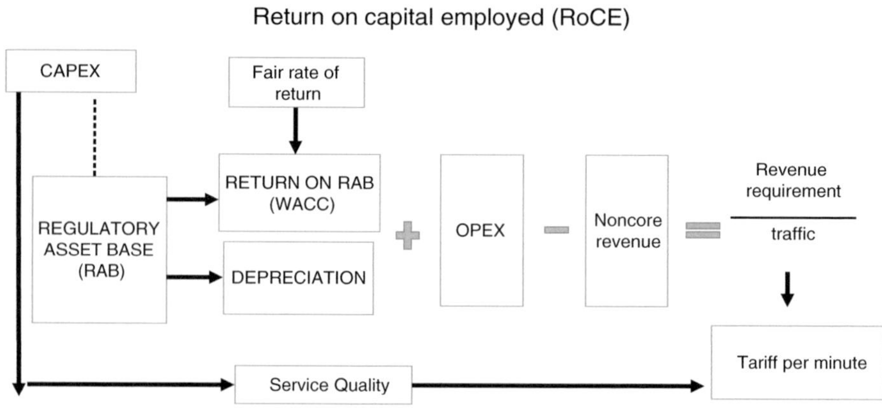


**Fig. 7.1** Regulatory building block approach. *Data Source* TRAI (2008), Sinha (2000)

capital (the return on RAB) and the other one is depreciation allowance (return of RAB). These two building blocks are then added to the projected level of operating expenditure (opex) to calculate the total revenue requirement for the business. This will be adjusted with any extra revenue accrued on account of value-added services (VASs) which are non-core revenue. (*Source: In the Matter of Normative Approach to Building Blocks in Economic regulation of Major Airports, AERA 2014.*)

In this approach, a rolling forward approach to RAB is adopted using the following formula.

$$\text{RAB year}\, t = \text{RAB year}\ t - 1 + \text{capital expenditure} - \text{depreciation}$$

This process is continued on an annual basis throughout and across regulatory periods. Some regulators apply an adjustment for inflation and make a compensating adjustment to the cost of capital. This is not an essential part of the process applied in India.

RAB generally does not include accounting adjustments such as prior year's gains or losses, or revaluation. Further, it does not necessarily correspond to the balance sheet as shown in the statutory accounts. RAB used in regulatory building block approach for tariff determination will reflect the amount of the capex base which has not been returned to investors.

An important characteristic of this methodology is that there is no possibility of equity owners getting their capital paid back more than once and providing a return once the investment has fully depreciated and has no value. Capital is returned through depreciation of the RAB and once removed from the RAB is not added back. It should also be noted that the model does not include the "liability" side of the balance sheet. Some regulatory jurisdictions follow a slightly different process which is called RoE method.

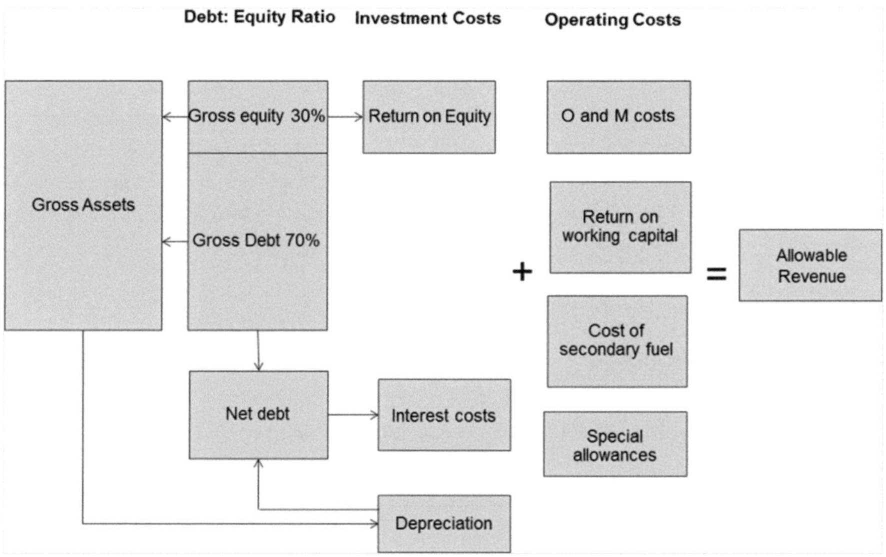


**Fig. 7.2** RoE Method. *Source* AERA website www.aera.gov.in, submission made by APAO on the consultation paper on normative approach

This is followed by the electricity regulator in India. It is explained in the following diagram (Fig. 7.2).

CERC applies a RoE process with a pass-through of interest costs though it regards return on assets as in some ways theoretically better. Most of the regulators applies a return on capital employed using a weighted average cost of capital (WACC). But CERC takes the cost of the return on gross equity plus passed through interest costs plus depreciation plus opex plus adjustments for tariff fixation. There is no direct role for a regulatory asset base. Others on the other hand apply return on net RAB and no pass-through of interest cost on debt.

In both the methods, the revenue entitlement for the service provider is the sum of cost of Capital + Depreciation + Opex + Tax. This will be divided by the number of expected unit of production (e.g. minutes of usage) and will give the unit price or price per minute. The unit price will decrease year after year as the RAB upon which the return is calculated is reduced by depreciation and also due to increase in volume of production.

Now let us examine what are the different cost concepts which are applied in tariff fixing. The regulator has to decide on the relevant definition of costs to be considered in cost models. The term "cost" is often used in different contexts with different meanings. When economists talk about costs, they are always concerned with economic cost. The economic cost of a decision depends on both the cost of the alternative chosen and the benefit that the best alternative would have provided if chosen. Economic cost differs from accounting cost because it includes opportunity cost. Accountants are concerned primarily with the proper recording and measuring of historical costs based upon a uniform set of rules. Engineering approaches for analysing cost behaviour are based on the use of engineering analysis of technological relationships between inputs and outputs. Economic costs are more relevant for developing advanced costing approaches for telecommunication services. Some of the generally applied costing principles are explained below.

### 7.1.1 Fully Allocated Cost (FAC) Approach

In the initial years after liberalization of the telecom sector, the costing of telecom services was mainly done using the FAC approach. Under this approach, the total cost that the firm incurs is allocated among the services that it provides. The cost of each service is derived using algorithms that allocate both direct and indirect costs to the service. The main advantage of this approach is its simplicity as it uses information in the accounting system, thus making this model easily auditable. The major drawbacks of the approach are that it fails to shadow market prices resulting in higher prices which may retard new entry of new players in the market. Also, the bases of some of the indirect allocations could be considered arbitrary and may cause cost distortion (AERA 2010).

### 7.1.2 Activity-Based Costing (ABC) Approach

ABC is the methodology by which costs are assigned based on the activities required to deliver a service based on the resources consumed by those activities.

ABC helps in making a more accurate determination of the time, cost and value related to specific activities. It also enables us to evaluate their individual contribution in meeting the overall objective. Therefore, several organizations are beginning to use this approach to formulate their cost estimates, instead of using the traditional elements of cost. The main advantage of this approach is that it is capable of influencing the design or structure of a product or service since it is able to break down the cost based on the activities involved. It is capable of highlighting how a relatively small increase in system performance can have a disproportionately heavy impact on final cost. It therefore can contribute to cost reduction by identifying cost drivers involved and substitute suitable alternatives wherever possible.

In the case of telecom services, the major cost drivers are the number of subscribers, volume of traffic, minutes of usage, number of messages, and data sent/received as well as the geographic area covered by the network. For many of the elements, there is more than one cost driver. Apart from the costs directly allocable to the activities, there are several common costs incurred by the network operator, viz. salaries of personnel, depreciation of network elements, cost of capital, depreciation of buildings and vehicles, marketing cost, power, raw bandwidth rentals and overheads. These common costs are apportioned to the cost elements of the services that the network provides (TRAI 2008).

### 7.1.3 Marginal Costing

Marginal cost is the amount at any given volume of output by which the aggregate variable costs are changed if the volume of output is increased or decreased by one unit. In practice, this is measured by the total variable cost attributable to one unit. Marginal cost is the sum of the prime cost [Direct Material + Direct Labour + Direct Expenses] and variable overhead.

Marginal costing is the computation of the incremental cost and ascertainment of the effect on profit on account of changes in volume of output by differentiating between fixed costs and variable costs.

The application of the marginal costing approach to the telecom sector poses several practical difficulties. For example, the network used for local, STD and ISD calls and many VASs is the same, and therefore, arriving at the marginal cost of these services is difficult. Most estimates of marginal cost are based on incremental cost. In case of the telecom sector, the minimal measurable change can be extremely small, viz. 1 mW of electricity, one second of calling duration or one local loop. It is difficult to estimate marginal costs on a microlevel in such cases. Accordingly, most practical estimates of marginal cost are based at least in part on a slightly larger increment of output than what is envisioned in economic theory.

As such, pricing services at marginal costs signal the efficiency of the operator to the consumers. This is because "incremental service and incremental cost" are the more appropriate measures of cost because they provide a close approximation to marginal cost if it is properly estimated (TRAI 2008, n.d.).

### 7.1.4 Ramsey Rule

When the operator has market power, the prices charged by it will exceed its marginal costs resulting in a profit. Since this causes a loss in welfare, the regulator has an interest in lowering prices to the level of marginal cost. However, marginal cost pricing may not be financially feasible for the operator because of economies of scale, or joint and common costs. In such cases, the pricing should be such that the quantities that consumers want to purchase deviate as little as possible from what customers would purchase with marginal cost pricing. This method of pricing is called Ramsey Pricing or the inverse elasticity rule. It raises prices above marginal cost in accordance with the price elasticity of demand. Markups above marginal cost are lower for services with more elastic demand, and conversely, markups are higher for services with more inelastic demand. The markup which is inverse to the elasticity of demand implies that such service or products could be loaded with higher markup and eventually higher price. The customer in such cases will be willing to pay more as they highly need the service. In the other situations where the elasticity of demand is very high where even a slight increase in prices will reduce the demand, the loading of markup will be less. An example in point is the incoming call versus outgoing calls. Markup to outgoing call has to be done very cautiously as a small increase will reverse the demand.

Telecommunication networks cost has a significant element of fixed common cost. In a competitive market, these common costs will be absorbed by product and services where consumers have a greater willingness to pay a markup over incremental cost. This also helps in maximizing the network usage (TRAI 2008, n.d.; AERA 2010).

### 7.1.5 Current Cost Accounting (CCA)

CCA means appraising the cost of assets by revaluing them at estimates of their present market price after allowing the necessary adjustments for wear and tear. CCA adopts the indexation approach or the absolute valuation. Under the indexation approach, appropriate indices are applied to asset book values to arrive at the current cost. Under the absolute valuation approach, the existing quantity of the asset is multiplied by its current acquisition price to arrive at the current cost.

To ensure a “level playing field”, the regulator should ensure that the cost base of an existing as well as a new operator and the regulated prices should be set according to CCA. Further, the asset considered for RAB and eligible for return should also reflect the current market price or the most efficient replacement cost which will vastly differ from the booked figure in the Book of Accounts (TRAI Consultation Paper on review of interconnection usage charges (IUC), Dec. 2008, various regulations and Tariff orders of TRAI).

### 7.1.6 Long-Run Incremental Cost (LRIC)

One of the most important reasons for the implementation of price regulation based on the use of LRIC models is related to the need to send the appropriate signals to the market and to become efficient, foster entry of efficient operator, adequate investments and innovation.

The LRIC can be defined in two ways (on starting a service or on stopping a service) that are complementary. On the one hand, it is the additional cost that a firm incurs over the long term in providing a particular service on the assumption that all of the other production activities remain unchanged. On the other hand, it is the total cost that the firm would avoid over the long term if it were to cease providing that particular service ("avoidable cost").

Forward-looking costs are generally preferred because they better reflect market conditions, but there may be some difficulties in determining them in which case one may have to use information from network operators on historical costs and adjust them for known inflation or price escalation. Determining or verifying the costs for telecommunications services is among the major challenges before the regulators. Regulators use cost analysis in setting or approving prices, including "retail" prices for consumers and "wholesale" prices for competitors. The main argument for an LRIC-based approach is that it provides a better measure of costs for price setting purposes. This is because it indicates the true level of costs associated with increasing or decreasing output because it is based on current cost. Regulators generally allow a markup on the LRIC for the firm to help it to recover all of its costs (TRAI 2008, n.d.; Sinha 2000).

### 7.1.7 Top-Down Methodology

Under a top-down modelling approach, actual (historical) accounting data (e.g. capital employed, traffic volumes and operating costs) of a specific firm is taken as a starting point parameters of the model. Such approach relies on actual network architectures and configurations in assuming their efficiency. After certain efficiency adjustments and a proper asset valuation, the historical cost–volume relationships of costs are projected forward to develop forward-looking incremental costs. The goal is then to take these aggregate costs and allocate them among all services provided by the firm. The advantage is that this method assures that all of the carrier's costs are accounted for. On the other hand, determining a suitable allocation formula poses problem. It can be used as a comparative check against a comprehensive bottom-up incremental cost analysis. Usually, owing to a lack of detailed data, the total cost of the company available is used to conduct a top-down analysis (TRAI Consultation Paper on review of interconnection usage charges (IUC), Dec. 2008, various regulations and tariff orders of TRAI).

### 7.1.8 Bottom-Up Methodology

A bottom-up approach model considers the network and cost structures of a hypothetical efficient operator who employs modern technology and operating methods and is not constrained by technology, systems and architectural decisions of the past. A bottom-up model identifies all components of the network necessary to produce the services in question. Based on engineering and economic experience and evidence, cost causation relationships are then defined to link the relevant quantities of network components with outputs and other relevant cost drivers. This method is expected to give good estimates of unit costs, assuming that complete disaggregated data on input costs arising from resources consumed in the provision of different services is available (TRAI 2008, n.d.). It will be ensured that there is no inefficiency inbuilt into the entire system and procedures.

## 7.2 Various Components of Cost

There are various components of cost elements which are considered for tariff fixation. They are mainly cost of capital (RoCE), depreciation, Opex, tax, licence fee and adjustment if any on account of recovery of non-core revenue such as VAS. Let us now examine these cost components.

### *7.2.1 Cost of Capital*

The most important and contentious element is cost of capital. It is known in different names such as WACC, RoCE, reasonable return or simply cost of capital. It is contentious because the regulators and operators mostly disagree with the rate of return.

Regulatory risk attached to determination of cost of capital is an important component of the total risk faced by the regulated firms, and both reward and risks should be taken into account by the regulators when they regulate the industry either by price caps, revenue caps or some other pricing regime. The determination of the cost of capital is an important part of any regulatory decision. Like any industry, the telecommunication firms are generally financed through a mixture of debt and equity. Since the cost of debt and equity capital is different, the overall measure of the cost of capital of a firm is the WACC. The WACC (%) is applied on the asset base of the service provider to calculate the eligible return which the operator is entitled to recover from the market by offering his services. Regulatory regimes that set the WACC too low may see a reduction or a delay of investment in infrastructure and the deployment of digital technologies. Both investors and telecommunications firms are seriously concerned by the approach adopted by regulators and the model they use to make an asset valuation that necessarily impacts the investment. The capital asset pricing model (CAPM) is the most widely used and the accepted technique for estimating the cost of equity. The returns are calculated using the discounted cash flow (DCF) methodology.

Since WACC calculations provide a range of estimates, the calculation of the cost of capital is often an area of contention between the firm and the regulator. The variation in estimates can have a significant impact on total costs.

The cost of capital is determined with reference to a number gearing of parameters such as risk-free rate, country risk premium, corporate risk premium, equity/asset beta, market risk premium and tax rate.

The following concepts are discussed further below:

- Weighted average cost of capital (WACC);
- Cost of equity;
- Cost of debt;
- Gearing.

(a) **Weighted Average Cost of Capital (WACC)**

The cost of capital represents the level of return expected by the investors on the investment made by them which makes that investment viable. The generally available sources of finance are debt and equity. The cost of debt is the rate at which the firm pays interest to its lenders of debt. The returns to equity investors are in the form of dividends and capital growth of the value of shares. The combination of cost of equity and cost of debt is commonly referred to as WACC. The formula is

$$\text{WACC} = g * \text{Rd} + (1-g) * \text{Re}$$

where $g$ is the gearing (debt/debt + equity), Rd is the cost of debt, and Re is the cost of equity.

In order to address the investors' expectations that the return would be net of tax, the following methods are adopted:

1. Post-tax forms of WACC assume that the company taxes are treated as a cost separate from the cost of capital.
2. Pretax forms of WACC account for the cost of taxation directly in the WACC estimate, and hence, company tax liabilities are included in the return on capital.

Further, the investors generally expect that the compensation mechanism provided by the regulator compensates for inflation by indexing the regulated asset base on which returns are allowed at a cost of capital which incorporates the inflationary trend. There are range of approaches used by the regulators domestically and internationally on the treatment of taxation and inflation. The generally accepted procedure is to calculate the tariff using a nominal post-tax cost of capital.

(b) **Cost of Equity**

The most commonly used approach to calculate the cost of equity is the CAPM. The basic premise of CAPM is that the investors expect their investment to yield at least a return equal to risk-free assets + a premium for the risk involved in the equity investment. This premium is equal to equity market risk premium. It is generally calculated by the return on riskier equities multiplied by equity beta for a particular investment, which measures the risk of a particular investment in relation to the average equity investment. Where the equity beta = 1, the investors will expect returns in line with the market. When the equity beta >1, it indicates that there are greater systematic risks associated with investment; therefore, there are greater expectations of returns by the equity investors.

The CAPM formula is defined as follows:

$$\mathrm{Re} = \mathrm{Rf} + \beta\mathrm{e} * \mathrm{EMRP}$$

where Re is the cost of equity, Rf is the risk-free rate, βe is the equity beta, and EMRP is equity market risk premium which is equal to Rm − Rf. Rm is the equity market return.

CAPM is the most appropriate approach for determining the cost of equity. However, the CAPM approach will potentially result in a wide range of results depending on the assumptions made in respect of the different components of CAPM.

While CAPM is the most common methodology for assessing the cost of capital, the following alternatives are also available for the pricing of infrastructure services:

(i) **Dividend Growth Model (DGM)**

This model assumes that the current quoted share price of a business is equal to the present value of all its future expected dividend payments. Given the current market share price and future dividend growth rate expectations, the cost of equity implicit in a share price can be determined by the following formula

$$\mathrm{Re} = (D_0 * 1 + g/P_0) + g$$

where Re is the post-tax cost of equity, $D_0$ is the current dividend, $g$ is the dividend growth rate, and $P_0$ is the current share price. Even though this method is not generally popular in price fixing, it has been used as a comparative check on the cost of equity derived from the CAPM.

(ii) **Arbitrage Pricing Model (APM)**

APM is a multifactor model which is based on the assumption that the return on the stock depends on pervasive macroeconomic influences or factors. Compared to other pricing models, the APM is simple and easy to calculate. However, it is rarely used in practice due to problems with data availability and specification of an appropriate model (AERA Consultation Paper on Regulatory Philosophy in Airports, Feb. 2010).

(c) **Cost of Debt**

The cost of debt is commonly expressed as the debt premium over the risk-free rate of return. The formula for calculating cost of debt is as follows:

$$\mathrm{Rd} = \mathrm{Rf} + \mathrm{DP}$$

where Rd is the pre-tax cost of debt, Rf is the risk-free rate, and DP is the corporate debt premium. The corporate debt premium represents the risk of default premium by investors in providing debt to a particular company. The higher the risk of default, the higher the corporate debt margin.

The regulators normally examine the cost of debt to ascertain whether it represents the most cost efficient option among the array of options available.

(d) **Gearing**

Gearing means the proportion of debt in the capital structure of a company and is normally calculated as a total value of debt as a proportion of the sum of the total value of debt and equity. The gearing has a wider impact on the overall cost of capital. A high level of gearing is likely to increase the risk to both equity and debt holders as the firm will require a high rate of return. Generally, the regulator takes an optimal approach to arrive at an efficient gearing (TRAI 2004, 2008; KPMG 2014).

### 7.2.2 *Depreciation*

The issue of depreciation is closely linked to the regulatory asset base and represents the "return of capital". The key determinants of depreciation are the life of the asset assumed and the method of depreciation followed. There are various methods of calculating depreciation. However, generally used method is straight line method. Depreciation is also governed by the Companies Act notified by the Ministry of Corporate Affairs in India.

### 7.2.3 *Operating Expenditure*

Operating expenditure is another important component of the regulatory building blocks and depends upon the operating efficiency and performance of a service provider. The regulatory treatment for operating expenditure in the tariff determination can have implications on incentives for the service provider with respect to achievement of efficiencies in operating costs. There are few approaches adopted by the regulators in considering the efficient Opex for tariff fixation. Some regulators consider a fixed percentage and some other consider as actual.

### 7.2.4 *Tax*

Tax is a mandatory expenditure and has to be factored in the pricing. Generally, the actual expenditure on tax is considered.

### *7.2.5 Non-core Revenue Adjustment*

A modern telecom network is engaged in a complex mix of services and some of which are complementary or by-products such as value-added service mostly without any extra expenditure or very less expenditure. Generally, an adjustment of such revenue is applied in determining the tariff of a particular product.

## 7.3 Pricing Approaches in the Telecom Sector

Having examined various cost components which are considered for fixing tariff for telecom services, let us now examine how the tariff fixation in done.

Tariff/price is a key strategic driver for telecom operators which directly impacts its ability to attract and retain consumers and also meeting its revenue and margin targets. As the market becomes competitive, the need for regulation decreases as market forces ensure that wide choices of services are available to the consumers at reasonable prices.

The following pricing approaches are discussed below:

- Cost plus pricing;
- Subsidized pricing;
- Demand-based pricing;
- Price floor and ceiling.

### *7.3.1 Cost Plus Pricing*

Under this approach, the cost of the service is calculated and then a markup (that accounts for profit margin) is added to the cost to arrive at the price to be charged to the consumers. Such price may be based on short-run marginal (or variable) costs, long-run incremental costs (which include investment costs) or FACs. All cost-based pricing requires considerable information and monitoring.

The advantages of this approach are that it is easy in application as it is based on actual cost information available from the accounting records. It is therefore easily auditable too. However, the major disadvantage is that it is difficult to rationally apportion the common cost (which forms a large part of the total cost in some cases) among the different services.

### 7.3.2 *Subsidy-Based Pricing*

Subsidies to price are normally given by the Government for achieving social objectives such as promoting the provision of telecom services or making telecom services accessible to the population living in the remote areas. Such subsidy could be given in terms of the access charges, rentals or price of the calls made. In the Indian context, subsidy was provided in respect of the access deficit charge (ADC). However, with the onset of liberalization and economic globalization, subsidy-based pricing is almost vanished in telecom sector.

### 7.3.3 *Demand-Based Pricing*

This approach considers the combined effect of the change in price and the corresponding change in demand volume and the consequent change of revenues. If the demand is price inelastic, the change in volume is smaller than the change in price, and therefore, revenues decrease with the reduction in price. If the demand is elastic, the change in volume is larger than the change in price, and therefore, revenues increase with the reduction in price. This is in otherwise discretionary price setting prevalent in India before TRAI comes into existence wherein the DoT decides the level of tariff for a telecom service and implement after the approval of parliament. There is no cost basis or other financial considerations, but only the affordability of consumers and revenue requirement for the Government are considered.

### 7.3.4 *Price Floor and Ceiling*

There could be an abuse of monopoly or market power by an operator. This could be by charging a high price (which includes a high profit margin) or a low price (at times even below cost) to limit competition from other players in the market. In order to deal with high prices, a price ceiling is prescribed, whereas a price floor is set to deal with low prices. Such price floor and ceilings help in creating a competitive environment which provides a level playing field for all players in the market (TRAI 2008, n.d.). This also acts an effective tool to check anti-competitive tendencies in the market.

## 7.4 Tariff Regulation of Telecom Services

According to TRAI, effective regulation results in many benefits, such as greater economic and technological growth, increased investment in the sector, cost reduction with improved efficiency, better quality of service, improved customer satisfaction, affordable prices delivering better value for money and improved access and availability of services (TRAI 2012). Hence, regulating the tariff is extremely important for the development of the sector.

Tariff regulation is discussed below under the following heads:

- Objectives of tariff regulation;
- Principles of tariff regulation;
- Regulatory approaches.

**Objectives of Tariff Regulation:**
Telecommunication tariff affects consumer interests, cost of other economic activities and the profitability of telecommunication enterprises. Hence, the objectives include financing, efficiency and equity objectives which are further explained below.

Tariff or price regulation has three primary objectives, namely

(a) **Financing Objective**:
The objective is to ensure that regulated operators are permitted to earn sufficient revenue to finance ongoing operations and future investments.
(b) **Efficiency Objective**:
The objective is to ensure that efficiency is achieved when prices equal the marginal cost of producing the service and/or when increased levels of output are realized through unchanged levels of input.
(c) **Equity Objective**:
The objective is to ensure the fair distribution of welfare benefits among members of society. Operator–consumer equity and consumer-to-consumer equity are desirable (TRAI 2008, n.d.).

**Principles of Tariff Regulation**:
For the telecom sector, the key principles in setting price/tariffs from a regulatory perspective include the following:

(a) **Cost basis**:
Cost-based tariffs imply that telecommunication services charges have to be aligned to the underlying costs of providing those services. This is to encourage operators to charge affordable prices effectively putting a ceiling on profitability.

(b) **Unbundling**:
The tariffs offered by the operators have to be sufficiently unbundled, so that customers do not pay for facilities, which are not part of their service package. This relates largely to the pricing of access services.

(c) **Transparency**:
Operators must publish details of tariffs and fees and make them easily available to the public.

(d) **Non-discrimination**:
An operator should offer customers the same tariff for identical services and offer discounts wherever it makes commercial sense, and such discount should be clearly disclosed in the published tariff. By this, the service providers cannot offer different tariff for the same service to different consumers of the same class (TRAI 2008, n.d.).

**Regulatory Approaches**:
The following approaches to tariff regulation are discussed below:

- Rate-of-return (ROR) approach;
- Price cap approach;
- Forbearance or light-touch regulation.

### *7.4.1 Rate-of-Return (ROR) Approach*

This is the traditional method of utility regulation where the regulated firm is allowed to charge prices that would cover its operating costs and give it a fair rate of return on the full value of its capital. If costs moved out of line with those prices, the firm would ask the regulator for a new set of prices. When rates are adopted in this manner, there will be an equitable and efficient balance between the interests of the utility and its investors and those of its customers.

One of the demerits of this approach is that there is a lack of incentive to minimize costs. The utility is normally given an opportunity to recover all of its prudently incurred costs, including a fair return on its invested capital. Therefore, as the firm spends more money, it will eventually be allowed to charge higher prices. Furthermore, since the regulated firm is allowed to earn a particular percentage return on its investment, it can increase its earnings simply by increasing its investment. This is virtually the opposite of what would occur in a competitive market, where unnecessary expenses and investment always translates into profit reductions. Thus, this approach does not provide an incentive to minimize costs. The other demerit is that over time, the ROR regulation does not provide the operator with a strong incentive to increase its productivity (TRAI 2008, n.d.; Sinha 2000).

### 7.4.2 Price Cap Approach

This is the most preferred form price regulation around the world. This approach was invented by Professor Stephen Littlechild of UK. In 1983, Professor Littlechild has recommended for adopting RPI-X price cap regulation for pricing the services of British telecom against the rate-of-return regulation (Bartle 2003). The recommendation was accepted by the UK Government and implemented. Since then, it slowly spread internationally as the most efficient price regulation and effective means of protecting consumer interest. This approach provides a flexible price range which imposes an upper limit on the average price increase for a basket of telecom services. It uses a formula to determine the maximum allowable price increase for a regulated operator's services for a specified number of years. The formula is designed to permit an operator to recover its unavoidable cost increase (e.g. inflation and tax increase) through price increases. Since the firm retains the benefits of cost reductions under price cap regulation, this regulatory regime provides a powerful incentive for improving efficiency.

The price cap formula is defined as follows:

$$\mathrm{PI}(t) = \mathrm{CPI}(t-1) + X,$$

where PI ($t$) is the maximum allowable price increase in the relevant year(s) for a given basket of regulated services as determined by the regulator; "$t$" is year; CPI ($t-1$), the consumer price index, is the inflation measure averaged for the previous calendar year ($t-1$). The average CPI in the previous calendar year has sole influence on the future CPI and is therefore a good predictor of future CPI. The "$X$" represents expected productivity gain of the operator over the relevant period.

Each price cap is for a specific period. Before the end of each given period, a review should be carried out by the operator to determine the new $X$ factor to be filed with the regulator for approval. When price caps are reset, attention is inevitably paid to the profits of the regulated firm and cost savings gained between reviews, at least partially, are passed on to the consumers. The price cap formula can further be improved by including quality and investment parameters. The expanded formula is as follows.

$$\mathrm{PI}(t) = \mathrm{CPI}(t-1) + X + K + Q$$

(where "$K$" is capital investment factor and "$Q$" represents the quality requirement factor).

Under the price cap regulatory framework, the service provider will be encouraged to operate the business in a manner that would be similar to a competitive market which constantly seeks to improve efficiency. Eventually, when the market opens up to allow full competition, the operator will be easily able to adapt to full liberalization than if he was required to change from a rate-of-return approach. RPI-X formula proved to be highly effective in attracting investment, and it motivates the industry to move to competition and hence reduction in the intrusive regulation. This model left dramatic changes in the network and infrastructure development not only in telecom but other infrastructures too.

**Evolution of Telecom Tariff Regulation in India and Role Played by TRAI**: The tariff regulation for the telecommunication services in India was initiated with the notification of Telecommunication Tariff Order 1999 (TTO 1999). This order provided the broad and long-term policy framework for telecommunication services in the country. The TTO 1999 specified standard tariff package (STP) which is a cost-based tariff using FAC mostly on historical cost basis consisting, inter alia, of monthly rental and call charges, for basic and cellular services and leased line circuits. Some of the services are kept under forbearance. Different approaches such as tariff ceiling and floor were also prescribed for certain services. The service providers were required to offer STP as mandated by TRAI (TRAI Consultation Paper, No. 01/2012). This has given a good starting point and a future direction for tariff regulation for entire telecom services in India.

Apart from the STP, the service providers were allowed flexibility to offer alternate tariff packages (ATPs). Various structural reviews were done there after and gradually moved to a light-touch regulation. Costing methodologies were also evolved from FAC (historic cost) to FAC (current cost) and then intended to move to FLLRIC (top down) and FLLRIC (bottom up) with necessary information wherever required (TRAI Consultation Paper, No. 01/2012).

The process evolved are by first fixing cost-based tariff for most of the telecom services and gradually taking note of the emerging market scenario, and after satisfying that the market forces could effectively regulate the prices and quality, TRAI started keeping the services under forbearance one after another giving freedom and flexibility to service providers to innovate and offer customer-specific tariff packages. However, while offering such packages they have to adhere to the principles set in by TRAI. Thus, as per the existing tariff regulatory framework, tariffs for all telecommunication services are forborne except for the following: (i) rural fixed-line services, (ii) national roaming services and (iii) leased circuits. Forbearance is also an important regulatory philosophy which is implemented when the competitive forces are effective in a market. The concept of forbearance is further explained in the following paragraphs.

### *7.4.3 Forbearance or Light-Touch Regulation*

The inherently intrusive process of regulation itself creates distortions that can be worse than the effect of monopoly abuse. The light-touch regulatory approaches can deliver better performing sectors than formal price control.

Light-touch regulation in other words "regulatory forbearance" is normally prescribed in matured markets. Under this approach, service providers are given the freedom to fix charges and design tariff plans and the regulator intervenes only if there is a violation of the set procedure or rules.

"Regulatory forbearance" is about enforcing regulation where it is needed and withdrawing from those parts of the market where it is no longer necessary. In simple words, regulatory forbearance means the ability of a regulator to forgo direct action at any point of time on the basis that the desired outcomes are already being achieved. However, even under forbearance, tariff for the service continues to be monitored and appropriate regulatory measures are put in place so that the interests of consumers are protected (TRAI 2012).

TRAI as a regulator closely watches the developments in the market. According to TRAI, since the time it took up the responsibility of regulating tariff for telecommunication services, there was continuous downward trend in the tariff levels and therefore there was no compulsion for the authority to revert back and forgo the principle of forbearance. As and when substantial reversal in the trend of tariff takes place and/or there are evidences of inadequate competition in any segment leading to high prices, the authority would be fully justified to intervene and even to set the prices for various telecommunication services.

In short, due to emergence of competition in Indian telecom sector, TRAI has gradually introduced forbearance in most of the products and services provided by the operators. This gives the required freedom and flexibility to service providers to offer competitive tariff plan suiting to specific needs of the consumers. Since there is effective competition, there is no requirement for TRAI to resort intrusive regulation. The basic policies of TRAI that the tariff should satisfy the principles of non-discriminatory, non-predatory or IUC complaint are to be strictly followed by the service providers. The operators need not take prior permission to offer such tariffs. The mandation of IUC complaint on all tariff proposals will effectively act as a floor and check the predatory pricing and similar unfair competitive tendencies in the market (TRAI 2008, n.d.; Sinha 2000).

## 7.5 Price Setting by TRAI—Few Examples

The following examples of price setting by TRAI are discussed in detail below:

- Landline and wireless call tariff under the forbearance regime;
- Cost-based interconnection usage charges—using FAC and LRIC approaches;
- Tariff fixation for International Private Leased Circuits (IPLCs)—FAC with historical costs—top-down approach;
- Tariff fixation for Domestic Leased Line (DLC)—current cost—bottom-up approach with normative approach.
- TRAI moving towards FLLRIC.

### 7.5.1 Landline and Wireless Call Tariff Under the Forbearance Regime

The New Telecom Policy, 1999 (NTP-99), liberalized the scope of cellular mobile service, fixed-line service and cable service, including the terms and conditions of licenses and the operational aspects. Interconnection had been a key concern among service providers and a cause of several disputes. Recognizing the importance of the issue, NTP-99 brought interconnection within the ambit of policy. It unequivocally asserted that interconnection shall be permitted between service providers in the mobile and basic service segments. It also covered resolution of problems faced by the existing operators, the restructuring of the DoT, spectrum management, universal service obligations and the role of the regulator. Most importantly, free entry into basic telecommunications replaced duopoly.

NTP-99 proved to be a catalyst for growth of the telecom sector. Such growth was characterized by significant penetration of telecommunications in India. One of the key contributors to the growth was the cost-based tariff for interconnection usage charges (IUC) which was constantly driven downwards due to increasing growth. The cyclical path started with volume growth which led to lower tariffs, falling tariffs enhanced affordability, which in turn led to exponential volume growth which further explained in subsequent paras.

In the case of basic services, the TTO 1999 had specified availability of STP a cost-based tariff which inter alia comprises of rental, call charges, free calls, etc., along with all other ATPs on offer by the service providers in the market. However, in the year 2003, TRAI decided that mandating a standard package was no longer necessary for urban basic service subscribers. In view of the overall competition and the implementation of ADC Regime, TRAI decided to forbear with respect to basic services except for rural subscribers where the STP was continued. The service providers were free to offer ATPs in addition to the STP (28th Amendment to TTO dated 5 November 2003) (TRAI 2012). Eventually, market responded with offering innovative tariff plans suiting to the specific needs of consumers.

Table 7.1 shows the comparative national long distance call tariffs prevalent in the years 1999 and 2006.

The above development shows that telecom penetration and competition can remove all artificial restrictions, and the limits imposed by time, distance and space

**Table 7.1** National long distance charges per minute

| Fall in tariff since 1999 death of distance | | |
|---|---|---|
| Distance | 1999–2000 | NLD tariff March 06 |
| Up to 50 km | 1.20 | 1.00 |
| Above 50 km and up to 200 km | 6.00 | 1.00 |
| Above 200 km and up to 500 km | 15.60 | 1.00 |
| Above 500 km and up to 1000 km | 21.60 | 1.00 |
| Above 1000 km | 30.00 | 1.00 |

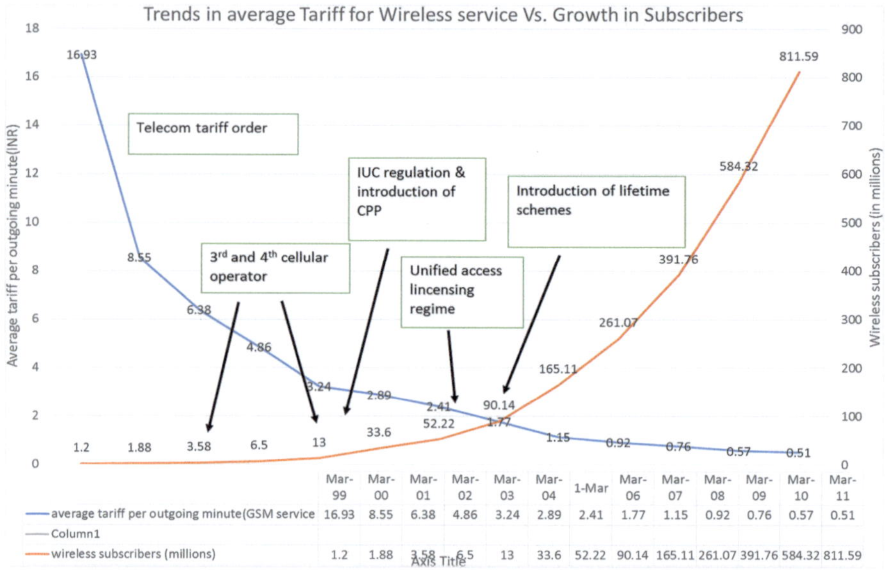


**Fig. 7.3** Trends in average tariff for wireless services versus growth in subscribers

are increasingly turning into memories of the past. "India One" tariff plan offers one rate across India irrespective of distance and time of the day (TRAI 2008, 2015).

Figure 7.3 shows the trends in average tariffs for wireless services vis-à-vis the growth in subscribers. It shows how fall in tariffs during the period March 1999 through March 2011 led to significant increase in the growth in subscribers.

The price reduction of telecom service contributed teledensity. Both have inversely proportionate relationship (TRAI 2008, n.d.).

There was also a significant decrease in the composite national roaming charges charged per minute.

Figure 7.4 shows the trend of composite national roaming charges for the period 2002 through 2009.

As per TRAI, the tariff should be IUC compliant meaning that the tariff should factor the interconnection usage charges of origination, carriage and termination costs. This led to a significant reduction primarily in the national long distance tariff. This is mainly on account of cost-based interconnection charges where the maximum cost for carriage is fixed at Rs. 0.65 which is far less even a rupee. The tariff for maximum distance slab also has aligned with this cost.

Figure 7.5 Average outgo per min is another indicator reflects the cost to a subscriber for using the telecom service. There is a sharp decline in cost.

This visible decline in tariff is directly attributable to effective regulation and pricing followed by TRAI.

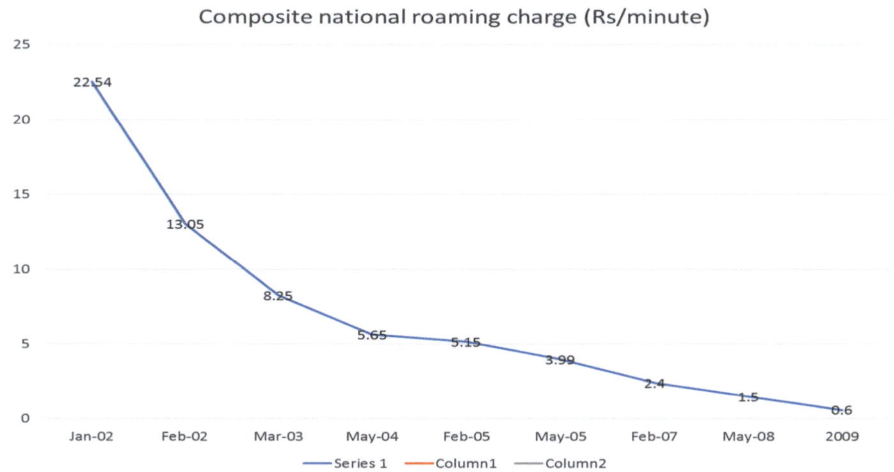


**Fig. 7.4** Composite national roaming charge (Rs/min). *Source* TRAI (n.d.)

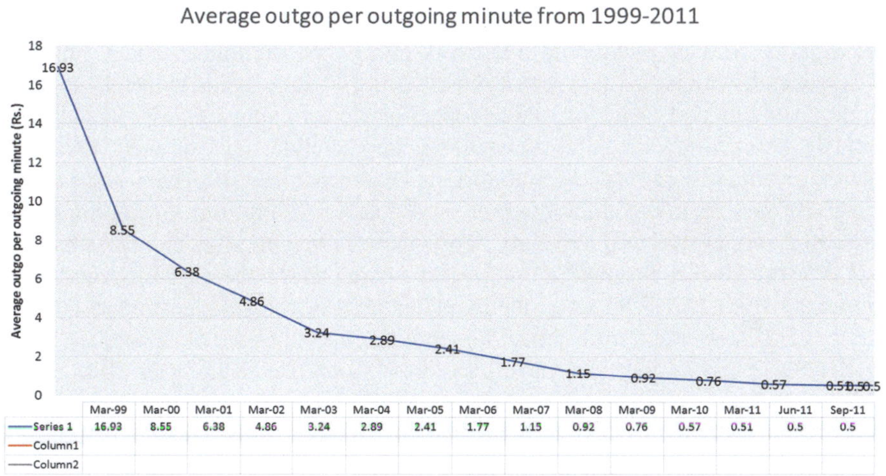


**Fig. 7.5** Average outgo per minute. *Source* TRAI (n.d.)

### *7.5.2 Costing of Interconnection Usage Charges—Using FAC and LRIC Approaches*

According to an International Telecommunication Union (ITU) survey, interconnection issues are the single most important problem in the development of a competitive marketplace for telecommunication services. TRAI has noted that the purpose of an interconnection usage charges (IUCs) regime is to ensure, on reasonable terms and conditions, that all service providers are able to gain access to the interconnection facilities and services necessary to provide efficient service to their customers. This allows dependent activities to flourish, creating a more robust market environment that is able to offer consumers more choice and value for money.

In India, cost-based interconnection usage charge regime for origination, transit and termination was first specified by TRAI in 2003 through the IUC regulation and followed by many amendments. Till such time, the interconnection usage charges are mostly decided by mutual agreements or bill and keep method. In such cases, the regulator will examine whether there is any discrimination or anti-competitive conduct rather than getting into the actual charges. The method of determining IUC in all regulations involved an assessment of the various cost items attributable to different network services.

Interconnection usage charges are part of the cost of carrying a call from a calling to the called party, and in this way, they are linked to determination of tariff. The right level of tariff is very important for sustainability of a telecom service provider. The authority had examined the appropriateness of implementing a hybrid forward-looking long-run incremental cost (FLLRIC) model for IUC while issuing the IUC consultation paper during December 2008. The authority noted that hybrid FLLRIC model is based on a hypothetical efficient operator and a number of assumptions, viz. the likely cost of network going forward, traffic pattern, presence of service providers in a given service area, coverage areas, towers, capacity requirement, market share of critical operators, conversion of SMS and data to minutes, estimation of capital expenditure, depreciation, cost of debt, beta estimation, effective corporate tax and various design parameters. There were apprehensions that any methodology that was based mainly on assumptions and projections could lead to uncertainty and would not be able to assure sustainability and growth. Hence, the authority decided not to adopt the FLLRIC model for setting the IUC. The tariff set by the regulator indicates that the costing of telecom services is based on a hybrid model which takes into consideration both FAC and LRIC after incorporating various adjustments in order to make it an efficient and forward looking. The internetwork termination charges in India are lower than many countries in the world which became possible due to the implementation of a cost-based IUC regime (TRAI 2008, n.d.).

### *7.5.3 Tariff Fixation for International Private Leased Circuits (IPLC)—FAC with Historical Costs—Top-Down Approach*

International Private Leased Circuit (IPLC) that offers global connectivity through submarine cable is a critical infrastructure for provision of broadband and Internet services, international long distance voice telephony and a number of key industries such as information technology (IT) and information technology enabled services

(ITESs). Software exporters, banks and other financial services companies use IPLCs. IPLC is also considered to be one of the basic requirements for IT and ITES industries such as business process outsourcing (BPO) and knowledge process outsourcing (KPO). India has emerged as one of the leading providers of ITES in the world and is fast acquiring a formidable reputation in this sector. In addition, Internet service providers (ISPs) use IPLC for their upstream connectivity abroad.

Based on a review of the market conditions, prices and the regulations, the TRAI felt that there was an immediate need to mandate ceiling tariff for IPLC based on the cost. This was necessary to promote a level playing field in the industry. Accordingly, TRAI through the 34th Amendment order dated 11 March 2005 notified the ceiling tariff for IPLC (half circuit). The ceiling tariff per annum was fixed for three different capacities, namely E-1: Rs. 13 lakhs; DS-3: Rs. 104 lakhs; and STM-1: Rs 299 laks. This ceiling tariff was applicable for all cable systems and all distances.

The authority adopted a top-down FAC (with historical cost) approach to arrive at the relevant cost estimate by using the cost data of the operator. TRAI mentioned that although the FLLRIC was used by most regulators, it felt that such an approach would give a major shock to the market and was also likely to make transition to competition difficult. Hence, it has decided to adopt the FAC approach based on historical cost in order to provide a buffer on the ceiling tariff.

The cost-based tariff has been determined by the authority on the basis of the investment cost after adjustments for depreciation and such other expenditure which are not relevant for setting up of IPLC. On such cost, a return on capital (ROC) of 14.42 % was applied based on a debt/equity ratio of the operator. The WACC of 14.42 % was higher than the WACC allowed in similar exercises previously done by TRAI.

Figure 7.6 shows that the E-1 price of Rs. 176 lakhs in 1998 has become 11.7 lakhs in 2006. Introducing competition and fixing a cost-based tariff facilitated this remarkable reduction in prices.

### *7.5.4 Tariff Fixation for Domestic Leased Line (DLC)—Current Cost—Bottom-Up Approach*

Leased circuits are considered to be a fast-growing segment in the telecom industry and are used by telecom service providers as well as other business organizations as input in their process. These cost-based tariffs were in the nature of price caps, and the service providers were free to offer discounts in a non-discriminatory manner.

According to TRAI, the leasing of circuits obviates the need for building the circuit, which requires heavy investment. Leasing of circuits ensures a dedicated channel/line for data and voice transfer across the connected point of presence and tends to even out expenses for the lessee. On the other hand, leased circuits involve upfront heavy capital investment and maintenance thereafter for the operators who

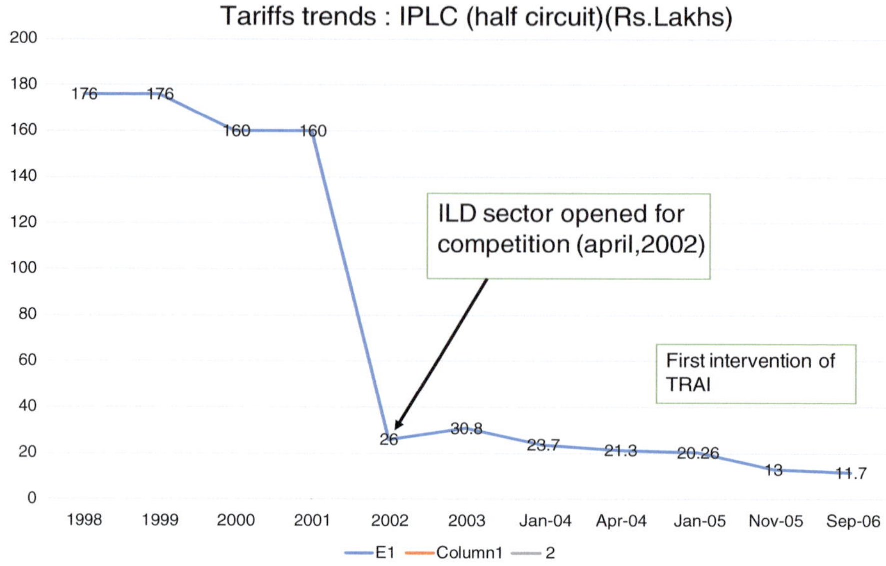


**Fig. 7.6** IPLC tariff trends. *Source* TRAI tariff order dated 8 September 2005 and various publications on IPLC, telegeography's bandwidth pricing report (2004) by Primetrica.Inc

build them. For the provider of these circuits, leasing allows additional income from their investments and is thus similar to any business with high initial capital costs. Hence, leasing offers potential advantages to the seeker and the provider and is a preferred alternative for many enterprises including telecom service providers.

TRAI observed that although the number of players increased, the competition was restricted to the areas where the new entrants built their networks. Even in areas where there were multiple service providers, tariff analysis revealed that new entrants simply followed the pricing of the incumbent operator.

In the tariff order issued in 2005, TRAI used a normative approach to derive the annual rental value for the DLC services. This approach enabled determination of cost-based tariffs for various capacities of DLCs and is a "bottom-up" approach. It used costs of disaggregated network elements submitted by operators to derive annual rental value.

The key characteristics of TRAI's normative pricing model are as follows:

(i) **Cost bases**

The cost bases were developed using an optical fibre cable (OFC) system. This being a widely used system provided a rational justification for deriving the ceiling tariff. For this purpose, TRAI collected the cost details from various operators. TRAI's bottom-up cost calculations of DLCs were based on the cost data provided by operators. However, examination of this data revealed significant variation across operators. Such variation occurred because the operators were at various stages of maturity and market penetration, and thus, their network and operations had reached different levels in their product cycle.

TRAI's goal was to use cost estimates to fix tariffs that provided continued incentive to new entrants for achieving greater efficiency and cost reduction, while ensuring the feasibility of deploying such a system in the market. It was necessary to ensure that the dominant operator did not have the opportunity to skew the market in his favour.

According to the TRAI methodology, for all categories of cost, namely fixed, semi-variable and variable, the second lowest value for each category was used. The operation and maintenance (O&M) cost was considered at 10 % of capital expenditure on equipment, cable and all other capital outlays. TRAI adopted annual depreciation rates of 5.28 and 11.88 % for capital expenditure in respect of cable and equipment, respectively. As regards the return on capital employed, a WACC of 13.93 % was adopted based on the data submitted by the operators. This WACC had also been used by TRAI earlier in the Telecommunication Interconnection Usage Charges Regulations.

(ii) **Capacity utilization and redundancy**

Capacity utilization is an important parameter affecting the prices since the capital expenditure as well as the operational expenditure is spread over the current volume of sale. Similarly, while using a normative network model, it is essential to account for redundancy in services for pricing the bandwidth between any two points as normally, operators provide alternate routes for point-to-point connectivity that tend to increase the expenditure. This is required to ensure the level of quality and uninterrupted service. TRAI adjusted these figures to reflect the market environment and factored cost for improving quality of services in tariff so that the service provider cannot offer an inferior quality product at a price determined by TRAI.

Figure 7.7 shows that by resorting to price fixing based on cost, the price of an E-1 capacity for a distance of more than 500 km is reduced by more than 95 %. The most important aspect is that the market has responded quickly with a lower price than the ceiling fixed by TRAI. This is also true in the case of all other capacities.

According to TRAI, the market for DLCs in the country has undergone several changes since the year 2005 when the tariffs for P2P-DLCs were last prescribed. Notably, demand and supply of DLCs have increased remarkably, and at the same time, the transmission technologies have become much more efficient, cost effective and versatile. Consequently, per unit cost of providing DLCs has reduced significantly particularly on the major routes. As a result, the TSPs are able to offer price discounts with respect to the ceiling tariffs prescribed by TRAI on many routes including the routes connecting metros and major commercial cities in the country. However, the benefit of reduction in underlying cost is not being passed on to the customers for those routes and geographic regions in the country where competitive

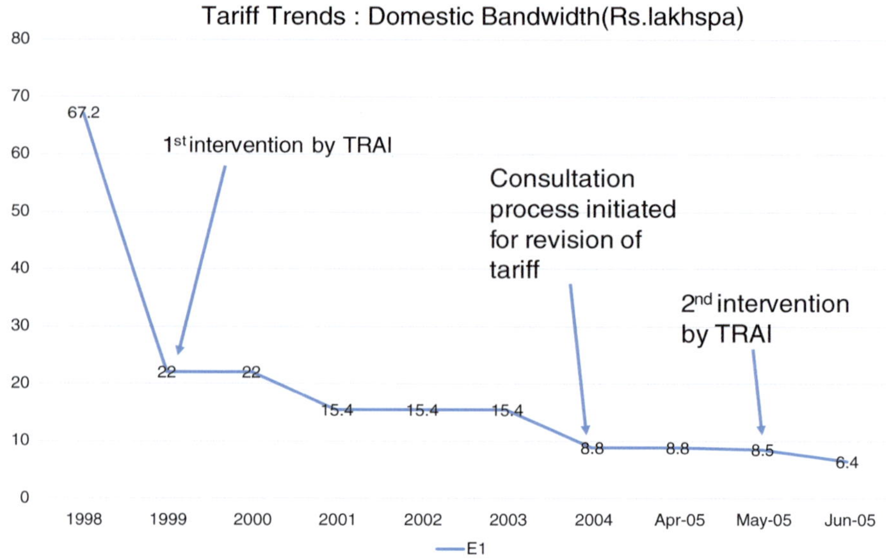


**Fig. 7.7** Trends of domestic bandwidth 1998–2005 (E-1). TRAI tariff order of domestic leased line April 2005 and various tariff orders of TRAI and various articles and price regulation of telecommunication service by Sidharth Sinha

activity is subdued. As a result, customers seeking DLCs to connect to such areas are forced to pay higher tariff (though within the ceiling tariffs prescribed by the authority) than those prevalent (TRAI 2014a).

TRAI after undergoing a detailed consultation process, the tariff for DLC services was further reduced in July 2014. The price ceiling determined by the authority will be an effective tool to check the abuse of market power and unfair competition in the market at the same time giving flexibility to operators to offer best tariff within the ceiling. This will also incentivize the operators to be efficient and reduce cost as the benefit of efficiency and cost reduction can be retained by the operator (TRAI 2014b).

### *7.5.5 Costing of Telecom Services—TRAI Moving Towards FLLRIC*

In most of the mature markets, regulators fix prices based on FLLRIC approach. This inter alia involves estimation of costs which consider the latest high-capacity equipment and technology. This in turn could imply a major reduction in costs compared to the cost of the equipment/technology presently in use. TRAI has while fixing the DLC tariff observed that the incumbent operator is already deploying the latest technology and using lower cost equipment in its expansion program.

Therefore, TRAI is emphasizing on sustaining this process so that a transition to long-run incremental cost (LRIC)-based prices may take place over time through market competition. Alternatively, such transition may be through the usage of LRAIC in setting new tariffs in case competition does not develop later. TRAI has observed that relying mainly or fully on LRAIC at present would give a much greater shock to the market and also likely to make transition to competition more difficult as in the case of IPLC observed by TRAI.

TRAI adopted the cost of the second most efficient operator as a normative basis for setting the prices in order to incentivise investments in the DLC market, while providing some cushion to relatively less efficient operators. Although the international practice is to adopt the cost of the most efficient operator, TRAI altered that approach for balancing the interests and ensuring fair play for the incumbent operator as well as the new entrants. Actual experience in subsequent years established that the TRAI's approach was appropriate which was evidenced by the choices in service providers available to the consumers and the positive effect of the market competition on pricing and quality of their services. It has therefore been a "win-win" situation for the service providers as well as the consumers. Lowering prices has increased volume and turnover of the sector.

It is also a fact that a large number of regulators worldwide are now adopting FLLRIC while determining cost-based tariffs. It can be reasonably presumed that the next tariff review by TRAI is expected to be based on FLLRIC.

## 7.6 Concluding Remarks

TRAI has fixed a cost-based tariff in 1999 and reviewed and revised subsequently with a clear objective that the telecom service and infrastructure facilities should be competitive. It should be cost based and maximize usage. Further, it should aim for a least regulatory intervention and a light-touch regulatory regime. Every regulatory intervention by TRAI had given a direction for future with a promise of shrinkage in regulatory overreach.

As per TRAI, the telecom sector's objectives cover a wide canvas including enhancing efficiency and flexibility of operations and financial viability of the sector, promoting investment and innovation, stimulating demand and competition, addressing unfair competition, providing high-quality service to consumers and meeting social objectives such as universal provision of telecom network services at fair, reasonable and affordable rates. It can be easily concluded that the introduction of cost-oriented tariffs by the regulator triggered the telecom revolution in India and contributed greatly in achieving the Government's objectives. It transformed the Indian telecom market into a fully competitive market by introducing forbearance or light-handed regulation wherein the operators have the flexibility to fix the tariff and report them after implementation. Such pricing is determined by market forces and provides consumers with a wide choice of services at reasonable prices. It also promotes effective competition by incentivizing the incumbents as well as the new entrants by ensuring regulatory predictability. The telecom industry has moved from the standard ARPU (average revenue per user) model to the MoU (minutes of usage) model. The focus of MoU is to derive maximum utilization of the network resources to increase productivity and prevent or reduce underutilization.

The selection of the appropriate approach for costing or pricing requires judgement, especially since the firms operate in a dynamic environment. Pricing decisions will be set to optimize profits over a period of time rather than at a single point in time. To insist that prices equal the costs at all times would be a deterrent for firms to undertake investments due to lack of incentive. Cost models require comprehensive data, and hence, it is imperative that there is access to detailed and accurate data by the regulator.

The main approaches of cost allocation are FAC and LRIC. Under FAC, all costs incurred by the operator are allocated to products following the allocation rules determined. This approach results in setting prices which are fairly consistent with investments made by the firm. However, it may result in inflating its asset base and consequentially lead to higher tariff. Under LRIC, a cost structure characterized by the scope and economies of scale is adopted which provides an incentive towards productive and dynamic efficiency as it only allocates the efficiently incurred cost.

The regulatory environment across countries prefers different cost modelling and pricing processes. It cannot be presumed that the choice of a particular costing methodology is appropriate for all markets. However, it is generally believed that the most appropriate costing methodology will be the combination of CCA and LRIC. FAC will be more preferred by incumbent operators, whereas LRIC would be preferred by new entrants. The costing principles and methodologies followed by TRAI also demonstrated that a combination of different methodologies is more appropriate than depending on any single methodology.

From a public policy standpoint of view, the price (tariff) needs to be economically efficient, ensure across the board connectivity, provide the right entry signals to investors, ensure fair cost recovery by an efficient operator and reflect the closest approximation of price in a fully competitive telecom market. There is a consensus among policy-makers and regulators that from among the various pricing theories and practices prevalent today, only the FLLRIC approach meets these criteria. This will also promote a forward-looking, efficient, progressive and dynamic perspective for the entire sector. The costing methodology followed by the telecom regulator in India for telecom services is moving on these lines.

## References

AERA (2010) Regulatory philosophy and approach in economic regulation of airports and air navigation services. Available at: http://aera.gov.in/upload/cp/544217b9d489030.pdf. Accessed 14 Feb 2015

Bartle I (2003) The UK model of utility regulation: a 20th anniversary collection to mark the 'Littlechild Report' 2003. Available at: http://www.bath.ac.uk/management/cri/pubpdf/Conference_seminar/31_Model_Utility_Regulation.pdf. Accessed 1 May 2015

Kathuria R (2004) Trade in telecommunication services: opportunities and constraints. Available at: http://icrier.org/pdf/wp149.pdf. Accessed 21 Jan 2015
Kearney AT (2013) The mobile economy 2013. Available at: https://www.atkearney.com/documents/10192/760890/The_Mobile_Economy_2013.pdf. Accessed 29 Nov 2014
KPMG (2014) Cost of capital study 2014. Available at: https://www.kpmg.com/DE/de/Documents/cost-of-capital-study-english-2014-kpmg.pdf. Accessed 11 Apr 2015
Melody W (1997) Telecom reform. Lyngby: den private ingeniørfond. Technical University of Denmark
Sinha S (2000) Price regulation of telecommunication services: TRAI's first tariff order. Vikalpa 25(1):43–54
TRAI (2004) Revision of ceiling tariff for domestic leased circuits. Available at: http://www.trai.gov.in/writereaddata/consultationpaper/document/conpaper22.pdf. Accessed 17 Jul 2014
TRAI (2008) Consultation paper on review of interconnection usage charge (IUC). Available at: http://trai.gov.in/WriteReaddata/ConsultationPaper/Document/cpaper31dec08.pdf. Accessed 18 Oct 2014
TRAI (2012) Review of policy of forbearance in telecom tariff. Available at: http://www.trai.gov.in/WriteReaddata/ConsultationPaper/Document/CP_Review-Policy-Forbearance-Telecom-Tariffs-2.pdf. Accessed 21 Feb 2015
TRAI (2014a) Consultation paper on review of tariff for domestic leased circuits. Available at: http://www.trai.gov.in/WriteReaddata/ConsultationPaper/Document/CP_on_Review_of_Tariff_for_DLC_24.03.2014_Final.pdf. Accessed 29 Mar 2015
TRAI (2014b) The telecommunication tariff (fifty seventh amendment) order, 2014. Available at: http://www.trai.gov.in/content/VerReg/97_0_2.aspx. Accessed 15 Apr 2015
TRAI (2015) Tariff orders. Available at: http://www.trai.gov.in/content/Regulation/0_2_REGULATIONS.aspx. Accessed 21 Sep 2015
TRAI (n.d.) Regulations on interconnection. Available at: http://www.trai.gov.in/content/VerReg/48_0_0.aspx. Accessed 15 July 2014

# Chapter 8
# Telecom Value Chain and Telecom Markets—Enterprise, Retail and Application Development

Value can be defined in many ways and is a function of the dimensions employed in a study. For the purpose of this chapter, the use of the word "value" is restricted to its common definition, as the amount buyers are willing to pay for a product or service. The concept of the value chain was first popularized by Michael Porter in a seminal work on the implementation of competitive strategies to enhance business performance. He defined value as the amount consumers are willing to pay for what a firm provides and conceived the "chain" as a combination of nine generic value-added activities operating within a firm. He also examined the interaction between these activities and classified a framework to provide value to customers (Porter 1985).

Porter identified the following primary and support activities that form the value chain for any enterprise. Inbound logistics, operations, outbound logistics, marketing and sales and service are the primary activities, whereas support activities include firm infrastructure, human resource management, technology development and procurement.

This model of a value chain has been revisited many times over, and in the present context of greater outsourcing and collaboration, the term now more closely reflects the linkages between multiple firms' value-creating processes and is sometimes also referred to as a "demand chain". The primary focus of modern value chains is on the benefits that accrue to customers, the interdependent processes that generate value and the resulting demand and fund flows (Feller et al. 2006).

The stellar growth of telecommunication services in India, especially over the last decade, can largely be attributed to a liberalized regulatory regime, structural reforms and hypercompetition. Such an environment enabled the telecom to grow and in turn act as a major catalyst in India's growth as a nation. There is no doubt that a majority of this growth has so far come from retail voice revenues. However, in today's changed scenario, as voice revenues continue to stagnate, operators are turning their attention to the potential of data services. As a possible solution to these declining margins, the data business was embraced by operators, but has yielded less-than-expected and desired results. The challenges that operators and regulators

© Springer India 2016

M.K. Medudula et al., *Telecom Management in Emerging Economies*,
DOI 10.1007/978-81-322-2749-6_8

face with this line of business are unique and demand unique solutions. Data, in and of itself, is many orders of magnitude higher than voice in terms of financial viability. This is due in part to the ability of data to mould itself to the needs of distinct customer groups. While voice revenues may not grow by much over the coming years, data revenues have real potential to drive, as well as sustain future growth.

## 8.1 Value Chains Versus Supply Chains

In the 1980s, supply chain management (SCM) emerged as a new integrative philosophy to manage the total flow of goods from suppliers to end consumers (Cooper et al. 1997). The term was coined by Keith Oliver in 1982 (Bacheldor 2003). A vice president at Booz Allen Hamilton, Oliver developed an integrated inventory management framework focused on managing the chain of supply as though it was a single entity and not a group of disparate functions (Laseter and Oliver 2003).

In essence, a supply chain and value chain are complementary views of an extended enterprise with integrated business processes enabling the flows of products and services in one direction and of value represented by demand and cash flow in the other (Ramsay 2005). Both chains apply to a similar network of companies, and in both cases, these companies interact with an objective of providing goods and/or services. The distinction between the two lies not in the structure of these chains, which are near identical in both cases, but rather in their fundamental objective. Supply chains focus upstream on integrating supplier and producer processes, improving efficiency and reducing waste, while value chains focus the other way, on creating value in the eyes of customers (Feller et al. 2006). To understand this concept better, consider the case of a supply chain from a farmer to a wholesaler to a retailer and finally to end consumers. In the case of fruit distributors like Dole and Chiquita operating on such a supply chain, if the distributed fruit passes through each cost optimized stage from the farmer to an end consumer, the chain is referred to as a supply chain. However, if value is added at each of these stages by employing standards for grading, sorting, packaging and cold storage, the resulting chain can be referred to as a value chain.

### *8.1.1 The Telecommunications Value Chain*

In an article on "Extending the concept of supply chains", Al-Mudimigh et al. (2004) demonstrated that value chain management (VCM) held the potential to deliver desired results, if and only if there was a clear emphasis on cooperation and collaboration. This focus requires that a new organizational mindset and new forms of behaviour be considered by all stakeholders, especially with respect to sharing information with the objective to improve strategic planning for future growth.

The key stakeholders in any telecommunications value chain include the following:

- **Telecom product/device manufacturers**—Handset manufacturers play a prominent role in the telecommunications value chain. The evolution of handsets over the last decade is a systemic response not only to the advancement of technology, but also to consumer preferences that have to an extent influenced technical progress. Device manufacturers hold a top of mind position in the minds of consumers. The value generally associated with Apple products is a testament to the fact that a well-managed value chain can reap huge benefits for manufacturers. The price premium that Apple products command is the result of the stability, ease of use and premium perceptions associated with these products.
- **Telecom service providers**—Service providers or operators enable telephony and data services on mobile handsets. In some developed markets, operators play a critical role in the distribution of handsets as well. Mobile phone bundled with service is a common feature in such markets, and in some cases, operators lead the value chain in terms of net sales (Giachetti and Marchi 2010). To enable services on handsets, service providers engage with respective licensors and regulators to acquire spectrum and offer access services. In addition, service providers invest heavily in infrastructure, a direct impact of which is an erosion of its margins. Of the entire set of stakeholders in the value chain, none, who are in the telecommunications business for profit, experience as much financial hardship as operators. Spectrum acquisition charges, spectrum usage charges, Universal Service Obligation levies and infrastructure are just some of the levies imposed on Indian service providers. It is important to note that while spectrum acquisition costs are treated as sunk costs, they effectively limit operators' ability to invest in infrastructure. Ineffective or prohibitive policies can have a severe negative impact on the health of the industry. Financial strain resulting from spectrum acquisition and leading to underinvestment in infrastructure has a measurable negative impact on the quality of services offered. In the absence of adequate spectrum, more telecom towers are required to offer an acceptable grade of service. If the spectrum procured is less and expensive, operators find it difficult, if not possible maintain a superior service portfolio.
- **Infrastructure providers**—These members of the value chain enable operators by setting up the physical infrastructure required to offer access services to consumers. The emergence of infrastructure providers brought great value to the entire industry. With their prime focus on infrastructure, these members have helped advance infrastructure sharing that, while lowering capital expenditure for operators, also has a positive impact on sustainability and environmental protection.
- **Content providers/aggregators/application service providers**—These members add value to the industry by creating content/applications for end consumers using handsets and access services from operators. Developed markets see greater participation from application providers, with significant revenues

coming from this segment. Analysys Mason in collaboration with IAMAI reported on the Indian evolution of mobile value-added services in 2011. The report revealed that the entire revenues generated from application services account for 11 % of total telecom revenues and that this figure is slated to grow to 31 % by 2015. Going forward, application service providers will play a critical role in bringing to market innovative applications that conform to the needs of consumers and would consequently generate great value for themselves, handset manufacturers, service providers and the customers.
- **Regulators and licensors**—Regulators play a critical role in the growth and sustainability of the telecommunications industry in any country. These members allocate spectrum rights to private and state players and ensure that a certain quality of service is consistently offered and that no entity secures monopolistic control and access over the market. In India, the regulator and licensor work together to supervise the telecommunications systems of the land. TRAI, the regulator, maintains sovereignty over matters related to tariffs and quality of service, while the licensor, DoT, has absolute control over licensing terms and spectrum allocation. The regulator, the licensor and the Industry, in any economy, need to work together to maintain and improve the health of telecommunications services in the country. Regulatory and licensing regimes would be sensitive to market realities, and these stakeholders work on a cooperative and collaborative model that adopts a consultative approach.
- **Consumers**—Consumers are the focus of any value chain, and the story is no different for telecommunications in India. As the focal members of the telecommunications value chain, consumers have the power to make or break the fortunes of for profit stakeholders in the value chain. The regulator in India, as in the case of many markets, places great importance on the needs of customers. Mobile number portability, implemented in India in 2010, afforded to consumers the flexibility to switch operators without having to change the number. Such policies that favour consumers demand operators to give greater focus to quality of services to minimize subscriber churn.

Giachetti and Marchi (2010) carried out a case study on the mobile phone industry from 1980 to 2009 and adopted a life cycle approach to understand the changes in product development in this industry. Based on primary and secondary research, they discovered that handset manufacturers had radically changed their product strategy in response to factors such as increased global competition and the need to respond rapidly to changing technology and consumer preferences.

An investigation of the distribution of value in the mobile phone supply chain conducted by Dedrick et al. (2011) used a framework based on theories of firm strategy to measure captured value in the case of three mobile phone models sold during the years 2004–2008 in various markets. The analysis revealed that in terms of net sales, mobile operators captured the greatest value from each of the three handsets studied, followed closely by handset/device manufactures, with suppliers coming in at a distant third. This situation, however, is reversed when the study is conducted in terms of operating profits. Operators carry the burden of network installation, upgrade and maintenance, which erodes much of the value recovered from monthly subscription fees. The study also revealed that manufacturer nationality directly influences supplier choice and is a key determinant of geographical value capture.

Dedrick et al. (2009), in an analysis of the distribution of value from innovation in the global supply chain of the Apple iPad and iPhone, studied the value dynamics of the undisputed leading mobile telecommunications company—Apple. Policies and economics of value systems implemented by the firm have allowed it to capture the largest share of value from product innovations, even though raw materials are sourced from and products are manufactured in China. With strict and unwavering control over the supply chain, Apple has been able to keep most of its design, software development, product management, marketing and other key functions in the USA. The authors of this paper applied analytics to Apple's supply chain so as to closely examine the distribution of value. This study revealed that China, while Apple's manufacturing hub, derives little value from the eventual sale of these goods. With a breakdown of value in the Apple products, Dedrick, Kraemer and Linden demonstrate that the assignment of profits to first-tier suppliers is based on the location of their corporate headquarters, and the main financial benefit to China is mostly limited to the wages paid for the manufacturing of the product.

## 8.2 Enterprise Market

The enterprise customers are by far the largest consumers of data services and are, by definition, a segment vastly different from the retail consumer. Fuelled by different and specific needs, enterprise consumers are demanding data connectivity throughout the country and the world. As an early adopter of telecommunications technology, this sector essentially promotes innovation. In order to fulfil the broadband penetration goals of NTP 2012 and Digital India, the telecommunications enterprise business will have to lead by conceptualizing a new set of data services to drive this growth. In the face of declining and saturated voice revenues, the enterprise business segment emerges as a real contender to provide a healthy stream of revenue to operators and help them usher in the next ICT revolution.

Over the last decade, industrial dependence on enterprise connectivity and access to data has increased exponentially. It would therefore be prudent to evaluate the enterprise consumer separately from the retail consumer and accordingly turn attention to the unique challenges faced by this group of customers.

The Indian enterprise segment has been growing at a healthy rate, owing primarily to two major factors—the increased adoption of IT and networking technology by Indian businesses and by international firms looking for connectivity to and from India. This growth, however, is for all intents and purposes, stunted. Global averages reveal that 35–50 % of revenues come from non-voice services, while India derives approximately 18 % of its telecommunication revenues from the same segment. This deficit points to the potential of data services and the role enterprise consumers will play in fuelling the required growth.

The following pie charts depict, as of December 2015, the NLD, ILD and ISP segments. This data has been compiled from the quarterly financial report (Q3, FY15-16) prepared and published by TRAI.

### 8.2.1 NLD Market Share

TRAI data reveals that of the entire NLD market, and the top five players collectively hold as much as approximately 75 % of the total market during Q3, FY15-16 (Fig. 8.1).

### 8.2.2 ILD Market Share

Bharti Airtel, Vodafone and Tata lead the market and collectively hold a market share greater than 50 % (Fig. 8.2).

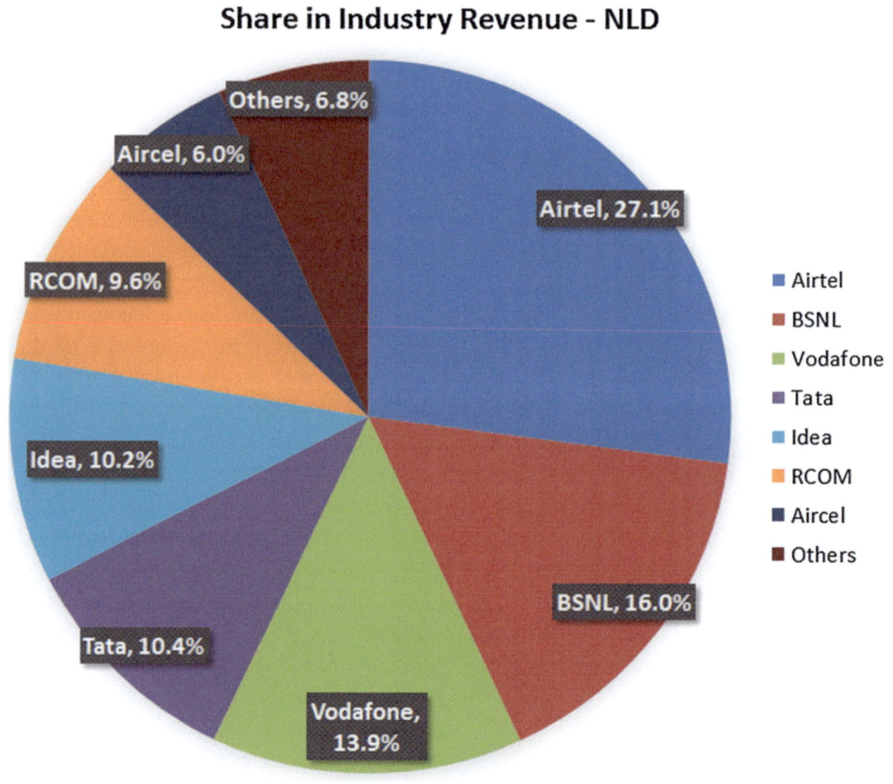


**Fig. 8.1** NLD market share—data and voice (TRAI financial data Q3, FY15-16)

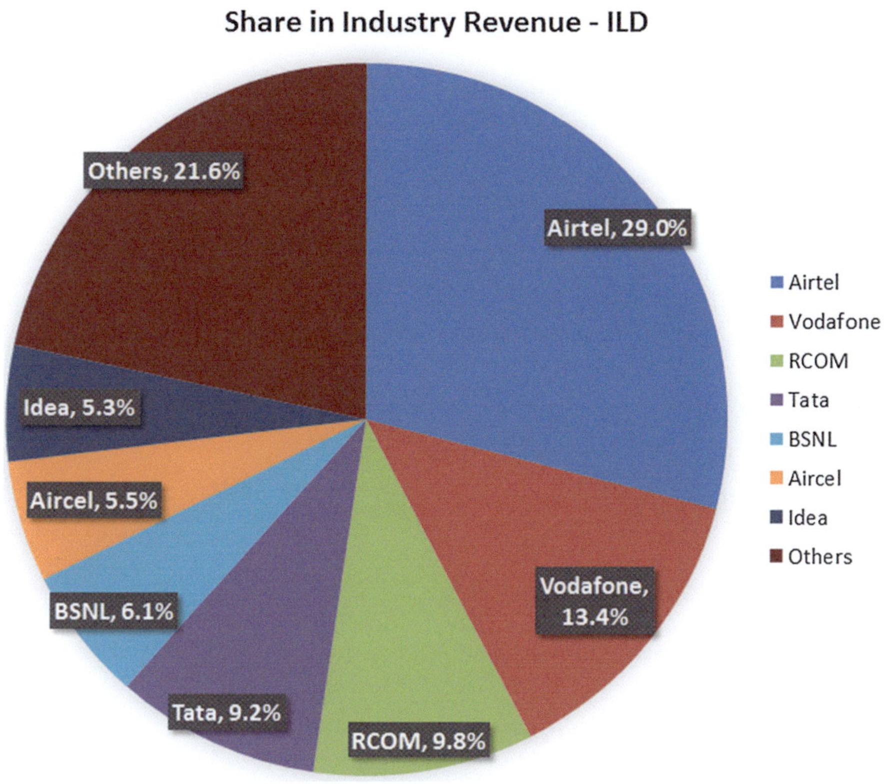


**Fig. 8.2** ILD market share—data and voice (TRAI financial data Q3, FY15-16)

### *8.2.3 ISP Market Share*

The state-run BSNL has a strong hold over the ISP business and holds a market share of 39.7 % (Fig. 8.3).

It is important to take note of the following when interpreting the market shares represented in the charts above: TRAI (Q3, FY15-16).

- The revenues reported by operators for their respective NLD, ILD, ISP and VSAT licences comprise revenues from voice as well as data.
- This is the only data in the public domain that offers an estimate of the enterprise market.
- The data projected in the previous pages reflects quarterly declarations by operators published by TRAI—Quarter 3 (October, November and December) for the financial year 2015–16.

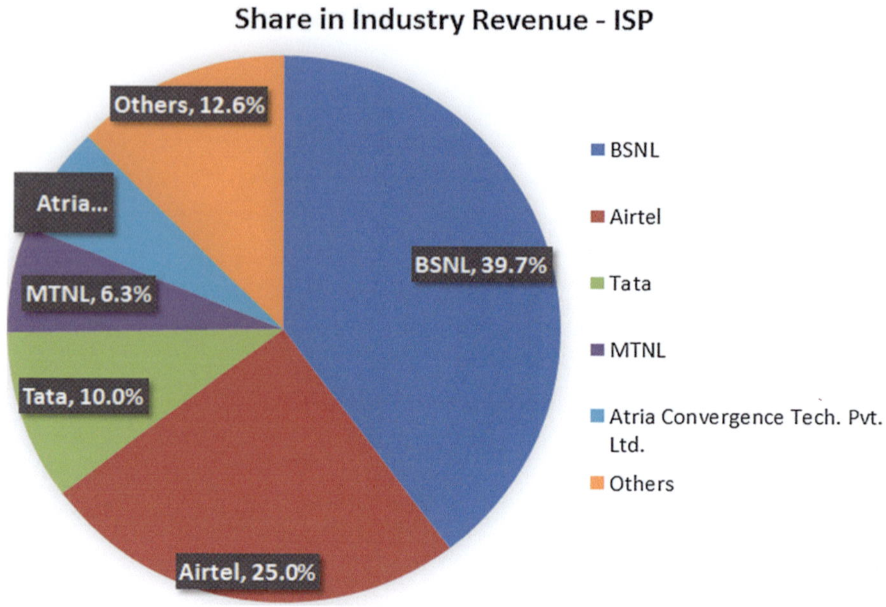


**Fig. 8.3** ISP market share (TRAI financial data Q3, FY15-16)

## 8.3 Growth of Enterprise Services

The growth of enterprise services in India can be described as healthy yet not entirely true to its potential. So far, the following can be attributed to the growth of this sector.

- **Economic growth**—The fast paced growth of the Indian economy has had a direct impact on the demand and growth of enterprise connectivity, and future growth will further stimulate demand for enterprise connectivity throughout the country.
- **Corporate expansion**—While Indian businesses, in pursuit of profits, continue to extend their businesses to other geographies, international firms are turning their attention towards India for similar reasons. The growing corporate expansion within and from the country will drive demand for enterprise data connectivity upwards.
- **Rural markets**—With an already saturated urban segment, rural markets certainly present new opportunities that can inject a healthy stream of revenues to sustain and help grow the enterprise data connectivity business. Initiatives to connect rural areas are already underway, and government initiatives such as the National E-Governance Plan have been set in motion to, among other things, bring Internet access to all villages. The scale of such initiatives leaves little doubt that higher bandwidth would be demanded in coming years.

## 8.4 Kinds of Enterprise Services

### 8.4.1 IPLC

An IPLC, or International Private Leased Circuit, is a private line used by companies to connect international locations with a point-to-point link and can be used for Internet access, business data exchange, video conferencing and/or any other form of telecommunications. The complexity of business arrangements for such links, especially with respect to business across borders, led the ITU to develop the one-stop shopping (OSS) framework. This framework simplifies the billing process with respect to such links by allowing an organization to place a single order with a single carrier for two IPLCs for two offices in two different countries.

### 8.4.2 DLC

A domestic leased circuit (DLC) is a point-to-point circuit used by companies to connect two locations within India. In 2007, TRAI issued regulations for the provision of DLCs or the local lead of DLCs. As per these regulations, a domestic leased circuit "is a leased circuit from the premise of one subscriber to the premises of other subscriber when both such premises are located within India". A leased circuit, in the licence, has been defined as "a virtual private network using circuit or packet switched (Internet Protocol) technology apart from point-to-point non-switched physical connections or transmission bandwidth and to which the public network is not connected". The current licensing regime also dictates that DLCs may be provided by NLD operators and access service providers (ASPs), viz. basic service operators (BSOs) and CMTS/UASL/UL licensees only.

A 2014 consultation exercise by TRAI, on tariff regulations for domestic leased circuits (TRAI 2014), engaged the industry in an extensive economic debate on price controls. A majority of operators presented tariff deregulation as the need of the hour as opposed to the regulator advocating the continued use of price controls to prevent price-gouging practices inherent in non-competitive markets. Some operators even proposed conditional deregulation for selected areas, subject to the discovery of effective competition. The consultation paper issued by the Authority also discussed how modern preferences tended towards VPNs over the traditional domestic leased circuit. This is discussed in greater detail in the next section.

### 8.4.3 MPLS

Technological progress over the last decade led to the development of MPLS networks that offer secured access over a shared network. This essentially renders the DLC market somewhat redundant, as enterprise customers can avail the same benefits offered by leased circuits. MPLS, or “multiprotocol label switching”, is a set of protocols that allow enterprise customers to securely connect distinct locations while greatly reducing costs and maintaining the same kind and quality of enterprise data connectivity (TRAI 2014).

### 8.4.4 VSAT

VSAT, or very small aperture terminal, is a satellite communications system for home and business use. Users of VSAT need a box (decoder) that acts as an interface between the customers’ computer and an outside antenna with a transceiver. This outdoor equipment is capable of broadcasting and receiving signals to and from a satellite transponder positioned in geostationary orbit. The satellite, on the other hand, broadcasts and receives signals from an earth station computer that acts as a hub for users connected to the network. These users are interconnected with the hub in a star topology, and communication between connected users is routed through the hub and delivered to recipients via the satellite. VSAT offers multiple advantages over traditional terrestrial services. Total control over the communications system and increased reliability and throughput are just some of the incentives for enterprise customers to operate their very own very small aperture terminals (VSATs) (Searchmobilecomputing, n.d.).

### 8.4.5 IP Transit/Peering Arrangements

The Internet is an interconnected network of networks—one that is built upon thousands if not millions of independent networks exchanging traffic with one another. ISPs routinely enter into such peering/interconnection agreements with other ISPs. As a general rule, if the amount of traffic exchanged between two ISPs is identical, agreements are cost neutral, i.e. accompanying no commercial considerations, and based entirely on the principles of equitable exchange between two parties. In other scenarios, where the traffic exchanged by one ISP exceeds the traffic exchanged by the other, the ISP with the larger amount of traffic pays the other on certain commercial terms. These transit agreements are quite common and have been in use since the inception of the public Internet.

While such arrangements may certainly sound uncontroversial, this is not the case. The dispute between Comcast & Netflix in the USA is essentially a dispute over such interconnection. As of latest analyses, Netflix accounts for the largest amount of American Internet traffic. This is to be expected, given Netflix’s business model. As a subscription video on demand (SVoD) provider over the Internet, Netflix is huge fan favourite and embraced by multiple platforms such as AppleTV and Roku. Such has been the success of this online video streaming service that the company today commissions studios to develop exclusive entertainment content (Orange is the new black, House of Cards, etc.). Exclusive content and the on-demand nature of the service have led to massive adoption by customers and have gradually led to this rise of this service provider as the largest carrier of traffic.

Reports of Netflix traffic being throttled, or slowed down, on Comcast networks was the smoking gun that kicked off a furious debate that eventually turned into an industry-wide consultation exercise on net neutrality. Netflix contended that net neutrality, the neutral nature of the Internet, has been compromised by the acts of Comcast (slowing down Netflix's traffic). It is important to take note of the underlying fundamental truths before evaluating such reports. It is an undisputable fact that the Internet is an interconnected network of networks, in which capacity is limited at any given point in time. Provisioning additional capacity requires investment that must eventually be passed off to consumers of this additional capacity.

## 8.5 Telecom Retail

A majority of historical growth of telecommunications industries across the world can be attributed entirely to the voice segment. However, modern requirements dictate that operators turn their attention to more lucrative lines of business, as the current state of voice revenues all over the world can best be described as lacklustre. Many, if not all, operators have recognized this shift in consumption patterns and are actively pursuing data as the new catalyst for growth.

TRAI routinely publishes a performance indicator report that best summarizes the adoption and growth of telecommunications services within and from India. More details about the current subscriber base and growth rate statistics are mentioned in Chap. 3.

## 8.6 Application Development

The evolution of telecommunications is not limited to the growth observed in revenues and subscriber bases, but also includes a drastic change in consumer expectations and consumption habits. From a time when the ability to make calls over mobiles was heralded as the crowning achievement of modern science and technology, consumers today expect their devices to be capable of much more. SMS, once clearly a value-added service, is now expected to be, and is, an out-of-the-box feature of handsets and network contracts/plans. To suggest otherwise would be ludicrous at best, and classify as no less than a marketing and technical failure on the part of a device manufacturer or an operator. Application services such as gaming, video and audio streaming, stock quotes, news, sports updates, chatting and several others are fairly common on many networks and need to be recognized for their true potential.

Application service providers will feature prominently in the future value chain and will play a critical role in the growth and adoption of mobile value-added services.

The growth of data services in India, envisioned and planned for by the regulator and the industry, demands a viable framework that helps realize the true potential of application development as a lucrative business opportunity with numerous social benefits.

The mobile value-added services market in India is growing at a healthy rate (IAMAIâ€ Analysys Mason 2011). In a study "Mobile Value Added Services Market in India 2014–2018", Technavio predicts that in India MVAS will grow at a compound annual growth rate (CAGR) of 22.13 % over the period of 2013–18.

Yet another area that is currently under study is the API business. Telecom firms can provide application developers with backdoors, or application programming interfaces into their networks, and offer a new range of service to both retail and enterprise customers. Applications designed specifically to interface with operator networks can potentially create novel use cases. Such applications need to be designed with ubiquity and an effective customer experience in mind. The OpenAPI standard is one such standard that allows for network interface, albeit at a basic level, with currently only a few interfaces available to developers. This field certainly merits the attention of operators, who should attempt to develop a monetizing strategy around this potentially lucrative line of business.

The growth so far will continue to be fuelled by better more functional hardware increasingly approaching affordable prices, increased adoption by younger citizens and innovative application development. The increased performance of networks over the coming years will enable higher data speeds ideal for the development and deployment of data-intensive applications. This growth, if engaged efficiently, would be beneficial to all stakeholders associated with the application services value chain. Mobile telecom service providers, application service providers, handset manufacturers, content developers, content aggregators and consumers all stand to benefit from application development. More details on mobile applications will be covered in Chap. 12.

## 8.7 Concluding Remarks

An evolution of the way in which the telecommunications business is conducted is imminent and needs to be embraced by all stakeholders. The future growth of the telecommunications industry hinges on a new system of cooperation and coordination between these stakeholders. It will also be of critical importance to keep business models flexible enough to exploit new opportunities. In April 2014, Microsoft announced a drastic shift in its business model. For an organization clearly driven by its operating system for most of its existence, to renounce market mechanisms and declare free distribution of its OS for devices with screen sizes less than 9 in., is a bold move in the least. In an effort to increase Windows' market share in mobile devices, this strategy is slated to give competition (iOS and Android), a run for their money.

Operators, equipment and device manufacturers, content providers, regulators and infrastructure providers need to work together to enhance the value created at every stage of the telecommunications value chain, all with the view to enhance value for the customer and, in pursuit of this target, improve the overall health of the industry as well as individual stakeholders. What will this new world of cooperation and coordination look like? Only time will tell.

## References


Al-Mudimigh A, Zairi M, Ahmed A (2004) Extending the concept of supply chain: The effective management of value chains. Int J Prod Econ 87(3):309–320

Bacheldor B (2003) Supply chain management still a work in progress—informationweek. Informationweek. Available at: http://www.informationweek.com/supply-chain-management-still-a-work-in-progress/d/d-id/1018682? Accessed 20 Apr 2015

Cooper M, Lambert D, Pagh J (1997) Supply chain management: more than a new name for logistics. Int J Logistics Manage 8(1):1–14

Dedrick J, Kraemer K, Linden G (2009) Who profits from innovation in global value chains?: a study of the iPod and notebook PCs. Ind Corp Change 19(1):81–116

Dedrick J, Kraemer K, Linden G (2011) The distribution of value in the mobile phone supply chain. Telecommun Policy 35(6):505–521

Feller A, Shunk D, Callarman T (2006) Value chains versus supply chains. Available at: http://www.ceibs.edu/knowledge/papers/images/20060317/2847.pdf. Accessed 9 May 2015

Giachetti C, Marchi G (2010) Evolution of firms' product strategy over the life cycle of technology-based industries: a case study of the global mobile phone industry, 1980–2009. Bus Hist 52(7):1123–1150

IAMAIâ€ Analysys Mason (2011) Evolution of mobile VAS in India: imperatives for exponential growth

Laseter T, Oliver K (2003) When will supply chain management grow up? Strategy Bus (32), pp. 1–5. Available at: http://www.manageris.com/files/articles/when_supply_chain_grow_up.pdf. Accessed 22 June 2015

Porter M (1985) Competitive advantage. Free Press, New York

Ramsay J (2005) The real meaning of value in trading relationships. Int J Oper Prod Manage 25 (6):549–565

Searchmobilecomputing, (n.d.). VSAT (very small aperture terminal) definition. Available at: http://searchmobilecomputing.techtarget.com/definition/VSAT. Accessed 22 Oct 2015

TRAI (2014) Consultation paper on review of tariff for domestic leased circuits. Available at: http://www.trai.gov.in/WriteReaddata/ConsultationPaper/Document/CP_on_Review_of_Tariff_for_DLC_24.03.2014_Final.pdf. Accessed 11 Mar 2015

# Chapter 9
# Telecommunication Policy—Concerns and Suggestions

The overwhelming growth of telecommunications in India can largely be attributed to the liberalization of the sector and the prolonged efforts of the licensor, the regulator and the Industry. Many of us have lived through an era of telecommunications when simply acquiring a fixed telephone line could take up to a whole year, and may be even longer depending on where it was to be situated. The same process can now be completed in no more than a few days. The ubiquitous availability of telecommunications services is often taken for granted, and we tend to forget about a time when owning a fixed line was considered a privilege.

This growth resulted from the liberalization of the sector, which facilitated the end of the state monopolies, and paved the way for privatization, competition and unprecedented progress at an increasingly accelerated pace. As would be expected, this transition came with its own set of challenges, many of which were essentially policy issues that were extremely prone to subjective interpretation, and had a measurable negative impact on telecom sector. This chapter is intended to provide a primer on the leading challenges and policy issues of the day, and possible resolutions to help propel the industry towards the next phase of growth.

It is important for the reader to take note that the issues discussed in the following pages are not the result of lapses in judgment on part of the industry or the authorities, but rather dynamic issues that emerge in the regulation of privatized yet critical public services such as telecommunications. The transition from a state-run monopoly in the sector to a healthy, sometimes hyper competitive environment has been a particularly challenging one and has brought with it the impetus to examine old systems and processes that were no longer suitable in a modern context. The need for such a transition was further warranted by the potential impact of telecommunications growth on national GDP. It is now an uncontentious fact that a growth in telecommunications has an associated positive impact on the GDP of a nation. Government of India, in pursuit of such goals, undertook the extensive task of liberalizing the state-run telecommunications monopolies and opened up the market to the wonders of competition.

© Springer India 2016

M.K. Medudula et al., *Telecom Management in Emerging Economies*,
DOI 10.1007/978-81-322-2749-6_9

Uncertainty in matters of telecommunications policy in India ranges from issues of spectrum assignment and its management, the need for licensing reforms, an overly complicated regulatory regime to a disproportionate level of taxation. While many of these issues would be unique to the Indian context, a majority would represent conditions that have at one time or another been tackled by other nations. There are lessons to be learnt from the many successes and failures of telecommunications globally, and the authorities along with members of the industry can benefit greatly from the experiences of others and gain valuable insights into how they may have aided in the growth of telecommunications in their nations.

Further growth of this industry in India would depend critically on the re-examination of certain policy issues as well as the institutionalization of progressive reform that creates a healthy business environment for all members of the value chain. The following sections of this chapter elaborate on these policy issues which are very important for the Indian telecommunications industry to set global benchmarks for others to strive for.

## 9.1 Spectrum Reforms

### *9.1.1 Overall Availability of Spectrum in All Bands*

One clearly articulated feature of the National Telecom Policy of 2012 is the recognition of telecommunications, including broadband connectivity as a basic necessity on par with education and health. Such is the focus on this industry that the policy idealizes the reach and growth of the Internet to the point of declaring, and correctly so, that everyone should have the "right to broadband". The policy places great emphasis on the power of "broadband information highways" and sets ambitious targets of bringing broadband to 175 million subscribers by 2017 and 600 million by 2020. Realization of such goals depends on the ability of service providers to reach customers in a cost-effective yet comprehensive manner. With over 1010.89 million wireless consumers and a mere 25.52 million wireline consumers (as on 31st Dec, 2015) (TRAI 2016), it is clear beyond any doubt that wireless is the stronger and may be only viable driver to achieve the ambitious broadband plans set by Indian Authorities.

Such growth, however, hinges on the availability of adequate spectrum, which is a major area of concern for telecommunications in India. Indian Telecom Service Providers (TSPs) hold approximately 13 MHz of spectrum, which contrasts significantly with global averages—EU (92.6 MHz), UK (82.2 MHz), France (138.5 MHz), Spain (100.6 MHz), and USA (96 MHz). The situation presents further problems when one considers the wide disparity between the traffic handled by Indian operators in comparison with their international counterparts. An approximately 10 times larger base of customers than global averages, as well as large targets, leaves little doubt that the Indian broadband revolution will depend critically on the sufficient and timely availability of radio spectrum across all permitted bands. In 2010, the Indian telecommunications regulator, TRAI, projected an overall requirement of 600 MHz of additional spectrum to address the growing needs of the industry by 2014 (TRAI 2012). As per their 12th Plan, the Telecom Sector Working Group has projected this need to rise to 800 MHz by 2015. Industrial estimates, however, stand at approximately 1000 MHz by 2015 and 2000 MHz by 2022. Such immense requirements are going to require a clear road map for spectrum availability in the near future. Non-commercial users with underutilized and in some cases even unutilized access spectrum in ideal bands should be relocated to other bands. Such spectrum refarming is possible and has been fervently proposed by all major telecommunications service providers in India. There is a need to increase the availability of spectrum across the 700, 800, 900, 1800, 2100, 2300, 2500 and 2600 MHz bands in conformance with global spectrum harmonization standards.

It is heartening to note that government of India has allowed spectrum trading and spectrum sharing. Detailed guidelines have also been provided. Globally, spectrum trading has proved itself as an effective tool to promote spectrum efficiency, a need that is just as critical as the allowance of trading. Spectrum sharing is considered as one of the most effective tools to enhance spectrum efficiency, network coverage and quality of service; spectrum sharing is vital to the future growth of telecommunications services in India. Associations and industry bodies had extensively represented that spectrum sharing should not only be permitted, but also should be structured in a manner that is not prohibitive, especially with respect to holding limits. While it is important for the government and regulatory authorities to prevent the emergence of an entity that can act as a significant market power, it is equally important to ensure that control procedures to prevent these emergences do not disincentivize progress.

### *9.1.2 Auction of Spectrum in 800 MHz Band*

The 800 MHz band in India is used primarily for CDMA, a technology that over the last few years has exhibited a precipitous decline in adoption and supporting ecosystem. A diminishing subscriber base and the associated erosion of investor confidence were just some of the reasons why the November 2012 spectrum auction for 800 MHz band spectrum saw zero participation from CDMA operators. This spectrum was once again put up for auction in March 2013. The repeated lack-lustre response from CDMA operators provided further evidence of the fact that modern-day consumer preferences were leaning significantly towards the GSM platform.

The 800 MHz band was auctioned in the recent auction, as a liberalized spectrum band with a spectrum lot of 5 MHz or more. The spectrum in this band was bought by the TSPs who may use it to provide broadband data services.

### 9.1.3 Availability of More Spectrum in 900 MHz Band

In 2015–2016, when many TSPs' licences came up for extension, 184.0 MHz of spectrum in the 900 MHz band was made available for auction. For providing newer technologies such as 4G/LTE, a minimum contiguous 5 MHz of spectrum is required. However, out of the likely 184 MHz, only 140 MHz could be provided in contiguous 5 MHz blocks and the remaining 44 MHz was auctioned as non-contiguous band. Only one circle, i.e. Punjab, had 3 blocks of 5 MHz. 9 circles (Andhra Pradesh, Gujarat, Himachal Pradesh, Haryana, Karnataka, Kerala, Maharashtra, Madhya Pradesh and Rajasthan) had only 2 blocks of 5 MHz. 7 other circles (Assam, Bihar, Northeast, Orissa, Tamil Nadu, Uttar Pradesh (West) and Uttar Pradesh (East)) had no more than one block of 5 MHz, and West Bengal did not have any contiguous 5 MHz blocks.

The above is the result of the government assigning 25 MHz in 900 MHz band for mobile services, but in reality allocating amounts in the range of 18.6–22.2 MHz across many service areas. Making available just the missing amounts would increase spectrum contiguity in 18 circles or service areas, from the current 28 blocks (140 MHz) to 46 blocks (230 MHz). This could have been achieved by clubbing together the spectrum held by non-commercial users, as well as provisioning the already vacant spectrum in 900 MHz.

### 9.1.4 Availability of More Spectrum in 2100 MHz Band

In 2010–11, DoT auctioned 3 blocks of 5 MHz in 2100 MHz band whereas one block was assigned to BSNL/MTNL at auction determined price. Of late, the TSPs have been demanding for further release of 4 blocks. However, only 1 block was put up for auction in 2015 auctions in 17 service areas. Additional spectrum in 2100 MHz band can help to ramp up India's mobile broadband connectivity, achieve broadband targets and trigger GDP growth. Now, DoT plans to auction 3 blocks in the upcoming 2016 auctions which is a welcome step.

### 9.1.5 Auction of Spectrum in 1800 MHz Band

Consequent to cancellation of access licenses in 2010, the auction in 1800 MHz band was conducted by DoT in November 2012 whereby the quashed licensee majorly bought spectrum. Subsequent spectrum auction also happened in February 2014 and March 2015 whereby 1800 MHz available with DoT as well as that becoming free from licenses expiring in 2014–16 was put to auction. However, not all spectrum sold was available in contiguous blocks which reduces its use for deployment of broadband technology. The industry has been demanding harmonization of spectrum assigned to TSPs and Defence, which will not only make the assigned spectrum contiguous but will also make available additional 200 MHz (paired) spectrum across 22 service areas. It is important that such an exercise is conducted at the earliest and spectrum becoming available be put to auction.

### *9.1.6 Auction of BWA Spectrum*

In 2010–11, DoT auctioned 2 blocks of BWA Spectrum (20 MHz—unpaired) in 2300 MHz band whereas one block was assigned to BSNL/MTNL in at auction determined price. However, the band lacked network/device ecosystem and even after lapse of 5 years, many TSPs have not yet launched their services. Further, BSNL and MTNL surrendered their BWA spectrum in all Metro and Class 'A' service areas citing their inability to utilize the spectrum. It is therefore important that spectrum in new bands be released/made available for auction once the network and device ecosystem matures. This will lead to optimum utilization of funds available with the TSPs.

## 9.2 Licence Reforms

### *9.2.1 Migration to Unified Licence Regime*

In August 2012, the government introduced a new unified licensing regime. While the Industry is keen to migrate to a "Unified Licence", in its current form, but the principle of "no worse off" has not been followed. Any migration to the Unified Licence should be a collaborative process that protects the interests of both parties.

#### 9.2.1.1 Licence Amendments Should Be Bilateral

A major point of contention routinely expressed by service providers relates to the unilateral amendment of licensing conditions by the licensor. Many one-sided amendments have been legally challenged by TSPs, and the Supreme Court of India agrees with their claim that a licence issued under the Indian Telegraph Act, 1885, is a legal contract between two parties and cannot be amended by one without the express consent of the other. Enshrining this principle in law and policy would not only enhance the confidence of investors in the sector but also aid in reducing unnecessary litigation.

#### 9.2.1.2 Active Infrastructure Sharing

Infrastructure sharing between telecom operators is currently limited to passive equipment such as the building, tower, dark fibre. In March 2009, DoT clarified that TSPs could share active infrastructure, provided it was limited to the antenna, feeder cable, Node B, Radio Access Network and transmission system (TRAI 2011). A formal policy to this effect has now been issued in February 2016.

#### 9.2.1.3 No Licence Fee on IP-1 Services

In October 2000, DoT allowed companies to provide assets such as tower, dark fibre, right of way, duct space to TSPs without holding a licence or an obligation to pay entry or licence fees (DoT 2010). Such companies were only required to register themselves with DoT as Infrastructure Providers—Category I (IP-I). In May and October 2008, TRAI recommended the imposition of licence fees on IP-I services, which was turned down by DoT. As per DoT, the activities of IP-I operators do not qualify for the grant of a licence. In May 2010, TRAI again recommended this imposition on IP-I services, but DoT vide a press-release dated 15.02.2012, deferred the decision till such time that this would be examined further.

It is also important to note that the intent of a revenue sharing arrangement in telecommunications is to charge licence fee as a part of the revenue generated by providing telecom services. Payments to IP-I operators represent costs of TSPs, on which a revenue share has already been paid. In the likely event of the imposition of a licence fee on IP-I services, pass through charges between IP-I and mobile operators should be allowed to prevent double taxation that would certainly have a negative impact on the growth of this sector.

The TRAI, in its recent recommendations, issued on the matter of "Definition of AGR for computation of licence fee and spectrum fee" has held that IP I should not be migrated to licensing regime. This comes as a welcome breather to the Industry.

#### 9.2.1.4 Review the Definition of Adjusted Gross Revenue

Currently, TSPs pay a percentage of their revenue as a licence fee. For calculating the amount of licence fee, a TSP has to pay, and the gross revenue of the company is treated as the gross revenue of telecom licence. A direct result of this is that TSPs are asked to pay licence fee on the revenue generated from non-licenced activities. In the past, TDSAT and TRAI have recommended that DoT should not levy licence fee on non-telecom revenue items.

There is a clear and present need to review and amend the definition of gross revenue and adjusted gross revenue, so licence fees are payable only on pure "telecom revenue". Another way to look at this is to consider licence fee as similar to service tax, in the case of which fees paid on input services are allowed to be set off against licence fees payable on output services. Such a policy would render moot the requirement of specific allow abilities of expenditure, as the licence fee would now be payable on gross revenue itself.

## *9.2.2 Simple, Clear and Predictable Regulatory Regime*

### 9.2.2.1 Resolution of Non-compliance Issues

Non-compliance in Indian telecommunications is a particularly tiresome concern, not because of the volume of violations, but rather the practice of levying a standard Rs. 50 Crs. (Rs 500 million) penalty for all violations, big or small. This inadvertently results in increased litigation since TSPs find little recourse but to challenge these penalty notices in a court of law. Media reports at the time of writing this book, spoke to the decision of the Telecom Commission to approve a proposal to rationalize the penalty regime and introduce a slab-based penalty structure starting from 1 Lakh all the way up to Rs 50 crs. Implementing such a policy would aid in the settlement of all violation cases (pending with DoT or under litigation).

### 9.2.2.2 Educational Program on Electro Magnetic Field

India has one of the toughest electromagnetic field (EMF) radiation standards for mobile towers and handsets in the world. The country has adopted strict limits that allow for only one-tenth of the non-ionizing radiation permitted internationally, and set as a standard by the International Commission for Non-Ionizing Radiation Protection (ICNIRP). Radiation can be classified as either ionizing or non-ionizing. As would be expected, ionizing radiation is generally considered to be the harmful kind, though its use in low quantities to treat different kinds of cancer with significant success need to be taken note of. Non-ionizing radiation on the other hand is known to pose little to no threat to humans exposed to it. The microwave ovens we all use today in fact heat our food with microwave radiation. The microwave radiation emanating from mobile towers is quite similar, only propagating at a different frequency range.

As highlighted above, Indian radiation norms are ten times as strict as those set by the International Commission for Non-Ionizing Radiation Protection (ICNIRP). However, local and state agencies continue to prohibit TSPs from putting up towers near residential colonies, schools, hospitals and other areas due to prevailing confusion and/or misguided campaigns on the potential risks of radiation to the human body. This adversely impacts the growth of telecom infrastructure and the quality of services offered. TSPs need government support to counter these misguided campaigns and to organize "educational programs" for state governments, local bodies and the public in general. Recent support from DoT as well as TRAI coming up with the campaign to address the fears in the mind of public regarding radiation from towers is appreciable.

## *9.2.3 Rationalize Regulatory Levies*

### 9.2.3.1 Uniform Licence Fee at 6 %

DoT used to charge licence fee @ 10, 8 and 6 % for different service areas and services. In May 2010, TRAI recommended DoT to progressively reduce the licence fee to a uniform rate of 6 % over a four-year period on a revenue-neutral principle (TRAI 2010). However, in June 2012, when the DoT moved to a uniform licence fee regime, the licence fee was set at 8 %.

### 9.2.3.2 Lower Uniform Spectrum Recurring Charge

Globally, TSPs pay nominal spectrum recurring charges in the range of 0.5–1 % of their revenue for auctioned spectrum. In India, however, TSPs are charged very high recurring spectrum charges, at 5 % of their adjusted gross revenue for auctioned spectrum. In October 2013, TRAI gave its no objection to DoT to keep spectrum recurring charges at 1 % of adjusted gross revenue across all spectrum bands. However, DoT has decided to go for a high spectrum charge of 5 %. This is even higher than the 3–4 % spectrum charge for administratively allocated spectrum in the 800 MHz and 900/1800 MHz bands. TRAI vide its recent recommendations on Spectrum Price and Valuation of Spectrum has again opined for spectrum to be at 3 %.

### 9.2.3.3 Reduce Operators' Contribution to Universal Service Obligation Fund

In April 2002, the government constituted a Universal Service Obligation (USO) Fund, under the requirements of which TSPs have been contributing 5 % of their adjusted gross revenue (which is one of the highest USO levies in the world). Till date, only 32 % of the collected amount has been disbursed to TSPs and more than Rs. 30,000 Crs. lies idle. This fund has essentially lost its relevance, as private TSPs have extended networks to rural areas (with 90 % market share) with negligible support from USO fund, and primarily at their own expense. TRAI has time and again recommended a reduction in the USO levy for those TSPs who expand networks into rural areas. In May 2010, TRAI recommended relaxations in the USO levy by 0.5–2 % depending upon the extent of rural coverage achieved by TSPs. In October 2008, DoT on prior recommendations by the regulator had decided to reduce the USO levy by 2 %, if TSPs cover more than 95 % development blocks. However, the proposal was never implemented because of reasons unknown to the industry.

#### 9.2.3.4 Support the Rising Cost of Security Requirements

Currently, TSPs bear the cost of meeting telecom network-related security requirements. Over the last few years, such costs have increased manifold. An analogy to understand what is being asked of the Indian TSPs would be the following—if security agencies need resources such as vehicles, weapons, they do not ask concerned private companies to provide these resources freely. On the contrary, security agencies want TSPs to bear the entire cost of meeting telecom network-related security requirements. Implementing systems such as "location-based service" in the telecom network is a costly proposition. The Industry has estimated a cost of Rs. 30,000 Crs for only the location-based service technology, which is humongous for TSPs by any standard. The government should seriously consider sharing the cost of meeting the telecom network-related security requirements. Such practices should not be limited to telecommunications alone and should apply to all industries.

### *9.2.4 Facilitate Growth by Creating Conducive Environment*

#### 9.2.4.1 3G Intra-Circle Roaming

In 2010, prior to 3G spectrum auctions, the government specifically permitted intra-circle roaming agreements between an operator holding 3G spectrum and another who did not. However, the government still challenged intra-circle roaming agreements, declaring these as illegal and imposed hefty penalties on TSPs. The matter went to Court. The telecom dispute settlement court, TDSAT, in its judgment dated 29.04.2014, held that intra-circle 3G roaming arrangement did not violate any provisions of the UAS licence and the government may not prohibit operators from carrying out the services mentioned in terms of the agreements. Further, the court held that 3G intra-circle roaming agreements promoted customers interest.

#### 9.2.4.2 Other Litigations

To enhance investors' confidence, in line with the steps taken in 1999 and 2003, the government should engage with Industry to reduce the litigations for telecom sector. Some of contentious issues are given as follows:

**One-Time Spectrum Charge**

Operators have been told to pay a one-time charge for spectrum beyond 4.4 MHz despite the fact that as per the policy, the government decided to take escalating spectrum recurring charge from operators rather than upfront charges. The government also increased the spectrum usage charge and microwave and backbone spectrum charge. In contrast, in its order dated 11.10.2011, the Supreme Court of India held that once a licence is issued under the provisions of the Indian Telegraph Act, the licence becomes a contract between the licensor and the licensee. The contract between two parties cannot be amended unilaterally by one party without the express consent of the other.

**Litigations Related to Demands of Licence Fee and Spectrum Usage Charge Raised by DoT**

TSPs have approached various courts over the issue of the demand note raised by DoT on account of licence fee and spectrum usage charges. Most demands have arisen due to differing interpretations of the definition of gross revenue and adjusted gross revenue. The demands raised by DoT on operators should be reviewed under the purview of new definition of gross revenue and adjusted gross revenue. This will enable operators to withdraw related petitions.

**Extension of the Licence Agreement**

The current validity of mobile licence is for an initial period of 20 years with a provision of further extension of "10 years at a time" along with bundled spectrum. However, DoT rejected the request of operators to extend their licence along with existing spectrum allocations and directed operators to buy spectrum through auctions. The operators certainly seem ready to pay a market-determined price for spectrum, but represent that they need legal assurances of continuity of their business via an extension of licence along with bundled spectrum.

**Maximum Penalty for Minor Violations/Non-compliance**

The DoT has levied maximum penalty for minor and unintended violations. As a result, operators have challenged these penalty notices in various courts. The slab-based penalty regime (as recommended by Telecom Commission) on past cases (pending with DoT and court) should be implemented. It would essentially enable operators to withdraw cases.

## 9.2.5 *Other Critical Issues*

### 9.2.5.1 Right of Way

The Telecom Operators have been assured Right of Way (ROW) under the Indian Telegraph Act of 1885 and as per the Act, the charges that can be levied for granting RoW shall be limited to the restoration of affected areas. However, State governments routinely impose varied, extensive and arbitrary RoW levies which increase the cost of laying a fibre network. Since a large part of the cost of deploying fibre networks is in form of RoW, there is a clear and present need for appropriate and uniform National policies that ensure access to right of way at reasonable prices. In addition, various municipalities and other State agencies have stipulated their own norms across the country for granting permission /access. State governments have started levying exorbitant charges not commensurate with restoration charges for the particular area. Such rates are often arbitrary and range from Rs. 1 lakh/- per km to Rs. 1 crore/per km. The imposition of such exorbitant RoW levies creates additional cost burdens for the telecom service providers and delays the expansion of networks, especially in the rural and remote areas. The government should bring out a uniform RoW policy and mandate all state governments to follow the same. These guidelines should lay down the principle for charging RoW, stipulate timelines for ROW approvals and specify common procedure across the country. These guidelines may also address the issue of the land conversion requirement for laying optical fibre connecting through the forest land for the purpose of establishing a telecom network.

#### 9.2.5.2 Infrastructure Status

In March 2012, the government announced the award of “infrastructure status” to tower companies, but associated benefits such as grid power availability on priority and at favourable rates, tax holidays, preferential debt interest and debt instruments were never afforded to operators. Because of critical national infrastructure, telecom towers are not powered by the national grid. Operators, at great cost to their companies, power their towers with diesel generators and expensive battery backup systems. Even in regions where grid availability is not an issue, telecom towers are not assured 24 × 7 power on priority and have to commit resources to generating power at virtually every telecom tower site in the nation. Policies that unnecessarily inflate cost burdens for operators should be revisited and redesigned to usher in the next telecom growth wave.

## 9.3 Concluding Remarks

The Indian Telecom sector has been a huge success story so far. The sector has witnessed unprecedented growth and in no time has climbed to world’s second largest telecom network in terms of number of subscribers. The credit very deservingly goes to the approach of the regulator and the government who have involved the telecom service providers in the decision-making process. The regime has been built on transparent, fair and just principles with a non-discriminatory approach. As a result, the consumers are enjoying one of the lowest telecom tariffs in the world.

However, there are some glitches, which remain to be addressed. There is a need to mandate a Nationwide Right of Way policy which streamlines the procedures and prescribes a nominal fee for laying of fibres, ducts and rolling out telecom towers. There is need to reduce litigation by introducing clarity in the revenue share principles and the slabwise penal norms in case of licence violation, which should be dependant on the seriousness of violation. The other aspect which needs immediate attention is the rationalization of various fees in terms of spectrum usage charges, licence fee and Universal Service Obligation fund—due to reasons elaborated in this chapter. With the ever-expanding growth in the demand for data services.

## References

DoT (2010) Annual report 2010–11. Available at: http://www.dot.gov.in/sites/default/files/English%20AR%202010-11_1.pdf Accessed 25 Mar 2015

TRAI (2010) Available at: http://www.trai.gov.in/WriteReadData/Recommendation/Documents/FINALRECOMENDATIONS952012.pdf. Accessed 2 Feb 2015

TRAI (2011) Consultation paper on issues related to telecommunications infrastructure policy. Available at: http://www.trai.gov.in/WriteReaddata/ConsultationPaper/Document/5-main.pdf. Accessed 15 Feb 2015

TRAI (2012) Consultation paper on valuation and reserve price of spectrum. Available at: http://www.trai.gov.in/writereaddata/consultationpaper/document/201308140649336549419bharti-final.pdf. Accessed 16 Feb 2015

TRAI (2013) Recommendations on valuation and reserve price of spectrum. Available at: http://www.trai.gov.in/WriteReadData/Recommendation/Documents/Recommendations%2009.09.2013.pdf. Accessed 3 Mar 2015

TRAI (2016) Press release on telecom subscription data as on 31st December, 2015. Available at: http://www.trai.gov.in/WriteReadData/WhatsNew/Documents/Press_Release_No_15.pdf. Accessed 26 Feb 2016

# Chapter 10
# Net Neutrality

A neutral Internet has assumed great importance in the modern public policy discourse and is the focus of a highly emotional debate in many nations. At the heart of the issue lies the concern that bottleneck control of the retail market would allow Internet service providers to discriminate against edge providers by either blocking or slowing down access to edge services over their networks. It is also claimed that this discrimination would ultimately cause irreparable harm to the Internet and somehow bring an end to this instrument of social change. It is however critical for all involved to understand how the Internet has evolved since its genesis and realizes that the issue is essentially much larger, and merits an in-depth analysis of the underlying economics and the administration of other similar information networks.

Proponents of net neutrality argue that the Internet and telecommunications service providers have every economic incentive to act as gatekeepers and that absent strict regulation, these SPs would certainly employ non-neutral business models to harm the Internet economy. The strictest interpretation of NN therefore calls for the application of a zero price rule on an existing peering market; that is, all content providers must be provided non-discriminatory access to all customers of all ISPs/TSPs. Currently, this peering market is subject to forces of competition and free market dynamics and exhibits the kind of characteristics observed in healthy industries. While on the face of it, a zero price rule may seem to be appropriate, and even socially desirable, there is little practical insight into what effect such a rule may have on the development of the Internet—especially when history and economics both suggest that free market structures have worked so far and do not demonstrate the need for strict regulation.

The following sections highlight some of the critical issues associated with NN, along with a historical context within which future debates must occur. Certain fundamental economic and technical conditions led to the development of an important public network, and fair access to this network must be preserved. However, misplaced mandates, such as the imposition of a zero price rule, would certainly have a chilling effect on further investment in broadband networks, which would not be ideal for any stakeholder in the Internet value chain.

© Springer India 2016

M.K. Medudula et al., *Telecom Management in Emerging Economies*,
DOI 10.1007/978-81-322-2749-6_10

## 10.1 Internet History

In 1962, the Advanced Research Projects Agency (ARPA) of the US Department of Defense (DoD) laid the groundwork for ARPANET, or what we today know and refer to as the "Internet". ARPANET was to be the first network to use Internet protocol, and the very first message over the network had to travel over 550 km from the University of California, Los Angeles to the Stanford Research Institute. Specifically, ARPANET has to its credit the accolade of the development of protocols for internetworking, a concept that was critical for the creation of the modern Internet. This set of protocols allowed multiple networks to be interconnected to create what was referred to in some circles as the network of networks.

At the time, the world's computers were primitive, exorbitantly expensive and with magnetic memory for barely a few thousand words. ARPANET connected such devices through protocols based on a best-effort principle; that is, the packets arriving at a node would be handled or transmitted towards their destination on a first-in–first-out (FIFO) basis. Information transmitted from these computers over ARPANET was generally latency insensitive with little assured quality of services in terms of timely delivery. The transmission and receipt of messages were driven solely by the best-effort principle.

The Internet of today, however, is a much larger ecosystem that is capable of transmitting myriad forms of information, some of which are extremely latency sensitive, i.e., require more reliable connections than what simple best-effort architectures are capable of providing. A practical example includes voice-over Internet protocol, in which latency losses would be far more noticeable (unreliable voice connection) than in the case of email.

## 10.2 Genesis of NN

NN is essentially dated common carrier regulation applied in a modern context. Anyone who has studied net neutrality in even low to moderate detail, would observe eerily similar characteristics with the following 120-year-old regulation

> [I]t shall be unlawful for any common carrier subject to the provisions of this act to make or give any undue or unreasonable preference or advantage to any particular person, company, firm, corporation, or locality, or any particular description of traffic, in any respect whatsoever, or to subject any particular person, company, firm, corporation, or locality, or any particular description of traffic, to any undue or unreasonable prejudice or disadvantage in any respect whatsoever (US federal Act 1887).

The above regulation, while quite similar in its approach and ideology to the current discourse over net neutrality, actually refers to US railways, which were exposed to common carrier back in 1887. There are important lessons to be derived from the historical use of this regulation.

Even under its imposition, US railroads continued to price discriminate, filing rates to charge different prices for transporting different commodities of the same weight. An economically rational argument can be used to support such discrimination; that is, the cost of transporting 1 kg of cotton is far lower than the cost of transporting 1 kg of radioactive material. As a result of the regulation, railroad tariffs in the USA grew larger and more complex each decade and also led to the emergence of highly discriminatory and dysfunctional regional transport cartels. In hindsight, antitrust or competition law that penalized undesirable behaviour would have been a far better tool to check the discrimination in this market (Owen 2007).

Many, such as Crowcroft (2007), have also opined that regulators who seek to impose rigid or static definitions of net neutrality would be well-advised to heed the lessons of the Internet history, and recognized that a strait-jacketed approach is hardly the right strategy. Hahn and Wallsten (2006) in their report on the economics of net neutrality demonstrate that mandating net neutrality would be likely to reduce economic welfare. Instead, governments should focus on creating competition in the broadband market by liberalizing more spectrum and reducing entry barriers created by certain local regulations. In cases where a broadband provider can exercise market power, the government should essentially use its antitrust or anti-competitive enforcement authority to police discriminatory behaviour (Wu 2003).

Net neutrality sadly has no one consistent definition. Defined first in 2003 by Colombia Law School Professor Wu (2003), the principle has today taken on different hues in different countries. At a fundamental level, NN seeks to promote a "free-and-open" Internet by restricting ISPs from acting in undesirable and especially anti-competitive ways. Simply put, net neutrality refers to the principle of neutral, non-discriminatory network access to all providers of content; that is, one agent offering a set of services shall not be treated differently (in terms of access to network, as well as speed with which its data is transmitted) than another agent offering services over the Internet. The literature classifies NN into strict and light sets of rules. Generally, strict NN prohibits most network management—e.g. "*Net Neutrality prohibits Internet Service providers from speeding up, slowing down or blocking internet traffic based on its source, ownership or destination*". Light rules however allow for some flexibility—e.g. *FCCs open Internet order* (2010) *with transparency*, *No blocking* and *No* ***Unreasonable*** *Discrimination* as the central tenets (FCC 2010).

## 10.3 Varying Approaches—USA Versus EU

In April, 2014, the European Parliament voted in favour of restricting ISPs ability to charge data hungry services for faster network access. Operators have voiced their concerns, especially with respect to network management. While the law still needs to be approved by Europe's council of Ministers, it would prohibit mobile networks and broadband providers from blocking services offered by OTT players. Slovenia and the Netherlands are the only two countries that currently enshrine the principle in law, where cable and telecom operators associations have taken official positions on the subject and have on gone on record to state the following—"Whilst we support an open Internet, a set of misconceptions about our industry, together with a rushed legislative process and a lack of technical analysis, risk transforming the Connected Continent Regulation into an anti-innovation and anti-consumer choice legislation". **Member states that have enacted legislation, such as The Netherlands and Slovenia, have adopted strict interpretations of net neutrality that forbid pricing flexibility as well as a wide array of network management opportunities**.

In striking contrast, the Federal Communications Commission in the USA up till now prescribed light regulations that offered a certain level of flexibility to network providers. The comprehensive NN rules (open Internet order) by the FCC were a light set of rules generally favoured by service providers in their submissions to the public consultation in 2014. Another difference between how the US and EU approach net neutrality stems from the treatment of wireless networks. The USA had up to this point excluded wireless Internet from certain aspects of NN regulation, with the bulk of regulations extending to fixed Internet access, primarily on the premise that sufficient competition in the wireless markets was adequate to address discrimination-related concerns. At the same time, the EU has treated fixed and wireless Internet on par and regulated them under similar terms and conditions. In the vote held on 27 Feb 2015, the FCC voted on the reclassification of Internet from an "information service" to a "telecommunications service", exposing it Title II of their Telecommunications Act, 1996. The proposal passed the vote with a 3–2 vote right down party lines—democrats voted for the proposal and republicans against. Title II of this act will now empower the FCC with the statutory authority it would need to regulate Internet services—this authority was absent at the time the FCC released the open Internet order in 2010, which was the premise for the rules to be struck down by the Supreme Court. The final proposal or net neutrality framework has yet to be released by the FCC and is expected to be released by April 2015.

### *10.3.1 Prioritization*

Prioritization of traffic based on source or kind of content has been repeatedly cited by proponents of net neutrality as a paramount evil that Internet service providers, if left unchecked, would employ entirely to their personal advantage and to act in anti-competitive ways with complete impunity. Proponents claim that if network providers/ISPs are free to prioritize traffic based on its source or description, they would use their bottleneck last mile access monopoly to favour content providers/edge companies who pay for the priority lane, and leave others who do not, in a perpetual slow-lane. The end result, according to supporters of NN, would be that content providers who pay for the priority lane would be able to offer a superior quality of service to end consumers, while run of the mill Internet start-ups that lack the financial appetite to purchase priority access would be rendered uncompetitive. As a result, Internet activist groups generally favour strict neutrality regulations that impose a complete ban on all prioritization of traffic over the Internet. While supporters of net neutrality would claim prioritization to be detrimental to the development of the Internet, and to innovation at the edges of the network, it is important to take note of evidence to the contrary, the history of the commercial Internet and possible roadmaps for a future public network that is orders of magnitude more sophisticated than today's best-effort Internet.

Prioritization of or differentiation between different kinds of traffic is not an ISP/TSP invented business model, but rather a concept that has been studied extensively by the very experts who drafted the standards for the development and commercialization of the public Internet.

The nexus of prioritization debates is rooted in how the Internet functions, especially with respect to its complete lack of assured quality of services. The current best-effort Internet provides what is sometimes referred to as a "send and pray" (Kumar et al. 1998) service in which packets arriving at a network node are forwarded towards their destination in a FIFO manner, and timely delivery is in no way guaranteed. It was this inability of the Internet to provide assured QoS that prompted the need for and debate surrounding scalable differentiated access services.

Historically, the need for prioritization of data packets on the Internet was recognized and addressed in communications standards such as TCP/IP. Prepared for Defense Advanced Research Project Agency (DARPA), the original TCP/IP standard (RFC791) from 1981 "*treat[ed] high precedence traffic as more important than other traffic*" and defined informational flags for prioritization of packets travelling on TCP/IP networks (DARPA 1981). This standards document was designed to automate policies for minimizing delays in transmission, maximizing throughput and maximizing reliability. The RFC791 standards were further expanded on by the Internet Engineering Task Force (IETF) standards documents [RFC2475 (Blake et al. 1998) and RFC2474 (Nichols et al. 1998)] published in 1998, which elaborated on the following—"*Differentiated services enhancements to the Internet protocol are intended to enable scalable service discrimination in the Internet without the need for per-flow state and signaling at every hop. A variety of services may be built from a small, well-defined set of building blocks which are deployed in network nodes. The services may be either* ***end-to-end or intra-domain****; they include* ***both those that can satisfy quantitative performance requirements (e.g., peak bandwidth) and those based on relative performance (e.g., "class" differentiation)***".

Concerns over how ISPs should be forbidden from prioritizing traffic can be traced back to the mid-1980s. Saltzer, Reed and Clarke, in their paper on "End-to-End Arguments in System Design" (Saltzer et al. 1984), reasoned for the very first time that the primary function of networks was to pass raw data from source to destination without inquiring as to that data's actual content. Essentially, the authors argued that networks should be "Dumb", and only servers and workstations at the edge of the network should be capable of performing intelligent functions. Although proponents of NN argue that networks were intended to be "Dumb", the specifications for communication over the Internet (TCP/IP), even after they were revisited by separate impartial parties, always included some form of prioritization. The "Smart" traffic filtering and prioritization systems specified under TCP/IP standards have long predated the "Dumb" design suggestions advocated by Saltzer et al. (Hass 2007) and others who have followed with that line of reasoning (Lee and Wu 2009).

Prioritization of data packets may not be as drastic a proposition as net neutrality proponents would make it out to be. Consider the fact that consumers can today purchase network routers, and using built in route filtering capabilities, prioritize the forwarding and delivery of certain favoured data packets over other unfavoured ones. Practically, these capabilities allow users to take control of how information flows over their networks and can be used, for example, to share wireless connectivity with a neighbour without worrying about degraded performance. This would be achieved by prioritizing own packets over those that serve outsiders. In essence, prioritization brings higher orders of efficiency into networks, and if such intelligent services could be deployed (in addition to what is already functioning) at the core of the network, we would observe increased usage across different kinds of Internet services as well as at an aggregate level.

Such prioritization would also be critical for the development of new specialized services such as driverless cars. Imagine a not so distant future with driverless public and private transit systems that allow for the automation of street lights, traffic management and vehicular control. Such systems will only be able to thrive if they have access to special highly reliable network access that extends beyond what we today refer to as the "best-effort" Internet.

## 10.4 Impact of NN

To understand the impact of net neutrality, one need not look any further than the experiences of nations that have enacted this principle in legislation. The Netherlands was the first European nation to enforce legislation on net neutrality in January 2012, which was consequently followed by an increase in data prices by operators. In 2011, customers of KPN, the largest mobile operator in The Netherlands, paid Euro 37.50 for 200 calls/SMS and 1 GB of data, whereas the same amount in 2013, one year after the imposition of the net neutrality rules, gave customers unlimited voice and SMS, but only half the amount of data (Layton 2013). In January 2015, Vodafone and KPN were both penalized for violations of net neutrality, with Vodafone having been found guilty of zero rating the HBO Go application in certain packages (Telegeography 2015) and KPN for blocking access to certain VoIP services over its free Wi-fi network. Both acts were determined to be against the principles of net neutrality and provide on-the-ground evidence of the true socio-economic impact of pre-emptive neutrality regulation.

Zero rating is the principle of providing free Internet access to certain applications and is essentially not a net neutrality issue since access to all content and applications remains open for all consumers. The principle is in fact no more than a packaging of services for targeted groups of customers. It is not a net neutrality issue since access to all content/applications remains open. Such arrangements increase social welfare by transferring the cost of Internet access from consumers to content providers. If a content provider deems its revenues to be substantial enough to subsidize access to its services by engaging in distribution arrangements with last mile access providers, then it should be allowed to do so. Pre-emptive or ex-post neutrality regulation should not come in the way of what can reasonably be defined as an evolution in service provisioning—that is, we are today capable of entering into complex commercial agreements with the goal to decrease retail prices and increase the usage of services. In the case of Vodafone, which was fined Euro 200,000 for zero rating, establishing a case for discrimination by the operator is untenable at best. Its users were in fact afforded access to a service for free, and at an aggregate level, the bundling generated additional welfare for consumers. Fining an operator for zero rating will effectively discourage it from providing free Internet access to consumers.

On the other hand, KPN's act of blocking certain VoIP services over its free Wi-Fi network earned it a fine of Euro 250,000. KPN provides free Wi-fi to its existing broadband customers with a Wi-fi network that covers entire cities. The company provides this service not out of a compulsion, but rather as a value addition which it should be allowed to offer in the manner it sees fit. Net neutrality was intended to protect the free-and-open Internet, but ironically, with penalties such as in the case of KPN, effectively discouraged another operator from offering free Internet to the consuming public.

The unintended consequences of net neutrality legislation can be observed in other nations as well. On 24th January 2015, the Slovenian telecommunications regulator fined Telekom Slovenije and Si.Mobil for zero rating the music streaming service "Deezer" and cloud storage service "Hanger Mapa", respectively (Mobileworldlive 2015). Deezer and Hanger Mapa are much smaller than rivals Spotify and Dropbox and, without the ability to enter into distribution arrangements with service providers, would find it challenging to take on established brands.

Net neutrality at its most fundamental level seeks to protect and promote a free-and-open Internet. In the above cases, however, unsubstantiated fears over how zero rating and blocking of certain Internet applications over free Wi-Fi networks would harm innovation on the Internet effectively caused service providers to stop providing free Internet access to consumers. Neutrality regulation, early origins of which can be traced back to 125-year-old common carrier law, can hardly be described as a time-tested approach. Mature structures such as the Internet require mature frameworks that certainly do not include dated legal frameworks that have little modern relevance and a questionable track record (Owen 2007).

### 10.4.1 Two-Tiered Markets

To fully appreciate the scope and impact of net neutrality as an enforceable law requires a clear understanding of how the Internet has evolved since its inception. The first Internet, or Internetwork, as it was referred to at that point in time, connected the networks of the University of California, Los Angeles, and the Stanford Research Institute. In the time since, many hundreds of thousands of networks across the world have been interconnected with what are known as IP transit/peering arrangements. Traditionally, such arrangements were almost entirely between two Internet service providers, each with a desire to exchange traffic with the other, and to connect to the World Wide Web. Take for instance two networks that need to be interconnected for users of each to access the content on the other. If the amount of traffic exchanged over the two networks is identical, then we have what is referred to as a cost neutral peering arrangement, i.e. free of any commercial considerations. However, if the amount of traffic that network A wishes to exchange with network B exceeds the amounts offered by B, then A must pay B on mutually negotiated commercial terms. This business model has evolved to include content providers such as Netflix as yet another stakeholder. Given the large amounts of traffic generated by some content providers, none of whom share the responsibility of creating infrastructure that would eventually carry information over the Internet, these content providers today routinely enter into peering arrangements in proportion to the costs incurred in the transmission of said content. It is important to note that such arrangements are hard to standardize, or reduce to a specific set of inputs, and as such should not be regulated. Leaving such arrangements to the free market would be a far more tenable proposition than regulating a complex structure, which may well do more harm than good.

Additionally, much research on investments in two-sided markets, such as Njoroge et al. (2013), reveal that ISPs' quality investment levels are driven by the trade-off they make between softening price competition on the consumer side and increasing revenues extracted from content providers (CPs). Essentially, investments are determined to be higher in cases where content providers pay for the bandwidth. Specifically, in the non-neutral regime, because it is easier to extract surplus through appropriate CP pricing, ISPs' investment levels are shown to be higher. Because CPs' quality is enhanced by ISPs' quality, their research suggests that larger investment levels ultimately lead to increases in CPs' profits. Similarly, consumer surplus increases as well. Overall, under the assumptions of their model, a thoroughly peer-reviewed game theoretic approach, social welfare is observed to be larger in non-neutral regimes.

Net neutrality proponents have consistently claimed that failure to enshrine the principle in law will harm innovation at the edge of the Internet, i.e. at the consumer level. Research by scholars such as Jamison and Hauge (2008) provides evidence to the contrary—that when a network provider optimally charges for and provides premium transmission for content providers, innovation is stimulated on the edges of the network and smaller content providers benefit more than larger content providers. Furthermore, the network provider increases its investment in network capacity when it offers premium transmission **without degrading service for content providers that do not purchase the premium service**. Also, the overall number of network subscribers increases when such "non-neutral" arrangements are permitted (Jamison and Hauge 2008).

Weisman and Kulick (2010) in their paper on "Price Discrimination, Two-Sided Markets and Net Neutrality Regulation" show that price discrimination is presumptively welfare-enhancing and that it is frequently a response to competitive market forces rather than the absence of such forces. They also demonstrate that the merits of price discrimination are likely enhanced in a two-sided markets frameworks, essentially because the platform provider must use prices to solve the "chicken-and-egg" problem—both sides of the market must be brought on board under conditions in which the relative valuations placed on the transaction can vary markedly across the two sides of the market. They conclude with the insight that price discrimination is necessary to unleash the full potential of broadband markets and access tiering, in which broadband providers market different levels of service quality to content providers is an example of differential pricing rather than discriminatory pricing. Prohibitions on such practices would likely serve to reduce consumer welfare, suppress competition and discourage investment in network infrastructure (Weisman and Kulick 2010).

The World Wide Web has evolved to its current state using the above principle, which has so far exhibited no signs of potentially breaking or harming the Internet. A peering arrangement lay at the heart of the infamous Comcast–Netflix dispute that placed net neutrality concerns at the top of the public policy agenda in many nations. While much is publicly professed about the arrangement, there is little that speaks of the arrangement between Netflix and Cogent, the peering provider who exchanged Netflix traffic with Comcast. Cogent has been the subject of many lawsuits related to un-negotiated amounts of traffic dumped on the networks of others such as Comcast. Cogent's failure to compensate Comcast for this imbalance was the reason Netflix had to personally engage with Comcast. Comcast offers services to its consumers with certain assured quality of services, and the kind of traffic Netflix can today boast of would choke even the most sophisticated networks, damaging the experience of the service for all subscribers. Economically, there is no justification for a content provider to keep increasing the traffic it exchanges with a network, without due consideration to the underlying economics that have so far made the Internet work as it does.

Similarly placed networks such as broadcast television and the PSTN provide further clues into what would make for appropriate Internet economics. Broadcast television is typically characterized by free-to-air (FTA) and paid channels. FTA channels are financed through advertising revenue, while paid channels are typically offered through a subscription-driven model. The distributors of broadcast television signals have always enjoyed the flexibility to create packages, bundling together FTA and paid channels, and the principle has historically been responsible for bringing down prices. Flexible pricing has allowed distributors to reach out to targeted groups of customers with tailor made solutions. There is no reason for a consumer who wishes to subscribe to just one set of channels to have to pay for every channel on the network. The inability to freely price broadcast signals, which would have made broadcast television a "neutral" network, would only serve to ensure that it would be a luxury few could afford.

The PSTN, or public switched telephone network, is in fact the oldest most neutral network one could study. The International Telecommunications Union has regulated this network for years. The network is characterized by numbering schemes and mandatory interconnection between countries, all to ensure that calls between any two parties connected to this global network are completed. Still, users of PSTN have the freedom to subscribe for tiers of services such tolled quality, priority connections for uses such as emergency response and nailed-up connections/leased lines. Operators also enjoy the freedom to package and price their services for targeted groups of customers. These conditions coexist with neutrality and do not prevent service providers or consumers from creating or choosing unique packages to suit their needs. There is no reason for this to not work for the Internet.

## 10.5 Concluding Remarks

In an era where services/applications over the Internet are substituting public telephony and to a large extent even broadcasting, it is becoming increasingly important to take note of what has so far made the latter platforms successful in their respective spaces, and to apply the principles that made them affordable for the consuming public.

The modern net neutrality agenda promotes a one size fits all approach that ignores the economics of the Internet access. This is apparent in the case of countries where net neutrality legislation exists, and because of it, operators have been discouraged from offering free Internet, a result that seems at odds with the goals and intent of the principle. Strict net neutrality, which would ensure that interconnection between stakeholders/networks is predicated on similar speeds, similar traffic and similar QoS, would in a sense lead to the militarization of the Internet and lead to the end of the democracy that has been fundamental to the development of the modern Internet. At the losing end of the battle would be consumer welfare, and as demonstrated by many scholars such as Becker et al. (2010), the interrelationships in the current internet ecosystem are more complex than claimed by net neutrality proponents and do not provide a compelling rationale for regulation.

## References

Becker GS, Carlton DW, Sider HS (2010) Net neutrality and consumer welfare. J Compet Law Econ 6(3):497–519

Crowcroft J (2007) Net neutrality: the technical side of the debate—a white paper. Int J Commun 567–579

FCC (2010) Open internet order. Available at: https://apps.fcc.gov/edocs_public/attachmatch/FCC-10-201A1.pdf. Accessed 8 Jul 2014

Hahn R, Wallsten S (2006) The economics of net neutrality. AEI-Brookings Joint Center for Regulatory Studies

Hass DA (2007) The never-was-neutral net and why informed end users can end the net neutrality debates. Berkeley Technol Law J 22(4):1565–1635

Information Sciences Institute (1981) RFC 791: DARPA internet program protocol specification 11. In: Postel J (ed) Available at: https://tools.ietf.org/html/rfc791

Jamison MA, Hauge JA (2008) Getting what you pay for: analyzing the net neutrality debate

Kathleen Nichols et al, IEFT Network Working Group, Request for Comments 2474: Definition of the Differentiated Services Field (DS field) In the IPv4 and IPv6 Headers (1998) Available at https://www.ietf.org/rfc/rfc2474.txt

Kumar VP, Laksman TV, Stiliadis D (1998) Beyond best effort: router architectures for the differentiated services of tomorrow's internet. IEEE Commun Mag, 152–164

Layton R (2013) Net neutrality in the Netherlands: Dutch solution or Dutch disease? In Proceedings of 24th European regional conference of the international telecommunication society, Florence, Italy, October 20–23, 2013

Lee RS, Wu T (2009) Subsidizing creativity through network design: zero-pricing and net neutrality. J Econ Perspect 23(3):61–76

News article found at https://www.telegeography.com/products/commsupdate/articles/2015/01/27/acm-fines-kpn-vodafone-for-net-neutrality-violations/

News article found at http://www.mobileworldlive.com/mobile-operators-slovenia-fall-foul-net-neutrality-rules

Njoroge P, Ozdaglar A, Stier-Moses NE, Weintraub GY (2013) Investment in two-sided markets and the net neutrality debate. Review of Network Economics 12(4):355–402

Owen BM (2007) Antecedents to net neutrality. Regulation 30(3):14–17

Saltzer JH et al (1984) End-to-end arguments in system design. ACM Trans Comput Syst 2:277. Available at: http://web.mit.edu/saltzer/www/publications/endtoend/endtoend.pdf

Section three of the US federal Act to Regulate Commerce (February 4, 1887, c. 104, 24 Stat. 379, 380)

Steven Blake et al, IETF Network Working Group, Request for Comments 2475: An Architecture for Differentiated Services (1998) [hereinafter RFC2475]. Available at https://www.ietf.org/rfc/rfc2475.txt

Weisman DL, Kulick RB (2010) Price discrimination, two-sided markets and net neutrality regulation. Tulane J Technol Intellect Prop 13:81

Wu Tim (2003) Network neutrality, broadband discrimination. J Telecommun High Technol Law 2:79–141

# Chapter 11
# Telecom Networks and Innovation

Telecom Industry is buzzing with huge growth of mobile users not only because of voice telephony but with increased pace of adoption of social media applications such as Twitter, Skype, Facebook, YouTube and WhatsApp.

People communication has changed from traditional two-way voice calls to sharing more things with each other over Internet. It is relevant for all segments, i.e., for individual or for business needs. Social media has changed the way people are connecting with each other. Video has become more pervasive and is the new way of engagement. Uploading pictures on social media, tweeting the updates and expressing likes/dislikes on Facebook have become a normal way of communication across the generations/societies across the globe.

Social media has grown beyond the individual space to public domain. Social media campaigns have started playing a catalyst role in building the future of nations. It is evident from the support extended to Malala Yousafzai of Pakistan, revolutions against dictatorship in Syria, Egypt and Tunisia and 2014 general elections in India.

All this is resulting into explosion of data on the Internet (the network of networks). New players are emerging and taking over the space staring from Google to WhatsApp, Snapchat and many more. It offers a challenge to the traditional operators of staying relevant on one side and tremendous opportunity to be the catalyst of change on the other. This chapter explains the challenges and opportunities for a telecom operator and is organized into several parts such as the changing paradigm, existing business model of a traditional Telco and opportunity landscape.

---

Contribution:
Mr. Divya Sethi
(Research Scholar—IIT Delhi)

© Springer India 2016

M.K. Medudula et al., *Telecom Management in Emerging Economies*,
DOI 10.1007/978-81-322-2749-6_11

## 11.1 Changing Paradigm of a Telecom Player

Data applications are replacing the traditional voice and messaging stronghold of a traditional telecom player. Reduction in cost of computing processor power, storage and bandwidth is driving in the new trends (Birudavolu and Nag 2011) such as follows: (a) end-user mobility (b) M2M (machine-to-machine) communications (c) cloud services (d) telecom mobility (e) social networking and (f) convergence.

More than 5 billion people are having mobile phones globally. 3G subscriber base has also crossed 1 billion mark a couple of years ago. It clearly establishes that the world is highly interconnected and mobile users are growing tremendously.

However, ARPU of Indian Telcos has been dropping as investigated by Wall Street Journal in 2011.

In summary, it is resulting in a paradigm shift for telecom players in individual and business segments equally:

**In Consumer Space**:

(a) Telcos will have to manage ocean of devices across millions of businesses and billions of lives—24 billion connected devices by 2020 are projected by GSMA (2012).
(b) Networks need to handle bandwidth floods as annual internet bandwidth will cross the zettabyte threshold in 2015 and will reach 1.6 zettabyte/year by 2018 with rapid increase in per capita Internet consumption—Source: Cisco VNI Research (Cisco 2015).
(c) Increasing adoption of on-demand high-definition TV over Internet on big (LCD/LED) screens shall further fuel the Internet demand. Therefore, traditional broadcasting models are being replaced by unicast models on Internet, while the revenue streams and business models are being developed.

And in **Business Segment**:

(d) Business needs are evolving around:

    i. High-speed, i.e., 40G/100G, interfaces to manage growing IP traffic (CAGR @23 %)—Cisco VNI, 2012.
    ii. 3× growth in mobile-based business applications—Source: Forrester Survey on North American Enterprises, 2012.
    iii. 50 % growth in employee-owned devices in Asia—Source: Cisco IBSG, 2012.
    iv. Desktop video conference (CAGR @43 %) in B2B space to take over room-based video conferencing (CAGR @16 %) by 2016—Source: Cisco VNI, 2012.

Various researches clearly indicate that existing business models of telecom player will have to go for a sea change to manage falling top-line and bottom-line pressures. It may result into consolidation (mergers and acquisitions) of businesses, but the success lies in services innovation. Operators have to abandon the “walled garden” model and embrace "open innovation and open business models" as it provides, an excellent leveraging power for telecom services (Raivio et al. 2011).

Adopting an open business model might call for varied degree of changes in Telco's eco-system, and therefore, it might take some time, but in the meanwhile, Telcos are exploring its significant asset: telecom networks, for developing new services.

## 11.2 Existing Business Models of a Typical Telecom Player

Telecom players invest heavily in terms of effort and money in developing their telecom networks. As a next step, products and services are developed by leveraging the telecom networks for consumers and business. Operators share their telecom infra with each other also. These products are classified under Telco products.

Telecom networks can be broadly classified in the following categories:

(i) Satellite networks,
(ii) Terrestrial networks,
(iii) Mobile networks,
(iv) Radio/microwave networks and
(v) Undersea/submarine networks.

A brief description of these networks and product/service offerings for various user categories is presented in the following section.

### *11.2.1 Satellite Networks*

There are broadly two types of satellite networks: two-way satellite networks called as VSAT networks and one-way satellite networks for TV broadcasting (Teleport and DTH networks):

(a) **VSAT Networks**: Very small aperture terminal (VSAT) networks provide connectivity for Internet to consumers and businesses. These networks operate typically in XC/C, KU, or KA bands in a STAR/TDMA or SCPC topology. A typical TDMA VSAT network (most popular version) consists of the following three network elements:
**HUB or Master Earth Station**: VSAT hub is the heart of a VSAT network as it controls, operates and manages all the VSATs on its networks centrally. It uses multiple frequencies for uplinking and downlinking of carriers to a satellite situated in geostationary orbit and eventually to a VSAT terminal. It consists of a large antenna, typically of 9.1 Mt, power amplifiers and other

electronics. Earth station is generally connected to an Internet gateway or a data centre (co-located at hub or at a customer location) for access to Internet and business applications for its users. A typical telecom operator invests in an earth station for its operations and deploys VSATs at the customer location for establishing the connectivity.

**Satellite**: A satellite is typically a frequency amplifier located around 36,000 ft above the ground in a geostationary orbit. Geostationary orbit is an orbit where the relative movement of the satellite to the earth is negligent. A satellite has multiple transponders with different frequencies for accepting and releasing signals from a single/multiple earth stations and VSATs. A satellite receives uplinks from one or more earth station on specific frequencies, amplifies the same and downlinks those to the VSATs on identified frequency slots. It does a reverse job on the signals uplinked by VSATs for the respective earth stations. Each satellite covers geography by virtue of its look-up angle and transmission power and is called as satellite footprint. It also has a typical power rating to handle the number of uplinks and downlinks in the said footprint and is measured in DB. A typical VSAT network is described in Fig. 11.1.

**VSATs**: VSATs are the CPE which are installed at the end-user location for establishing end-to-end connectivity between a hub and the remote location. It complements the hub and satellite in terms of band of operations and offers connectivity to the users for Internet or business applications or both. It gets installed in the satellite footprint alike to hub. It is capable of receiving the hub uplink called as out route and is able to uplink for hub called as in route. A typical Ku-band VSAT will have an antenna size varying from 0.9 to 1.2 mt depending upon its location in the satellite footprint and the link speed.

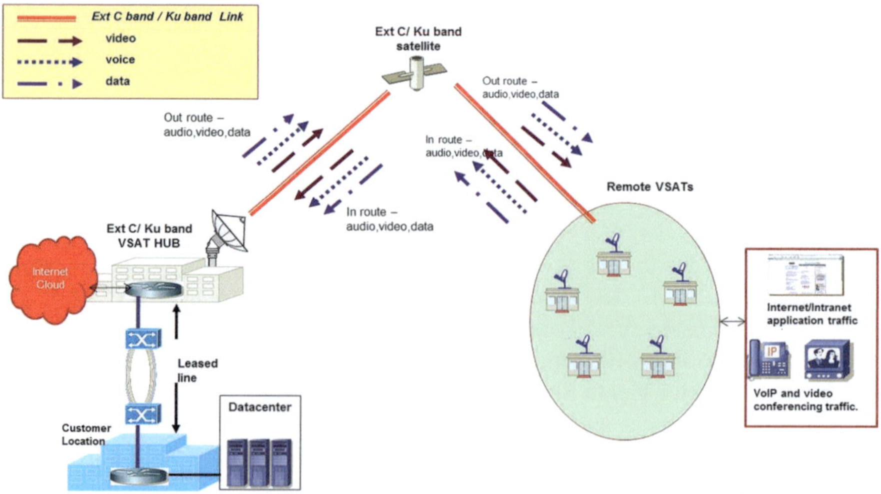


**Fig. 11.1** A typical VSAT network (author)

Combination of VSAT RF power and antenna size is derived through a scientific study called as link engineering. It factors in hub and satellite parameters also.

**Applications**: VSAT networks are suitable for carrying voice, data and video traffics at different speeds.

**Segment**: Individual consumers and business deploy VSATs for Internet access at remote and far-flung locations. A typical, business use case example is banking ATM network. The SCPC variant of VSAT networks is used for point-to-point high-capacity backhaul links for extending terrestrial networks for multiple reasons, e.g., data centre connectivity, redundancy on alternate medium and mobile network extension to difficult terrain.

(b) **Teleport Networks**: Many operators invest in setting up a teleport for uplinking the TV channels to a cable operator. It is called as head end and distributes the feed to its consumers over a cable network. When the transmission is meant for consumers directly, then it is called as a DTH network. Teleport networks have following three key network elements:

**Teleport HUB**: Alike to VSAT hub station, it consists of uplinking electronics only, as there is no need of two-way communication. It is connected to the live feeds from the TV channels and typically has the capability for play-out and content editions. It again consists of a large antenna oriented towards a satellite with power amplifiers and frequency modulators, etc., for uplinking the channels.

**Satellite**: Alike to VSAT networks, there is a satellite located in the geostationary orbit for distributing the uplink from a teleport to the cable head ends in its footprint.

**Head end**: Cable head end receives the channels meant for itself on a specific frequency for further distribution to its users on cable.

**Applications**: Video (TV channels) carriage for cable operators.

**Segment**: Business for teleport and DTH for consumers.

### *11.2.2 Terrestrial Networks*

Terrestrial networks are deployed by the telecom operators for offering different types of services, e.g., voice, data (Internet) and video to its users. These networks are deployed with a huge investment in terms of money, effort and time. A typical terrestrial network is deployed with a mix of copper (for access) and fibre (for core). However, these days, operators are deploying fibre even for access networks. In terms of classification, a terrestrial network can be divided in three subcategories as explained in the following section:

(a) **Access Network**: Access networks are deployed on copper/fibre for extending connectivity to the end-user at their homes and offices. Access network is also called as last-mile network. It follows through a route of MSU to RSU to pillar to subpillar to distribution box at a distribution point (DP). A twisted copper

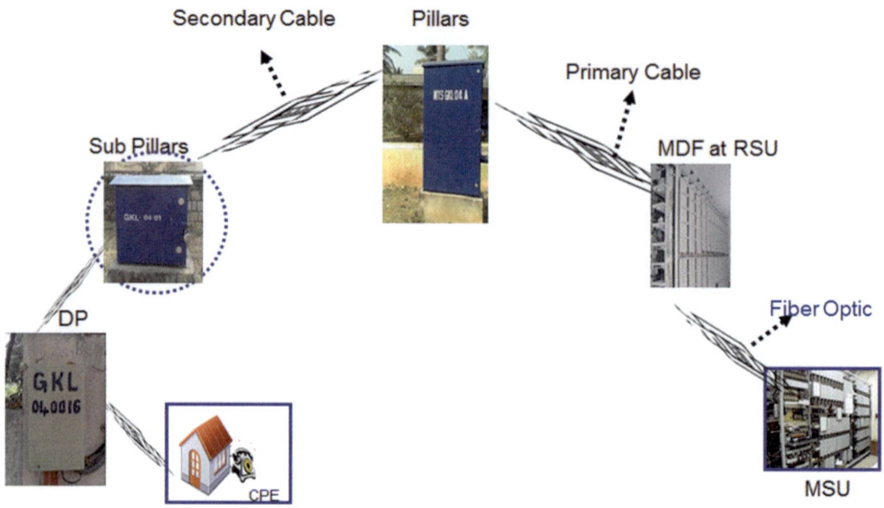


**Fig. 11.2** Access network elements (author)

pair is pulled from the nearest DP to the user location for extending telecom services as shown in Fig. 11.2.

However, with drop in cost of fibre and to address the high-speed data connectivity demands of consumers, access networks are now deployed on optical fibre to connect the homes or offices. It is called fibre to the home (FTTH) concept also. Optical line termination equipment (OLTE) replaces the traditional modem at user end. FTTH enables high speed and deeper reach for access networks for multiple applications.

(b) **Aggregation Networks**: Various access networks get aggregated at different points in an area at relevant concentration points which then get extended to a core. Aggregation networks are deployed on fibre.

(c) **Core Networks**: Core network of a Telco is the core footprint of its network spread across a geography or a country. It is built on high-capacity optical fibre cables pulled in cable ducts spreading across multiple hundred/thousand kilometres in the form of multiple rings. A Telco spends heavily in spreading its core network to different cities or places of its business interest.

#### 11.2.2.1 Technology of Terrestrial Networks

Traditional telecom networks are deployed using electrical topology. SDH technology and DWDM technology are used to create multiple network rings for covering a typical geography. There is a migration to optical transmission using OTN technology platforms for creating additional capacities, high-speed interfaces and for building resilience in the terrestrial networks. Additionally, OTN platform

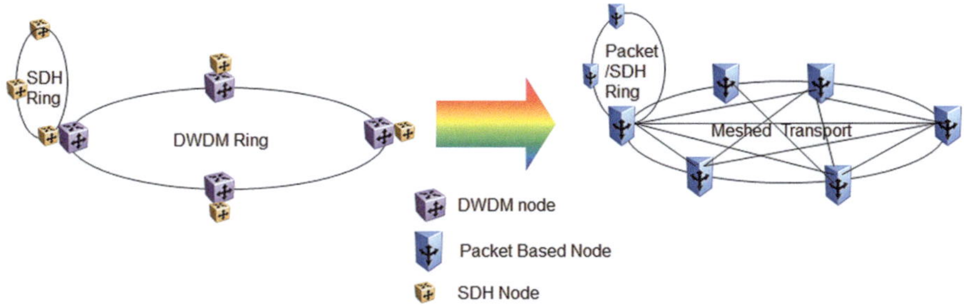


**Fig. 11.3** OTN evolution (author)

helps the telecom operator in driving network efficiencies and for extending deeper reach. Terrestrial networks are capable of carrying high volumes of data from one city/geography to other and are dug in the ground. Some of the other benefits derived from OTN technology are (a) native support for IP and TDM traffic (b) subchannel granularity (c) Layer 0/Layer 1 restoration (d) 40 Gig/100 Gig interface support and (e) crossconnect scalability in terabytes. Figure 11.3 explains the concept and evolution of OTN technology in terrestrial networks.

#### 11.2.2.2 Key Applications on Terrestrial Networks

**Voice** Terrestrial networks were initially built to carry voice through deployment of voice switches on TDM platforms on it. Almost all legacy access networks were deployed on copper initially and for carrying a single TDM (analog) voice channel, i.e., basic telephony. In between, ISDN technologies were deployed for carrying multiple channels of voice and data in a digital format.

**Data** Terrestrial networks deployed for voice initially were later on used for extending Internet connectivity to its user by deploying appropriate technology at the back end. Same last mile which was used to carry voice now is enabled to carry voice and data (Internet). It was made possible by using a different frequency band on copper last mile by deployment of DSLAMs, IP routers among other service provisioning and billing elements in the core and a modem at the user end. VDSL technology was deployed to address the high-speed requirements on the same copper last mile later.

Data channels for business applications for clear channel or Ethernet connectivity between the user locations are derived from investments made in multiplexers and ATM switches in the terrestrial core. MPLS networks are built as next-generation connectivity solution for assuring application-level quality of service and high availability. E1/T1 interfaces at customer end are possible with these investments on the terrestrial networks.

**Video** Terrestrial networks are enabled to deliver video for TV viewing/ entertainment with deployment of cable hub and head end along with other

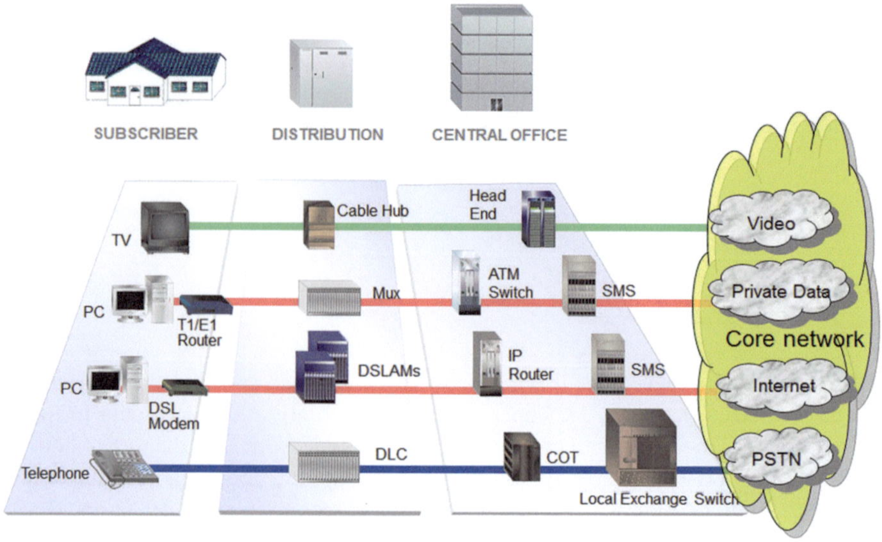


**Fig. 11.4** Terrestrial networks with multiple applications (author)

elements for service provisioning and billing at the backend and by using fibre/copper for high-speed content. IPTV bundled with voice + data is the result of such upgradation. A Telco is fully enabled to offer triple play of voice data and video for its consumers on terrestrial networks.

Figure 11.4 explains the evolution of voice to data to video carriage capability in terrestrial networks with deployment of associated technology at the back end as well at end-user location.

**Segments and Products**:

**Consumer Segment** Voice telephony, voice and DSL combos, voice and DSL and IPTV combos.

**Business Segment** Voice telephony, ISDN, Internet Leased Line, local loop, national long-distance (NLD) connectivity, multiprotocol label switching (MPLS) connectivity, etc.

**Telco Segment** Telecom players are mandated to establish point of interfaces (POIs) for seamless continuity of voice/data and video services between consumers irrespective of their subscription with any telecom operator in a geography/country. Therefore, operators interconnect with each other and carry traffic for or of each other depending upon the licences they have acquired for business in that particular geography, e.g., NLD provider in a territory is allowed to provide connectivity to any ISP/basic telephony and UL licensee in India. All basic telephony/UL holders are mandated by the regulator to establish POI for continuity of basic telephony and mobile services.

Additionally, telecom players share their terrestrial infra with other operators in many other ways, e.g., dark fibre sharing, bulk Internet capacity sale from an upstream ISP to downstream ISP (Class A, B, C category ISP) on commercial basis.

It is important to note that voice, data and video offerings have evolved over a period of time and thus operated and managed differently and independently of each others. They follow different protocols and thus are carried differently on access/aggregation and at times even on the core, e.g., MPLS, NLD and IP backbones are created differently between themselves and also with reference to TDM voice and video carriage networks.

### 11.2.3 Mobile Networks

Telecom operators deploy mobile networks for enabling mobile communication in a circle/geography/country. Key elements of a typical mobile network are shown in Fig. 11.5.

Key mobile technology components are mobile station controller, base station controller, BTS and provisioning and billing components. Mobile networks ride on terrestrial networks wherever possible for interconnecting these elements as well connecting the mobile networks with the PSTN (basic telephony networks) for seamless connectivity between mobile and fixed-line consumers through POIs.

Mobile networks were initially deployed for extending voice telephony to the consumers. It started with 2G/CDMA for voice and low-speed data followed by 3G/4G and now 5G for delivering high-speed data for mobile users. Mobile technologies followed through the evolution from CDMA/2G to 3G to 4G and 5G now. In the voice-dominant era, the focus of the network planners was to maximize EPS efficiency. However with the focus changing to data, mobile networks are

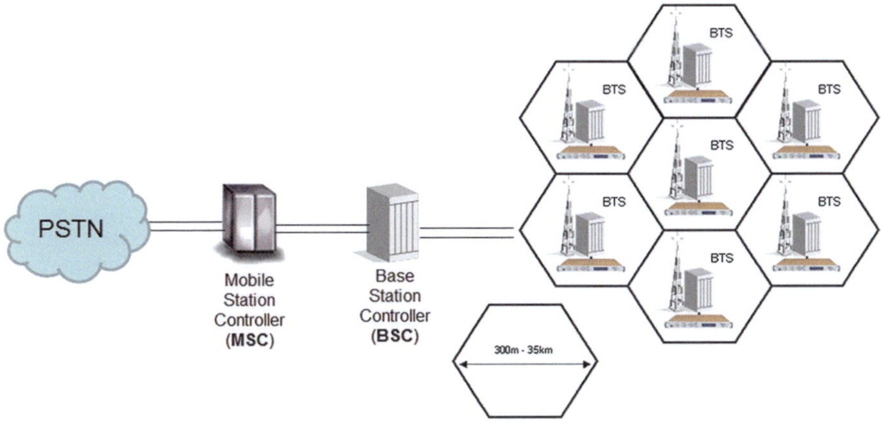


**Fig. 11.5** Mobile network elements (author)

designed to supply high-speed and high-quality Internet at low cost. 4G offers the lowest-cost and highest-speed Internet as compared to 3G and 2G networks.

It may be interesting to note that voice is still carried as TDM voice though the networks have the capability to carry VoIP and VoLTE and at a lower cost. Data and video is carried on IP. OTT (over the top) applications, e.g., WhatsApp, Twitter, messenger apps and Hike, are also a function of IP enablement on mobile networks though typically falling under freemium category. As described above, mobile networks have their own topology and thus operating independent and management modules with huge investments involved.

**Segments and Products**:

**Consumer Space** Mobile telephony, mobile data (Internet) and dongle (2G, 3G and 4G).

**Business Space** Mobile telephony, mobile value-added services, mobile data and dongle.

### *11.2.4 Radio/Microwave Networks*

Radio frequency (RF) networks are deployed by the telecom players for extending the voice, data and MO networks to the difficult and far-flung areas. RF networks complement the copper or fibre networks in terms of extending the capabilities either in the form of backhaul network in the core/aggregator levels and at times as last-mile connectivity to the end-users for data connectivity.

RF networks are deployed either in unlicensed band or in licensed frequency bands.

**Segments and Products**:

**Consumer Space** Broadband wireless access (BWA) for Internet, Wi-fi hot spots.

**Business Space** VSAT hubs to DC connectivity.

**Telco** Backhaul on MW for MO networks.

### *11.2.5 Submarine Networks*

Submarine cables are the undersea cables deployed across the globe through the 5 continents to provide connectivity for voice, data and video traffic. These networks are undersea fibre cables deployed with huge investments and time either by a single telecom operator/entity or a conglomerate of multiple operators. A single entity/operator may keep the capacity of itself (which is a rare occasion), or it may

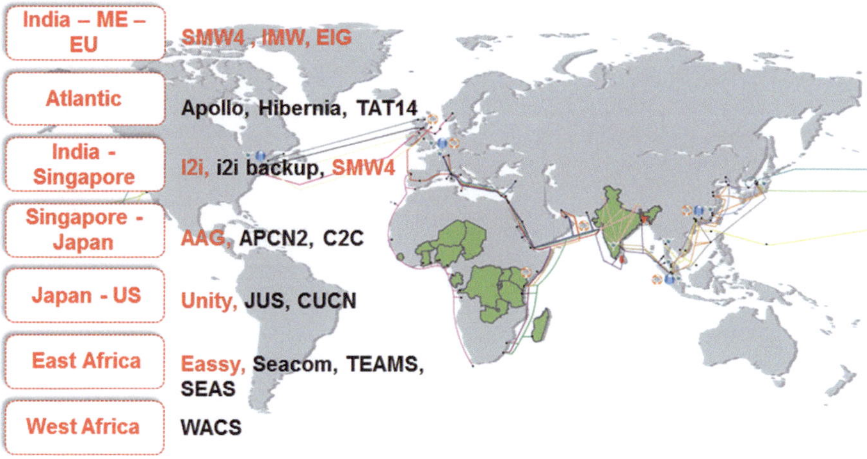


**Fig. 11.6** Undersea cables (author)

share it with other operator commercially. In case of a joint asset, each participating operator gets a dedicated capacity based on the investment proposition which it can use for its own captive use or for commercial benefit with other participating operators or any other operator as per the conglomeration agreements. Operators carry voice, data or video traffic for themselves, their customers or for another one, depending upon their respective business models across the globe. Figure 11.6 shows some of the undersea cables with their names, routes and countries it touches through. A few examples of these cables are SMW4, which traverses through India, Middle East and Europe; i2i from India to Singapore; AAG between Japan and Singapore.

**Segments and Products**:

**Consumer Segment** ISD calling and Internet.

**Business Segment** ILD (International Leased Lines), IPLC connectivity, iMPLS, global VC, ITFS, etc.

**Telco** Voice minutes, VC minutes, dark fibre (IRU) sharing, etc.

Telecom network is the most important asset of any telecom operators. Different types of operators develop different types of the network out of the five different types depending upon its business model, technology evolution and market demands over a period of time. An overall network segment—telecom technology mapping—is summarized in Fig. 11.7a.

It is worth noting that all the network segments (access, aggregator, core) are thickly integrated with each other which results into an integrated telecom infrastructure though may be on different technologies and access mediums. Many Telcos have deployed high-speed express networks (on OTN or next-generation

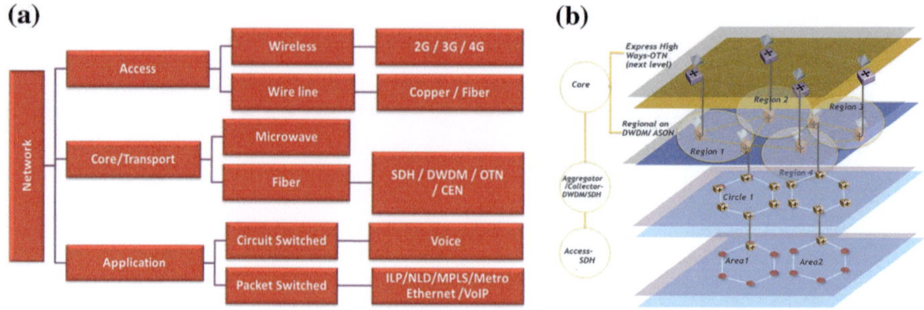


**Fig. 11.7** **a**, **b** Network segment—telecom technology map

technology) in their backbone (Fig. 11.7b) which cuts across the traditional (ASON, DWDM, SDH) rings to establish a low-latency (<40 ms), high-capacity ($n \times$ STM1s), highly available (multiple paths) networks for bandwidth hungry and mission critical applications, e.g., video carriage for TV broadcasting and high-speed Internet experience for any type of consumers.

Application-based core networks are deployed by leveraging the integrated telecom network infrastructure. Architecture of a typical application network—MPLS network—is described in the next section (Fig. 11.8).

All other networks such as mobility networks, national long-distance network, Internet service network and voice telephony networks are also built on similar lines with their own respective network elements and NOCs though leveraging the same core and access network assets.

**Fig. 11.8** MPLS network architecture (author)

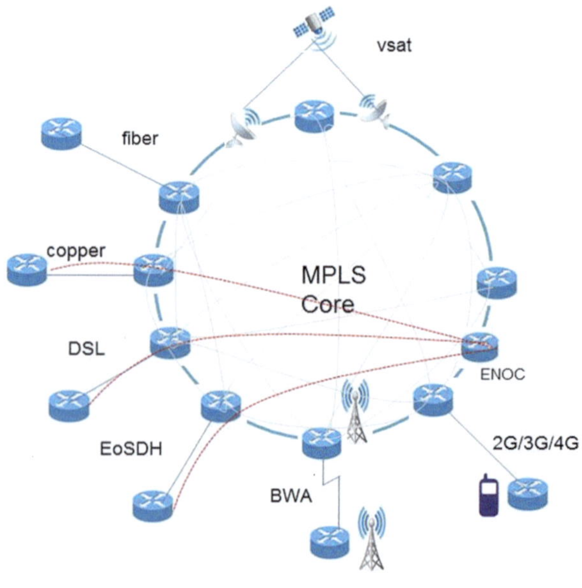

## 11.3 Opportunity Landscape

Telecom network infrastructure of a typical Telco spreads over multiple hundred thousands of kilometres. These networks are traditionally leveraged for services as described earlier. Operators are attempting to augment the basic service offerings with top-ups or bundle, e.g., MPLS core is enhanced with telepresence, managed video conference (VC) and application quality management (AQM) infrastructure for offering bundled MPLS with VCS or MPLS with AQM solutions (Fig. 11.9).

MPLS Networks: MPLS networks (typically a Layer-3 service) are created on the core network by overlaying a dedicated layer of technology in the form of MPLS POPs. It is called as the MPLS core and is managed through a ENOC (MPLS e-NOC is a separate NOC than the core/access network NOCs, though they work in tandem). MPLS connectivity to an end-user is offered by extending the MPLS ring through a last mile which can be on any type of access medium.

However, there is a huge opportunity emerging in the telecom space with establishment of Internet protocol (IP) as the default medium for all applications.

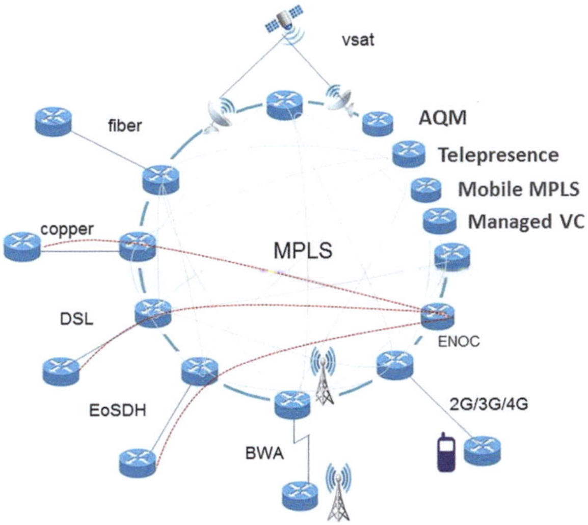


**Fig. 11.9** MPLS core (author)

**Fig. 11.10** Supercore

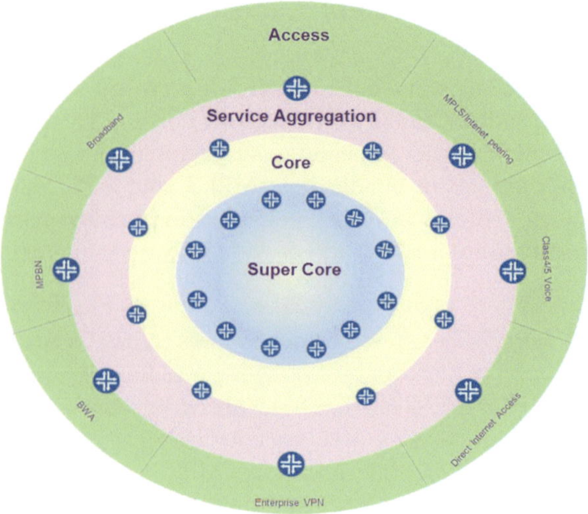


In order to leverage the IP momentum, the traditional telecom infrastructure (independent voice and data—ISP/NLD/MPLS, etc.) is being transformed to a converged supercore, accessible by all types of access technologies, i.e., fibre, coaxial, copper, RF and Satcom. It is an expensive and time-consuming journey. Many operators have already initiated for the migration.

Supercore is a converged core on optical technology ready for carrying huge volumes of IP traffic. It is overlapped by extended core, which is overlapped by service aggregation layer which further is overlapped by access networks for extending reach. All these are attempted to be managed by a super-NOC for an integrated view of application performance, network performance and user analytics as described in Fig. 11.10.

Through this converged telecom infrastructure, applications can be managed smoothly. All types of traffic (voice, data and video) will be treated as an integrated payload on the supercore. The key difference between super- and extended cores is the load carrying capacity and associated investments. Application sensitivities, configurations, SLAs, etc., are managed at the service aggregation layer. And lastly, access network integration happens at the access layer. Many operators are undertaking the IP-fiction of their access networks to realize the dream of a converged IP infrastructure (Fig. 11.11).

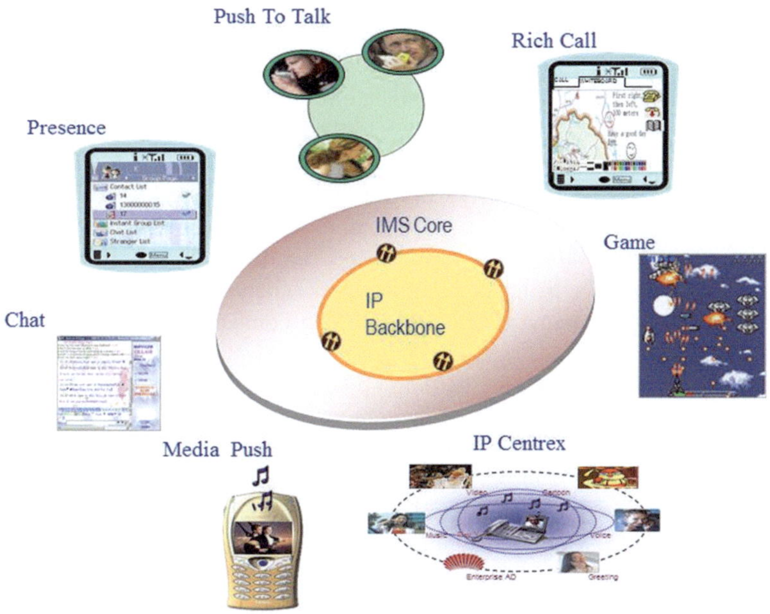


**Fig. 11.11** Unlocking the long tail of services

IP centrex replacing TDM Centrex, gaming solutions and presence solutions, push to talk, etc., by using telephone numbers as identifiers. It may be termed as new-generation telecom solutions. New-generation services stem out from a platform called as integrated management services (IMS) platform alike to traditional voice, data application cores over and above IP backbone or super-IP core. Various models for IMS are under evaluation by the operators depending upon their macroeconomic environment.

Interplay of networks, devices, applications is envisaged to create the future of telecom industry, in which integrated and application-sensitive telecom networks shall play a catalyst role. Even TMF has proposed a futuristic model of telecom industry for a comprehensive view.

*In Summary:* Telecom networks serve as the most important business parameter of a telecom operator. Operators are busy in upgrading their telecom infrastructure for ocean of devices across millions of businesses and billions of lives in the zettabyte age with application sensitivity management. However, the success lies with the ability of the operator to build new-generation telecom services derived from next-generation telecom networks.

## 11.4 Concluding Remarks

There is a paradigm shift in telecommunication world with the evolution of mobile devices, education becoming more social, video has started playing more dominant role be it for downloads or uploads or for collaboration. Virtual world has a telling impact on the real world. Networks need to handle bandwidth flood to the tune of petabyte/exabyte/zettabyte because of the afore-stated paradigm shift. IP is in the centre of everything, and telecom networks are evolving to IP-ready access, aggregator and core for better application-level sensitivity management. Telecom networks are also expanding to provide 100 Gig connectivity with better network resilience models.

Telecom service providers are coming up with innovative products and solutions for moving up in the value chain by leveraging the modern-day telecom networks. It may be in the form of hard bundles of modern-day networks, devices, and managed services, e.g., managed video conferencing service (A bundle of highly resilient MPLS network, video conferencing equipment and bridge services). OVCC (Open Visual Communications Consortium) is another example wherein video networks of multiple telecom service providers and created a Global Video Conferencing Exchange. SLAs for such services are in the form of continuity of high-quality video conference (telepresence) to the users, which is derived from various ingredients from networks, equipment and bridge. Another example is video carriage networks which provide high quality of service for high-definition television broadcast from remote locations for events and news from various last-mile access mediums. Teleeducation and telemedicine solutions are some other examples wherein such interplay of modern-day networks and technology (equipment) is visible globally.

In the mobile world, solutions such as vehicle tracking solutions, point of service Kiosks, real-time inventory management, video surveillance, mobile valet are some other examples of such innovations. Telecom service providers are betting on innovations spreading over modernization of telecom networks, IP-ready platforms, new products and services to emerge as a catalyst of change which would enable them to stay ahead of new entrants, i.e., OTT operators and likes of Google, Microsoft and Apple, in their domain.

## References

Birudavolu S, Nag B (2011) A study of open innovation in telecommunication services: a review of literature and trends. Available at http://cc.iift.ac.in/research/Docs/WP/09.pdf. Accessed 14 Jun 2014

Cisco (2015) Cisco global cloud index: forecast and methodology, 2013–2018. Available at: http://www.cisco.com/c/en/us/solutions/collateral/service-provider/global-cloud-index-gci/Cloud_Index_White_Paper.pdf. Accessed 18 Mar 2015

GSMA (2012) GSMA announces the business impact of connected devices could be worth US $4.5 trillion in 2020| newsroom. Available at: http://www.gsma.com/newsroom/press-release/gsma-announces-the-business-impact-of-connected-devices-could-be-worth-us4-5-trillion-in-2020/. Accessed 3 Sept 2014

Raivio Y, Luukkainen S, Seppälä S (2011) Towards open telco—business models of API management providers. In: IEEE proceedings of the 44th Hawaii international conference on system sciences

# Chapter 12
# Mobile Device: Applications, Over the Top Services, Identity Protection and BYOD Policy

A vital constituent of the rapidly growing global telecommunication industry is the Indian telecommunication industry. As per the TRAI press release ending 31 July 2015, active mobile subscriber base on the date of peak VLR in July 2015 was 885.15 million and the total wireless subscriber base stood at 983.21 million. There is a trend of increased rural subscription and decreased urban subscription in recent times. The overall teledensity stood at 78.02 with urban and rural teledensities at 145.13 and 47.84, respectively. Delhi has the highest teledensity of 238.59 when compared to the other circles. Even though the mobile subscriptions growth rate has decreased, there has been an increasing trend in the usage of smartphones by the Indian subscribers. India is the 2nd largest mobile handset market in the world and the smartphone market grew by 12.2 % during 1H 2012 vis-à-vis 1H 2011 (CMR's India Mobile Handsets Market Review, 2012) with a shipment of 5.05 million.

With the increasing trend of usage of smartphones by the Indian subscribers and implementation of several services on the mobile platform, subscribers face a real challenge of making sure that the mobile platform is secure enough to prevent any data and identity thefts. Mobile has become the smart platform for all computing and data access needs for both consumers and enterprises. This chapter presents an overview of various mobile application categories and the need for having OTT policy framework in India. With increasing adoption and usage of app based services the identity protection mechanisms have gained importance along with various risk mitigation strategies.

© Springer India 2016

M.K. Medudula et al., *Telecom Management in Emerging Economies*,
DOI 10.1007/978-81-322-2749-6_12

## 12.1 Mobile Phone Utility/Mobile Apps and Ecosystem/Mobile Ecosystem

When mobile phone was first introduced the basic utility derived is calling and SMS functionality. With the introduction of app-driven ecosystem, the utility of the device increased manifold. Today, we think of mobile as the most useful and widely used device in daily life. Devices which once delivered basic utility have now been upgraded to deliver the functionalities of a computer and are known as smartphones.

### *12.1.1 Smartphone Classification*

Smartphones are classified based on several parameters such as cost, operating system which it runs, screen size and the generation of technology it supports. The cost-based classification was initially visible during the introductory stage of the smartphone devices, but this classification was no longer significant during the growth stage when the device cost was reduced to make it available to all economic sections. Today there are many smartphones available in low prices which provide plethora of services. The term “smartphone” was associated with mobiles as early as 1997, but it was only when Apple launched the iPhone in 2007, the real significant change in terms of consumer adoption and market for application developers was witnessed. The app ecosystem was very important for the development of smartphone usage and growth.

### *12.1.2 App Ecosystem*

Till 2001, the app ecosystem was mainly limited to the applications which have come pre-installed in the phone. The software was not open to any third-party applications. The launch of Symbian OS which was majorly adopted by the mobile manufacturer Nokia and other players helped the developers to install third-party applications developed on Symbian platform onto mobile. The need of further interactivity and user-friendly apps has led to the development of apps store by Apple. The app ecosystem got the necessary push with the launch of apps store by Apple which has redefined the way the customers perceive, use and maintain apps on their device. With the launch of Software Development Kit and Apps store transformation took place in value-added service industry.

After Apple introduced its operating system to support iPhone, another operating system Android was introduced as robust open-source platform for mobile which was later owned by Google. Android operating system further propelled the industry (both application developers and mobile manufacturers) to come out with smarter and cheap mobile phones which were more user-friendly and high mobile computing power.

The operating system is the most vital part of any mobile smartphone because it defines all the features, performance, applications, security, etc., of the smartphone. In today's world, a lot of operating systems are available on which the whole system runs as such Android, BlackBerry, iOS, Windows, Symbian to name few and also there are new ones being developed. Consumer absorption and adoption of mobile apps has led to the development of ecosystem with several product innovations. Today, we have app for any type of service that we can imagine. We have several app store that provide more than billion apps. The adoption would not have been possible without two significant changes in the telecom industry. The 1st change is the development of better cellular networks that support greater data speeds. The usage of mobile Internet and apps have risen significantly with introduction of 3G cellular networks in India. The 2nd change is the reduction of smartphone prices and development of smartphone by Indian manufacturers.

### *12.1.3 Smartphone Manufacturers*

The major smartphone manufacturers currently in market are Samsung, Apple, Lenovo, LG, Xiaomi, Lava, Nokia, Motorola, etc. Based on the sales of the smartphones of these companies, it was found that most of them have more service centres in the countries in which they are manufactured. The availability and quality of after sales service is one major aspect that a customer will look at when he/she is purchasing the smartphone. In India, Lava and Micromax have established themselves as an emerging player.

The IDC report showing the sales volumes of various smartphone manufacturing companies in the last quarter is given in Table 12.1. It also compares these figures with the same quarter last year.

**Table 12.1** Quarterly smartphone sales of handset manufacturers

| Vendor | 2014 Q3 shipment volumes (in millions) | 2014 Q3 market share (in %) | 2013 Q3 shipment volumes (in millions) | 2013 Q3 market share (in %) | Q3 '14/Q3'13 change (in %) |
|---|---|---|---|---|---|
| Samsung | 78.1 | 23.8 | 85.0 | 32.5 | −8.2 |
| Apple | 39.3 | 12.0 | 33.8 | 12.9 | 16.1 |
| Xiaomi | 17.3 | 5.3 | 5.6 | 2.1 | 211.3 |
| Lenovo | 16.9 | 5.2 | 12.3 | 4.7 | 38.0 |
| LG | 16.8 | 5.1 | 12.0 | 4.6 | 39.8 |
| Others | 159.2 | 48.6 | 113.0 | 43.2 | 40.8 |
| Total | 327.6 | 100 | 261.7 | 100 | 25.2 |

*Source* IDC worldwide quarterly mobile phone tracker, 29 October 2014

In the digital world, dependency on Internet is increasing rapidly. A recent survey of purchase patterns of smartphone users indicates that more customers prefer buying their smartphone online, thus adding to the increased revenue of e-commerce giants (60 % of Flipkart's revenue come through the sale of smartphones).

A trend that can be observed these days is because of the fact that more and more companies are launching their latest smartphones through online channels only (e.g. Moto E and Moto G, Nexus 5 and Xiaomi handsets). The hassle-free user experience and the ease of cash transfer can be considered the major factors for this rising trend. The provision for the other owners to share their user experience and feedback on the sales and after sales services in the same online portal will also give some most needed insights to potential buyers. From the manufacturer's point of view, they have substantial savings as they do not have to go through dealers, resellers or own retail stores. Increased usage of smartphones is primarily due to the access to faster data speed and improved Internet penetration among both rural and urban areas.

### *12.1.4 Mobile Services: Applications and Crowdsourcing*

Usage leads to adoption and this is very true in case of smartphones. Customers across different segments in telecom market use smartphones in their daily life. The technological barriers have been reduced due to improved application interface and smoother access to data. Improved features and reduced handset costs enabled greater affordability for the users. Mobile once used for voice calling and basic text message is being used for high end computing and commerce presently. The growth of applications on smartphones is possible due to availability of strong network infrastructure and apps distribution platforms. To promote the growth of locally relevant mobile apps, the government can act as an enabler especially in the pursuance of socio-economic development and inclusive growth for benefit of multiple fronts which include but are not limited to, agriculture, healthcare, education, finance and governance.

However, to promote the holistic development of the apps economy, Indian developers will need to focus more on user interface design as well as on business model innovation. The market must realize the latent potential of uniquely developed Indian apps. This potential can be unlocked only if network coverage increases to remote areas, smartphone penetration continues to rise and the "absorptive capacity" of the Indian population towards new technology also grows through schemes that promote digital awareness and literacy. Without these preliminary conditions and support infrastructure, the user base of the Indian apps economy will remain short of its true potential.

All major stakeholders have a role to play in achieving the growth of locally relevant content. Telecom operators have an imperative to increase 3G network deployment or leapfrog into new generation technologies. Original equipment manufacturers and app developers need to collaborate to create and ensure that locally relevant apps are compatible with a variety of mobile devices sold across the country. The Government and Reserve Bank of India need to ensure that the policy framework is favourable by re-evaluating telecom regulations and mobile payment policies, respectively.

In short, app developers, distributers, government, device manufacturers, telecom companies and other stakeholders must work together to ensure that Indian app economy continues on its upward growth trajectory and the needs of Indians at the bottom of the pyramid are addressed and international competitiveness is achieved.

#### 12.1.4.1 Mobile Application Categories

There exists more than a billion of apps which provide plethora of services. Mobile apps are provided by application distribution platform where app developers make them available. We shall look at the main categories of applications which we generally use in daily life. Here, the applications have been used for representing the utility and no preference is done in mentioning the application over others. The various categories of applications on mobile include:

(a) M-Commerce Applications
Buying and selling is an important activity for meeting our needs and wants. Mobile has helped the users in making these activities in a more user friendly way. Today, we can buy anything we want through mobile. Mobile commerce is all about buying and selling goods and service through mobile platforms. Internet has provided the means to get the required information whenever we require and helps us to take informed decisions in life. Mobile commerce today is a picture of dynamism. Consumers are using mobile to fill the gap between the online and offline world. While it started out with consumers using their mobile phones as an alternative to window shopping, the scenario has turned on its head with customers using brick and mortar shops to identify and analyse their products and then make a purchase online. M-commerce boom has also been aided by the availability of affordable smartphones. Introduction of 3G technology has also enabled the growth of m-commerce services. All the organizations want to make their presence felt on mobile platforms. M-commerce has impacted retail sector to some extent due to changing time spending patterns of consumers. M-commerce provides the ease to users to order what they want at the convenience of their residence or workplace. Improved optimization, availability of cash on delivery payment options, easy return policies, ability to track your order and discounts have slowly worked their way in increasing m-commerce market presently. One interesting change which we notice is some of the ecommerce Websites have now transformed to purely m-commerce such as Myntra which no longer has any e-commerce business and became purely app-driven business. Flipkart another major commerce Website is planning to move entirely to mobile

platform. Some other apps include Amazon, Snapdeal, eBay, ShopClue, Yepme and Naaptol.

(b) Embedded Games
Improved graphics and processing power on mobile platforms enabled mobile to run embedded games. These games are embedded in the Web page code itself and the user can play them in the browser.

(c) Imaging Applications
Imaging/photography applications provide the users to enhance the quality of the image. There are applications such as Google Photos which helps in storing, retrieving, editing and sharing the pictures. These applications help you with cropping and transforming tools to get the perfect aesthetic image. Several other OTT applications do provide these facilities.

(d) Video streaming Apps
These apps helps us in viewing different forms of videos and also provide remote controls for other streaming devices. Some video streaming apps also gives the ability to broadcast your video live, share videos and interact with other people. YouTube is the popular app in this category.

(e) Music and Radio Apps
There are several apps which play different formats of music. These apps provide music on demand services. Music industry has seen the magnetic tapes, CDs, DVDs, iPods and MP3 players as the means to service. Now mobile has become a converged device with the capability of triple-pay services. Music is free on many apps, and paid apps give the comfort of add free experience. Apps such as Wynk, Gaana, Google Play Music, Hungama, Saavn Music and Radio come in this category.

(f) Education/Digital Media apps
Mobile is being used as platform for education in many regions of the world. In particular, in India where the broadband penetration is low, mobile is seen as the solution by the government to provide education for the rural regions. Some of the apps in this category include Khan Academy, WordFlex Touch Dictionary and TED.

(g) Messaging, Text, Image and video sharing apps
Many OTT players provide the capability of sending text, images, voice and video through their apps. Messaging apps prove the ability to group chat, multimedia messaging, language support and real-time locations. Some of the apps which are popular in this category are WhatsApp, Hike Messenger, Instagram, Snapchat, Facebook Messenger, BlackBerry Messenger, Line, Viber, Wechat, Skype and QQ Mobile.

(h) Productivity Apps
These apps aim at improving the efficiency at performing the task and keep track of the daily activities. These apps also aim at motivating the user in completing the task and improve on further. Some of the apps in this category include Microsoft Office, CamScanner, File Manager Apps, Google Calendar, Security apps and Optimization apps.

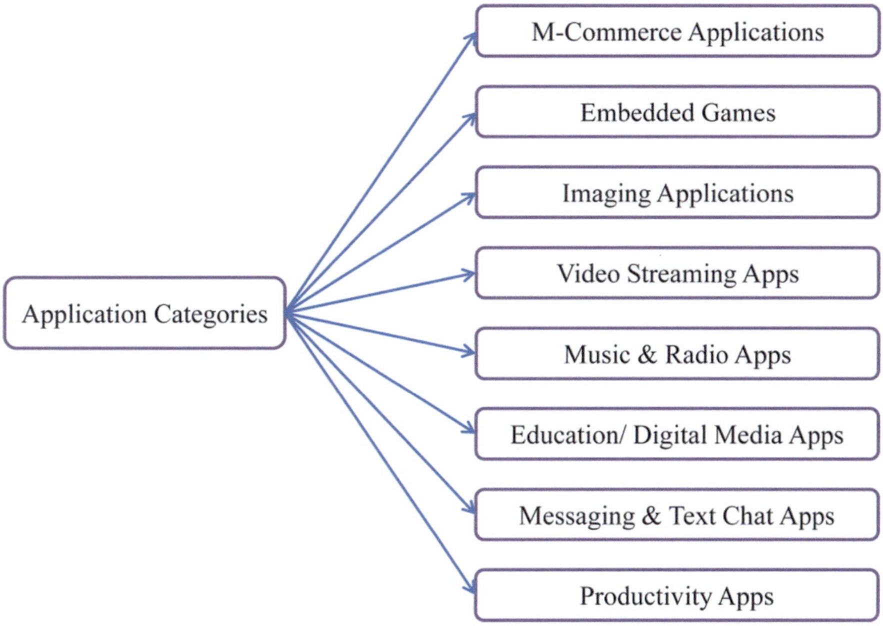


**Fig. 12.1** Categories of mobile-based applications

Mobile application industry facilitates the adoption of smartphones by the users. This industry has come a long way starting with proprietary platforms and later on with open-source platforms leading the way towards more development in this field (Fig. 12.1).

#### 12.1.4.2 Crowdsourcing

Many applications are not just driven and maintained only by the staff of the organization. There are applications which require help from volunteers to update the information. Such practice of making use of external people who volunteer or work part-time with the organization is known as crowdsourcing. The compensation to solve the problem or main the application can be monetary, reward or just intellectual satisfaction of the volunteer. The advantage of outsourcing is solution-centric at low cost. Mobile crowdsourcing is a term that describes crowdsourcing activities that are processed on smartphone or other mobile devices. Contribution is key to crowdsourcing and that makes it essential to look at it from the human-centric perspective. Research in the field of crowdsourcing systems has been able to derive four basic component of any crowdsourcing system which can be applied to the design and development of MCS as well. The four components are user management, task management, contribution management and workflow management.

User management component consists of functions such as registering users, evaluating user groups, forming user groups and establishing coordination mechanisms. Registering user deals with acquiring user account details, e.g. through social network sites, while evaluating user takes care of ensuring if the user is trustworthy and competent to contribute. It is important to form communities of users and establish a coordination mechanism so as to facilitate the interaction of contributors and targeted distribution of tasks and incentives or rewards. Task management comprises of important functions such as designing and assigning tasks. Task design involves the size, question, phrasing and reward. Allocating right task to the right person at the right time with the right reward is key to the success of crowdsourcing. Next component contribution management takes care of functions such as evaluating and selecting tasks. Feedback to the contributor can be given while evaluation is done. Avoiding cheat submissions is a challenge in selecting contributions. Data processing and machine learning algorithms can be used to preprocess, combine and select results. Workflow management grows in importance with the complexity of tasks. This component takes care of functions such as defining the inputs and outputs pertaining to each contribution. The interdependencies between tasks are also managed by designing efficient workflows that help to achieve the ultimate result.

With social media providing immense potential and wider reach through mobile phones, crowdsourcing systems are now built around social media platforms. Image-based mobile translation/search dominates the systems prevalent today. Camera phone applications help in translating texts written in unfamiliar formats or scripts. An example of such an application is the ***UbiAsk***, which is a crowdsourcing application that leverages the power of social media. *UbiAsk* provides translation services to mobile users in unfamiliar environments with the help of ordinary people who have volunteered for the service on social media (Liu et al. 2011).

Small organizations like ***Waze*** are making use of crowdsourcing to build up a network of around 70,000 volunteer map editors who update the real-time traffic data that helps around 15 million users to get to work on time. New features are added that provide detailed information on unpleasant incidents along the preferred path such as road work, speed traps, accidents (http://www.crowdsourcing.org/2014).

Geolocation aware mobile crowdsourcing apps are also employed to alert medical help when life-threatening situations such as heart attacks and road accidents occur. Sickness forecasting applications like ***SickWeather*** makes use of crowdsourced data to forecast sickness and potential outbreaks. *GeoChat*, an application deployed during 2010 earthquake relief activities in Haiti helped in coordinating relief and support activities. Similarly other applications such as ***Ushahidi*** and ***Crowdmap*** can be used to crowdsource information regarding crisis in real time.

To touch the lives of the workers living at the bottom of the pyramid, mobile crowdsourcing platforms like ***MobileWorks***, aim at providing employment to workers in the developing nations. They provide optical character recognition tasks that workers can undertake using low-end phones with limited screen resolutions too. (*MobileWorks: A Mobile Crowdsourcing Platform for Workers*.)

The future of mobile crowdsourcing looks promising with the next step being crowdcreation and crowdcuration. This would enable workers to search through their social networks and connections for already existing content and also creating content that their employers are looking for.

## 12.2 Over the Top Services (OTT): Policy Framework and Revenue Models (Swaroop 2015)

A communication service provider's ecosystem consists of the technology driving it, applications built around this technology, compatible devices and the policy framework that defines standards for smooth functioning. OTT is a service delivery model. It is called "over the top" because the services are offered over the Internet involving clusters of several managed and unmanaged networks. OTT services are delivered without any dependence on TELCOs managing the underlying network.

E-mail is an OTT service delivered over the Internet. Advent of e-mail many years back made the snail mail (physical mail services by P&T) redundant. Other popular services delivered over the top are messaging, audio and video calling, etc.

OTT streaming is the delivery of video and audio media streams over Internet, anywhere, anytime and on any device. Cable TV and IPTV providers are offering services over the smartphones and tablets. They have moved a step beyond the traditional set-top box and TV sets. On the other hand, the smart TVs are serving Internet content over the TV screen. Conventional IPTV is delivered over a dedicated infrastructure provided by the operator whereas OTT video gets transported over the open Internet spanning managed and unmanaged networks. In case of OTT services, ISP is responsible only for transporting the content loaded in IP packets. ISP may or may not be aware of the OTT content and hence are not responsible for the quality/appropriateness of the content being delivered. They do not manage the content and also do not have redistribution rights. This scenario is in contrast to the purchase/rental of video/audio content from an ISP, such as video on demand or messages delivered by WhatsApp.

OTT services deliver third-party content to an end-user device. Desktops, laptops, tablets, smartphones, set-top boxes, smart TVs and gaming consoles are all examples of Internet-connected devices. Out of all the devices mentioned here, the one indeed fuelling OTT demand is the smartphone. The package which we refer to as a smartphone offers advanced computing capabilities of a PDA, a media player, a digital camera and/or a GPS navigation unit. Another important attribute of a smartphone is its connectivity: over Wi-fi and cellular data. It facilitates mail management, syncing of personal and professional e-mail accounts, instant messaging and a lot more.

Consumers can access latest and innovative apps available in the app stores. That addresses two aspects related to consumer experience: easy availability and user-friendly graphics/interfaces. Innovations revolve around need and technology acts just as an enabler. Same need if met through a better offering may result in extinction of already established or evolving products. Post SMS and before OTT messaging, industry also witnessed a phase when few Web portals offered free SMS services to registered users. OTT services can take many forms, but voice and message apps have been the most popular with the consumers. Voice and messaging OTT apps have hit the TELCOs hard. Users prefer Skype, WhatsApp, Rebtel, Viber and Voxer, etc., to send messages, videos or to make VOIP calls at almost zero/nominal cost. This is likely to be the industry future as we increasingly move from "circuit switched" to "packet switched".

If we study cases like "e-mail versus P&T Departments" or "Amazon versus book stores" we can see an underlying common phenomenon. Consumers had the same services delivered more efficiently through a new delivery mechanism and older methods were discarded. Interestingly, voice/messaging-based OTTs were available over PCs/laptops since a decade almost. In other words a small percentage of voice/messaging services were getting delivered OTT and not through conventional TELCO route. The older handsets did not offer interfaces to get hooked to Skype or other OTTs and hence Skype's scope remained limited to PCs/laptops. It is the availability of apps over smartphones that gave prominence to the term "OTT". Smartphones/apps combo has been a mixed bag for mobile operators. Data usage has increased significantly with access to games, videos and social networks. At the same time, it has opened the door to disruptive newcomers, the OTT providers, who are offering similar voice and messaging services and have become a formidable competition.

- Skype over laptop did not concern TELCOs much, but Skype over smartphone is an established threat.
- Skype over data connection is a breather but Skype over Wi-fi leads to revenue leakage.

### *12.2.1 The Need for OTT Policy Framework*

CSP's offer services at the national and international level. CSP industry plays a pivotal role in a country's technological and business growth. "National security", "Consumer right's protection" and "equal opportunity for entrepreneurs" are important issues that demand for clear guidelines and policies. Unavailability of a robust and well-defined policy framework is a gap area identified after literature review. Though lots of research is being done around OTT Policy Framework and relevant papers have been published by researchers, but it is yet under consideration of the DoT and regulators. Absence of a policy framework is the problem that needs to be addressed. And as OTT is here to stay a framework is required that ensures win–win situation for all stakeholders in the OTT ecosystem. Proposed framework has to ensure rights of all stakeholders and at the same time it has to facilitate industry growth.

Major stakeholders affected by the absence of a policy framework in OTT ecosystem are as follows:

(i) Government/regulator,
(ii) Service providers,
    (a) Content provider,
    (b) Network provider and
(iii) Consumer.

**Stakeholder 1: Government/Regulator**
Regulator's treatment towards the services offered by OTT players and those offered by TELCOs should be uniform. Net neutrality is an issue between TELCOs and OTT operators. Over the top companies are in an advantageous position because current regulatory framework on data protection does not ask them, like TELCOs, to follow rules for the treatment and retention of users' data.

**Stakeholder 2-A: Content Provider**
Content providers are traditional application service providers selling VAS services through TELCO channel and OTT service providers, not controlled by TELCOs. Both content providing channels, traditional VAS and OTT, need to be brought under common norms and rules.

Sources of great revenue, the VAS partners might be given preference by the TELCOs over the OTT players. Different treatment might give rise to issue of TELCO biasedness towards preferred content.

Lower revenue share has been a major concern among the traditional VAS players. Major chunk of VAS revenue goes to the TELCOs because of the current on-deck business model. Off-deck business model requires lots of standardization and coordination. This segment needs clear guidelines for the players.

**Stakeholder 2-B: Network Provider**
TELCOS and OTT players are at a different-level playing field when it comes termination charges and obligations. In case of OTT players offering voice and messaging there is no termination obligation left anymore. Directives and regulations put the pressure of maintaining data privacy and date retention on TELCOs whereas OTT players are free from such obligations. OTT players are not restricted by market geographies. Traditional TELCOs have to comply with the tax laws and international trade norms if they want to spread their wings outside the home geography. TELCOs together present a one network picture for smooth telecommunication between any two geographies on the earth. This is achievable due to interoperability standards. There are no such compliances existing for OTT players. TELCOs are committed to offer a minimum level of QoS and follow all the regulations put into effect by the regulator. Financial setbacks being faced by TELCOs are hampering the investments that are required in putting up new infrastructure and new networks together to handle the data surge. Hence, TELCOs are asking for an

arrangement through which they can get into commercial agreements according to the QoS offered with the OTT companies.

**Stakeholder 3: Consumer**

In order to understand consumer's state in an OTT ecosystem, we would first identify the rights or privileges a consumer is given in traditional TELCO world. QoS is monitored by TRAI through audits and consumer surveys. TRAI asks for point of interconnection (POI) congestion report also from the TELCOs on a monthly basis. Interconnection is reliability of termination of calls no matter which operator's network the dialled party belongs to. Emergency services like dial 100 are made available by all TELCOs. Customers have a right to inter-circle MNP. Intra-circle too will be available soon. Customers can avail NDNC services which ensure filtering of unwanted calls. TELCOs follow TRAI prescribed uniform code of metering and billing. Service providers are supposed to get their metering and billing systems audited. Tariff plans are well defined and standardized for longer validity, roaming services, etc.

**Inferences drawn regarding Stakeholder's Rights**

Based on the review of above-mentioned scenarios reported in telecom industry worldwide following inferences have been drawn which seem relevant to Indian telecom industry. As mentioned above, the inferences drawn revolve around the major stakeholders of a communication ecosystem, the regulator, the consumer and the service provider. The inferences drawn are captured in the table given below. These inferences provide a foundation for the policy framework.

<table>
<tr><th colspan="5">Stakeholders</th></tr>
<tr><th rowspan="2">Regulator (to ensure)</th><th rowspan="2">Consumer (right to)</th><th colspan="3">Application service provider</th></tr>
<tr><th>Content providers (right to)</th><th colspan="2">Network providers (right to)</th></tr>
<tr><td>Security (national level)</td><td>QoS</td><td>Net neutrality</td><td rowspan="6">Fair play (in erms of)</td><td>(a) Data privacy laws</td></tr>
<tr><td>Security (consumer level)</td><td>Data privacy</td><td>Off-deck business model</td><td>(b) Data retention laws</td></tr>
<tr><td>Fair play</td><td>Fair billing</td><td></td><td>(c) Tax laws</td></tr>
<tr><td>Market growth</td><td>Interconnection reliability</td><td></td><td>d) International trade norms</td></tr>
<tr><td>Advanced technologies</td><td>Emergency calls</td><td></td><td>(e) Interoperability standards</td></tr>
<tr><td>Revenue loss</td><td>National directive-based services—MNP, NDNC</td><td></td><td>(f) QoS norms</td></tr>
</table>

Services will be delivered over Internet and the market should be open to the extent possible. Net neutrality is to be maintained, national security is to be guarded. Hence, regulation is required from the perspective of "fair play" aspect. That offers an unbiased ecosystem to all players.

### 12.2.2 Strategy Behind OTT Revenue Models

Revenue model forms an integral part of a business model. A business model details strategies employed for excellence in manufacturing, distribution and promotion, etc. These factors collectively lead to revenue generation avenues. A business model can be plain vanilla, or it can be highly complex. A simple food service business generates revenue by selling products at a profit margin over the costs it incurs. However, an online venture might monetize using a combination of multiple streams, revenue generating as well as non-revenue generating, working in close coordination.

IT industry business models differ significantly from those adopted by conventional businesses. Product and service delivery models have undergone major changes at a fast pace. Industry has taken a leap from desktops to cloud computing. OTT is one of the latest delivery mechanism. It is about the services getting delivered over the Internet. These services could range from e-mail, messaging, networking to online shopping and e-commerce. This necessitates the need for defining business strategies, making OTT an integral part of it.

Today, Internet offers information, music, videos, games, mailing, messaging, chatting and a lot more to consumers, at minimal charges or free of cost. However, companies providing these services are generating great revenues too. How it works out for them? And when many provide free services than what would make an offer look more compelling over its competitors? Answer to these questions lies in the well thought strategy of the companies offering these services. In order to understand the strategy, we need to consider the following points.

Customers perceive that services available over Internet are always free. Even promise of offering assured QoS does not pull masses to join a paid service over a free one lookalike. Premium customer base for specialized services will always be there but would have limitations on size it can attain. Disruption is not happening only on the technology front, it is as well being experienced at stages of bundling, distribution and in form of product features. Replication of products and services, its distribution and supporting its post-delivery is much easier in IT/Internet space compared to the traditional industries. Considering these points, the revenue models should ensure monetization through one stream or the other. The old saying "change is the only constant" supports well, the strategy, of OTT players (Internet majors) as they have to keep evolving always. OTT players makes use of various business models such as Freemium, Royalty, Advertising etc.

## 12.3 Mobile Identity Management and Risk Mitigation Practices

Every innovation has the downside and same is the case with smartphone and improved technology and access. Security and privacy concerns would really matter to the smartphone users, and identity management is the key to prevent unauthorized access. Tokens that are unique within a given scope, be it locally and globally or within a specific domain, defines a specific digital identity. Mobile identity is an extended version of the digital identity which may be classified as device-to-device, location-to-location and context-to-context.

In device-to-device identity, mobile identity is used to attest the authority of a particular individual to gain access to a specific resource while using different devices. In location-to-location identity, the mobile identity is used in the certification process to determine the authority of a particular individual to gain access to a specific service while moving in different geographical areas. In context-to-context identity, the device needs to select the most preferable identity depending on the context, e.g. the people in their proximity.

### *12.3.1 Threats to Mobile Identity Management*

**Identity theft** It is done by stealing the security credentials by using a trusted mobile device as a proxy. The digital footprint of a user is, thus, compromised revealing a range of personal information including biometric data.

**Eavesdropping or spyware** Not only is it difficult to detect, but the cheapest method for any attacker. Vulnerability is presented by WLANs and GSM networks with 802.11 encryption. Information at risk includes geographical locations, financial transactions, communications, preferences, purchases, critical personal information and profile information.

**Surveillance** Traffic data or localized EMEI data can be monitored. Such unintended disclosure can reveal large amounts of personal information and give an elaborate profile of an unsuspecting user if the network monitoring is not secure. Mobile device users can be monitored both via network monitoring and also by sensors in their physical surroundings.

**Phishing** It is the method of acquiring confidential information by posing as a trustworthy entity. It can be done by the use of malicious software, forged e-mails or by network attacks.

**Man-in-the-middle attacks (MITM)** An attacker operates as an intermediary between a mobile device and its trusted services. The attacker can, thus, monitor the user or steal his identity.

**Illegitimate utilization of interception software** Communication service providers are required to maintain appropriate technical measures to allow lawful interception of communications. The communication service provider is expected by law to allow the competent enforcement authority to intercept the communications. This may be delegated to the service provider itself and allow malicious intruders working for the service provider to unlawfully gather information.

**Collection and storage of private information beyond the stated purpose** Service providers may obtain more personal information than required to perform the service. This is especially risky when appropriate security mechanisms are not present.

**Threats to protocols** GSM has several such weaknesses: for example, the encryption is applicable to the wireless transmissions, i.e. the messages are sent in text format from the base station to the gateways. The mobile station has to periodically transmit its current location to the base station. This can be used to track the movement of a subscriber.

**Lack of user awareness** This is a challenge especially in the context of online social. Users need to be made aware of the extent to which personal data is revealed to service providers.

## *12.3.2 Mobile Identity Protection Mechanisms*

### 12.3.2.1 EU Projects

The Privacy and Identity Management for Europe (PRIME) is the major mobile identity protection mechanism in Europe. It provides solutions for enhancing the privacy identity management. Its goal is to develop a framework and working prototype for collaborative mechanism for privacy and identity protection. It provides solutions for privacy enhancing identity management that supports end-user sovereignty over their private sphere and enterprises.

### 12.3.2.2 FIDIS Network of Excellence

It focuses on framework for identifying individual, digital identities. It also investigates interoperability, ID theft, privacy, security and forensic implications. MODINIS project is a prospective study of possible initiatives and solution in e-government. The identification in mobile ad hod networks is achieved by certificates, public private key, anonymous credentials.

#### 12.3.2.3 Identity Management in Cellular Networks and GSM

GSM supports two types of identity management, i.e. International Mobile Subscriber Identity (IMSI) and International Mobile Equipment Identity (IMEI). The IMSI identifies the subscriber and is stored on the SIM. These two attributes are identifiers and not an identity. The identity in fact is composed of home location register (HLR) which is a database kept by cell phone providers which in turn associates these IMSI with the subscriber data. Similar to the HLR, a provider maintains an Equipment Identity Register (EIR) that stores the IMEIs of banned or monitored cell phones. All the identity management within the network including authentication and revocation is completely managed by the provider.

In order to prevent hacking through tracking of devices, a form of pseudonym, namely the Temporary Mobile Subscriber Identity (TMSI), is assigned to a mobile device when it connects to a location area and replaces the IMSI.

#### 12.3.2.4 Use of Federated Identity Management Tools

Federated identity management models can be used to perform the management of identity. Such models can be identity management "meta-systems", such as the Windows CardSpace or the OpenID (En-Nasry and El Kettani 2011).

#### 12.3.2.5 Biometric Authentication

Biometric tools such as face, hand geometry, voice recognition, iris scan and keystroke dynamics. can be used for authentication. For example, Motorola's Mobile Automated Fingerprint Identification System (AFIS) is a handheld biometric tool that can capture fingerprint and facial images, analyse the data and can even be used to match this information against databases stored locally on the device, in centralized biometric matching system, or on smart cards.

#### 12.3.2.6 Secure Hardware on Mobile Devices

"**Secure Element**" (SE) where secret or private keys are stored is needed for mobile devices with a high level of end-to-end security. There are three categories of SEs which include removable hardware (SMC, Chip, SIM, ASUSB), non-removable hardware (such as embedded chip) and security on non-dedicated hardware (Mobey Forum 2008).

#### 12.3.2.7 BlackBerry Security

BlackBerry has been able to provide state-of-the-art security by using innovative device data leak prevention wherein workspace and personal space are separated and all data transfer between work space and personal space goes through strict data leak control checks to make sure that no app uses data from work space.

### *12.3.3 Risk Mitigation Strategies*

The ability of smartphones to store, retrieve and compute data has transformed the mobile to be a data hub for the users. As a result, risk mitigation practices become important in order to prevent data leak. All the practices can be classified under three strategies as depicted in Fig. 12.2 where several identity management tools discussed earlier and applications based security come under the device oriented strategy. These three strategies are not meant to be practised in isolation as the system requires more than one of these strategies to ensure safe access.

Consumer-oriented strategy deals with mainly the operational-level practices when the device is being used. This includes the device usage, sharing and handling practices that are best for risk mitigation. This is one of the important strategies which the organization expect the employees to follow when their device is

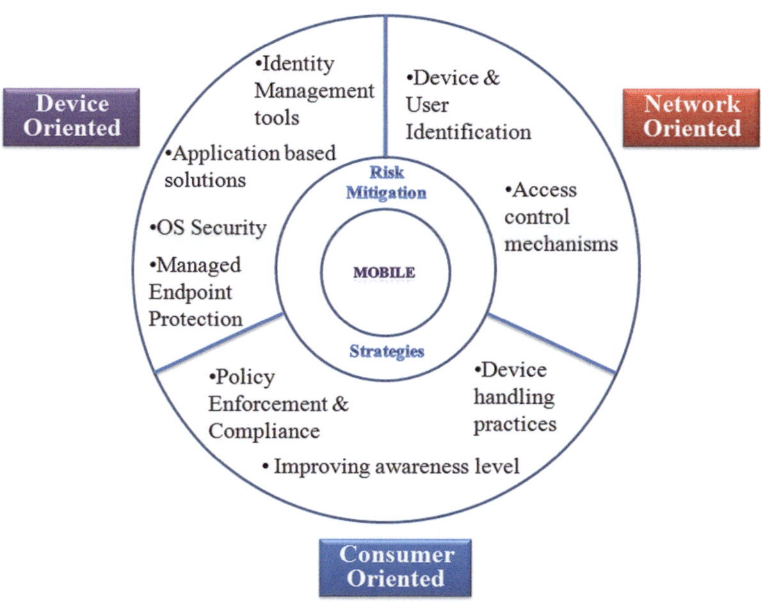


**Fig. 12.2** Risk mitigation practices

subscribed to BYOD (bring your own device) policy. Ensuring policy compliance from the users is an important condition of BYOD subscription.

## 12.4 BYOD: A Step Towards Consumerization

The term BYOD is used for "bring your own device", and this has been linked to increased productivity in organizations. In many organizations, the employees are encouraged to bring their own device (mobile/tablet/laptop) and have the company data synced to the personal device. Organizations may have separate policy (BYOM) mobile devices. Organizations have given the employees liberty to use any device which is compatible and which can run softwares/virtual interface which provides the necessary office tools to work. Employees are encouraged to use their personal devices through monetary benefits and other incentives towards the recurring charges during usage.

### *12.4.1 Implementation Challenges and Benefits*

BYOD has been identified to be at the peak of inflated expectations on the 2012 Gartner Emerging Technologies Hype Cycle Curve (Gartner 2012). This states that early publicity of such technologies results in many success stories and also do result in enough cases of failures. Organizations have debated whether to allow employee access social media websites and personal e-mail services at work. Many organizations in several industries have understood the importance of being adapted to the consumerization of IT at workplace and have been trying to find the right balance in allowing their employees to access the tools and information they need to do their work efficiently (Thomson 2012).

### *12.4.2 Steps in Creating BYOD Policy*

(a) **Establishing minimum requirements for device**

Many organizations state that the device which becomes a part of BYOD policy should used by the employee who owns the device. Employee should not share his device with others as per the policy agreement. The user shall be restricted from third-party applications or softwares depending upon the policy terms. The company would specify the list of softwares which can be installed on the device. The device requirements should be met in terms technical features (both hardware and operating system) as per the policy.

(b) **Mentioning minimum user requirements/eligibility conditions**

Employee would be eligible to subscribe to BYOD policy once he/she meets the mentioned criteria in the policy. Organizations decide the eligibility based on the job description, title and nature of work. In many organizations, the employees at managerial level are eligible to subscribe to BYOD policy.

(c) **Clearly articulating security protocols and rules in the policy agreement (during authorization and termination of BYOD service)**

The policy document must clearly state the protocols that the employee should follow before subscribing the policy and as well as after the policy is in effect. The policy document should also include clearly explain the minimum security protocols which the employee should adhere to and the steps he should take once his device gets mismanaged or lost. The document should clearly state whom to be contacted if the device gets lost. The document should mention the limits for acceptable use and mention the risks and liabilities which the employee has by adhering to the policy. Every mobility device is prone to attack from hackers through malware; hence, the policy document should mention the user action for timely update for security software updates on the device. Most of the threats to company data lies at the point of transaction (end-user's browser); hence, the security policy should educate the end-users/employees as many data leaks in the organization happen due to careless and are not malicious in nature (Morrow 2012). Organizations can provide clarity on the type of information that is accessible through BYOD policy by categorizing the information according to the confidentiality level. Generally, organizations can make use of four- or five-level categorization of information to protect the confidentiality. A four-level classification is stated below:

(i) Public data: Non-sensitive information can be categorized in this category. This may include the company vision, mission statements and all the information which is published on the company Website.
(ii) In-house data: This type of information would be accessible only by the employees of the organization. The access can be given to all employees irrespective of the functionality or region where the employee belongs to. Usually, most of the information in the knowledge group of the organization pertain to this category. Employees can access this data but sharing the data with other people who are not the part of organization is usually restricted.
(iii) Project/restricted data: This data can be accessible only by a group of employees who are involved in a project/assignment together. This data is also accessible by the vendors and clients who are involved in the project/assignment.
(iv) Extremely private data: This data is highly confidential and accessible only by the group of employees who are part of the top-level management of the organization. This data may include trade secrets and financial plans.

Termination rules also become an important part of the document which should clearly state the eligibility for the device to get terminated from the policy.

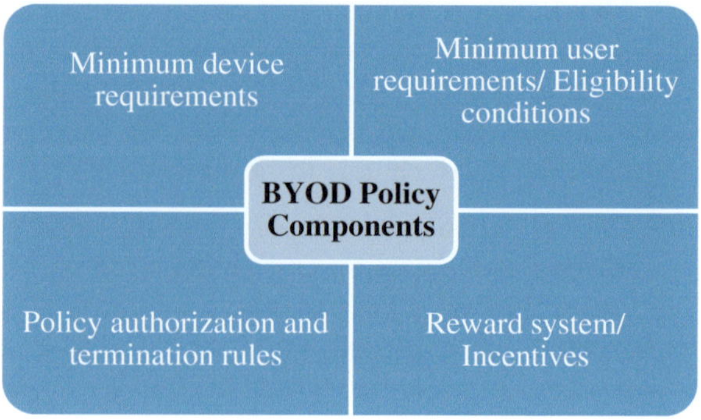


**Fig. 12.3** Important components of BYOD policy

Generally, the termination will be accepted by all the organizations before the employee resigns. Many organizations mention the minimum time period which the employee has to put his/her device on the policy after subscription. If the employee wishes to terminate before the minimum subscription time, then organizations would not be willing to provide the incentives/benefits as per the policy. The termination rules would call for deletion of all the organization data and softwares which the employee got installed as per the policy. The employee would also agree that no data has been saved on his/her device after the termination of the policy.

(d) **Establishing reward system/incentives to encourage the adoption**

Though BYOD policy would bring challenges to the organization in terms of securing the data, it also cannot be neglected due to the value and benefits it brings to both the organization and the employees. The attitude towards and perceived benefits of BYOD would significantly influence the employees intention to use BYOD device (Lebek et al. 2013). Organizations promote use of BYOD policy by their employees by establishing a reward system/incentives. Organization provides financial incentives on timely basis till the subscription of the policy and would also reimburse any recurring charges on monthly or quarterly basis for the device used under this policy. Clearly establishing the rules for the reward system/incentives is an important step towards encouraging adoption (Fig. 12.3).

## 12.5 Concluding Remarks

Improved data speeds by 3G and 4G technologies which are being used by the subscriber enabled the adoption of several value-added services on mobile. The quality of life is improved through quicker information delivery and use of plethora of applications on mobile platform. Both the consumers and the application industry had benefited by the changes in the sector. Regulatory concerns exist as a result of changing telecom business environment by the entry of OTT players. This emphasizes the importance of having proper regulatory framework to overcome any unhealthy scenario for the business environment and promoting technology and innovation in this sector. Organizations have brought friendly policies such as BYOD so that the users can benefit the flexibility the policy offers. Every technology is not void of the negativity it brings with it, and mobile platform is not exception in this case. Every user has to be aware of possible threats due to improper usage practices with the mobile. Industry has made considerable progress in mitigating the risk through identity management solutions. But equal action from the user through best practices is required to ensure both the device and data safety.

## References

En-Nasry B, El Kettani M (ed) (2011) Towards an open framework for mobile digital identity management through strong authentication methods. In: Secure and trust computing, data management, and applications, 1st edn. Springer, Berlin, pp 56–63

Gartner (2012) Gartner's 2012 hype cycle for emerging technologies identifies. Available at: http://www.gartner.com/newsroom/id/2124315. Accessed 6 Jun 2015

Lebek B, Degirmenci K, Breitner M (2013) Investigating the influence of security, privacy, and legal concerns on employees' intention to use BYOD mobile devices. In: Proceedings of the nineteenth Americas conference on information systems

Liu Y, Lehdonvirta V, Alexandrova T, Nakajima T (2011) Drawing on mobile crowds via social media. Multimedia Systems 18(1):53–67

Mobey Forum (2008) Best practice for mobile financial services: enrolment business model analysis. Available at: http://www.mobile-ecosystem.org/wp-content/uploads/downloads/2010/03/Best-Practices-for-MFS-Enrolment-Business-model-analysis-final.pdf. Accessed 22 Jul 2015

Morrow B (2012) BYOD security challenges: control and protect your most sensitive data. Netw Secur 2012(12):5–8

Swaroop M, Sagar M (2015) Over the top services (OTT): policy framework and revenue models. IIT Delhi, Working Paper

Thomson G (2012) BYOD: enabling the chaos. Netw Secur 2012(2):5–8

# Appendix A

See Table A.1.

© Springer India 2016

M.K. Medudula et al., *Telecom Management in Emerging Economies*,
DOI 10.1007/978-81-322-2749-6

**Table A.1** Global telecom information database (acts and laws/ministry/regulator/operators)

| Country | Region (country code) | Sub region | Laws/policies/ acts/events (in chronological order) | Government/ministry/ department | Regulator | Incumbent operator | Other operators (MNOs/fixed-line) | Sources (Weblink) |
|---|---|---|---|---|---|---|---|---|
| Afghanistan | Asia (93) | Southern Asia | Telecom and Internet Policy (2003), Telecommunication Law (2006), Broadband Access License (2012) | Ministry of Communications and Information Technology (MCIT)—1955 | Afghanistan Telecommunication Regulatory Authority (ATRA) | Afghan Telecom (Afghan Wireless Communication Company (AWCC)) | Etisalat, MTN, Roshan (TDCA), Wasel Telecom and Salaam | http://mcit.gov.af/en; http://atra.gov.af/en |
| Albania | Europe (355) | Southern Europe | TRE Establishment (1998), Law On Telecommunications in the Republic of Albania (1995) | Ministry of Public Works, Transportation and Telecommunications | Electronic and Postal Communications Authority (AKEP) | Albanian Telecom (Eagle Mobile) | AMC (OTE), Plus Communication, Vodafone | http://www.akep.al/en/ |
| Algeria | Africa (213) | Northern Africa | ARPT Creation and Liberalization (2000), General Telecommunications Law (2000-2003) | Ministère de la Poste et des Technologies de l'Information et de la Communication | Autorité de régulation de la poste et des télécommunications (ARPT) | Algerie Telecom (Mobilis) | Ooredoo (NMTC), Orascom Telecom Algerie (OTA)/ Djezzy, Wataniya Telecom Algerie/Nedjma | http://www.arpt.dz/ |
| American Samoa | Oceania (1) | Polynesia | Telecommunication Act (1996) | NA | Federal Communications Commission (FCC) | American Samoa Telecommunications Authority (ASTCA) | BlueSky Communications, Digicel | http://astca.net/ |
| Andorra | Europe (376) | Southern Europe | Creation of Telecommunications Service Andorra (975) | Ministry of Public Administration, Transport and Telecommunications | Servei de Telecomunicaciones d'Andorra (Andorra Telecom) | Andorra Telecom | NA | http://www.andorratelecom.ad/; https://www.govern.ad/ |
| Angola | Africa (244) | Middle Africa | INACOM Establishment (1999), Basic Telecommunication Law (2001) | Ministério das Telecomunicações e Tecnologias de Informação | Institut Angolias des Communications (INACOM) | Angola Telecom (Formerly known as Servei de Telecomunicacions d'Andorra) | Movicel (Mobile brand of Angola Telecom), Unitel, Mercury Telecom (MS Telecom) | www.inacom.gov.ao; http://www.mtti.gov.ao/ |
| Anguilla | Americas (1) | Caribbean | Public Utilities Act (2003), Telecommunications Act(2003), | Ministry of Infrastructure, Communications, Utilities and Housing | The Public Utilities Commission | Cable and Wireless (West Indies) Limited (C and W) | Digicel Anguilla, Lime | http://www.pucanguilla.org/; http://www.gov.ai/ministry.php?id=5 |

(continued)

**Table A.1** (continued)

| Country | Region (country code) | Sub region | Laws/policies/ acts/events (in chronological order) | Government/ministry/ department | Regulator | Incumbent operator | Other operators (MNOs/fixed-line) | Sources (Weblink) |
|---|---|---|---|---|---|---|---|---|
| | | | Telecommunications code (2004) | | | | | |
| Antigua and Barbuda | Americas (1) | Caribbean | The Telecommunications Act (2007) | Ministry of Telecommunications, Science and Technology | Telecommunications Division of the Government of Antigua and Barbuda | Antigua Public Utilities Authority (APUA) | Digicel, Lime | http://telecom.gov.ag/ |
| Argentina | Americas (54) | Southern America | Telecommunications Act (1972) | SeCom | La Autoridad Federal de Tecnologías de la Información y las Comunicaciones (AFTIC) | Empresa Nacional de Telecomunicaciones (ENTel) | Claro Argentina, Movistar Argentina, Telecom Personal (Argentina) | http://www.aftic.gob.ar/ |
| Armenia | Asia (374) | Western Asia | Telecommunication Law (1998) | The Ministry of Transport and Communication of the Republic of Armenia | Public Services Regulatory Commission (PSRC) | ArmenTel | Beeline (Armentel), Orange, VivaCell (MTS), Ucom | http://www.psrc.am/en/; http://www.mtc.am |
| Aruba | Americas (297) | Caribbean | | Minister of Finance, Communication, Utilities and Energy | Directie Telecommunicatie Zaken | SETAR N.V. | DIGICEL ARUBA, MIO wireless, Scarlet Aruba | http://www.dtz.aw |
| Australia | Oceania (61) | Australasia | Telecommunications Act (1997) | Department of Communications | Australian Communications Authority (ACMA) | Telstra | Optus (Singtel), Vodafone | http://www.acma.gov.au |
| Austria | Europe (43) | Western Europe | Telecommunications Act (2003) | Federal Ministry of Transport, Innovation and Technology (BMVIT) | Austrian Regulatory Authority for Broadcasting and Telecommunications (RTR) and Telecom Contrl Commission (TKK) | Telekom Austria | 3 Austria (Hutchison), Lycamobile, T-Mobile Austria (Deutsche Telekom) | https://www.rtr.at/en; https://www.bmvit.gv.at/en/ |
| Azerbaijan | Asia (994) | Western Asia | Law of the Republic of Azerbaijan on Telecommunication (2005) | Ministry of Communications and High Technologies | Ministry of Communications and High Technologies | Aztelekom | Azercell, Bakcell, Azerfon, Caspian Telecom, Delta Telecom | http://www.mincom.gov.az/home/ |

(continued)

**Table A.1** (continued)

| Country | Region (country code) | Sub region | Laws/policies/ acts/events (in chronological order) | Government/ministry/ department | Regulator | Incumbent operator | Other operators (MNOs/fixed-line) | Sources (Weblink) |
|---|---|---|---|---|---|---|---|---|
| Bahamas | Americas (1) | Caribbean | Telecommunications Act (1999), Utilities Regulation and Competition Authority Act (2009), Communications Act (2009) | Government of The Commonwealth of The Bahamas | Utilities Regulation and Competition Authority (URCA) | The Bahamas Telecommunications Company Ltd (BTC) | NIL | http://www.urcabahamas.bs/ |
| Bahrain | Asia (973) | Western Asia | Telecommunications Law (2002) | Ministry of Industry and Commerce | Telecommunications Regulatory Authority (TRA) | Bahrain Telecommunications Company | VIVA, Zain, Batelco | http://www.tra.org.bh/ ; http://www.moic.gov.bh/En |
| Bangladesh | Asia (880) | Southern Asia | Telegraph Act (1885), Wireless Telegraph Act (1933), National Telecommunication Policy (1998), Telecommunication Act (2001), National Broadband Policy (2009) | Ministry of Post, Telecommunications and Information Technology | Bangladesh Telecommunication Regulatory Commission (BTRC) | Bangladesh Telecommunications Company Ltd (BTCL) | Grameen Phone Ltd. (GP), Banglalink Digital Communications Limited, Robi Axiata Limited (Robi), Airtel Bangladesh Limited (Airtel), Pacific Bangladesh Telecom Limited (Citycell) and Teletalk Bangladesh Ltd. (Teletalk) | http://www.btrc.gov.bd/; www.ptd.gov.bd |
| Barbados | Americas (1) | Caribbean | Telecommunications Act (2001), Telecommunications Regulations (2003, 2004, 2005) | The Division of Energy and Telecommunications, Prime Minister's Office | Telecommunications Unit, Division of Energy and Telecommunications | Cable and Wireless Barbados Ltd. | Digicel Barbados Limited | www.telecoms.gov.bb |
| Belarus | Europe (375) | Eastern Europe | Law of the Republic of Belarus (2005) | Ministry of Posts and Telecommunications | Ministry of Posts and Telecommunications | Beltelecom | Turkcell (Life), Telekom Austria (Velcom), MTS | www.mpt.gov.by/en/ |

(continued)

**Table A.1** (continued)

| Country | Region (country code) | Sub region | Laws/policies/ acts/events (in chronological order) | Government/ministry/ department | Regulator | Incumbent operator | Other operators (MNOs/fixed-line) | Sources (Weblink) |
|---|---|---|---|---|---|---|---|---|
| Belgium | Europe (32) | Western Europe | Law on Electronic Communications (2005), Telecom Act (1999) | Institut Belge des Services Postaux et des Télécommunications (IBPT) | Belgian Institute of Postal services and Telecommunications (BIPT) | Belgacom | Proximus, Mobistar and Base | www.bipt.be/en |
| Belize | Americas (501) | Central America | The Belize Telecommunications Act (2002, 2009) | Ministry of Energy, Science, Public Utilities, Transport, Communications and National Emergency Management | Belize Public Utilities Commission | Belize Telecommunications Ltd (BTL)/Belize Telemedia (Digicell) | Speednet Communications | www.puc.bz |
| Benin | Africa (229) | Western Africa | Civil society and National NICT policy (2003) | Ministry of Communications | Autorité De Régulation Des Communications Électroniques Et De La Poste (ARCEP) | Benin Telecoms (Libercom) | Glo Mobile (Globacom), Moov (Maroc Telecom), MTN and Bell Benin | http://arcep.bj/ |
| Bermuda | Americas (1) | Northern America | Telecommunications Act (1986), Electronic Communications Act (2011) | Ministry of Energy, Telecommunications and e-Commerce | Bermuda Regulatory Authority (RA) | Bermuda Telephone Company (BTC) | Digicel, CellularOne Bermuda | http://www.rab.bm/ |
| Bhutan | Asia (975) | Southern Asia | Bhutan Telecommunications Act (1999), Bhutan Information, Communications and Media Act (2006) | Ministry of Information and Communication (MoIC) | Bhutan InfoComm and Media Authority | Bhutan Telecom (B-Mobile) | TashiCell | http://www.bicma.gov.bt/ |
| Bolivia | Americas (591) | Southern America | Bolivian Telecommunications Act (1995) (Ley No. 1632) | Ministerio de Comunicación/Ministry of Communications | Superintendencia de Telecomunicaciones (SITTEL) | Bolivian National Telecommunications Company | Entel, Telecel, NuevaTel PCS (Viva) and Cotas, Telefonica Celular de Bolivia S. A. (Tigo) | https://www.osiptel.gob.pe |
| Bonaire, Sint Eustatius and Saba | Americas (599) | Caribbean | BT&P (2001), BES Telecommunications Act | Ministry of EZ for the Telecommunications Sector | Bureau of Telecommunication and Post (BT&P) | Telefonia Bonairiano N.V. (Telbo) | Digicel Bonaire, UTS Mobile | |

(continued)

**Table A.1** (continued)

| Country | Region (country code) | Sub region | Laws/policies/acts/events (in chronological order) | Government/ministry/department | Regulator | Incumbent operator | Other operators (MNOs/fixed-line) | Sources (Weblink) |
|---|---|---|---|---|---|---|---|---|
| Bosnia and Herzegovina | Europe (387) | Southern Europe | The Communication Regulatory Agency (2001), Implementation of Communications Law (2002), Telecom Policies (2000, 2002, 2006 and 2009) | Minister for Telecommunications, Posts, IT and Communication | The Communication Regulatory Agency (CRA) | BH Telecom, Telecom Srpske(M: tel), Croatian Telecom | NA | http://rak.ba/eng/ |
| Botswana | Africa (267) | Southern Africa | Botswana Telecommunications Corporation Act (1980), Telecommunication Policy (1995), BTA Establishment (1996), Communications Regulatory Authority Act (2012) | Minister of Communications, Science and Technology | Botswana Communications Regulatory Authority | Botswana Telecommunications Corporation (BTC) | BeMobile (BTC), Mascom Wireless, Orange Botswana | http://www.bocra.org.bw/ |
| Brazil | Americas (55) | Southern America | General Telecommunications Law (1997) | Ministry of Communications | Agência Nacional de Telecomunicações (ANATEL) | Telebras divided into 4 incumbents (Telemar, BRASIL TELECOM, Embratel and Telefonica) | Oi, Claro (América Móvil), Telefônica Brasil (Vivo) and TIM Brasil | http://www.anatel.gov.br |
| British Virgin Islands | Americas (1) | Caribbean | Telecommunication Policy (2007), Telecommunication Act (2006) | Minister of Communications and Works | Telecommunications Regulatory Commission (TRC) | Lime (Cable and Wireless Communications) | Digicel, Caribbean Cellular Telephone (CCT) | http://www.trc.vg/ |
| Brunei Darussalam | Asia (673) | South-Eastern Asia | Jabatan Telekom Brunei establishment (1952) | Ministry of Communications/Kementerian Perhubungan | Authority for Info-communications Technology Industry (ATIT) | Jabatan Telekom (Telekom Brunei Berhad- TelBru) | Progresif Cellular Sdn Bhd (PCSB), DST Communications Sdn Bhd (DST) | www.aiti.gov.bn/ |

(continued)

**Table A.1** (continued)

| Country | Region (country code) | Sub region | Laws/policies/ acts/events (in chronological order) | Government/ministry/ department | Regulator | Incumbent operator | Other operators (MNOs/fixed-line) | Sources (Weblink) |
|---|---|---|---|---|---|---|---|---|
| Bulgaria | Europe (359) | Eastern Europe | Electronic Communications Act (2007) | Ministry of Transport, Information Technology and Communications | Communication Regulation Commission (CRC) | Bulgarian Telecommunications Company (Vivacom AD) | Mobiltel (M-Tel), Telenor (earlier branded as GLOBUL) | www.crc.bg/; https://www.mtitc.government.bg/ |
| Burkina Faso | Africa (226) | Western Africa | Telecomminication Act No. 051/98/AN (1998) | Ministère des Postes et Télécommunications | Autorité de régulation des communications éléctroniques (ARCE) | Onatel (Telmob) | Bharti Airtel (Acquired Zain), Moov (Telecel) | www.arce.bf/ |
| Burundi | Africa (257) | Eastern Africa | DecreeLaw No. 1/011 (1997); Presidential Decree No. 100/97 (2014) | Ministere Des Transports, Postes Et Telecommunications | Agence de Régulation et de Contrôle des Télécommunications (ARCT) | Onatel (ONAMOB) | U-COM Burundi (TelecelGlobe), Econet, Lacell SU, Africell | www.arct.gov.bi/ |
| Cambodia | Asia (855) | South-Eastern Asia | Regulator Establishment (2012) | The Ministry of Posts and Telecommunications (MPTC) | Telecommunication Regulator of Cambodia (TRC) | Telecom Cambodia (TC) | MobiTel, Smart Axiata, Metfone, qb (CADCOMMS), Excell (GT Cell) | www.trc.gov.kh/ |
| Cameroon | Africa (237) | Middle Africa | Law N° 2010/013 (2010), Law N° 98/014 (1998) | Ministere Des Postes Et Des Telecommunications | Agence de Regulation des Telecommunications (ART) | Cameroon Telecommunications Corporation (CAMTEL) | MTN, Orange, Viettel | www.art.cm/ |
| Canada | Americas (1) | Northern America | Canadian Radio-television and Telecommunications Commission Act (1985), Telecommunications Act (1993) | Minister of Industry | Canadian Radio Television and Telecommunications Commission (CRTC) | Bell Canada, Telus (Telus Mobility), Manitoba Telecom Services (MTS), SaskTel and Shaw Communications | Rogers Communication, Vidéotron, WIND Mobile, Eastlink | www.crtc.gc.ca/eng |
| Cape Verde | Africa (238) | Western Africa | Privatization (1995) | Ministry of Infrastructure, Transport and Communications | Agencia Nacional das Comunicações/ National Communications Agency (ANAC) | Cabo Verde Telecom (CVT) | T+ (Unitel) | www.anac.cv/ |

(continued)

**Table A.1** (continued)

| Country | Region (country code) | Sub region | Laws/policies/ acts/events (in chronological order) | Government/ministry/ department | Regulator | Incumbent operator | Other operators (MNOs/fixed-line) | Sources (Weblink) |
|---|---|---|---|---|---|---|---|---|
| Cayman Islands | Americas (1) | Caribbean | Information and Communications Technology Authority Law (2002) | Ministry of Communications, Works and Infrastructure | Information and Communications Technology Authority (ICTA) | Cable and Wireless (Lime) | Digicel | www.icta.ky/ |
| Central African Rep. | Africa (236) | Middle Africa | The Telecommunication Act No. 96/008 (1996) | Ministre des Postes et télécommunication | Agence de Régulation des Télécommunications (ART) | Société Centrafricaine de Télécommunications (Socatel) | Telecel Centrafrique, Atlantique Telecom (Maroc Telecom), Orange | www.art-rca.org/ |
| Chad | Africa (235) | Middle Africa | Telecommunications Act (1998) | Ministry of Communications and Spokesperson | Office Tchadien de Regulation des Telecoms (OTRT) | Société des Télécommunications du Tchad (Sotel Tchad) | Airtel Chad (Formerly known as Celtel), Tigo Chad (Millicom) | www.otrt.td/ |
| Chile | Americas (56) | Southern America | The General Telecommunications Act (Act No. 18.168 of 1982) | Ministerio de Transportes y Telecomunicaciones | Subsecretaria de Telecommuni-cacaiones (SUBTEL) | Telefónica Chile (Movistar) | Claro (América Móvil), Entel PCS, VTR Móvil, Nextel (Novator) | www.subtel.cl/ |
| China | Asia (86) | Eastern Asia | Establishment of Ministry of Information Industry (MII) (1998), Foreign Investment Regulations (2001), Establishment of Ministry of Industry and Information Technology (2008) | Ministry of Industry and Information Technology (MIIT) | Ministry of Industry and Information Technology (MIIT) | China Mobile | China Telecom, China Unicom | www.miit.gov.cn/ |
| Colombia | Americas (57) | Southern America | The Public Utility Services Law (1994) | Ministerio de Tecnologías de la Información y las Comunicaciones (MINTIC) | Comisión de Regulación de Comunicaciones (CRC) | Telefónica (Formerly known as Colombia Telecom) | Empresa de Telecomunicaciones de Bogotá (ETB), Claro Colombia (América Móvil), Colombia Movil (Tigo), | https://www.crcom.gov.co/ |

(continued)

**Table A.1** (continued)

| Country | Region (country code) | Sub region | Laws/policies/acts/events (in chronological order) | Government/ministry/department | Regulator | Incumbent operator | Other operators (MNOs/fixed-line) | Sources (Weblink) |
|---|---|---|---|---|---|---|---|---|
| Comoros | Africa (269) | Eastern Africa | Electronic Communications Law No. 14-031 (2004) | Ministry of Transportation, Post, Telecommunications, Communication and Tourism | Autorite Nationale de Regulation des Tics (ANRTIC) | Comores Telecom (Comtel)- Formerly known as Societe Nationale des Postes and Telecommunications (SNPT) | NA | www.anrtic.km/ |
| Congo (Dem. Rep.) | Africa (243) | Middle Africa | High Council of Broadcasting and Communications Act (2011), Telecommunications Act (1940, 2002) | Ministre des Postes, Télécommunications, Nouvelles Technologies de l'Information et de la Communication (PT-NTIC) | Autorite de Regulation de la Poste et des Telecommunications du Congo (ARPTC) | Office Congolais des Postes et des Télécommunications (OCPT) | Supercell, Oasis Telecom, Vodacom DRC, Orange RDC, Tigo, Airtel DRC (Acquired Celtel) | http://arptc.gouv.cd/ |
| Congo (Rep.) | Africa (242) | Middle Africa | Telecommunications Act No. 11-2009 (2009), Telecommunication Law No. 14-97 (1997) | Ministry for Post and Electronic Communications | Regulatory Agency for Electronic Communications and Post (ARPCE) | Société des Télécommunications du Congo (Congo Telecom) | Azur (Equateur Telecom Congo), Airtel Congo, MTN (Accueil), Warid Congo | http://www.arpce.cg |
| Cook Islands | Oceania (682) | Polynesia | Telecommunications Act (1989) | Ministry of Finance and Economic Management | Government of the Cook Islands | Telecom Cook Islands (Bluesky) | NA | http://www.parliament.gov.ck |
| Costa Rica | Americas (506) | Central America | SUTEL Establishment (2008) | Ministerio de Ciencia Tecnología y Telecomunicaciones de Costa Rica (MICITT) | Superintendencia de Telecomunicaciones (SUTEL) | I.C.E. (Instituto Costarricense de Electricidad) | Claro CR, Movistar | http://sutel.go.cr/ |
| Côte d'Ivoire | Africa (225) | Western Africa | Telecommunications Act (1995), Telecommunications Decree No. 2012-293 (2012) | Ministère de la Communication | Autorité de Régulation des Télécommunications/Tic de Côte d'Ivoire (ARTCI) | Côte d'Ivoire Telecom | MTN, Orange, Moov (ATLANTIQUE TELECOM), Oricel | www.artci.ci/ |
| Croatia | Europe (385) | Southern Europe | Electronic Communications Act (2008), Electronic Communications Act Amendment (2011) | Ministry of Maritime Affairs, Transport and Infrastructure | Croatian Post and Electronic Communications Agency (HAKOM) | T-Hrvatski Telekom | Orange, Tele2, Optima Telecom (Fixed-line), H1 Telekom (Fixed-line) | www.hakom.hr/ |

(continued)

**Table A.1** (continued)

| Country | Region (country code) | Sub region | Laws/policies/ acts/events (in chronological order) | Government/ministry/ department | Regulator | Incumbent operator | Other operators (MNOs/fixed-line) | Sources (Weblink) |
|---|---|---|---|---|---|---|---|---|
| Cuba | Americas (53) | Caribbean | Digital and Telecommunications Advancement Act (2015) | Ministério de la Informática y las Comunicaciones de Cuba (MIC) | Ministério de la Informática y las Comunicaciones de Cuba (MIC) | Empresa de Telecomunicaciones de Cuba S.A. (SA ETECSA) | NIL | http://www.cubagob.cu/ |
| Cyprus | Asia (357) | Western Asia | Electronic Communications and Postal Services Law (2004) | Ministry of Transport, Communications and Works | Office of the Commissioner of Electronic Communications and Postal Regulation (OCECPR) | Cyprus Telecommunications Authority (CYTA) (Mobile brand: Cytamobile-Vodafone) | MTN Cyprus | www.ocecpr.org.cy/ |
| Czech Republic | Europe (420) | Eastern Europe | Electronic Communications Act No. 127 (2005) | Ministry of Industry and Trade | Czech Telecommunications Office | Telefonica 02 | T-Mobile, Vodafone (formerly Oskar Mobil), U:fon (Mobilkom) | www.ctu.eu/ |
| D.P.R. Korea | Asia (850) | Eastern Asia | Telecommunication Act Amendment (2001) | Ministry of Post and Telecommunications | Ministry of Post and Telecommunications | Korea Post and Telecommunications Corporation (KPTC) | Koryolink | http://www.korea-dpr.com/ |
| Denmark | Europe (45) | Northern Europe | Telecom Policy (1994), Electronic Communications Act (2011) | The Danish Government | Danish Business Authority | TDC (Tdc Mobil) | Telenor, Telia (TeliaSonera), Hi3G (Hutchison) | http://danishbusinessauthority.dk/ |
| Djibouti | Africa (253) | Eastern Africa | Djibouti Telecom SA Incorporation (1999) | Ministere De La Communication, Charge Des Postes Et Des Telecommunications | Ministere De La Communication, Charge Des Postes Et Des Telecommunications | Djibouti Telecom | NIL | www.presidence.dj/ |
| Dominica | Americas (1) | Caribbean | Telecommunications Act 8 (2000) | Ministry of Information, Science, Telecommunications and Technology | The National Telecommunications Regulatory Commission of the Commonwealth of Dominica (NTRC) | Cable and Wireless (Dominica) limited (LIME) | Digicel | www.ntrcdom.org/ |

(continued)

**Table A.1** (continued)

| Country | Region (country code) | Sub region | Laws/policies/acts/events (in chronological order) | Government/ministry/department | Regulator | Incumbent operator | Other operators (MNOs/fixed-line) | Sources (Weblink) |
|---|---|---|---|---|---|---|---|---|
| Dominican Rep. | Americas (1) | Caribbean | General Telecommunications Law No. 153-98 (1998) | Ministry of Public Works and Communication | Instituto Dominicano de las Telecomunicaciones (Indotel) | Compañía Dominicana de Teléfonos (Codetel) (Presently known as Claro) | Orange, Viva | www.indotel.gob.do/ |
| Ecuador | Americas (593) | Southern America | Communications Law/LEY ORGÁNICA DE COMUNICACIÓN (2013), Telecommunications Act/LEY ORGÁNICA DE TELECOMUNI CACIONES (2015) | El Ministerio de Telecomunicaciones y de la Sociedad de la Información/The Ministry of Telecommunications and Information Society | Agencia de Regulación y Control de las Telecomunicaciones (ARCOTEL) | Corporación Nacional de Telecomunicaciones (CNT) | CNT Mobile (Formerly known as Alegro), Claro/Conecel (América Móvil), Movistar (Telefoníca) | www.arcotel.gob.ec/ |
| Egypt | Africa (20) | Northern Africa | Egypt Telecommunication Regulation Law No. 10 (2003) | Ministry of Communications and Information Technology (MCIT) | National Telecom Regulatory Authority (NTRA) | Telecom Egypt | MobiNil, Vodafone, Etisalat Misr | http://www.tra.gov.eg/english/main.asp |
| El Salvador | Americas (503) | Central America | Liberalization(1997), Legislative Decree No. 808 (1996), Telecommunications Act (1997), Telecommunications Act (2010) | NA (Data Not Available) | Superintendencia General de Electricidad y Telecommunicaciones (SIGET) | Compañía de Telecomunicaciones de El Salvador (Claro) | Digicel, Tigo, Movistar (Telefónica Móviles) | www.siget.gob.sv/ |
| Equatorial Guinea | Africa (240) | Middle Africa | Telecommunications Act: LEY No. 7 (2005) | The Ministry of Transport, Technology, Posts and Telecommunications | Órgano Regulador de las Telecomunicaciones (ORTEL) | Getesa-Orange | Guinea Ecuatorial de Comunicaciones Sociedad Anonima (GECOMSA), Muni Telecom | www.ortel-ge.org/ |

(continued)

**Table A.1** (continued)

| Country | Region (country code) | Sub region | Laws/policies/acts/events (in chronological order) | Government/ministry/department | Regulator | Incumbent operator | Other operators (MNOs/fixed-line) | Sources (Weblink) |
|---|---|---|---|---|---|---|---|---|
| Eritrea | Africa (291) | Eastern Africa | Eritrea Communications Proclamation no. 102/98 (1998) | Ministry of Transport and Communications | Eritrean Communications Regulatory Authority —ECRA | Eritrea Telecommunication Services Corporation (EriTel) | Nil | http://www.tse.com.er/ |
| Estonia | Europe (372) | Northern Europe | Telecommunications Act (2000), Electronic Communications Act (2005) | Ministry of Economic Affairs and Communications | Estonian Competition Authority | Elion Enterprises Limited (Elion) (Eesti Telekom) | Tele2, Elisa | www.konkurentsiamet.ee/?lang=en |
| Ethiopia | Africa (251) | Eastern Africa | Telecommunication Proclamation No. 49 (1996), No. 73 (1997), Regulations No. 47 (1999) | Ministry of Communication and Information Technology | Ethiopian Telecommunications Agency (ETA) | Ethio Telecom (Ethiopian Telecommunications Corporation) | Nil | http://www.ethionet.et/, www.mcit.gov.et |
| Falkland (Malvinas) Is. | Americas (500) | Southern America | GSM Services (2005) | Falkland Islands Government | Law and Regulation Directorate | Cable and Wireless (LIME) | Nil | http://www.falklands.gov.fk/ |
| Faroe Islands | Europe (298) | Northern Europe | Telecommunications Act (1997) | Ministry of Trade and Industry | Telecommunication Authority of the Faroe Islands | Faroese Telecom | Kall P/F (Vodafone) | www.fjarskiftiseftirlitid.fo/fo/english/about-us/ |
| Fiji | Oceania (679) | Melanesia | Telecommunications Act (1999), National Broadband Policy (2011) | Ministry of Information and Communications | Telecommunications Authority of Fiji (TAF) | Telecom Fiji Limited | Digicel, Vodafone | http://www.taf.org.fj |
| Finland | Europe (358) | Northern Europe | Telecommunications Act No. 396 (1987), Finland's Radio Act No. 1015 (2001), Communications Market Act No. 393 (2003) | Ministry of Transport and Communications | Finnish Communications Regulatory Authority (FICORA) | Telia Sonera | Elisa, Alands Mobiltelefon (AMT), DNA, Elisa | https://www.viestintavirasto.fi/en/ |

(continued)

**Table A.1** (continued)

| Country | Region (country code) | Sub region | Laws/policies/acts/events (in chronological order) | Government/ministry/department | Regulator | Incumbent operator | Other operators (MNOs/fixed-line) | Sources (Weblink) |
|---|---|---|---|---|---|---|---|---|
| France | Europe (33) | Western Europe | Telecommunications Act (1996), Creation of Autorité de Régulation des Télécommunication (1997) | Minister of Culture and Communication/ Ministre de la Culture et de la Communication | Autorité de Régulation des Communications Electroniques et des Postes (ARCEP) | France Telecom (Orange) | SFR, Bouygues Telecom, Free Mobile | www.arcep.fr/ |
| French Guiana | Americas (594) | Southern America | NA | Ministère des Outre-Mer (French Ministry of Overseas) | Autorite de Regulation des Communications Electroniques et des Postes (ARCEP)—Paris | Orange Caraïbe (France Telecom) | Digicel, Outremer Telecom (SFR) | http://www.guyane.pref.gouv.fr/; http://www.outre-mer.gouv.fr/; www.arcep.fr/ |
| French Polynesia | Oceania (689) | Polynesia | NA | Government of French Polynesia | Government of French Polynesia | Office des Postes et Télécommunication (OPT) | Tikiphone (Vini), Vodafone | |
| Gabon | Africa (241) | Middle Africa | Telecommunication Law No. 4, 5 and 6 (2001) | Ministère de l'Economie Numérique et de la Poste | Agence De Regulation Des Communications Electroniques Et Des Postes (Arcep) | Gabon Telecom | Moov Gabob, Airtel, Azur Telecom (Bintel) | www.arcep.ga/ |
| Gambia | Africa (220) | Western Africa | Public Utilities Authority Act (2001), Information and Communication Act (2009) | Ministry of Communication, Information and IT | Gambian Public Utilities Regulatory Authority (PURA) | Gambia Telecommunications Company (Gamtel/Gamcell) | Comium, Qcell, Africell | www.pura.gm/ |
| Georgia | Asia (995) | Western Asia | Telecom Act (1995), Law on Broadcasting (2004), Law on Electronic Communications (2005) | Ministry of Economic and Sustainable Development of Georgia | Georgian National Communications Commission (GNCC) | Telecom Georgia Ltd. | MagtiCom, Geocell, Mobitel (Beeline) and AT&T | www.gncc.ge/en/ |

(continued)

**Table A.1** (continued)

| Country | Region (country code) | Sub region | Laws/policies/acts/events (in chronological order) | Government/ministry/department | Regulator | Incumbent operator | Other operators (MNOs/fixed-line) | Sources (Weblink) |
|---|---|---|---|---|---|---|---|---|
| Germany | Europe (49) | Western Europe | Telecommunications Act (1996) and (2004) | Federal Ministry for Economic Affairs and Energy | Federal Network Agency—Bundesnetzagentur | Deutsche Telekom (T-Mobile) | Vodafone (D2), O2 and E-Plus (Telefónica) | www.bundesnetzagentur.de/ |
| Ghana | Africa (233) | Western Africa | Ministry of Transport and Communications | Ministry of Communications | National Communications Authority | Ghana Telecom (Presently Vodafone Ghana) | MTN, Airtel, Glo, Expresso, Tigo | www.nca.org.gh/ |
| Gibraltar | Europe (350) | Southern Europe | Regulatory Authority Act (2000), Communications Act (2006) | Minister for Economic Development, Telecommunications and the GSB | Gibraltar Regulatory Authority | Gibtelecom | CTS Gibraltar Ltd (Fixed), Shine Mobile | www.gra.gi/ |
| Greece | Europe (30) | Southern Europe | Telecommunications Act 2867 (2000), Telecommunications Law 3431 (2006), Law 4070 (2012) | Ministry of Infrastructure, Transport and Networks | EETT (National Telecommunications and Post Commission) | Hellenic Telecommunications Organization S.A. (OTE) | Cosmote (OTE), Vodafone, Wind | www.eett.gr/ |
| Greenland | Americas (299) | Northern America | Creation of TELE Greenland (1997) | Government of Greenland | Government of Greenland | Tele Greenland (Tele-Post) | Nil | http://naalakkersuisut.gl/en/Naalakkersuisut |
| Grenada | Americas (1) | Caribbean | Telecommunications Act 31 (2000) | Ministry of Communications, Works, Physical Development, Public Utilities, ICT and Community Development | National Telecommunications Regulatory Commission (NTRC) | Cable and Wireless (Lime) | Digicel | http://ntrc.gd/ |
| Guadeloupe | Americas (590) | Caribbean | NA | Ministère des Outre-Mer (French Ministry of Overseas) | Autorite de Regulation des Communications Electroniques et des Postes (Arcep)—Paris | Orange Caraïbe (France Telecom) | Digicel, Outremer Telecom (SFR), Dauphin, TelCell | www.arcep.fr/; http://www.outre-mer.gouv.fr/ |

(continued)

**Table A.1** (continued)

| Country | Region (country code) | Sub region | Laws/policies/ acts/events (in chronological order) | Government/ministry/ department | Regulator | Incumbent operator | Other operators (MNOs/fixed-line) | Sources (Weblink) |
|---|---|---|---|---|---|---|---|---|
| Guam | Oceania (1) | Micronesia | Telecommunications Act (2004) | NA | Guam Public Utilities Commission | GTA Teleguam (Pulse Mobile) | Docomo Pacific, IT and E (MTC), iCONNECT | www.guampuc.com/ |
| Guatemala | Americas (502) | Central America | Ley General de Telecomunicaciones/ General Telecommunications Law (1996) | Ministerio de Comunicaciones, infraestructura y vivienda | Superintendencia de Telecomunicaciones de Guatemala (SIT) | Telecomunicaciones de Guatemala (TELGUA) (Currently subsidiary of América Móvil)- Mobile brand 'Claro' | Tigo (Millicom), Movistar, Red | www.sit.gob.gt/ |
| Guernsey | Europe | Northern Europe | The Telecommunications (Bailiwick of Guernsey) Law (2001), UK communications authority-Ofcom's Wireless Telegraphy Act (2006) and Communications Act (2003) | Commerce and Employment Department | Channel Islands Competition and Regulatory Authorities (CICRA) | Sure (Formerly known as Guernsey Telecoms) | Airtel-Vodafone | www.cicra.gg/ |
| Guinea | Africa (224) | Western Africa | New Law of Telecommunications No. 018 (2015) | Minister of Posts, Telecommunications and New Information Technologies (MPTNTI) | Autorité de Régulation des Postes et Télécommunications (ARPT) | Societe des Telecoms de Guinee (Sotelgui) | Intercel Guinée (Acquired by Expresso Telecom), Orange, Cellcom, MTN | http://www.arpt.gov.gn/ |
| Guinea-Bissau | Africa (245) | Western Africa | Basic Law of Information and Communication Technologies—Law No. 5 (2010) | NA | Autoridade Reguladora Nacional das Tecnologias de Informação e Comunicação (National Regulatory Authority of | GuineTelecom (Moble brand GuineTel) | Spacetel (MTN), Orange | http://arn.gw/ |

(continued)

**Table A.1** (continued)

| Country | Region (country code) | Sub region | Laws/policies/ acts/events (in chronological order) | Government/ministry/ department | Regulator | Incumbent operator | Other operators (MNOs/fixed-line) | Sources (Weblink) |
|---|---|---|---|---|---|---|---|---|
| | | | | | Information and Communication Technologies) | | | |
| Guyana | Americas (592) | Southern America | Public Utilities Commission Act No. 26 (1990), Public Utilities Commission Act No. 10 (1999) | Office of the President | Guyana Public Utilities Commission (PUC) | Guyana Telephone and Telegraph Company Limited (GT&T) | Cellink (GT&T), Digicel | www.puc.org.gy/ |
| Haiti | Americas (509) | Caribbean | Telecommunication Decree No. 105 (1969), Telecommunication Act (1977) | Ministère des Travaux Publics, Transports et Communications | Conseil National des Télécommunications (CONATEL) | Natcom (Télécommunications d'Haiti S.A.M.) | Digicel, Voilà (Comcel), Haitel | http://conatel.gouv.ht/ |
| Honduras | Americas (504) | Central America | Telecommunications Decree 185/95 (1995) | NA | Comision Nacional de Telecomunicaciones (Conatel) | Empresa Hondureña de Telecomunicaciones, HONDUTEL | Tigo (Telefónica Celular (Celtel)), claro (América Móvil), Digicel (Acquired by América Móvil) | www.conatel.gob.hn/ |
| Hong Kong, China | Asia (852) | Eastern Asia | Telecommunications Ordinance (2012) | Commerce and Economic Development Bureau (CEDB) | Office of the Communications Authority (OFCA) | PCCW (Formerly known as Hong Kong Telephone Company Ltd.) | Smartone-Vodafone, China Mobile HK, Hutchison 3, csl Limited | www.ofca.gov.hk/en/ home/ |
| Hungary | Europe (36) | Eastern Europe | Telecommunications Act LXXII (1992), Communications Act No. XL (2001), Electronic Communications Act (2003) | NA | National Media and Info-communications Authority | Magyar Telekom (T-Mobile) | Vodafone, Telenor | http://english.nmhh. hu/ |
| Iceland | Europe (354) | Northern Europe | Electronic Communications Act No. 81 (2003), Post | Ministry of the Interior | Post and Telecom Administration | Siminn (Formerly known as Iceland Telecom Ltd) | Vodafone, Nova | www.pfs.is/english/ |

(continued)

**Table A.1** (continued)

| Country | Region (country code) | Sub region | Laws/policies/acts/events (in chronological order) | Government/ministry/department | Regulator | Incumbent operator | Other operators (MNOs/fixed-line) | Sources (Weblink) |
|---|---|---|---|---|---|---|---|---|
| | | | and Telecom Administration Act No. 69 (2003) | | | | | |
| India | Asia (91) | Southern Asia | Indian Telegraph Act (1885), Indian Wireless Telegraphy Act (1933), National Telecom Policy (1994), New Telecom Policy (1999), Broadband Policy (2004), National Telecom Policy (2012) | Ministry of Communications and Information Technology | Telecom Regulatory Authority of India (TRAI) | Bharat Sanchar Nigam Limited Portal (BSNL) and Mahanagar Telephone Nigam Limited (MTNL) | Bharti Airtel, Vodafone, Idea, Reliance, Aircel, Tata, MTS (Sistema Shyam TeleServices Limited), Telewings, Videocon | www.trai.gov.in/; http://www.dot.gov.in/ |
| Indonesia | Asia (62) | South-Eastern Asia | Telecommunication Act No. 5 (1964), Act No. 3 (1989) and Act No. 36 (1999) | Ministry of Communication and Informatics (Kementerian Komunikasi dan Informatika) | Badan Regulasi Telekomunikasi Indonesia/Indonesian Telecommunications Regulatory Authority (BRTI) | Telkom—PT. Telekomunikasi Indonesia | Indosat, XL Axiata (Acquired Axis Telekom Indonesia), 3 (Hutchison), Telkomsel, Bakrie Telecom (CDMA), Smartfren Telecom (CDMA) | www.brti.or.id/ |
| Iran (I.R.) | Asia (98) | Southern Asia | Duties and liabilities Act of Ministry of Information and Communications Technology (2003) | Ministry of Information and Communications Technology | Communications Regulatory Authority (CRA) of Iran | Telecommunication Company of Iran (TCI) | Hamrahe Aval (MCI), Irancell (MTN), RighTel, Taliya Mobile | http://www.cra.ir/ |
| Iraq | Asia (964) | Western Asia | Spectrum Management Policy (2013) | Ministry of Communications | Commission of Media and Communications (CMC) | Iraqi Telecommunication and Post Company (ITPC) | Asia Cell, Zain (fomerly MTC), Korek Telecom | www.cmc.iq/en/ |
| Ireland | Europe (353) | Northern Europe | Postal and Telecommunications Services Act (1983), | Department of Communications, | Commission for Communications Regulation (ComReg) | Eircom (Meteor)-Privatized | Hutchison 3, O2, Vodafone | www.comreg.ie/ |

(continued)

**Table A.1** (continued)

| Country | Region (country code) | Sub region | Laws/policies/ acts/events (in chronological order) | Government/ministry/ department | Regulator | Incumbent operator | Other operators (MNOs/fixed-line) | Sources (Weblink) |
|---|---|---|---|---|---|---|---|---|
| | | | Communications Regulation Act (2002) | Energy and Natural Resources | | | | |
| Isle of Man | Europe | Northern Europe | Telecommunications Act (1984), Wireless Telegraphy Act (2006) | Department of Home Affairs | Communications Commission | Manx Telecom | Sure (Batelco Group) | https://www.gov.im/cc/ |
| Israel | Asia (972) | Western Asia | Communications Law (Telecommunications and Broadcasting) (1982) | Ministry of Communications | Ministry of Communications | Bezeq | Cellcom, Orange, Pelephone, Hot Mobile, Golan Telecom | www.moc.gov.il/ |
| Italy | Europe (39) | Southern Europe | Competition Act No. 287 (1990), Telecommunications Act No. 249 (1997) | Il Ministero dello Sviluppo Economico/The Ministry of Economic Development | Italian Communications Authority/Autorità per le garanzie nelle comunicazioni (AGCOM) | Telecom Italia | 3 Italia, TIM, Vodafone, Wind | www.agcom.it/ |
| Jamaica | Americas (1) | Caribbean | The Telecommunications Act (2000) | Ministry of Science Technology, Energy and Mining (MSTEM) | Office of Utilities Regulation Jamaica (OUR) | LIME | Digicel | www.our.org.jm/ |
| Japan | Asia (81) | Eastern Asia | Telecommunications Business Act (1984) | Ministry of Internal Affairs and Communications | Ministry of Internal Affairs and Communications | Nippon Telegraph and Telephone (NTT) | KDDI, NTT DoCoMo, SoftBank Mobile | www.soumu.go.jp/english/ |
| Jersey | Europe | Northern Europe | Competition Regulatory Authority (Jersey) Law (2001), The Telecom munications (Jersey) Law (2002) | Minister for Treasury and Resources | Jersey Competition Regulatory Authority (JCRA) | Jersey Telecom | Airtel-Vodafone, Sure (Batelco Group), | www.cicra.gg/ |
| Jordan | Asia (962) | Western Asia | Telecommunications Law No. 13 (1995) | Ministry of Information and Communications Technology (MoICT) | Telecommunications Regulatory Commission (TRC) | Jordan Telecom Group (JTG) | Orange Jordan (JTG), Zain (Jordan Mobile Telephone Services), Umniah (Batelco Group) | www.trc.gov.jo/ |

(continued)

**Table A.1** (continued)

| Country | Region (country code) | Sub region | Laws/policies/acts/events (in chronological order) | Government/ministry/department | Regulator | Incumbent operator | Other operators (MNOs/fixed-line) | Sources (Weblink) |
|---|---|---|---|---|---|---|---|---|
| Kazakhstan | Asia (7) | Central Asia | Telecommunications Law No. 382 (1999), Law on Communication No. 567-II (2004) | Minister of Investment and Development of the Republic of Kazakhstan | Minister of Investment and Development of the Republic of Kazakhstan | Kazakhtelecom | Kcell (TeliaSonera), Tele2, Beeline, Altel (Kazakhtelecom) | http://info-con.mid.gov.kz/en |
| Kenya | Africa (254) | Eastern Africa | Information and Communications Act (1998), The Kenya Communications Regulations (2001) | Ministry of Information, Communication and Technology (ICT) | Communications Authority of Kenya (CA) | Telkom Kenya | Airtel Kenya Limited, Orange (Telkom Kenya), Safaricom (Telkom Kenya) | www.ca.go.ke/ |
| Kiribati | Oceania (686) | Micronesia | Telecommunication Act (2004), Communications Act (2012) | Ministry of Communication, Transport and Tourism Development | Communications Commission of Kiribati (CCK) | Telecom Services Kiribati Limited (TSKL) (Acquired by Amalgamated Telecom Holdings (Fiji's ATH)) | Nil | www.cck.ki/ |
| Korea (Rep.) | Asia (82) | Eastern Asia | Telecommunications Business Act (2008) | Korea Communications Commission. | Korea Communications Commission. | KT Corporation | SK Telecom (SKT), LG U+ | http://eng.kcc.go.kr/user/ehpMain.do |
| Kosovo (Rep.) | Europe | Southern Europe | Law on Telecommunications No. 16 (2003) | Ministry of Transport and Communications | Telecommunications Regulatory Authority (TRA) | Post and Telecom of Kosovo (PTK)-Mobile Brand (Vala) | IPKO | http://www.arkep-rks.org/ |
| Kuwait | Asia (965) | Western Asia | Telecommunications Law No. 26 (1996), Communication Law No. 37 (2014) | Ministry of Communications | Ministry of Communications | Zain (Formerly known as MTC) | Ooredoo (Formerly Wataniya Telecom), Kuwait Telecom Company (VIVA) | http://moc.kw/English/ |
| Kyrgyzstan | Asia (996) | Central Asia | Law on Licensing System (2012) | Ministry of Transport and Communication | State Communications Agency | KyrgyzTelecom | Sky Mobile, Alfa Telecom(Megacom), Nur Telecom (O!), Beeline (VimpleCom brand) | http://www.nas.gov.kg/ |

(continued)

**Table A.1** (continued)

| Country | Region (country code) | Sub region | Laws/policies/acts/events (in chronological order) | Government/ministry/department | Regulator | Incumbent operator | Other operators (MNOs/fixed-line) | Sources (Weblink) |
|---|---|---|---|---|---|---|---|---|
| Lao P.D.R. | Asia (+856) | South-Eastern Asia | Telecommunication Law (2001) | Ministry of Communication Transport Post and Construction (MCTPC) | National Authority of Posts and Telecommunications (ANPT) | Lao Telecom | Beeline, ETL, Unitel (STC), Sky Telecom | http://www.ilp.gov.la/Lao_Law/Telecommunications_Law.pdf |
| Latvia | Europe (371) | Northern Europe | Electronic Communications Law (2005) | Satiksmes Ministrija/Ministry of Transport | Latvian Public Utilities Commission / Sabiedrisko pakalpojumu regulēšanas komisija (SPRK) | Lattelecom (Latvian Mobile Telephone) | Bite, Tele2, Triatel | www.sprk.gov.lv/ |
| Lebanon | Asia (961) | Western Asia | Telecom Law 431 (2002) | Ministry of Telecommunications | Republic of Lebanon Telecommunications Regulatory Authority (TRA) | Ogero | Touch, Alfa. | www.tra.gov.lb/ |
| Lesotho | Africa (266) | Southern Africa | Telecommunications Policy (1999), Telecommunications Authority Act (2000), ICT Policy (2005), Communication Policy (2008) | Ministry Of Communications, Science and Technology | Lesotho Communications Authority (LCA) (formerly Lesotho Telecommunications Authority (LTA)) | Telecom Lesotho (Presently known as Econet Telecom Lesotho) | Vodacom | www.lca.org.ls/ |
| Liberia | Africa (231) | Western Africa | Telecommunications Act (2007) | Ministry of Posts and Telecommunications | Liberia Telecommunications Authority (LTA) | Liberia Telecommunications Corporation (LIBTELCO) | Cellcom, Comium, Lonestar (MTN) | www.lta.gov.lr/ |
| Libya | Africa (218) | Northern Africa | Law No. 16 (1984) | Ministry of Communications and Infomatics | General Telecommunication Authority (GTA) | General Post and Telecommunications Company (GPTC) | Al Madar, Libyana Mobile Phone (GPTC) | http://cim.gov.ly/ |
| Liechtenstein | Europe (423) | Western Europe | Media Act (2005), Communications Act (2006) | NA | Amt für Kommunikation (AK)/The Office for Communications | Telecom Liechtenstein | Orange, Swisscom, Mobilkom (merged with Telecom Liechtenstein) | http://www.llv.li/#/11109 |

(continued)

**Table A.1** (continued)

| Country | Region (country code) | Sub region | Laws/policies/acts/events (in chronological order) | Government/ministry/department | Regulator | Incumbent operator | Other operators (MNOs/fixed-line) | Sources (Weblink) |
|---|---|---|---|---|---|---|---|---|
| Lithuania | Europe (370) | Northern Europe | Law on Radio Communication (1995), Law on Electronic Communications (2004) | Ministry of Transport and Communications | The Communications Regulatory Authority)/Ryšių Reguliavimo Tarnyba (RRT) | Teo LT | Omnitel, Mediafon, UAB Bite Lietuva, UAB TELE2 | www.rrt.lt/en |
| Luxembourg | Europe (352) | Western Europe | Telecommunications Law (1997), Law on Networks and Electronic Communications Services (2011) | The Ministry for Communications and Media/Service des médias et des communications (SMC) | Institut Luxembourgeois de Régulation (ILR) | P&T Luxembourg (P&T) (Mobile brand: LuxGSM) | Tango, Orange, LOL Mobile | www.ilr.public.lu/ |
| Macao, China | Asia (853) | Eastern Asia | Basic Telecommunications Law (2001) | Department of Lands, Public Works and Transport | Bureau of Telecommunications Regulation/Direcção dos Serviços de Regulação de Telecomunicações (DSRT) | Companhia de Telecomunicações de Macau (CTM) | Hutchison Telephone (3 Macau) Company Limited, China Telecom (Macau) Company Limited, Smartone—Mobile Communications (Macau), Limited | http://www.dsrt.gov.mo/web/en |
| Macedonia | Europe | Southern Europe | Telecommunication Act (2004), Law on Electronic Communications (2005) and (2014) | Minister of Information Society and Administration | Agency for Electronic Communications (AEK) | Makedonski Telekom | T Mobile (Deutsche Telekom), VIP Operator, One (Telekom Slovenije) | www.aek.mk/en/ |
| Madagascar | Africa (261) | Eastern Africa | Law No. 93-001 (1994),Decree No. °99-143 (1999) | Ministere Des Telecommunications, Des Postes Et De La Communication | Autorité de Régulation des Technologies de Communication (ARTEC) (Earlier sector was regulated by OMERT) | Telecom Malagasy (Telma) | Orange, Airtel (Formerly Celtel) | http://www.omert.mg/ |

(continued)

**Table A.1** (continued)

| Country | Region (country code) | Sub region | Laws/policies/ acts/events (in chronological order) | Government/ministry/ department | Regulator | Incumbent operator | Other operators (MNOs/fixed-line) | Sources (Weblink) |
|---|---|---|---|---|---|---|---|---|
| Malawi | Africa (265) | Eastern Africa | Communications Act (1998) | Ministry of Information | Communications Regulatory Authority (MACRA) | Malawi Telecommunications Limited (MTL) | Airtel, Telekom Networks Malawi (TNM), G-Mobile (GAIN), Celcom Ltd | www.macra.org.mw/ |
| Malaysia | Asia (60) | South-Eastern Asia | Telecommunication Act (1950), Digital Signature Act (1997), Communications and Multimedia Act (1998) | Ministry of Communications and Multimedia/ Kementerian Komunikasi Dan Multimedia Malaysia (KKMM) | Malaysian Communications and Multimedia Commission (MCMC) | Telekom Malaysia | Celcom Axiata, DiGi Telecommunications, Maxis Communications, U Mobile | www.skmm.gov.my/; http://www.kkmm.gov.my/ |
| Maldives | Asia (960) | Southern Asia | Telecommunications Regulation (2003), Telecommunication Policy (2006–2010), National Broadband Policy (2014–2018) | Minister of Transport and Communications | Communications Authority of Maldives | Dhiraagu | Ooredoo (Previously known as Wataniya Telecom) | www.cam.gov.mv/ |
| Mali | Africa (223) | Western Africa | Telecom Act No. 2001-005 (2001) | Ministère de l'Economie Numérique, de l'Information et de la Communication | Autorité Malienne de Régulation des Télécommunications/ TIC et des Postes (AMRTP) | Societe des Telecommunications du Mali—SOTELMA (Mobile brand-Malitel) | Orange (France Telecom) | http://amrtp-mali.org/ |
| Malta | Europe (356) | Southern Europe | Electronic Communications (Regulation) Act (1997), Communications Authority Act (2000) | Ministry for the Economy, Investment and Small Business Portfolio | Malta Communications Authority (MCA) | Maltacom (Currently known as GO plc) | Mobile Communications (GO Mobile), Vodafone, Melita Mobile | https://www.mca.org.mt/ |
| Marshall Islands | Oceania (692) | Micronesia | NTA Act (1990), Radio Communication Act (1993) | Ministry of Transportation and Communications | Ministry of Transportation and Communications | National Telecommunications Authority (NTA) | Nil | http://www.ntamar.net/ |

(continued)

**Table A.1** (continued)

| Country | Region (country code) | Sub region | Laws/policies/acts/events (in chronological order) | Government/ministry/department | Regulator | Incumbent operator | Other operators (MNOs/fixed-line) | Sources (Weblink) |
|---|---|---|---|---|---|---|---|---|
| Martinique | Americas (596) | Caribbean | NA | Ministère des Outre-Mer (French Ministry of Overseas) | Autorite de Regulation des Communications Electroniques et des Postes (Arcep)—Paris | Orange Caraïbe (France Telecom) | Digicel, Outremer Telecom (SFR) | www.arcep.fr/; http://www.outre-mer.gouv.fr/ |
| Mauritania | Africa (222) | Western Africa | Telecommunications Act 99-019 (1999) | Minister of Employment, Vocational Training, Information Technology and Communications/ Ministère de l'emploi, de la formation professionnelle et des TIC | Autorite de Regulation | Mauritel | Chinguitel (Expresso Telecom), Mattel | www.are.mr/ |
| Mauritius | Africa (230) | Eastern Africa | The Telecommunications Act (1998) | Ministry of Technology, Communication and Innovation | Information and Communication Technologies Authority (ICT) | Mauritius Telecom (MT) | Orange (Cellplus), Emtel, Mahanagar Telephone Mauritius Limited (MTML) | https://www.icta.mu/ |
| Mayotte | Africa | Eastern Africa | NA | Ministère des Outre-Mer (French Ministry of Overseas) | Autorite de Regulation des Communications Electroniques et des Postes (Arcep)—Paris | | Outremer Telecom | www.arcep.fr/ |
| Mexico | Americas (52) | Central America | Federal Telecommunications Law (1995), Federal Telecommunications and Broadcasting Law (2014) | Secretaría de Comunicaciones y Transportes (SCT) | Instituto Federal de Telecomunicaciones (IFT) | Telmex (American Movil) | Nextel Mexico (Acquired by AT&T), Movistar (Telefónica), Telcel (Telmex), Iusacell (Acquired by AT&T) | www.ift.org.mx/ |
| Micronesia | Oceania (691) | Micronesia | Telecommunications Act (1981), Radiocommunications Act (1991), ICT Policy (2012) | Department of Transportation, Communications and Infrastructure (TC&I) | Communications Division, FSM TC&I | Federated States of Micronesia Telecommunications Corporation (FSMTC) | | www.ict.fm/ |

(continued)

**Table A.1** (continued)

| Country | Region (country code) | Sub region | Laws/policies/ acts/events (in chronological order) | Government/ministry/ department | Regulator | Incumbent operator | Other operators (MNOs/fixed-line) | Sources (Weblink) |
|---|---|---|---|---|---|---|---|---|
| Moldova | Europe (373) | Eastern Europe | Electronic Communications Act no. 241-XVI (2007) | Ministry of Information Technology and Communications | National Regulatory Agency for Electronic Communications and Information Technology (ANRCETI) | Moldtelecom (Mobile Brand: Unité) | Orange, Moldcell, Interdnestrcom | http://en.anrceti.md/ |
| Monaco | Europe (377) | Western Europe | | Ministry of Public Works, the Environment and Urban Development | Direction des Communications Electroniques | Monaco Telecom | | http://www.nic.mc/ |
| Mongolia | Asia (976) | Eastern Asia | Communications Act (2001) | NA | Communications Regulatory Commission (CRC) | Mongolia Telecom Company (MTC) | G-Mobile, Skytel, Mobicom, Unitel | www.crc.gov.mn/en/ |
| Montenegro | Europe (382) | Southern Europe | Law on Electronic Communications (2013) | Ministry for Information Society and Telecommunications | Agency for Electronic Communications and Postal Services (EKIP) | Crnogorski Telekom | T-Mobile (Crnogorski Telekom), Mtel, Telenor | www.ekip.me/eng/ |
| Montserrat | Americas (1) | Caribbean | Telecommunications Act Revised (2008), Info-Communications Development Act (2009) | Ministry of Communications, Works, Energy and Labour | Montserrat Info-Communications Authority (MICA) | Lime (Cable and Wireless) | Digicel | www.mica.ms/ |
| Morocco | Africa (212) | Northern Africa | Telecommunication Act (1997), postal and telecommunications. Law No. 24 (1996) and Law No. 55-01 (2004) | Ministère des Postes et des Télécommunications (MPT) | Agence Nationale de Réglementation des Telecommunications (ANRT) | Maroc Telecom/IAM (Earlier known as Office National des Postes et Télécommunications) | Inwi, Meditel | www.anrt.ma/en |
| Mozambique | Africa (258) | Eastern Africa | General Telecommunications Framework—Lei No. 8 (2004) | Ministerio dos Transportes e Comunicacoes (MTC) | Instituto Nacional das Communicacoes de Mozambique/ Mozambique National Communications Institute (INCM) | Telecomunicações de Moçambique (TDM) | Vodacom, Movitel (Viettel Group), mcel (Moçambique Celular) | www.incm.gov.mz/ |

(continued)

**Table A.1** (continued)

| Country | Region (country code) | Sub region | Laws/policies/ acts/events (in chronological order) | Government/ministry/ department | Regulator | Incumbent operator | Other operators (MNOs/fixed-line) | Sources (Weblink) |
|---|---|---|---|---|---|---|---|---|
| Myanmar | Asia (95) | South-Eastern Asia | Telecom Law (2013) | Ministry of Communications and Information Technology (MCIT) | Myanmar Posts and Telecommunications (MPT) | Myanmar Posts and Telecommunications (MPT) | Telenor, Ooredoo (Formerly Q-Tel), Digicel | www.mpt.com.mm/en/ |
| Namibia | Africa (264) | Southern Africa | MINISTRY OF WORKS, TRANSPORT AND COMMUNICATION | Ministry of Information and Communications Technology | Communications Regulatory Authority of Namibia (CRAN) | Telecom Namibia (Fixed-line), MTC (Mobile) | Telecom Nambia (TN Mobile) | www.cran.na/ |
| Nauru | Oceania (674) | Micronesia | Wireless Telegraphy Act (1974), Telecommunications Act (2002) | Ministry of Telecommunication | Ministry of Telecommunication | | Digicel | http://www.naurugov.nr |
| Nepal | Asia (977) | Southern Asia | Telecommunication Act.2053 (1997) | Ministry of Information and Communications | Nepal Telecommunications Authority | The Nepal Telecom Company | Ncell (Spice Nepal) | www.nta.gov.np/ |
| Neth. Antilles | Americas (599) | Caribbean | NA | Minister of Transportation and Telecommunication | Bureau Telecommunications and Post (BT&P) | EUTEL (Former incumbent, now it is part of Netherlands) | Digicel (Curacao Telecom N.V.), Telcell, Uts (Setel Nv), Antialliano Por | www.btnp.org/ |
| Netherlands | Europe (31) | Western Europe | Telecommunications Act (1988) | Ministry of Economic Affairs | Netherlands Authority for Consumers and Markets (ACM) | Koninklijke PTT Nederland (KPN/KPN Mobile) | T-Mobile, Vodafone | https://www.acm.nl/en/ |
| New Zealand | Oceania (64) | Australasia | The Commerce Act (1986), Telecommunications Act (2001) | Ministry of Business, Innovation and Employment | Commerce Commission | New Zealand Limited (TelecomNZ) | Vodafone (Formerly TelstraClear), 2degrees | www.comcom.govt.nz/ |
| Nicaragua | Americas (505) | Central America | General Law on Telecommunications and Postal Services No. 200 (1995), Telecommunications Decree No. 128 (2004) | Ministry of Transportation and Infrastructure (MTI) | Instituto Nicaragüense de Telecomunicaciones y Correos (Telcor) | Empresa Nicaragüense de Telecomunicaciones, S.A. (ENITEL) (Currently Operating as Claro) | Movistar (Telefónica Móvil) | www.telcor.gob.ni/ |

(continued)

**Table A.1** (continued)

| Country | Region (country code) | Sub region | Laws/policies/acts/events (in chronological order) | Government/ministry/department | Regulator | Incumbent operator | Other operators (MNOs/fixed-line) | Sources (Weblink) |
|---|---|---|---|---|---|---|---|---|
| Niger | Africa (227) | Western Africa | Ordinance No. 99-045 (1999), Telecommunications Sector Policy (1999) | Ministère des Postes, des Télécommunications et de l'Economie Numérique | Autorité de Régulation des Télécommunications et de la Poste | Société Nigérienne des Télécommunications (SONITEL) (Mobile brand- Sahelcom) | Airtel, Orange (France Telecom), Telecel (Moov) | www.armniger.org/ |
| Nigeria | Africa (234) | Western Africa | The Wireless Telegraphy Act (1990), Nigerian Communications Act (2003) | Federal Ministry of Communication Technology | Nigerian Communications Commission | Nigeria Telecommunications (NITEL) (Acquired by Mtel) | Airtel, Etisalat, Glo, Globacom, Visafone (Acquired by MTN), M-Tel, MTN | www.ncc.gov.ng/ |
| Niue | Oceania (683) | Polynesia | Communications Act (1989) | Ministry of Infrastructure | NA | Telecom Niue | | http://www.gov.nu/ |
| Norfolk Islands | Oceania | Australasia | Telecommunication Act (1992), Telecommunications Amendment Act (2004) | Ministry of Finance | NA | Norfolk Telecom | | |
| Northern Marianas | Oceania (1) | Micronesia | Commonwealth Telecommunications Act (2000) | NA | NA | IT&E (Micronesian Telecommunications Corporation- MTC) | Docomo Pacific | |
| Norway | Europe (47) | Northern Europe | Electronic Communications Act 83 (2003) | Ministry of Transport and Communications | Norwegian Post and Telecommunication Authority/Nasjonal kommunikasjons-myndighet (Nkom) | Telenor Group | Netcom, Network Norway (Acquired by ICE) | www.nkom.no/ |
| Oman | Asia (968) | Western Asia | The Telecom Act (2002) | Ministry of Transport and Communications | Sultanate of Oman Telecommunications Regulatory Authority (TRA) | Oman Telecommunications Company (Omantel) | Ooredoo Oman, Oman Mobile (OMTC) | https://www.tra.gov.om/ |
| Pakistan | Asia (92) | Southern Asia | The Pakistan Telecommunication Ordinance (1994), Telecom Reorganization Act (1996) | Ministry of Information Technology (MoIT) | Pakistan Telecommunication Authority | Pakistan Telecommunication Company Ltd (PTCL) (Mobile Brand-Ufone) | Mobilink, Telenor, Warid, Zong (China Mobile Pakistan) | www.pta.gov.pk/ |

(continued)

**Table A.1** (continued)

| Country | Region (country code) | Sub region | Laws/policies/ acts/events (in chronological order) | Government/ministry/ department | Regulator | Incumbent operator | Other operators (MNOs/fixed-line) | Sources (Weblink) |
|---|---|---|---|---|---|---|---|---|
| Palau | Oceania (680) | Micronesia | The Telecommunication Act (1982) and (2013) | NA | NA | Palau National Communications Corporation (PNCC Wireless) | Palau Mobile Corporation (PMC) | |
| Palestine | Asia | Western Asia | NA | Ministry of Telecommunications and Information Technology (MTIT) | Ministry of Telecommunications and Information Technology (MTIT) | Palestinian Telecommunication Company (PalTel) (Mobile brand- Jawwal) | Wataniya Telecom | |
| Panama | Americas (507) | Central America | Telecom Law No. 31 (1996) | Ministry of Communications and Information Technology (MCIT) | Autoridad Nacional de los Servicios Públicos (ASEP) | Cable and Wireless Panamá (CWP) | Claro (América Móvil), Digicel, Movistar | www.asep.gob.pa/ |
| Papua New Guinea | Oceania (675) | Melanesia | Telecommunications Act (1996) | Ministry of Communication and Information Technology | National Information and Communications Technology Authority (NICTA) | Telikom PNG Ltd (Mobile Brand- Citifon) | Digicel, Vodafone (bmobile) | http://www.nicta.gov.pg/ |
| Paraguay | Americas (595) | Southern America | Telecommunication Law No. 642 (1995) | Ministry of Public Works and Communications | Comisión Nacional de Telecomunicaciones (Conatel) | Corporación Paraguaya de Comunicaciones (Copaco) | Tigo (Millicom), Claro (América Móvil), Personal (Núcleo), Vox (Hola Paraguay) | www.conatel.gov.py/ |
| Peru | Americas (51) | Southern America | NA | Ministerio de Transportes y Comunicaciones (MTC) | Organismo Supervisor de Inversión Privada en Telecomunicaciones (OSIPTEL) | Telefónica del Perú S. A (Mobile brand- Movistar) | Claro (América Móvil), Entel (formerly Nextel Peru), Bitel | https://www.osiptel.gob.pe/ |

(continued)

**Table A.1** (continued)

| Country | Region (country code) | Sub region | Laws/policies/ acts/events (in chronological order) | Government/ministry/ department | Regulator | Incumbent operator | Other operators (MNOs/fixed-line) | Sources (Weblink) |
|---|---|---|---|---|---|---|---|---|
| Philippines | Asia (63) | South-Eastern Asia | Public Telecommunications Policy Act (Republic Act No. 7925) (1995) | Department of Transportation and Communications (DOTC) | National Telecommunications Commission (NTC) | Philippine Long Distance Telephone Company (PLDT) (Smart Communications) | Globe Telecom (Touch Mobile), Express Telecom (Exetel), Digital Telecommunications/ Sun Cellular (Owned by PLDT), Bayan Telecommunications (Acquired by Globe), Bell Telecommunication (Vega Telecom), Now Telecom (Formerly Next Mobile) | www.ntc.gov.ph/ |
| Poland | Europe (48) | Eastern Europe | Telecommunication Act (2004) | Ministry of Administration and Digitization | Office of Electronic Communications (UKE) | Telekomunikacja Polska S.A. (Polish Telecom) | T-Mobile, Orange (Formerly PTK Centertel), Polkomtel (PLUS), Play (P4) | www.en.uke.gov.pl/ |
| Portugal | Europe (351) | Southern Europe | Telecommunications Act (1989) | Minister of Economy | Autoridade Nacional de Comunicações (ANACOM) | Portugal Telecom | Meo, Optimus, Vodafone, Zon Mobile | www.anacom.pt/ |
| Puerto Rico | Americas (1) | Caribbean | Telecommunication Act (1996) | NA | Junta Reglamentadora de Telecomunicaciones de Puero Rico | Puerto Rico Telephone Company (PRTC) | AT&T Mobility, Sprint PCS, Open Mobile, T-Mobile, Claro (América Móvil) | www.jrtpr.gobierno. pr/ |
| Qatar | Asia (974) | Western Asia | Telecommunication Law No. 34 (2006) | Ministry of Information and Communications Technology (ictQATAR) | The Supreme Council for Communication and Information Technology (SCICT)/ Communications Regulatory Authority (CRA- Independent Regulator) | Qatar Telecom (Qtel/Ooredoo) | Vodafone | www.cra.gov.qa; www.ictqatar.qa/en |

(continued)

**Table A.1** (continued)

| Country | Region (country code) | Sub region | Laws/policies/ acts/events (in chronological order) | Government/ministry/ department | Regulator | Incumbent operator | Other operators (MNOs/fixed-line) | Sources (Weblink) |
|---|---|---|---|---|---|---|---|---|
| Réunion | Africa | Eastern Africa | NA | NA | Autorite de Regulation des Communications Electroniques et des Postes (Arcep)—Paris | | Orange, Outremer (SFR) | http://www.arcep.fr/ |
| Romania | Europe (40) | Eastern Europe | Regulatory Framework for Communications (Ordinance No. 79) (2002), Law no. 239 (2005) | Ministry of Communications and Information Society | The National Authority for Management and Regulation in Communications (ANCOM) | Romtelecom (Telekom Romania) | Vodafone, RCS and RDS, Orange | www.ancom.org.ro/ en/ancom_106 |
| Russian Federation | Europe (7) | Eastern Europe | The Federal Law on Communication (2003) | Ministry of Telecom and Mass Communications of the Russian Federation (MINSVYAZ) | Ministry of Telecom and Mass Communications of the Russian Federation (MINSVYAZ) | Svyazinvest (Currently known as Rostelecom) | MTS, Beeline (VimpelCom), MegaFon, Tele2 | http://www.minsvyaz. ru/en/ |
| Rwanda | Africa (250) | Eastern Africa | Telecommunications Law No. 44/2 (2001) | The Minister of Youth and ICT (MYICT) | Rwanda Utilities Regulatory Authority | Rwandatel (Acquired by Liquid Telecom) | Airtel, MTN, Tigo | www.rura.gov.rw/ |
| S. Tomé and Principe | Africa (239) | Middle Africa | Telecommunications Law No. 3 (2004) | Ministère des Travaux Publiques, Infrastructures, Transports et Communications | Autorité Générale de Régulation (AGER) | Companhia Santomense de Telecomunicacoes (CST) | | www.ager-stp.org/ |
| Samoa | Oceania (685) | Polynesia | Telecommunications Act (2005), Telecommunications Amendment (2008), Broadcasting Act (2010) | Ministry of Communications and Information Technology | Office of the Regulator of Samoa (OOTR) | Bluesky Samoa Limited (Formerly SamoaTel) | Digicel | http://www.regulator. gov.ws/ |
| San Marino | Europe (378) | Southern Europe | NA | Segreteria di Stato Territorio e Ambiente | | San Marino Telecom (SMT) | | www.territorio.sm/ |

(continued)

**Table A.1** (continued)

| Country | Region (country code) | Sub region | Laws/policies/ acts/events (in chronological order) | Government/ministry/ department | Regulator | Incumbent operator | Other operators (MNOs/fixed-line) | Sources (Weblink) |
|---|---|---|---|---|---|---|---|---|
| Saudi Arabia | Asia (966) | Western Asia | The Telecommunications Act (2001) | Ministry of Communications and Information Technology | Saudi Communications and Information Technology Commission (CITC) | Saudi Telecom Company (STC Group) | Mobily (Etihad Etisalat), Zain, Public Telecommunications Company (BRAVO, PTC) | www.citc.gov.sa/ |
| Senegal | Africa (221) | Western Africa | Law on Telecommunications No. 96-03, No. 2001-15 and No. 2011-01 | Ministere De La Communication | Autorité de Régulation des Télécommunications et des Postes (ARTP) | Sonatel (Orange) | Expresso (Sudatel), Alizé, Tigo (Sentel GSM), Hayo Telecom | www.artpsenegal.net/ |
| Serbia | Europe (381) | Southern Europe | Telecommunications Law (2007), Electronic Communications Law (2010) | Ministry of Trade, Tourism and Telecommunications | Republic Agency for Electronic Communication (RATEL) | Telekom Srbija (MTS) | Telnor, VIP Mobile (Mobilkom Austria Group) | http://www.ratel.rs/home.136.html |
| Seychelles | Africa (248) | Eastern Africa | Broadcasting and Telecommunication Act (2000) | Ministry of Information Technology and Communication (MITC) | Department of Information Communications Technology | | Airtel Seychelles, Cable and Wireless (Seychelles) Ltd | www.ict.gov.sc/ |
| Sierra Leone | Africa (232) | Western Africa | The Telecommunications Act (2006) | Minister of Information and Communications | National Telecommunications Commission (NATCOM) | Sierra Leone Telecommunications Company (Sierratel) | Bharti Airtel, Ambitel, Comium, Africell, Sierratel, Datatel, Cellcom, Smart Mobile (InterGroup Telecom) | www.natcom.gov.sl/ |
| Singapore | Asia (65) | South-Eastern Asia | Telecommunications Act 43 (1999) | Ministry of Communications and Information (MCI) | Infocomm Development Authority of Singapore (IDA) | Singapore Telecommunications (SingTel) | MobileOne (M1), StarHub | https://www.ida.gov.sg/ |
| Slovakia | Europe (421) | Eastern Europe | Electronic Communications Act No. 351 (2011) | Ministry of Transport, Posts and Telecommunications of the Slovak Republic (MDPT) | Regulatory Authority for Electronic Communications and Postal Services (Regulatory Authority—RÚ) | Slovak Telekom (T-Mobile) | Orange Slovensko, Telefónica O2 | http://www.teleoff.gov.sk/index.php?ID=9 |

(continued)

**Table A.1** (continued)

| Country | Region (country code) | Sub region | Laws/policies/acts/events (in chronological order) | Government/ministry/department | Regulator | Incumbent operator | Other operators (MNOs/fixed-line) | Sources (Weblink) |
|---|---|---|---|---|---|---|---|---|
| Slovenia | Europe (386) | Southern Europe | Law on Telecommunications (1997), Electronic Communications Act (2011) | NA | Agency for communication networks and services of the Republic of Slovenia | Telekom Slovenije | Mobitel, Si.Mobil, Tušmobil, T-2 | www.akos-rs.si/akos-ang |
| Solomon Islands | Oceania (677) | Melanesia | Telecommunications Act (2009) | Ministry of Communications and Aviation | Telecommunications Commission of Solomon Islands | Solomon Telekom (Ourr Telekom) | bmobile-Vodafone | http://www.tcsi.org.sb/ |
| Somalia | Africa (252) | Eastern Africa | National Communications Act (2012) | Ministry of Posts and Communication | Ministry of Posts and Communication (No independent regulator exist) | | Hormuud Telecom (Hortel), Nationlink, Telesom, Somali Telecom Group, Somafone, Golis, Somtel | www.mopc.somaligov.net/ |
| South Africa | Africa (27) | Southern Africa | Telecommunications Act (1996 and 2000), Independent Broadcasting Act (1993), Electronic Communications Act (2005 and 2014) | Ministry of Telecommunications and Postal Services | Independent Communications Authority of South Africa (ICASA) | Telkom SA (Telkom Mobile/8ta) | Vodacom, MTN, Cell C | https://www.icasa.org.za/ |
| South Sudan | Africa (211) | Southern Africa | National Communications Act No. 24 (2012) | Ministry of Telecommunications and Postal Services | Ministry of Telecommunications and Postal Services | Sudatel | MTN, Gemtel (Green Netwroks), Zain, Vivacell | www.motps.goss.org/ |
| Spain | Europe (34) | Southern Europe | General Telecommunications Act No. 9 (2014) | Ministerio de Industria, Energía y Turismo | Spain's National Authority for Markets and Competition (CNMC)/Comisión Nacional de los Mercados y la Competencia | Telefonica | Orange, Vodafone, Movistar, Yogio | www.cnmc.es/ |

(continued)

**Table A.1** (continued)

| Country | Region (country code) | Sub region | Laws/policies/ acts/events (in chronological order) | Government/ministry/ department | Regulator | Incumbent operator | Other operators (MNOs/fixed-line) | Sources (Weblink) |
|---|---|---|---|---|---|---|---|---|
| Sri Lanka | Asia (94) | Southern Asia | Telecommunications Act No. 25 (1991), Telecommunication Levy Act No. 21 (2011) | Ministry of Telecommunication and Information Technology | Telecommunications Regulatory Commission of Sri Lanka (TRCSL) | Sri Lanka Telecom (SLT) | Mobitel (SLT), Airtel, Hutch, Etisalat (Celltel), Dialog (Axiata Group) | www.trc.gov.lk/ |
| St. Kitts and Nevis | Americas (1) | Caribbean | Telecommunications Act 2 (2000) | Ministry of International Trade, Labour, Social Security, CARICOM Affairs, and Telecommunications and Technology | The National Telecommunications Regulatory Commission (NTRC) | Cable and Wireless (LIME) | Digicel | http://ntrc.kn/ |
| St. Lucia | Americas (1) | Caribbean | Telecommunications ACT 27 (2000) | Ministry of Infrastructure, Port Services and Transport | The National Telecommunications Regulatory Commission (NTRC) | Cable and Wireless (LIME) | Digicel | www.ntrc.org.lc/ |
| St.Maarten | Americas (1) | Caribbean | NA | Ministry of Tourism, Economic Affairs, Telecommunications and Transport (Ministry TEATT) | Bureau Telecommunications and Post | | | http://www. sxmregulator.sx/ |
| St. Pierre and Miquelon | Americas (508) | Northern America | NA | NA | Autorite de Regulation des Communications Electroniques et des Postes (Arcep)—Paris | SPM Telecom (Ameris) | | www.arcep.fr/ |
| St. Vincent and the Grenadines | Americas (1) | Caribbean | Telecommunications ACT 1 (2001) | The Ministry of Foreign Affairs, Foreign Trade, Commerce and Information Technology | The National Telecommunications Regulatory Commission (NTRC) | Cable and Wireless (LIME) | Digicel | www.ntrc.vc/ |
| Sudan | Africa (249) | Northern Africa | The Telecommunication Act (2001) | Ministry of Information and Communications | National Telecommunications Corporation (NTC) | Sudan Telecom Company (Sudatel) | Canartel, MTN, Zain Sudan | www.ntc.gov.sd/ index.php/en/ |

(continued)

**Table A.1** (continued)

| Country | Region (country code) | Sub region | Laws/policies/ acts/events (in chronological order) | Government/ministry/ department | Regulator | Incumbent operator | Other operators (MNOs/fixed-line) | Sources (Weblink) |
|---|---|---|---|---|---|---|---|---|
| Suriname | Americas (597) | Southern America | Telecommunication Act (2004) | Ministerie van Transport, Communicatie en Toerisme—TAS | Telecommunicatie Autoriteit Suriname (TAS) | Telesur (TeleG) | Uniqa (Intelsur UTA), Digicel | www.tas.sr/ |
| Swaziland | Africa (268) | Southern Africa | Post and Telecommunications Corporation Act No. 11 (1983), The Electronic Communications Act (2013) | Ministry of Tourism, Environment and Communications | Swaziland Post and Telecommunications Corporation (SPTC) | Swaziland Post and Telecommunications Corporation (SPTC) | MTN Swaziland | www.sptc.co.sz/ |
| Sweden | Europe (46) | Northern Europe | Electronic Communications Act (2003) | Ministry of Enterprise and Innovation | Swedish Post and Telecom Authority (PTS) | Telia Sonera | Telenor, Tele2, Hi3G | www.pts.se/en-GB/ |
| Switzerland | Europe (41) | Western Europe | Telecommunications Act No. 784.10 (1997) | Federal Department of Environment, Transport, Energy and Communications (DETEC) | Federal Office for Communications (OFCOM/BAKOM), The Federal Communications Commission (ComCom)-Independent Regulator | Swisscom AG | Sunrise, Orange | www.ofcom.admin.ch/ |
| Syria | Asia (963) | Western Asia | Syrian Telecommunication Regulatory Authority | Ministry of Communications and Technology | Syrian Telecommunication Regulatory Authority (SYTRA) | Syrian Telecom | MTN, Syriatel | http://www.moct.gov.sy/ |
| Taiwan, Province of China | Asia (886) | Eastern Asia | Telecommunications Act (1996), Fundamental Communications Act (2004 | Ministry of Transportation and Communications of the Republic of China | National Communications Commission | Chunghwa Telecom | Ambit, Asia-Pacific Telecom, FarEasTone, Taiwan Mobile,Taiwan Star Telecom, vibo Telecom | www.ncc.gov.tw/english/ |

(continued)

**Table A.1** (continued)

| Country | Region (country code) | Sub region | Laws/policies/acts/events (in chronological order) | Government/ministry/department | Regulator | Incumbent operator | Other operators (MNOs/fixed-line) | Sources (Weblink) |
|---|---|---|---|---|---|---|---|---|
| Tajikistan | Asia (992) | Central Asia | NA | Ministry of Communications | The Communications Regulatory Agency (CRA) | Tajiktelecom | Babilon Mobile, Tcell, Beeline (Tacom), TK Mobile, MegaFon (TT Mobile) | |
| Tanzania | Africa (255) | Eastern Africa | Tanzania Communications Act No. 18 (1993), TCRA Act No. 2 (2003), Electronic and Postal Communications Act No. 3 (2010) | Ministry of Communication, Science and Technology | Tanzania Communications Regulatory Authority —TCRA | Tanzania Telecommunications Company Limited (TTCL) | Zantel (Fixed-line), Vodacom, Airtel, Tigo, Smart Telecom, Benson Informatics Limited | https://www.tcra.go.tz/ |
| TFYR Macedonia | Europe (389) | Southern Europe | Electronic Communications Law (2005) | Ministry of information society and administration | Agency for Electronic Communications | Makedonski Telekom (T- Mobile) | Vip (Telekom Austria), One (Telekom Slovenije) | http://www.aek.mk/en/?lang=en |
| Thailand | Asia (66) | South-Eastern Asia | Telecommunications Business Act, B.E. 2544 (2001), Telecommunications Act (1996) | The Ministry of Information and Communication Technology | National Broadcasting and Telecommunications Commission (NBTC) | Telephone Organization of Thailand (TOT) and Communication Authority of Thailand (CAT) | AIS, DTAC, TrueMove H, True Corporation (Fixed-line), TT&T (Fixed-line) | www.nbtc.go.th/wps/portal/Eng |
| Timor-Leste | Asia | South-Eastern Asia | Telecommunication Decree-Law no. 15/2012 (2012) | Ministry of Transport and Communication | The National Communications Authority | Timor Telecom | Telin (Telkomcel) | http://anc.tl/ |
| Togo | Africa (228) | Western Africa | Electronic Communications Law No. 2012-018 (2012) | Ministry of Posts and Telecommunications | Autorite de Reglementation des Secteurs de Postes et Telecommunications (ART&P) | Togo Telecom/Togo Cellulaire | Atlantique Telecom (Moov) | www.artp.tg/ |
| Tonga | Oceania (676) | Polynesia | COMMUNICATIONS ACT (2000) | Ministry of Information and Communications of Tonga | Ministry for Information and Communications of Tonga | Tonga Communications Corporation | Digicel | http://www.mic.gov.to/ |

(continued)

**Table A.1** (continued)

| Country | Region (country code) | Sub region | Laws/policies/acts/events (in chronological order) | Government/ministry/department | Regulator | Incumbent operator | Other operators (MNOs/fixed-line) | Sources (Weblink) |
|---|---|---|---|---|---|---|---|---|
| Trinidad and Tobago | Americas (1) | Caribbean | Telecommunications Act 2001 | Ministry of Trade, Industry, Investment and Communications | Telecommunications Authority of Trinidad and Tobago | Telecommunications Services of Trinidad and Tobago (TSTT) (B-Mobile) | Digicel | www.tatt.org.tt/ |
| Tunisia | Africa (216) | Northern Africa | Telecommunication Code (Law No. 2001-1) | Ministre des Technologies de l'Information et des Communications | Instance Nationale des Télécommunications (Accueil) | Tunisie Telecom (Tunicell) | Ooredoo (Qtel), Orange (France Telecom) | www.intt.tn/ |
| Turkey | Asia (90) | Western Asia | Telegram and Telephone Law No. 406 (1924), and Telecommunications Law No. 4502 (2000), Telecommunications Law No. 4673 (2001), Electronic Communications Law (2008) | Ministry of Transport, Maritime and Communication | Information And Communication Technologies Authority (ICTA)/ Bilgi Teknolojileri ve İletişim Kurumu (BTK) | Türk Telekom | Vodafone, Avea | www.btk.gov.tr/en-US/ |
| Turkmenistan | Asia (993) | Central Asia | NA | Ministry of Communications | Ministry of Communications | Turkmen Telecom/Altyn Asyr (TM Cell) | MTS Turkmenistan | http://www.mincom.gov.tm/tk |
| Turks and Caicos Is. | Americas (1) | Caribbean | Telecommunications Policy(2003), Telecommunications Ordinance (2004) | NA | Telecommunications Commission | NA | Cable and Wireless West Indies Ltd Turks and Caicos<br>Digicel (Turks and Caicos) Limited<br>Islandcom Telecommunications | www.telecommission.tc/ |
| Tuvalu | Oceania (688) | Polynesia | Telecommunications Corporation Act (1993) | Ministry of Works Communications and Transport | NA | NA | | |
| Uganda | Africa (256) | Eastern Africa | Communications Act (1997, 2000, 2013) | Ministry of Information and Communications Technology | Uganda Communications Commission | Uganda Telecom | MTN, Airtel, Smile, Warid, Smart, Africell (Acquired Orange), Vodafone | www.ucc.co.ug/ |

(continued)

**Table A.1** (continued)

| Country | Region (country code) | Sub region | Laws/policies/ acts/events (in chronological order) | Government/ministry/ department | Regulator | Incumbent operator | Other operators (MNOs/fixed-line) | Sources (Weblink) |
|---|---|---|---|---|---|---|---|---|
| Ukraine | Europe (380) | Eastern Europe | Telecommunications Act No. 1280-IV (2003) | Ministry of Infrastructure | National Commission for the State Regulation of Communications and Informatization | Ukrtelecom | Kyivstar, MTS, life:) | www.nkrzi.gov.ua |
| United Arab Emirates | Asia (971) | Western Asia | Federal Telecom Law No. 3 (2003) | Ministry of Interior MOI —E-Services and Telecom | Telecommunications Regulatory Authority (TRA) | Etisalat Group | Du | www.tra.gov.ae/en |
| United Kingdom | Europe (44) | Northern Europe | Telecommunication Act (1981, 1984), Communication Act (2003) | Minister for Culture, Communications and Creative Industries | Office of Communications (Ofcom) | British Telecom (BT) | Cellnet, o2 (Telefónica), Vodafone, Everything Everywhere(EE), Hutchison | www.ofcom.org.uk/ |
| United States | Americas (1) | Northern America | Communications Act (1934), Telecommunications Act (1996) | Ministry of Communications | Federal Communications Commission (FCC) | | Verizon, AT&T, Sprint, US Cellular, T- Mobile etc. | https://www.fcc.gov/ |
| Uruguay | Americas (598) | Southern America | NA | Ministry of Industry, Energy and Mining | Unidad Reguladora de Servicios de Telecomunicaciones (URSEC) | Administración Nacional de Telecomunicaciones (ANTEL) | Claro (América Móvil), Movistar | https://www.ursec.gub.uy/ |
| Uzbekistan | Asia (998) | Central Asia | NA | Ministry of Development of Information Technologies and Communications | Ministry of Development of Information Technologies and Communications | Uzbektelecom (UzTelecom) | Beeline, Ucell (COSCOM), CDMA Uzbekistan (Perfectum Mobile) | https://my.gov.uz/en/authority/48 |
| Vanuatu | Oceania (678) | Melanesia | Telecommunication Act (1989), Telecommunication Act Amendment (1993) | Ministry of Infrastructure and Public Works Utilities | Telecommunications and Radiocommunications Regulator (TRR) | Telecom Vanuatu Ltd | Digicel | www.trr.vu/ |

(continued)

**Table A.1** (continued)

| Country | Region (country code) | Sub region | Laws/policies/acts/events (in chronological order) | Government/ministry/department | Regulator | Incumbent operator | Other operators (MNOs/fixed-line) | Sources (Weblink) |
|---|---|---|---|---|---|---|---|---|
| Vatican | | | NA | Vatican City State | Department of Telecommunications | NA | Telecom Italia, Omnitel—Vodafone, Wind (Italy) | |
| Venezuela | Americas (58) | Southern America | Ley Orgánica de Telecomunicaciones/Telecommunications Act (2011) | Ministerio del Poder Popular para la Comunicación y la Información (Minci) | Comisión Nacional de Telecomunicaciones (CONATEL) | Compañía Anónima Nacional de Teléfonos de Venezuela (Cantv)-Movilnet | Movistar, Digitel, Telecom Venezuela | www.conatel.gob.ve/ |
| Viet Nam | Asia (84) | South-Eastern Asia | Law on Telecommunications (2009) | Ministry of Information and Communications | Vietnam Telecommunication Authority (VNTA) | Viettel Group | Vinaphone, MobiFone (VNPT), Vietnamobile, Gmobile, S-Fone (SK Telecom) | www.vnta.gov.vn |
| Yemen | Asia (967) | Western Asia | NA | The Ministry of Telecommunications and Information Technology (MoTIT) | The Ministry of Telecommunications and Information Technology (MoTIT) | Public Telecom Corporation (PTC) | MTN, Sabafon, Hits-Unitel (Y-Tel), Yemen Telecom | |
| Zambia | Africa (260) | Eastern Africa | Electronic Communications and Transactions Act No. 21 (2009), Information and Communications Technologies (ICT) Act No 15 (2009) | Ministry of Transport, Works, Supply and Communications | Zambia Information and Communications Technology Authority (ZITCA) | Zambia Telecommunications Company (Zamtel) | MTN, Airtel | www.zicta.zm/ |

# Appendix B

See Table B.1.

© Springer India 2016

M.K. Medudula et al., *Telecom Management in Emerging Economies*,
DOI 10.1007/978-81-322-2749-6

**Table B.1** Intergovernmental organizations/telecom unions/associations and agencies

| S. No. | Organization (year of establishment) | Committees/suborganizations/groups | Expanded title | Weblink |
|---|---|---|---|---|
| 1 | AMTA | | Australian Mobile Telecommunications Association | http://www.amta.org.au/ |
| 2 | ANSI | | American National Standards Institute | http://www.ansi.org/ |
| 3 | APEC | | Asia-Pacific Economic Cooperation | http://www.apec.org/ |
| | | APEC TEL | APEC Telecommunications and Information Working Group | http://www.apectelwg.org/ |
| 4 | APT (1979) | | Asia-Pacific Telecommunity | http://www.apt.int/ |
| | | AWG | APT Wireless Group | http://www.apt.int/APTAWG |
| 5 | ARIB | | Association of Radio Industries and Businesses | http://www.arib.or.jp/english/ |
| 6 | ATIS | | Alliance for Telecommunications Industry Solutions | www.atis.org/ |
| 7 | ATU | | African Telecommunications Union | www.atu-uat.org/ |
| 8 | BEREC | | The Body of European Regulators for Electronic Communications | http://berec.europa.eu/ |
| 9 | BIS | | Bureau of Indian Standards | www.bis.org.in/ |
| 10 | CCSA | | China Communications Standards Association | www.ccsa.org.cn/english/ |
| 11 | CENELEC (1973) | | The European Committee for Electrotechnical Standardization | http://www.cenelec.eu/ |
| 12 | CEPT (1959) | | The European Conference of Postal and Telecommunications Administrations | www.cept.org |
| | | ECC | Electronic Communications Committee | www.cept.org/ecc |
| | | ECO | European Communications Office | www.cept.org/eco |

(continued)

**Table B.1** (continued)

| S. No. | Organization (year of establishment) | Committees/suborganizations/groups | Expanded title | Weblink |
|---|---|---|---|---|
| | | Com-ITU | Committee for ITU Policy | http://www.cept.org/com-itu |
| 13 | CITEL | | Inter-American Telecommunication Commission | https://www.citel.oas.org |
| 14 | COAI | | Cellular Operators Association of India | www.coai.com/ |
| 15 | CTO | | Commonwealth Telecommunications Organisation | http://www.cto.int/ |
| 16 | CTU (1989) | | Caribbean Telecommunications Union | http://ctu.int/ |
| 17 | EU | | European Union | http://europa.eu/index_en.htm |
| | | ENISA | European Network and Information Security Agency | https://www.enisa.europa.eu/ |
| 18 | FIRST | | Forum of Incident Response and Security Teams | http://www.first.org/ |
| 19 | GSMA | | GSM Association | http://www.gsma.com/ |
| 20 | IEC (1906) | | International Electrotechnical Commission | www.iec.ch/ |
| | | CISPR | International Special Committee on Radio Interference | www.iec.ch/cispr |
| 21 | IEEE | | Institute of Electrical and Electronics Engineers | http://www.ieee.org/index.html |
| 22 | IMPACT | | International Multilateral Partnership Against Cyber Threats | http://www.impact-alliance.org/ |
| 23 | INTUG | | International Telecommunications Users Group | http://intug.org/ |
| 24 | ISO | | International Organization for Standardization | http://www.iso.org/ |
| 25 | ITSO | | International Telecommunications Satellite Organization | http://www.itso.int/ |

(continued)

**Table B.1** (continued)

| S. No. | Organization (year of establishment) | Committees/suborganizations/groups | Expanded title | Weblink |
|---|---|---|---|---|
| 26 | ITU | | International Telecommunication Union | http://www.itu.int |
| | | ITU-T | ITU Telecommunication Standardization Sector | www.itu.int/en/ITU-T/ |
| | | ITU-R | ITU Radiocommunication standards | www.itu.int/en/ITU-R/ |
| | | ITU-D | ITU Telecommunication Development Sector | www.itu.int/en/ITU-D/ |
| 27 | NIST | | National Institute of Standards and Technology | http://www.nist.gov/ |
| 28 | OMA | | Open Mobile Alliance | http://openmobilealliance.org/ |
| 29 | RCC (1991) | | Regional Commonwealth in the field of Communications | http://www.en.rcc.org.ru/ |
| 30 | TEC | | Telecom Engineering Centre (TEC) | www.tec.gov.in/ |
| 31 | TIA | | Telecommunications Industry Association | www.tiaonline.org/ |
| 32 | TSDSI | | Telecommunications Standards Development Society | www.tsdsi.org/ |
| 33 | TTA | | Telecommunications Technology Association | www.tta.or.kr/English/ |
| 34 | TTC | | Telecommunications Technology Committee | www.ttc.or.jp/e/ |
| 35 | USITUA | | The United States ITU Association | http://www.usitua.org/ |
| | | ITAC | International Telecommunication Advisory Committee | http://www.usitua.org/itac.htm |
| 36 | WTO | | World Trade Organization | https://www.wto.org/ |

MIX
Papier aus verantwortungsvollen Quellen
Paper from responsible sources
FSC® C105338

If you have any concerns about our products,
you can contact us on
**ProductSafety@springernature.com**

In case Publisher is established outside the EU,
the EU authorized representative is:
**Springer Nature Customer Service Center GmbH**
**Europaplatz 3, 69115 Heidelberg, Germany**

Printed by Libri Plureos GmbH
in Hamburg, Germany